GENDER AND DISCOURSE

SAGE Studies in Discourse

Consultant editor: TEUN A. VAN DIJK

The study of discourse has become a major development in all disciplines of the humanities and the social sciences. *Studies in Discourse* will feature introductory books for the key domains and most relevant topics in this exciting new cross-discipline. The series aims to stimulate teaching and research on discourse in linguistics, literature, sociology, anthropology, psychology, communications studies, history, law and other disciplines.

The focus of this series is to examine the structures and functions of text and talk in the multiple contexts of social fields, and the discourse analytical approach to important social issues and societal relationships, such as those of gender, ethnicity, inequality and power.

The books are authored by leading international specialists in their fields and will review the literature, current theoretical ideas, explain methods, and demonstrate these in extensive discourse analyses.

GENDER AND DISCOURSE

Edited by
Ruth Wodak

SAGE Publications
London • Thousand Oaks • New Delhi

First published 1997

 SAGE Publications Ltd
6 Bonhill Street
London EC2A 4PU

SAGE Publications Inc.
2455 Teller Road
Thousand Oaks, California 91320

SAGE Publications India Pvt Ltd
32, M-Block Market
Greater Kailash – I
New Delhi 110 048

British Library Cataloguing in Publication data

A catalogue record for this book is available
from the British Library.

ISBN 0 7619 5098 2
ISBN 0 7619 5099 0 (pbk)

Library of Congress catalog card number 97–069196

Typeset by Mayhew Typesetting, Rhayader, Powys
Printed in Great Britain by Redwood Books, Trowbridge, Wiltshire

CONTENTS

NOTES ON EDITOR AND CONTRIBUTORS

RUTH WODAK is Professor of Applied Linguistics in the Department of Applied Linguistics, University of Vienna. Her research interests include text linguistics, language in politics, prejudice and discrimination and gender studies. Current research includes communication in institutions (power and discourse), minority languages and studies in public and private discourse in Austria since 1945 with special focus on manifestations of anti-semitism and racism towards foreigners. Ruth Wodak is on the advisory boards of several journals including, *Discourse and Society*, *Multilingua* and *Applied Linguistics Journal*. She has published extensively in journals and her book publications in English include *Language Behavior in Therapy Groups* (1986), *Language, Power and Ideology* (1989), *Disorders of Discourse* (1996) and *Communicating Gender in Context* (with Helga Kotthoff, 1997).

DEBORAH CAMERON is Professor of English Language at the University of Strathclyde, Glasgow. She has researched and has published in areas of feminist theory and practice, but is best-known for her work on language and gender. Among other publications she is the author of *Feminism and Linguistic Theory* (1992) and *Verbal Hygiene* (1995).

JENNIFER COATES is Professor of English Language and Linguistics at Roehampton Institute, London. Her published work includes *Women, Men and Language* (originally published 1986, 2nd edition 1993), *Women in their Speech Communities* (1989) (co-edited with Deborah Cameron) and *Women's Studies: An Introduction* (1995) (co-edited with Beryl Madoc-Jones). Her new book, *Women Talk*, an account of her long-term research into conversation between women friends, was published in October 1996, and her *Language and Gender Reader* will appear in 1997.

DAVID CORSON is Professor in the Department of Theory and Policy Studies, and in the Modern Language Center at the Ontario Institute for Studies in Education. He is the founding editor of the journal *Language and Education* and general editor of *The Encyclopedia of Language and Education*. Recent publications include *Discourse and Power in Educational Organizations* (1995) and *Changing Education for Diversity* (1997).

VICTORIA DeFRANCISCO is an Associate Professor in Communication Studies and Director of Women's Studies at the University of Northern Iowa. Her research has appeared in *Discourse and Society, Women and Language* and *Language in Society*. She co-authored *Women's Voices in Our Times: Statements by American Leaders* and guest-edited a special issue of *Women's Studies in Communication*.

SUZANNE EGGINS lectures in semiotic approaches to text/discourse in the School of English at the University of New South Wales. Her research interests include conversation analysis, cohesion in text, and theory and analysis. Her publications include *An Introduction to Systemic Functional Linguistics* (1994) and *Analysing Casual Conversation* (co-authored with Diana Slade, 1997).

JANET HOLMES holds a personal Chair in Linguistics at Victoria University of Wellington, New Zealand. She teaches linguistics and sociolinguistics courses, specializing in New Zealand English and language and gender issues. Her publications include a textbook, *An Introduction to Sociolinguistics* and the first sociolinguistics book on New Zealand English, *New Zealand Ways of Speaking English*, co-edited with Allan Bell.

RICK IEDEMA is Research Fellow at the Centre for Hospital Management and Information Systems Research (University of New South Wales). He operates a consultancy for a major magazine publisher and television production company through his business 'Meaning Research'.

SHARI KENDALL is a doctoral candidate in linguistics with a concentration in sociolinguistics at Georgetown University. In addition to her research on workplace communication, she has presented papers on the representation of gay men and lesbians in media coverage of gay rights controversies, interpersonal communication in lesbian couples, and the creation of authority in religious discourse.

BONNIE McELHINNY is Assistant Professor of Anthropology at the University of Toronto. Her work focuses on language, gender and political economy. She has published chapters and articles in *American Speech, Gender Articulated, The Clinical Law Review* and *Sociolinguistics and Language Teaching*. She is completing an ethnography currently entitled 'Policing Gender', based on her fieldwork with the Pittsburgh police department.

NORA RÄTHZEL is Researcher at the University of Bremen and at the Institut für Migration und Rassismusforschung in Hamburg. Her research interests include everyday racism, gender relations and ethnic relations. She is co-author of *Female Sexualization* and is a member of the editorial board of *Social Identities* and the *International Association for the Study of Racism*.

AMY SHELDON is a professor in the Department of Speech-Communication at the University of Minnesota, where she is also on the graduate faculties of Linguistics and Feminist Studies, and is an Affiliate of the Center for Cognitive Sciences. Her research has focused on child and adult first and second language acquisition. In 1996 she was guest editor of an issue of the journal *Research on Language and Social Interaction*.

ALYSON SIMPSON lectures in language, literature and gender studies. She combines her interests in critical discourse theory with feminist poststructuralism to examine the construction of gendered subject positionings in children's interactions. She is presently completing her doctoral studies with a thesis entitled '"It's my turn!": a critical discourse analysis of the construction of gendered subjectivity in children's games' at the University of Western Sydney.

DEBORAH TANNEN is University Professor and Professor of Linguistics at Georgetown University. In addition to gender and language, her research interests include conversational style, spoken and written language, and cross-cultural communication. Her publications include *Conversational Style: Analysing Talk Among Friends* (1984), *Talking Voices: Repetition, Dialogue and Imagery in Conversational Discourse* (1989), *You Just Don't Understand* (1990), *Talking From 9 to 5: Women and Men in the Workplace: Language, Sex and Power* (1994) and *Gender and Discourse* (1994).

INTRODUCTION: SOME IMPORTANT ISSUES IN THE RESEARCH OF GENDER AND DISCOURSE

Ruth Wodak

Aims and goals

Research on gender and sex in sociolinguistics and discourse analysis started in the early 1970s. Investigators examined two domains of language behaviour in particular: speech behaviour of men and women on the phonological level, and interactions (conversational styles) between women and men in discourse. In this introduction, I will first discuss some concepts of 'gender/sex' and 'discourse' and suggest possible working definitions. In addition, I would like to trace briefly the theoretical development of gender studies in feminist linguistics, thereby providing a general introductory framework for this volume (see Wodak and Benke, 1996; Holmes, 1996).

Studies of gender-specific language behaviour are often contradictory and depend on the author's implicit assumptions about sex and gender, methodology, samples used, etc. As a result, as stated by Eckert and McConnell-Ginet, 'women's language has been said to reflect their conservatism, prestige consciousness, upward mobility, insecurity, deference, nurturance, emotional expressivity, connectedness, sensitivity to others, solidarity. And men's language is heard as evincing their toughness, lack of affect, competitiveness, independence, competence, hierarchy, control' (1992: 90).

Owing to the many contradictory approaches, assumptions and results, it is necessary to develop a critical approach to this vast literature. All the claims made about women and men at different times, in different circumstances and with totally different samples, on the basis of different implicit ideologies about gender, must be analysed carefully and viewed in relation to the development of gender studies in the social sciences.

In my view, many empirical studies have neglected the context of language behaviour and have often analysed gender by merely looking at the speakers' biological sex (see the arguments in Nichols, 1983; Eckert,

1989; Cameron and Coates, 1990; Henley and Kramerae, 1991; Duranti and Goodwin, 1992; Crawford, 1995; Kotthoff and Wodak, 1997). Some of the research has isolated the variable of sex/gender from other sociological or situational factors and has made hasty generalizations about genderlects. Instead, I would like to propose that a context-sensitive approach which regards gender as a social construct would lead to more fruitful results (see Harres, 1996; Wetschanow, 1995). Moreover, I would like to suggest a look at gender in connection with the socio-cultural and ethnic background of the interlocutors, and in connection with their age, their level of education, their socio-economic status, their emotions and the specific power-dynamics of the discourse investigated.

Gender and sex

Basic assumptions

The point of departure for gender studies is (or was) the critique of the assumption of binary sexuality, the presupposition that the differentia-tion between the two 'sexes' is a natural fact, 'evidently' represented in the body. The feminist movement criticized not this assumed biological, binary concept of sex but the frequently accepted biological determina-tion of culturally conditioned traits as 'gender-typical qualities'. Here, above all, feminists criticized those traits employed in justifying the unequal and unjust treatment of women. On the one hand, they dismantled myths of femininity which, from an evolutionary viewpoint, were derived from traditional stereotypes such as the myth that all women are 'caring' from birth in a biologically determined way. On the other hand, they criticized that, through its constant reiteration, the traditional division of labour between the sexes contributes towards the reinforcement and perpetuation of these myths about biologically conditioned gender traits (Wetschanow, 1995: 12).

> By contrast, here the sociologically reasoned view is advocated that the gender roles allotted by society are based on the anatomical difference between the sexes, but that their manifestations evince such enormous differences over different historical eras and in different cultures that the attempt to legitimize them by recourse to 'nature' seems untenable and – wherever it is never-theless undertaken – ideologically highly suspicious. . . Painstaking investiga-tions, including intercultural comparisons, have not to date produced any evidence of the biological determination of those 'typically' male and female traits and forms of behaviour which constitute the sexual characters in the common understanding. . . To name just one example, this applies to Freud's idea that 'activity' is male and 'passivity' female. (Rohde-Dachser, 1991: 25ff)

To avoid such a naturalization of characteristics and attributes, research-ers differentiated between 'sex' and 'gender'. This sex/gender concept results from the assumption that a cultural sex – a gender – takes on a culturally specific form against the background of biological sex. Such an understanding implies that the sex/gender concept operates on the principle that, while the binarity of the sexes is an immutable fact, the traits assigned to a sex by a culture are cultural constructions, that they are socially determined and therefore alterable.

Recently, critics of gender studies have aimed their attacks at the 'construction of a basic binary structure' as such. The category of gender has itself become the centre of analysis and the deconstruction of difference has become a subject (see Cameron, Chapter 1; Simpson, Chapter 8 in this volume; and see the section on 'The constructedness of the sexes' in this chapter, 11–12).

Some definitions

The British sociologist Anthony Giddens defines 'sex' as 'biological or anatomical differences between men and women', whereas 'gender' 'concerns the psychological, social and cultural differences between males and females' (1989: 158). On the basis of these characterizations, it seems relatively easy to distinguish between the two categories. However, the definitions miss the level of perception and attribution, the way gender stereotypes often influence the interaction of self- and other assessment. Giddens does mention some syndromes of 'abnormal' development, such as the testicular feminization syndrome and the androgenital syndrome, that is where infants designated as 'female' at birth, even if chromosomally male, tend to develop female gender identity, and vice versa (see Cameron's discussion in Chapter 1 in this volume; Wodak and Benke, 1996: 128ff).

In a social construction perspective not only gender, but even sex is seen as a socially developed status (Lorber and Farrell, 1991a). In this context sex is understood more as a continuum constructed of chromosomal sex, gonadal sex, and hormonal sex – all of which 'work in the presence and under the influence of a set of environments' (Fausto-Sterling, 1985: 71). It makes no sense therefore to assume that there is merely one set of traits that generally characterizes men and thus defines masculinity; or likewise, that there is one set of traits for women which defines femininity. Such an unitary model of sexual character is a familiar part of sexual ideology and serves to reify inequality between men and women in our society. It also makes possible numerous socio-biological explanations relating neurological facts with linguistic behaviour (Chambers, 1992).

In contrast to such biological ideologies, Connell (1993: 170ff) proposes a non-unitary model of gender. Both femininity and masculinity vary and understanding their context-dependent variety is regarded as central to the psychology of gender. He argues also that, since masculinity and femininity coexist in the same person, they should be seen not as polar natural opposites but as separate dimensions. 'Femininity and masculinity are not essences: they are ways of living certain relationships. It follows that static typologies of sexual character have to be replaced by histories, analyses of the joint production of sets of psychological forms' (Connell, 1993: 179).[1]

In addition to such a perspective Lewontin stresses the relevance of the socialization process: the development of a person's gender identity 'depends on what label was attached to him or her as a child. . . Thus biological differences became a signal for, rather than a cause of, differentiation in social roles' (1982: 142). This definition connects the impact of societal norms and evaluations, power structures and the role of socialization remarkably well (see also Sheldon, Chapter 9 in this volume; Wodak, 1986; Wodak and Schulz, 1986; Wodak and Vetter, forthcoming; and the 'Social-psychological Theory of Text Planning', proposed in the latter studies, which will not be elaborated upon here).

In the context of this perspective, it is more coherent to talk of gender as the understanding of how what it means to be a woman or to be a man changes from one generation to the next and how this perception varies between different racialized, ethnic, and religious groups, as well as for members of different social classes (see Gal, 1989: 178; Stolcke, 1993: 20; Lorber and Farrell, 1991a: 1ff). Gender categories thus are seen as social constructs. They institutionalize cultural and social statuses and they serve to make male dominance over women appear natural: 'gender inequality in class society results from a historically specific tendency to ideologically "naturalize" prevailing socio-economic inequalities' (Stolcke, 1993: 19).

Discourse

The term 'discourse' integrates a range of occasionally contradictory or exclusionary meanings in its daily and philosophical uses (Vass, 1992: 1; Maas, 1988). Fairclough (1992: 3) points to several ways in which the concept appears, stressing how they arise in modern discourse analysis: 'samples of spoken dialogue, in contrast with written texts', 'spoken and written language'; 'situational context of language use'; 'interaction between reader/writer and text'; and 'notion of genre' (newspaper discourse, for example). In 'discursive psychology' (Harré and Stearns, 1995: 2ff), moreover, 'discourse' refers to the totality of signs that carry meaning: the mind is seen as the product of the signs encountered, including non-verbal signs.

These various meanings of 'discourse' are usually employed in an unreflecting way. It is frequently unclear as to whether a short text sequence is meant or a whole variety of text, or if a very abstract phenomenon is to be understood under this heading.[2] Consequently, I shall try to clearly distinguish between the concepts of discourse, text and discourse analysis.

It is not possible in this chapter to provide an extensive overview of all developments in discourse analysis or all the different notions of 'discourse' established in divergent paradigms (see van Dijk, 1985: 4; 1990; Schiffrin, 1993: 21; Renkeema, 1993; Vass, 1992: 9; Titscher et al., 1997). Instead, I would like to focus only on definitions that are important for the contributions presented in this book. I will begin by differentiating between 'text' and 'discourse'. I shall then offer my own approach to the concept of 'discourse' which has developed and changed over many years of studying gender, institutions and political discourse from a discourse sociolinguistic point of view (Wodak, 1996; Wodak et al., 1997a) and which shares elements, but is not identical, with the approaches of Teun van Dijk (1990: 163ff; 1993) and Norman Fairclough (1992: 62ff; Fairclough and Wodak, 1997).

Discourse and text

Gisela Brünner and Gabriele Graefen (1993: 7–8) characterize the main differences between 'text' and 'discourse' in the following way:

> By *discourse* are to be understood units and forms of speech, of interaction, which can be part of everyday linguistic behaviour, but which can equally appear in an institutional sphere. Orality, admittedly, is not a feature which holds true for *all* forms of discursive behaviour . . . but is very much the typical case. Regarded systematically, discourse requires the co-presence of speaker and listener ('face-to-face interaction'); this can, however, be reduced to a temporal co-presence (on the telephone).

Brünner and Graefen also define discourse as the totality of interactions in a certain domain (medical discourse, for example) which appears similar to the definition offered by Foucault (see Wodak, 1996: 24). 'Text', however, has different roots, in both philology and literature:

> In the context of a theory of linguistic behaviour, it is an essential determination of the text that the linguistic behaviour, which is made material in the text, is detached from the overall common speech situation just as is the receptive behaviour of the reader – the common ground being understood in a systematic, not a historical sense. In a text, speech behaviour assumes the quality of knowledge, which is in the service of transmission and is stored for later use . . . the written form, which is constitutive for the everyday use of the term, and today is frequently regarded as almost synonymous with 'text', is therefore not a necessary feature of a text.

Text does not have to be written, according to Brünner and Graefen (1993) who rely on the theory of 'functional pragmatics', founded by Konrad Ehlich. There Ehlich also speaks of the 'extended speech situation' (1983) (*zerdehnte Sprechsituation*) which, in his opinion, is characteristic for 'texts', in contrast to 'discourse'. Discourse must not be oral. The main difference lies in the function of 'handing down' (*Überlieferung*) and in the simultaneous existence (or absence) of a situational context. Thus, discourse may be defined as 'text in context' (van Dijk, 1990: 164) on the one hand, and as a 'set of texts' on the other (Dressler and Merlini-Barbaresi, 1994: 6).[3]

Van Dijk also points to a decisive aspect, which is that discourse should also be understood as action: 'I understand "discourse" . . . both as a specific form of language use, and as a specific form of social interaction, interpreted as a complete communicative event in a social situation' (1990: 164; see also Eggins and Iedema, Chapter 7 in this volume). The behavioural aspect is very important and relates to Ludwig Wittgenstein's concepts of 'language game' and 'form of life' as well as to Jürgen Habermas's concept of 'ordinary language' (Leodolter, 1975: 27; Wodak, 1996: 12). Both are also of crucial significance to the development of speech act theory of D.A. Austin and John Searle (see Schiffrin, 1993: 49; Wodak, 1986: 229). These approaches emphasize the integration of non-verbal and verbal language behaviour, as well as the definition of discourse to be seen as action (*Sprachhandlung*). Discourse is thus inseparable from other forms of social practice.

Discourse as social practice

In most studies, the self-contained communicative act is the centre of interest. This points to a fundamentally more difficult and complex question – the extent to which a unit of discourse may be defined as self-contained at all. We shall return to that question again (see Chapters 3, 4 and 5 in this volume). At this point, it only needs to be noted that, in terms of the range of the concept of discourse, there is no objective beginning and no clearly defined end. *In principle* – because of intertextuality – every discourse is related to many others and can only be understood on the basis of others. The limitation of the research area and on a specific discourse therefore depends on a subjective decision by the researcher, on the formulation of the questions guiding the research (Kress, 1993).

Taking all these considerations into account, I would like, above all, to emphasize the behavioural aspect and therefore suggest the following definition of discourse (see Fairclough, 1992: 62; Fairclough and Wodak, 1997):

> *Critical Discourse Analysis sees discourse – the use of language in speech and writing – as a form of 'social practice'.* Describing discourse as social practice implies a dialectical relationship between a particular discursive event and the situation, institution and social structure that frame it: the discursive event is shaped by them, but it also shapes them. That is, discourse is socially constituted, as well as socially conditioned – it constitutes situations, objects of knowledge, and the social identities of and relationships between people and groups of people. It is constitutive both in the sense that it helps sustain and reproduce the social status quo, and in the sense that it contributes to transforming it. (Wodak, 1996: 17)

This provides a direct link to our discussion of organizations and institutions (see Chapters 2, 5 and 6 in this volume) in which the reality constituting element of discourse is emphasized.[4] In addition, it becomes evident that questions of power and ideology[5] are connected with discourse, every interaction is thus influenced by power relationships resulting in the speech-situation and the overall context.

The distortion of discourse (in Habermas's sense: see Wodak, 1996: 28) leads to 'disorders of discourse' in everyday interaction. Understanding seems to be an exception; misunderstanding and conflict are frequently to be detected. Critical discourse analysis in my view, is an instrument whose purpose is precisely to expose power structures and 'disorders of discourse'.

Feminist linguistics

Analogous to the term 'racism', the word 'sexism' was invented in the 1960s. It refers to discrimination within a social system on the basis of sexual membership. In Western culture, as in most other social systems, this means, in concrete terms, that there are exactly two sexes in binary opposition to each other: female and male. The relationship between these two categories is not an equal or egalitarian one but a hierarchical one, where the category 'man' or 'male' is the norm and the category 'woman' or 'female' represents the 'other' and the 'abnormal', that is the 'marked version' – logically following the normativeness of the male (Wetschanow, 1995: 18ff; Crawford, 1995; Coates, 1993; Chapters 1 and 2 in this volume). With the concept of 'sexism', women defined themselves for the first time as a social group and as a suppressed minority. As such, they sought to reveal the mechanisms of suppression, making others aware of and fighting these devices. Social groups often define themselves by means of their common language which plays an important role in identity creation and, for subcultures, serves as a means of differentiating themselves from the outside world. This specific identity manifests itself in certain conversational styles, manifestations of emotions etc. (see Coates, Chapter 10 in this volume).

Research conducted by feminist-oriented women should by no means be equated with either research conducted by women or research on women. Feminist scholarship in every discipline is characterized by its criticism of science and its criticism of the androcentric view within 'traditional science'. Feminist linguistics (FL) developed within linguistics. Many proposals and basic assumptions of FL relate to and overlap with principles of critical linguistics and critical discourse analysis (see Fairclough and Wodak, 1997; Wodak, 1996: 17ff) as well as with the qualitative paradigm in the social sciences (Cicourel, 1992). It would be beneficial to investigate these parallel developments from the standpoints of the theory of knowledge, history and sociology to find reciprocal influences (which, unfortunately, cannot be accomplished in the course of this introduction). Throughout this volume, however, some intersections and influences of critical discourse analysis and FL with and on each other are mentioned (see especially Chapters 2 and 5).

According to Marlis Hellinger, FL is distinguished from all other disciplines by the following three aspects, which similarly analyse the relationship between language and gender:

1. FL places female and male linguistic behavior and the linguistic phenomena connected with the designations of women and men at the centre of its considerations.
2. FL interprets persons-related asymmetries in the field of language systems and language use as expressions of the linguistic discrimination of women (sexism) and links these directly to the plane of social discrimination. Traditional studies usually make do with descriptive results . . . .
3. FL does not accept phenomena as given, but seeks alternatives in keeping with the principle of the linguistic equal treatment of women and men. It pursues explicitly political goals by criticizing ruling linguistic norms and understanding the linguistic change it advocates as part of an overall change in society. (Hellinger, 1990: 12)

For FL researchers, both the system-oriented and the behaviour-related approaches to language are of interest as the following two questions must be answered:

1. How are women represented in the existing language system?
2. How does the linguistic behaviour of the group of women differ from that of men?

'Language has never been seen by feminists as a detached system and speaking never as a detached technique' (Günther and Kotthoff, 1991: 17). Representatives of FL do not have a 'purely scientific' interest in investigating the connection between language and sex, that is in describing this connection, but they are concerned with assessing this relationship. FL is an explicitly partisan form of linguistics. It goes beyond analysis. It produces concrete proposals for change and makes socio-political claims (Wodak et al., 1997b; Postl, 1991: 27).

Sociolinguistic studies of sex/gender

In the 1970s, 'sex' was established within sociolinguistic research as a social variable next to the already-existing variables of social stratum, age, nationality, ethnic affiliation, religion, class and region. In correlative-quantitative sociolinguistic investigations on the prestige and stigma variants of languages (see Kotthoff, 1992) the sex variable became a factor which significantly affected the use of language. The best-known representatives of this quantitative-correlative approach in sociolinguistics, with its focus on urban groups of persons, are William Labov, Peter Trudgill and Lesley Milroy.[6] The working methods within this sociolinguistic approach diverge considerably from one another in certain aspects (unlike Trudgill and Labov, Milroy works with network analyses) but in one respect they are identical: their methodology. All of them operate quantitatively, that is linguistic variables are defined that are realized in different forms and in different varieties (Kotthoff, 1992). Then, the different variants are correlated with sociological parameters.

Several other studies have taken very different approaches and have used methodologies other than the approaches mentioned above. In particular, a lot of criticism related to the implicit chauvinistic ideologies in these first studies and also to the undifferentiated analysis of the two sexes which totally neglected the range of variation in each of the genders under observation. In my own study of the language of mothers and daughters in Vienna, for example (Wodak, 1983; 1984; 1985), I showed that, apart from these sociological parameters, other variables, such as psychological ones, are also responsible for the variation concerning each gender. Based on this research, I proposed the 'Theory of the Socio-Psychological Variation' (see also Wodak, 1984; Wodak and Schulz, 1986). This study stressed in particular the variation that was found *among* the women and girls investigated, one which relativized the factor of 'sex'.

Thus, the empirical study of variation showed that the linguistic differences in the speech behaviour between mother and daughter were greater than those between mother and son, even in stable and friendly relationships. Moreover, upwardly mobile daughters spoke hypercorrectly, in specific demarcation from their mothers and their social class. One of the most significant results was the determination that some upper middle class daughters spoke the most dialectical style as a result of the bad relationship with the mother and not because of the class factor.

Another approach of considerable importance in recent sociolinguistics is the concept of 'communities of practice' (Eckert and McConnell-Ginet, 1992: 92ff). 'Communities of practice are defined as an aggregate of people who come together around mutual engagement in some common endeavour. Ways of doing things, ways of talking, beliefs, values, power relations – in short, practice – emerge in the course of their joint activity around that endeavour' (1992: 95).

Gender is produced and reproduced in differential membership in such communities of practice. Women define themselves in respect to other women, men to men. Women and men differ in the paths they take to obtain greater social status. Women are under constant pressure to display their persona (Eckert, 1989: 247ff). Both Eckert and McConnell-Ginet argue very convincingly and provide many examples to support their view that survey studies are too general and their level of abstractness too great. As a result, many subtle and important intervening variables have been neglected, including the context, that is the communities of practice.

Sexism and the language system

Feminists conceive language as 'a symbolical reflection of androcentric structures' (Günther and Kotthoff, 1991: 7), as one of the means of patriarchal society to discriminate, disregard and incapacitate women.[7] In their view, the language system already reflects the patriarchal structure of Western societies.

> The language system was analyzed as regards the treatment of women, and language was exposed as a means of legitimizing male structures with the intention, above all, of extracting women from being subsumed under general and male categories. Together with the language system, linguistic behaviour was made into the object for analysis of the new research discipline and the issue of gender-specific differences was investigated in styles of communication. (1991: 32)

The assumption that an individual language system has lexical elements and morphological and grammatical rules that are already sexist is based on the premise that 'due to their long history as public decision-makers, men not only determine the economic, political and social orientation of social life, but also influence the functioning and the semantic contents of each individual language' (Postl, 1991: 89).

Once the language system has become the object of investigation for feminist linguists, it is interesting to note how the linguistic structure of an individual language is connected to the structure of society, how the structure of the language is conditioned by the structure of society and vice versa. Unlike studies investigating the divergent gender linguistic behaviour, studies on the sexist use of language focus on the possibilities of reference to both genders or their practice that exist in an individual language. According to Pusch, the objects of 'feminist system linguistics' are 'partriarchalisms in diverse language systems':

> As a feminist linguist I reject part of these 'latent laws' (i.e. clotted sexisms) and when speaking and writing employ my 'ungrammatical' inventions and deliberate violations of the rules intentionally and as often as possible, with the aim of establishing them as grammatical and gradually making the old misogynist laws alter their status to 'deviations'. (1990: 13)

A solution, an opportunity to create awareness, is seen by feminist linguists as a break with tradition, a deliberate violation of the traditional and conventional linguistic rules which enables reflection on these rules, assumed to be given or 'extraconscious'. This, so their argument continues, creates the potential for change (see Pusch, 1990: 16; Frank, 1992: 121). In the 'Guidelines to Prevent the Use of Sexist

Language' (Guentherodt et al., 1982: 2) this desire for individual action is very clearly expressed. The authors of the article word their objective as follows:

> The aim of these guidelines for the non-sexist use of language is to identify sexist language and to offer alternative uses that are neither hostile to women nor discriminating.

The analysis of conversation and discourse

Unlike the above-mentioned research field, FL – which examines the use of language – concerns itself with gender differences in conversation and discourse (oral as well as written). Differences are investigated in the following fields of language use: voice, pronunciation, intonation, choice of words, argumentation, lexicon, syntax, interactional and conversational behaviour, as well as visual features and modes and non-verbal communication. The gender-induced differences in the use of language were and are not treated simply as divergent variants standing side by side. By virtue of a patriarchally organized society, the interpretation of the differences ascertained is of major significance.

The interpretation of the diverse linguistic indicators (like turn-taking, indirectness, interruptions and overlaps) varies according to the specific gender theory and ideology which underlie the studies. Probably the two best-known theories about the gender-induced use of language are those of 'difference' and 'dominance'. I will not elaborate upon them here as they have been treated extensively elsewhere in this book (see Chapters 1, 2 and 4; see also Henley and Kramerae, 1991; Wodak and Benke, 1996; Kotthoff and Wodak, 1997; Harres, 1996).

Whereas investigations following the 'dominance model' have interpreted the use of such indicators as manifestations of 'powerless language of women', research in the paradigm of the 'difference model' views the linguistic behaviour of men and women as originating in opposed modes of socialization and equal in their meaning and impact. Hedging, tag questions or indirectness can be viewed 'negatively' or 'positively', either as signs of female insecurity or as supporting conversational work, depending on the context of the discourse and the theoretical approach adopted.

Recent theoretical approaches in the feminist study of discourse

The constructedness of the sexes Judith Butler expresses the significance of the 'sex' category in its most varied dimensions in the following way:

as 'identity' is assured through the stabilizing concepts of sex, gender, and sexuality, the very notion of 'the person' is called into question by the cultural emergence of those 'incoherent' or 'discontinuous' gendered beings who appear to be persons but who fail to conform to the gendered norms of cultural intelligibility by which persons are defined. (1990: 17)

In her arguments against the tenability of the categories of 'women' and 'sex', Judith Butler (1990) has referred more explicitly to postmodernist theories. In the manner of Foucault she ascribes normative power to the idea of gender identity and the attempt to describe it. By the mere act of defining a gender identity many bodies, practices and discourses are excluded or devalued, whereas the constructed and hence upright character of this gender identity is simultaneously concealed (Young, 1994: 226).

Although I agree with some of the proposals made in these approaches, one also has to take into account that in our societies biological sex is still used as a powerful categorization device: for example, in many occupations women are still paid less than men for the same achievements and positions. In these contexts, biological sex as a 'natural factor' is still salient and certainly not only a variable social construct. Therefore, it has to be repeated that all these assumptions and analyses are context dependent: they are valid for some aspects of social and institutional life, but not for all. However, in these recent feminist theories (Butler, 1990) the idea of two sexes is criticized as being a construction, a prediscursive factor taking the place of reality. Following this interpretation, 'sex' cannot be separated into a biologically inherent aspect and a socially acquired one. The category of 'sex' itself is a purely cultural product of discourse. It is denied that it is a 'universal, suprahistorical and extrasocial entity'; it is understood to be an 'integral component of every form of life'. More recently, some authors have differentiated Butler's dogmatic position: it is a question of revealing 'the reproduction mechanisms, networks and institutional compulsions that ensure that constructions become persistent and resistant and appear timeless, immovable and identical with themselves' (Hirschauer, 1992: 333). It is a matter of exposing the arbitrary construction of this binary opposition and hence also its mutability, and not of criticizing the binarily organized perception as unreal. For:

Even if there is no such thing as natural biological sexual bodies and the anatomical definition is contingent on the state of knowledge in biology, the constructions of 'male' and 'female' bodies are effective. They become part of physical perception and gain reality through 'physical practices'. (Lorey, 1993: 20)

Doing gender Unlike a research approach that accepts sexual differences as an aggregation of qualities and deals with the qualitative behavioural tendencies of women and men, ethnomethodologically oriented studies produced a new focus of research: 'doing gender'. A conception of gender as an aggregation of attributes is concerned with investigating and displaying the peculiarities of women and interpreting them as 'gender-specific or gender-typical attributes' so as to reveal the asymmetry of the difference between the sexes, to criticize it and to make it politically visible. Such a paradigm of characteristics complicates or renders impossible an interactional approach since attributes are 'entities' and not processes. A further problem raised by the concept of gender as a concept of attributes is the possibility of individualization; that is the individual who has been seen to possess or not to possess certain attributes becomes the centre of attention, and the level of the social system is neglected.

Unlike this non-interactive approach, 'doing gender' regards membership of a gender not as a pool of attributes 'possessed' by a person, but as something a person 'does'. In this sense, membership of a gender constitutes a performative act and not a fact. Gender is continually realized in interactional form. Gender is created not only in the everyday activities which characterize 'doing gender', but also in the asymmetry of the relationship between the sexes, the dominance of the 'male' and its normativeness. Patriarchal inequality is produced and reproduced in every interaction (Wetschanow, 1995: 15; Harres, 1996: 18ff; West and Zimmermann, 1991). This concept of 'doing gender' stresses the creative potential and the embedding of gender-typical behaviour in a social context. Thus, according to Hagemann-White, for the practice of feminist research this would mean that attributes stated to be gender-typical must be reinterpreted as 'means of producing, perpetuating and personally performing the polarity of the sexes' (1993: 20).

Presentation of the volume

What connects the diverse, ideologically and theoretically distinct approaches in this volume is the clear basic assumption that the context of the respective discourse has to be included and integrated into the study of gender and discourse.

The first three chapters are dedicated to general and basic inter-disciplinary issues surrounding the topic of gender and discourse. Deborah Cameron investigates the debates about the concepts of sex/gender and its relationship to language and language use, and the implications of that relationship. She positions herself as a feminist linguist, defined as having a critical view of the arrangement between the sexes. In an extensive and critical study, she reviews the development of the studies of gender and discourse and the diverse theoretical and ideological approaches and assumptions underlying this research, finally presenting her own position relating to Eckert and McConnell-Ginet's (1992) concept of 'communities of practice' (see earlier). Victoria

DeFrancisco investigates the many intersections between discourse, gender and power, integrating several important sociological concepts (such as Pierre Bourdieu, Jürgen Habermas, Hannah Arendt and Steven Lukes). She focuses on the importance of resistance to power and societal norms, and believes that feminist linguists should find social and discursive practices which enable women in different cultures to resist dominance and power.

Using data from Germany, university students' discussions about Turks, men and women, and their images and perception among the German population, Nora Räthzel addresses another central dimension in this field: the relationship of racism, gender and discourse. The 'foreigner problem' has grown to enormous proportions in Central and Western Europe, owing to the fall of the 'Iron Curtain' in 1989–90. This chapter offers many political and practical implications for everyday dealing with 'the other' and with practices of everyday racism.

The next six chapters deal with our societies' different institutions and organizations, analysing conversations between women and men, or observing interactions of the genders. Shari Kendall and Deborah Tannen summarize the research on gender, discourse and the workplace while presenting their own framework for understanding the relationship between power, gender and workplace communication. The framing approach that Deborah Tannen proposes draws on Erving Goffman to point out that the relationship between gender and language is 'sex-class linked': ways of speaking are associated with women or men as a class in a given society. This concept is related then to the sociolinguistic theory of power and solidarity.

Bonnie McElhinny analyses extensively some sequences of public and private language, illustrating that the traditional distinctions between the public and the private have become obsolete. She includes a very elaborated and extensive critique on conversational analysis and the understanding of context. The data are drawn from several of her own empirical studies conducted in police and welfare institutions. David Corson focuses on the institution of school and the relationships of boys and girls in classrooms. Based on his discussion of 'options' and 'ligatures' as the two consequences which people draw from education, he suggests that the access to options and ligatures is linked to power and gendered discursive practices and norms which are produced and reproduced through the institution of education.

Suzanne Eggins and Rick Iedema present the only contribution dealing with written discourse with their examination of women's magazines. They compare two Australian magazines in all their dimensions, visual and verbal, applying the Hallidayan framework of functional systemics linguistics. This chapter provides insight into the social perceptions and images of women, as well as their impact on the potential readership. The authors apply Bernstein's control theory in explaining the different semiotic modes of the two magazines and the impact of an elaborated or

restricted coding orientation on the readership and their choice of meanings. Two contributions then deal with children's discursive practices,
but from very different theoretical positions and underlying assumptions.
Alyson Simpson analyses tape recordings from family interactions and
explores issues of power and subjectivity while members of the family
play games. She applies a post structuralist framework to highlight the
position of power which exists in this family and the relationship of
power to gender and generation. She is also specifically concerned with
the role of the 'mother' in this interaction. Through her data from peer
group interactions, Amy Sheldon illustrates that both boys and girls have
conflicts and strategies for conflict solving, but that these are different for
the two genders. These results contradict many stereotypes about girls
and women (such as that they do not act out their aggressions). Through
this 'double-voicing' framework, she shows that girls utilize very specific
discursive styles when arguing with each other.

The final two chapters concern different gendered discursive practices in everyday situations in diverse cultures. They are more ethno-
graphically oriented than the other contributions. Jennifer Coates
analyses conversations between women friends. She places emphasis on
the discursive practices which are used in 'doing friendship' which she
claims differ between men and women. The primary goal of talk
between women friends, she suggests, is the construction and maintenance of close and equal social relationships. She draws on a huge
corpus of conversation and interviews with women.

Janet Holmes presents a wide range of data from interviews with
women and men, focusing on the narratives and the distinct differences
between these narratives in New Zealand – a very traditional culture
where gender roles are concerned. She provides a model for analysing
narratives, content and form, and extrapolates the everyday practices
used in relating experiences to each other. She succeeds in finding very
typical narrative genres and discursive gender practices.

This volume addresses a wide audience of scholars and non-specialists.
The very different approaches, methodologies and authentic data present
the openness and wide variety of this field. In addition, very central
questions and issues surrounding gender identity and gender politics are
discussed which serve to raise awareness about gender, power,
ideologies, institutions, everyday practices, culture and discourse.

Notes

I would like to thank Gertraud Benke and Karin Wetschanow for sharing their
ideas with me, especially for the section on feminist linguistics, and Rick Iedema,
Martin Reisigl and David Corson for their comments on this chapter. I am also
very grateful to Alexandra Thurman for correcting my English. I am naturally
solely responsible for the final version.

1. Discursive psychologists (like Rom Harré) talk about 'positioning' – a unique intersection of discursive relationships for all of us (see Corson, 1995).

2. We cannot deal, in this context, with the convergence of developments within text linguistics and discourse analysis. See Vass (1992: 10), Beaugrande and Dressler (1981).

3. See also Fairclough: 'my attempt at drawing together language analysis and social theory centres upon a combination of this more social-theoretical sense of discourse [in Foucault's sense: author] with the "text-interaction" sense in linguistically-oriented discourse analysis' (1992: 4). Fairclough continues in defining three dimensions of 'discourse': any discursive event is seen as an instance of discursive and social practice. 'Text' relates to the linguistic analysis, 'discourse' to the interaction, to processes of text production and interpretation. The 'social practice' dimension relates to the institutional context of the discursive event. Any transcript of discourse, according to Fairclough, however, would be labelled 'text'. Fairclough himself is very influenced by Foucault and Pêcheux, but mostly also by Hallidayan linguistics (Fairclough, 1992: 55ff).

4. An example of the reality constituting characteristics of discourse would be the various guidelines for non-sexist use of language (Wodak et al., 1987). By the use of both male and female forms, it is hoped that ultimately the consciousness of users will be changed and not just language use. Making women visible in discourse would, therefore, also result in a different evaluation of women.

5. The whole notion of 'ideology' and its relationship to discourse is far too complex to discuss extensively in this introduction (see Chapters 3 and 5 in this volume). I would just like to propose a definition which could serve as a basis for what follows: 'ideologies are particular ways of representing and constructing society which reproduce unequal relations of power, relations of domination and exploitation. Ideologies are often (though not necessarily) false or ungrounded constructions of society' (Wodak, 1996: 18). See also Wodak et al. (1989), Corson (1993), and van Dijk (1997) for other conflicting definitions and diverse approaches to the concept of ideology.

6. See Labov (1966), Trudgill (1972; 1974) and Milroy and Milroy (1978). See also Cameron (1990), Coates and Cameron (1990), Coates (1993), Kotthoff (1992), and Wodak and Benke (1996) for critical discussions of sociolinguistic gender studies.

7. See Wetschanow (1995: 20ff), Mills (1995), Wilkinson and Kitzinger (1995), Samel (1995), Schissler (1993) and Gräszel (1991) for overviews in these domains of FL.

References

Beaugrande, Robert and Dressler, Wolfgang (1981) *Einführung in die Textlinguistik*. Niemeyer: Tübingen.

Brünner, Gisela and Graefen, Gabriele (1993) 'Einleitung: zur Konzeption der funktionalen Pragmatik', in Gisela Brünner and Gabriele Graefen (eds), *Texte und Diskurse*. Opladen: Westdeutscher Verlag. pp. 7–24.

Butler, Judith (1990) *Gender Trouble: Feminism and the Subversion of Identity*. New York: Routledge.

Cameron, Deborah (1990) 'Introduction', in Jennifer Coates and Deborah

Cameron (eds), *Women in their Speech Communities: New Perspectives on Language and Sex*. London: Longman. pp. 3–12

Cameron, Deborah and Coates, Jennifer (1990) 'Some problems in the sociolinguistic explanation of sex differences', in Jennifer Coates and Deborah Cameron (eds), *Women in their Speech Communities: New Perspectives on Language and Sex*. London: Longman. pp. 13–26.

Chambers, Jack, K. (1992) 'Linguistic correlates and gender in sex', *English World Wide*, 2: 173–218.

Cicourel, Aaron (1992) 'The interpenetration of communicative contexts: examples from medical encounters', in Alessandro Duranti and Charles Goodwin (eds), *Rethinking Context: Language as an Interactive Phenomenon*. Cambridge: Cambridge University Press. pp. 291–310.

Coates, Jennifer (1993) *Women, Men and Language*. London: Longman.

Connell, R.W. (1993) *Gender and Power: Society, the Person and Sexual Politics* (1987). Oxford: Polity.

Corson, David (1993)'Discursive bias and ideology in the administration of minority group interests', *Language in Society*, 22: 165–91.

Corson, David (1995) *Using English Words*. Amsterdam: Kluwer.

Crawford, Mary (1995) *Talking Difference: on Gender and Language*. London: Sage.

Dressler, Wolfgang U. and Merlini-Barbaresi, Livia (1994) *Morphopragmatics*. Berlin: Mouton.

Duranti, Alessandro and Goodwin, Charles (eds) (1992) *Rethinking Context: Language as an Interactive Phenomenon*. Cambridge: Cambridge University Press.

Eckert, Penelope (1989) 'The whole woman: sex and gender differences in variation', *Language Variation and Change*, 3: 245–67.

Eckert, Penelope and McConnell-Ginet, Sally (1992) 'Communities of practice: where language, gender, and power all live', in Kira Hall, Mary Bucholtz and Birch Moonwomon (eds), *Locating Power: Proceedings of the Second Berkeley Women and Language Conference*. Berkeley, CA: Berkeley Women and Language Group, University of California–Berkeley. pp. 89–99.

Ehlich, Konrad (1983) 'Text und sprachliches Handeln', in Aleida Assmann, Jan Assmann and Christoph Herdmair (eds), *Schrift und Gedächtnis*. Munich: Fink. pp. 24–43.

Fausto-Sterling, Anthony (1985) *Myths of Gender: Biological Theories about Women and Men*. New York: Basic Books.

Fairclough, Norman (1992) *Discourse and Social Change*. London: Polity.

Fairclough, Norman and Wodak, Ruth (1997) 'Critical discourse analysis: an overview', in Teun van Dijk (ed.), *Discourse and Interaction*. London: Sage. pp. 258–84.

Frank, Karsta (1992) *Sprachgewalt: die sprachliche Reproduktion der Geschlechter-hierarchie*. Tübingen: Niemeyer.

Gal, Susan (1989) 'Between speech and silence: the problematics of research on language and gender', in Micaela di Leonardo (ed.), *Gender at the Crossroads of Knowledge: Feminist Anthropology in the Postmodern Era*. Los Angeles: University of California Press.

Giddens, Anthony (1989) *Sociology*. Oxford: Blackwell/Polity.

Gräszel, Ulrike (1991) *Sprachverhalten und Geschlecht*. Pfaffenweiler: Centaurus Verlag.

Guentherodt, Ingrid, Hellinger, Marlis, Pusch, Luise and Trömel-Plötz, Senta

(1982) 'Richtlinien zur Vermeidung sexistischen Sprachgebrauchs', in Martha Heuser (ed.), *Frauen-Sprache-Literatur*. Paderborn: Schöningh. pp. 84–91.

Günther, Susanne and Kotthoff, Helga (1991) 'Von fremden Stimmen: Weibliches und männliches Sprechen im Kulturvergleich', in Susanne Günther and Helga Kotthoff (eds), *Von fremden Stimmen. Weibliches und männliches Sprechen im Kulturvergleich*. Frankfurt: Suhrkamp. pp. 7–52.

Hagemann-White, Carol (1993) 'Die Konstrukteure des Gechlechts auf frischer Tat ertappen. Methodische Konsequenzen einer theoretischen Einsicht', *Feministische Studien*, 11 (2): 68–78.

Harré, Rom and Stearns, Peter (eds) (1995) *Discursive Psychology in Practice*. London: Sage.

Harres, Annette (1996) 'Tag questions and gender in medical consultations', PhD thesis, Department of Linguistics, Monash University.

Hellinger, Marlis (1990) *Kontrastive feministische Linguistik*. Ismaning: Hueber.

Henley, Nancy M. and Kramarae, Cheris (1991) 'Gender, power and miscommunication', in Nick Coupland, Howard Giles and John Wiemann (eds), *'Miscommunication' and Problematic Talk*. London: Sage. pp. 18–43.

Holmes, Janet (1996) 'Sex and language', in Hans Goebl, Peter H. Nelde, Zdenek Stary and Wolfgang Wölck (eds), *Kontaktlinguistik – Contact Linguistics – Linguistique de contact*. Berlin: de Gruyter. pp. 720–5.

Kotthoff, Helga (1991) 'Der Tamada gibt am Tisch den Ton an', in Susanne Günther and Helga Kotthoff (eds), *Von fremden Stimmen. Weibliches und männliches Sprechen im Kulturvergleich*. Frankfurt: Suhrkamp. pp. 229–61.

Kotthoff, Helga (1992) 'Unruhe im Tabellenbild? Zur Interpretation weiblichen Sprechens in der Soziolinguistik', in Susanne Günther and Helga Kotthoff (eds), *Die Geschlechter im Gespräch: Kommunikation in Institutionen*. Stuttgart: Metzler. pp. 126–46.

Kotthoff, Helga and Wodak, Ruth (eds) (1997) *Communicating Gender in Context*. Amsterdam: Benjamins.

Kress, Gunter (1993) 'Against arbitrariness: the social production of the sign', *Discourse and Society*, 4(2): 169–93.

Labov, William (1966) 'Hypercorrection by the lower middle class as a factor in linguistic change', in William Labov (1991) *Sociolinguistic Patterns*. Philadelphia: University of Pennsylvania Press. pp. 122–43.

Leodolter (Wodak), Ruth (1975) *Das Sprachverhalten von Angeklagten bei Gericht*. Kronberg: Scriptor.

Lewontin, Richard (1982) *Human Diversity*. London: W.H. Freeman.

Lorber, Judith and Farrell, Susan A. (1991a) 'Preface', in Judith Lorber and Susan A. Farrell (eds), *The Social Construction of Gender*. London: Sage. pp. 1–6.

Lorber, Judith and Farrell, Susan A. (eds) (1991b) *The Social Construction of Gender*. London: Sage.

Lorey, Isabell (1993) 'Der Körper als Text und das aktuelle Selbst: Butler and Foucault', *Feministische Studien*, 11(2): 68–78.

Maas, Utz (1988) 'Probleme und Traditionen der Diskursanalyse', *Zeitschrift für Phonetik, Sprachwissenschaft und Kommunikationsforschung*, 41(6): 717–29.

Mills, Sara (1995) *Language and Gender*. London: Longman.

Milroy, James and Milroy, Lesley (1978) 'Belfast: change and variation in an urban vernacular', in Peter Trudgill (ed.) *Sociolinguistic Patterns in British English*. London: Arnold. pp. 19–36.

Nichols, Patricia C. (1983) 'Linguistic options and choices for black women in the rural South, (1976), in Barrie Thorne, Cheris Kramarae and Nancy Henley (eds), *Language, Gender and Society*. Cambridge: Newbury House. pp. 54–68.

Postl, Gertrude (1991) *Weibliches Sprechen*. Frankfurt: Suhrkamp.

Pusch, Luise (1990) *Alle Menschen werden Schwestern*. Frankfurt: Suhrkamp.

Renkeema, Jan (1993) *Discourse Studies*. Amsterdam: Benjamins.

Rohde-Dachser, Christa (1991) *Expedition in den dunklen Kontinent: Weiblichkeit im Diskurs der Psychoanalyse*. Berlin: Springer.

Samel, Ingrid (1995) *Einführung in die feministische Sprachwissenschaft*. Frankfurt: Erich Schmidt Verlag.

Schiffrin, Deborah (1993) *Approaches to Discourse Analysis*. London: Blackwell.

Schissler, Hanna (ed.) (1993) *Geschlechterverhältnisse im historischen Wandel*. Frankfurt: Campus.

Stolcke, Verena (1993) 'Is sex to gender as race to ethnicity?', in Teresa De Valle (ed.) *Gendered Anthropology*. London/New York: Sage. pp. 16–36.

Titscher, Stefan, Wodak, Ruth, Meyer, Michael and Vetter, Eva (1997) *Methoden der Textanalyse*. Opladen: Westdeutscher Verlag.

Trudgill, Peter (1972) 'Sex, covert prestige, and linguistic change in the urban British English of Norwich', *Language in Society*, 1: 179–96.

Trudgill, Peter (1974) *The Social Differentiation of English in Norwich*. Cambridge: Cambridge University Press.

van Dijk, Teun (1985) *Handbook of Discourse Analysis*. New York: Academic Press.

van Dijk, Teun (1990) 'Social cognition and discourse', in Howard Giles and W. Peter Robinson (eds), *Handbook of Language and Social Psychology*. New York: Wiley. pp. 163–86.

van Dijk, Teun (1993) *Elite Discourse and Racism*. London: Sage.

van Dijk, Teun (1997) *Topics in the Theory of Ideology*. London: Sage.

vass, Elisa (1992) 'Diskursanalyse als interdisziplinäres Forschungsgebiet', MA thesis, University of Vienna.

West, Candace and Zimmerman, Don H. (1991) 'Doing gender', in Judith Lorber and Susan A. Farrell (eds), *The Social Construction of Gender*. London: Sage. pp. 13–37.

Wetschanow, Karin (1995) '"Als wenns a Grammatikfehler wär": Splittingver- halten einer Gruppe mit links-alternativ feministischer Unisozialisation', MA thesis, University of Vienna.

Wilkinson, Sue and Kitzinger, Celia (1995) *Feminism and Discourse*. London: Sage.

Wodak, Ruth (1983) 'Die Beziehung zwischen Mutter und Tochter bei schwierigen Kindern: Erstellung einer Typologie aus sozio- und psycholinguis- tischer Sicht', *Wiener Linguistische Gazette*, no. 2.

Wodak, Ruth (1984) *Hilflose Nähe? Mütter und Töchter erzählen*. Vienna: Bundesverlag.

Wodak, Ruth (1985) 'Aspekte des schicht-, geschlechts- und generationsspezi- fischen Lautwandels in Wien: eine Untersuchung zum Sprachverhalten von Müttern und Töchtern', in Marlis Hellinger (ed.) *Sprachwandel und feministische Sprachpolitik: Internationale Perspektiven*. Opladen: Westdeutscher Verlag.

Wodak, Ruth (1986) *Language Behavior in Therapy Groups*. Los Angeles: University of California Press.

Wodak, Ruth (1996) *Disorders of Discourse*. London: Longman.

Wodak, Ruth and Benke, Gertraud (1996) 'Gender as a sociolinguistic variable', in Florian Coulmas (ed.), *The Handbook of Sociolinguistics*. Oxford: Blackwell. pp. 127–50.

Wodak, Ruth, De Cillia, Rudolf, Blüml, Karl and Andraschko, Elisabeth (1989) *Sprache und Macht – Sprache und Politik*. Vienna: Bundesverlag.

Wodak, Ruth, De Cillia, Rudolf, Reisigl, Martin, Liebhart, Karin, Hofstätter, Klaus and Kargl, Maria (1997a) *Zur diskursiven Konstruktion nationaler Identitäten*. Frankfurt: Suhrkamp.

Wodak, Ruth, Kargl, Maria and Wetschanow, Karin (1997b) *Richtlinien zur sprachlichen Gleichbehandlung*. Project report, Department of Linguistics, University of Vienna.

Wodak, Ruth, Moosmüller, Sylvia, Doleschal, Ursula and Feistritzer, Gert (1987) *Sprachliche Gleichbehandlung von Mann und Frau*. Vienna: Bundesministerium für Arbeit und Soziales.

Wodak, Ruth and Schulz, Muriel (1986) *The Language of Love and Guilt*. Amsterdam: Benjamins.

Wodak, Ruth and Vetter, Eva (forthcoming) 'Diplomats, politicians, and journalists: the construction of professional identities', in Bessie Dedrinos (ed.), *Critical Discourse Analysis*.

Young, Iris M. (1994) *Geschlecht als serielle Kollektivität: Frauen als soziales Kollektiv*. Frankfurt: Suhrkamp.

1

THEORETICAL DEBATES IN FEMINIST LINGUISTICS: QUESTIONS OF SEX AND GENDER

Deborah Cameron

The theoretical debates which I will examine are debates about sex/gender, its relationship to language and language use, and the implications of that relationship. All these are matters on which feminist scholars disagree – an important point to make, because outsiders often see feminist scholarship as a homogeneous category, defined by assumptions which all feminists must share. In fact, feminist scholarship encompasses diverse views, and not infrequently conflicting ones.

For the purposes of this discussion, 'feminist linguistics' will be taken to mean something different from the study of language and gender *per se*. In practice the two overlap significantly – most contemporary language and gender research is also feminist in orientation – but in principle the subject-matter can be treated without reference to feminism, either as a political movement or as a body of theory. Indeed, it can be treated from an overtly *anti-feminist* perspective. What distinguishes a feminist approach is not merely concern with the behaviour of women and men (or of women alone): it is distinguished, rather, by having a critical view of the arrangement between the sexes. It should also be said here that this 'arrangement between the sexes' cannot be reduced to 'the differences between women and men'. From a feminist standpoint, male–female differences are of interest only as part of a larger picture, and they need to be theorized rather than simply catalogued.

This chapter deals with *theoretical* debates, and will not therefore have much to say about debates on methodology. 'Feminist linguistics' has never in fact been confined to departments of linguistics, but is a multidisciplinary enterprise to which anthropologists, sociologists, psychologists, cultural/semiotic theorists and philosophers have all contributed along with linguists (mainly sociolinguists and discourse analysts). Not surprisingly, there has been debate on the differing methodologies associated with these different (sub)disciplines: experimental work as practised in psychology versus the naturalistic approach of conversation analysis, not to mention introspection as practised by philosophers and (some) linguists; quantitative methods as used in psychology, some sociology and some sociolinguistics versus the qualitative or 'holistic' methods preferred in anthropology and discourse analysis. In many disciplines, too, orthodox methodologies have been subject to feminist critique from within. The issues raised are not irrelevant theoretically, since the methods a researcher uses embody theoretical assumptions (a point discussed at greater length in Cameron et al., 1992). But issues of method lie for the most part beyond my scope here.

Sex and gender: 'Are there women, really?'

Modern feminist thinking has distinguished between 'sex', the bio-logical phenomenon, and 'gender', the social one. The starting point is Simone de Beauvoir's observation, made in 1949, that you may be born female, but you *become* the kind of social being your society defines as 'a woman' (the same is of course true of males/men). De Beauvoir's point is by now familiar, but it is less often appreciated that the sex/ gender distinction is conceived by feminists in varying ways, and that some of them have questioned its usefulness.

It was also Simone de Beauvoir who asked, on the very first page of her introduction to *The Second Sex*, 'Are there women, really?' (1972: 13). Does the category 'women' have, in the terms used by today's decon-structionists, any 'ontological status'? Half a century on, the subject of most feminist theory is no longer simply 'women' but the gender relations which produce both women and men. Implicitly, however, and sometimes explicitly, these relations may be conceptualized in a number of ways, with a particular point of dispute being how far gender relations should be taken to have a basis in irreducible *sexual* difference.

Nicole-Claude Mathieu (1989), an anthropologist who is identified with the same theoretical current in feminism that Simone de Beauvoir represented, has suggested that there are three main paradigms for conceptualizing the sex/gender relationship. She does not mean that every society, or every social scientist, explicitly proclaims allegiance to one or other of these paradigms. On the contrary, in most cases they operate as implicit background assumptions. The aim of Mathieu's paper is to foreground these assumptions so that conflicts about sex and gender (within feminism as well as outside it) may be clarified.

The first paradigm is what Mathieu calls 'homology': gender is seen as a socially mediated expression of the biological given, sex. Indi-viduals learn 'feminine' or 'masculine' behaviour depending on their prior categorization as biologically 'male' or 'female', with the social elaborating on the biological. This is not the same as saying that all aspects of our behaviour are directly determined by biology, but it does suggest that sex is the foundation on which gender-related behaviour is built (for example, the greater degree of aggression displayed by boys compared with girls may be socially learnt, but it elaborates on a pre-existing biological tendency for males to be more aggressive than females). Gender in this paradigm 'translates' sex into the social behaviours we call gender.

The second paradigm is 'analogy': gender *symbolizes* sex. Gender identity in this paradigm is based on the collective social experience of living as a member of the group 'women' or 'men' – taking on particular 'gender roles' in order to conform to cultural expectations. These roles and expectations may differ significantly in different societies and periods of history even though male and female biology *per se* shows no such variation. Because of this variability, the 'analogy' approach rejects the first paradigm's assumption that there is a direct and straightforward relation between sex and gender, emphasizing that gender is a symbolic marking of sexual difference rather than an elaboration on biological characteristics. In support of this it is also pointed out that people can live successfully as members of a gender that does not match their anatomical sex. Historically, women have 'passed' for men; currently, individuals of both sexes may seek surgery to bring their bodies into conformity with the social role with which they have identified. Mathieu notes that this privileging of social roles over biological traits has been the standard approach of the social sciences. In some versions (such as structural functionalism) the roles are treated as complementary; in feminist versions they are more often treated as hierarchical, involving male dominance and female subordination, and some degree of conflict between the two groups.

Mathieu's third paradigm is 'heterogeneity': sex and gender are different in kind. The idea that their relationship is either homologous or analogous, or in other words that sex is in some sense the foundation for gender, is regarded within this approach as an ideological fiction. We should not take for granted that the world is 'naturally' divided into two groups, 'women' and 'men', but should see this division as something produced historically for the purpose of securing one group's domination over the other. In this paradigm, *gender constructs sex, not vice versa*.

This argument may become easier to understand if we make an analogy with social class. Only an extremist fringe regards pre-given (genetic) traits as determining whether someone belongs to the ranks of the exploiters or the exploited. Wealth and poverty may be inherited, certainly, but this is a cultural matter. Class divisions arise in the first place from acts of exploitation: one group enslaves another, or manages to accumulate a larger share of the available resources (land, property, money) so that people left without these resources are forced to go to work for the more privileged on disadvantageous terms (for example as serfs for a feudal master or wage-labourers for a capitalist). A similar analysis may be applied to what looks at first glance like a more plausible instance of biological division, namely 'race'. Although the physical markers of race, such as skin colour, are genetically trans-mitted, racial categories have consistently been found not to map on to biologically distinct populations. They map much more readily on to divisions created by the historical exploitation of some groups by others through enslavement, colonization, and indentured and migrant labour.

Some feminists, including both French materialists in the tradition of de Beauvoir like Mathieu, Monique Wittig and Christine Delphy and, from a rather different perspective, postmodernist theorists like the US philosopher Judith Butler, suggest that if it were not for our gendered *social* arrangements, 'sex' as we know it – a strict bipartite classification of people on the basis, usually, of their genitals – would not have its present significance. That is not to deny human sexual dimorphism; the point is rather (as it also is with race) that human biological variations assume importance for us when for social, economic and political reasons they become a basis for classifying people and ordering them into hierarchies. No society is ordered on the basis of variations in blood group, and therefore we do not regard 'people with group O blood' as a natural kind – though in purely biological terms it would be easier to identify this 'kind' than it is to identify classes or races. Sex may be more straightforward to identify, but arguably the significance we attach to the identification follows from the significance of gender divisions in the organization of our societies.

For materialist feminists gender, like race and class, is constituted by exploitation (of women's domestic and other work, their sexuality and their reproductive capacities). For such feminists, the ultimate political goal is therefore not to make women and men 'more equal' but to eliminate gender divisions. As Susanne Kappeler (1995) observes, equality between groups which are constituted by the dominance of one over the other is by definition impossible. You cannot, for instance, tackle class inequality by proposing to make everyone a capitalist, for without workers' labour to extract surplus value from, there are no capitalists. Other feminists would however disagree with the material-ists' analysis: some would see sexual difference as finally irreducible, while many would dispute that difference has to mean hierarchy, and would propose that it could and should be positively valued.

The answer to de Beauvoir's question 'Are there women, really?' is not, then, as straightforward as it might seem. If the question means, 'Do women exist as a natural kind?', then feminists disagree. Some would say 'Yes, and they should get a better deal', others 'Yes, but we could change what it means to be a woman', and still others 'No, and the sooner we get rid of "women" the better!' What, though, does any of this have to do with language and linguistics? The answer I would give is that all the most important theoretical debates within feminist linguistics have their roots in disagreements about gender, and the relationship of language to it.

Language and gender: is there a 'women's language'?

Feminist linguists have posed a question analogous to Simone de Beauvoir's 'Are there women, really?': to wit, 'Is there a women's language?' The terms in which this question is formulated have changed over the past twenty years, but there remains a basic concern with the question of what, if anything, characterizes the use of language by women, and how particular characteristics of 'women's language' may be linked to the gender relations of a given society.

At a literal level, the term 'women's language' is obviously problematic. As Sally McConnell-Ginet (1988) notes, no one would answer the question 'What language do you speak?' by saying 'women's language', or for that matter 'women's English'. Even the less radical term 'genderlect', coined on the analogy with 'dialect', 'sociolect' and 'idiolect', is problematic because women and men do not in most cases form distinct speech communities. Some degree of segregation and exclusion on the basis of gender is found in many or most societies, but typically men and women will nevertheless participate in at least some of the same key social institutions (such as the family or household, the workplace, the village) while being differently positioned within them. As the sociolinguist Penelope Eckert has noted, gender works in a different way from race, ethnicity or class:

> Gender and gender roles are normatively reciprocal, and though men and women are expected to be different . . . this difference is expected to be a source of attraction. Whereas the power relations between men and women are similar to those between dominated and subordinated classes and ethnic groups, the day to day context in which these power relations are played out is quite different. It is not a cultural norm for each working-class individual to be paired up for life with a member of the middle class or for every black person to be so paired up with a white person. However, our traditional gender ideology dictates just this kind of relationship between men and women. (1989: 253–4)

The question of what 'women's language' is thus becomes a question about how the norm of gender 'reciprocity' operates to differentiate 'women' linguistically from 'men' in one speech community.

In considering the answers which have been given to that question, Mathieu's paradigms of sex and gender are once again relevant. Early pre-feminist discussions (for example, Jespersen, 1922) vacillated between the view that gendered language 'translates' innate biological dispositions and the view that it 'symbolizes' gender roles which are fundamentally social. Feminist linguists, in common with most social scientists, have preferred the 'social roles' approach. Talking like a woman – or a man, though women have more often been the focus for research on gender – is treated as one part of a social gender role.

This assumption led pioneering feminist linguists like Robin Lakoff (1975) to suggest that 'women's language' was a product of early childhood socialization. Parents and other authority figures encourage little girls to adopt a gender-specific way of speaking which displays their femininity linguistically in the same way that wearing frilly dresses, playing with dolls, 'throwing like a girl' and avoiding 'rough' play displays (one culture's norm of) femininity physically. And this femininity is not just an arbitrary collection of traits whose function is to mark off girls as different from boys, it is a symbolic enactment of powerlessness: about taking up less space, making fewer demands, appearing weaker and less aggressive than boys. 'Women's language', as Lakoff conceived it, is distinguished in particular by the use of mitigating devices which reduce the force of utterances, and by the avoidance of strong or aggressive language.

One question much asked in relation to Lakoff is how far her generalizations about 'women's language' (WL) will hold empirically. Her evidence is anecdotal, and she has often been criticized for implicitly taking some women – white, relatively privileged anglophone US suburbanites – as the norm for all. Even within the same society, the USA, there are many women – working class or of non-Anglo ethnicity – who have been unable to identify with Lakoff's description of WL. There have also been many studies which have failed to confirm the accuracy of the description.

While this is not the place to review all the empirical evidence and counter-evidence, it bears pointing out that in assessing Lakoff's argument *theoretically* we need not fixate on issues of substance (what features WL might or might not consist of) to the exclusion of the more abstract point being made. This, I take it, is that women's ways of speaking in any community, or for that matter the ways of speaking that are folk-linguistically associated with women, whether accurately or not, constitute a symbolic display of that community's concepts of the norms for femininity. The actual substance of the latter can vary considerably: the ethnographic literature shows, for example, that whereas some communities (like Lakoff's) regard indirectness as typically a feminine speech trait, others (like the Malagasy speakers described by Ochs, 1974) associate women with direct styles and men with indirectness. But the overarching claim would be that if a community identifies a particular speech style or genre as typical of women, it will also tend to see that style as indexical of 'what women are (naturally) like'. The evidence for this more general proposition seems to me much stronger than the evidence for Lakoff's substantive hypotheses about WL (for a survey that underlines the point, see Sherzer, 1987). And the proposition itself can be interpreted in line with a more radical conception of the sex–gender relationship, as will be discussed below.

The model which has emerged, especially among anglophone scholars, as the main alternative to a Lakoff-style view of WL as symbolic powerlessness is the so-called 'difference' or 'subcultural' model whose best-known proponent is Deborah Tannen (1990; 1993; 1994). In this model, gender differences are treated as similar to the cultural differences that complicate and may frustrate intercultural or interethnic communication (cf. Gumperz, 1982). They are viewed as stemming in the first place from the pervasive segregation or separation of boys and girls in the peer groups of childhood and adolescence. Since these groups are organized differently, participate in different activities and orient to different values, immersion in them gives rise to differing repertoires of communicative practices – or perhaps more accurately, *preferred* communicative practices (see Goodwin, 1992, who shows that girls are able to adopt the 'masculine' practice when it is necessary for confronting boys in a dispute). Susan Gal (1991) has remarked on the apparent non-reciprocity of the shifting: when gender norms conflict it appears masculine norms typically prevail.

The 'difference' model resembles the Lakoff model in treating gendered speech as part of a broader gender role, and in locating its genesis in early childhood socialization; but it differs in the aspect of socialization that is emphasized (Lakoff focuses on the family, Tannen on the peer group), and also in the way the role itself is conceptualized. For Lakoff, as noted before, what is displayed in WL is femininity as a kind of stylized powerlessness. For Tannen what is displayed in the speech of both women and men is orientation to a particular set of values: for men the central one is status, for women it is connection or affiliation. These differing values arise out of the collective social experience of living in a particular group which is to a considerable extent separate and distinct from others: thus in Mathieu's terms the approach exemplifies the 'gender as analogy' model.

In much recent discussion, Lakoff and Tannen have been made to stand for diametrically opposed views of the relationship between language, gender and power – in shorthand, the 'dominance' and 'difference' approaches. Yet while the differences between them are significant, from the point of view adopted here they are really more similar then different. Both exemplify Mathieu's 'analogy' paradigm; both assume that 'women's language' is, in essence, the language characteristically used by women. A presupposition here is that the 'women' pre-exist the 'language'. 'Women's language' is the language of subjects who are already, definitively, women. Which brings us back to Simone de Beauvoir's question . . .

But what else, one might ask, could 'women's language' possibly be? One answer has been suggested by the anthropological linguist Susan Gal (1991; 1995). Discussing the variationist sociolinguistic approach which concentrates on discovering correlations between linguistic and demographic variables, Gal comments:

What is missing in such work is the understanding that the categories of *women's speech, men's speech*, and *prestigious* or *powerful speech* are not just indexically derived from the identities of speakers. Indeed, sometimes a speaker's utterances create her or his identity. These categories, along with broader ones such as *feminine* and *masculine*, are culturally constructed within social groups; they change through history and are systematically related to other areas of cultural discourse such as the nature of persons, of power, and of a desirable moral order. (1995: 171)

From this point of view, there *is* something 'women's language' could be apart from just the sum total of linguistic features whose frequency of use distinguishes (subjects already constituted as) women from (subjects already constituted as) men. It could be a discursive construct, an order of meaning, which serves as a resource for the ongoing construction of gender identity by members of a particular culture. Gal wants linguists to attend more carefully to 'ideological-symbolic aspects of talk – the cultural constructions of language, gender, and power that shape women's and men's ideas and ideals about their own linguistic practices' (1995: 173).

This proposal marks a theoretical shift. Although Gal refers to 'what is missing' in orthodox sociolinguistics, in fact this 'missing' understanding cannot simply be added on to the orthodox model, for the relationship it suggests between language and gender (or any other social category) is more or less the opposite of what orthodox linguists assume. 'Women's language' as a category is no longer seen to be derived indexically from the social identity of those who use it ('women'), but has become an 'ideological-symbolic' construct which is potentially *constitutive* of that identity. 'Being a woman' (or a man) is a matter, among other things, of talking like one. Subjects produce their own linguistic behaviour, and judge the behaviour of others, in the light of the gendered meanings attached by the culture to particular ways of talking.

As I hinted earlier, one could reinterpret Lakoff's account of WL along these lines (the point is developed in more detail by Bucholtz and Hall, 1995). The phenomenon Lakoff 'describes' in *Language and Woman's Place* might be less an empirical reality than a symbolic ideal, which helps to shape, as Susan Gal says, ideas about how women and men *ought* to speak and to some extent therefore (though this will be more variable) how they actually do speak in particular instances. If this reinterpretation is accepted, it might mute the criticism that Lakoff's generalizations have not always been confirmed empirically. At the same time, it would suggest that the relation between symbolic understandings and representations of gender and the negotiation of gender identity in everyday social behaviour is an important area for further research.

One implication of Gal's remarks for the planning and execution of empirical work is that linguistic behaviour cannot be the only object of the researcher's attention: it needs to be related to some more broadly ethnographic (and often also historically informed) description of the local contexts and belief systems within which language use is embedded. There does currently seem to be movement in this direction among feminist researchers, exemplified for instance by many of the papers in the collection where Gal's piece appears (Hall and Bucholtz, 1995). Another implication of the emphasis Gal places on 'cultural constructions of language, gender and power' is that two domains of research which have often been considered separate – the investigation of 'ordinary' or 'natural' gendered speech behaviour and the investigation of gender ideologies as they are (re)produced in media representations – could be more systematically related to one another.

Performing gender: linguistics and postmodernism

Gal's emphasis on the 'ideological-symbolic' nature of gender construction has some affinities with the feminist postmodernist 'performativity' thesis advanced most influentially by Judith Butler (1990); though it has been pointed out that a somewhat similar set of ideas can be found in the much earlier work of symbolic interactionists and ethnomethodologists in the traditions of Erving Goffman and Harold Garfinkel. Some feminist linguists argue for a feminist appropriation of the earlier formulations because of problems they perceive in feminist postmodernism (see, for example, Kotthoff and Wodak, forthcoming). This too is an emergent theoretical debate, and I will return to it below after first outlining the postmodernist approach.

In Nicole-Claude Mathieu's terms, Judith Butler proposes a version of the 'heterogeneity' paradigm, in as much as she rejects any account in which sex is a foundation for gender (she proposes that sex, as we understand it, is discursively produced by the social relations of gender). At the same time, Butler describes gender as 'performative', a matter of repeatedly performing certain acts which are seen conventionally as merely outward expressions of a prior identity, but are really constitutive of that identity. 'Gender is the repeated stylization of the body, a set of repeated acts within a rigid regulatory frame which congeal over time to produce the appearance of substance, of a "natural" kind of being' (1990: 33).

Although Butler does not discuss language using in these terms, it is easy to see how speech in particular might be analysed as a 'repeated stylization of the body', and some recent research has taken performativity and performance as potentially useful concepts for investigating the relationship of language and gender. For instance, Kira Hall (1995) describes how telephone sex workers make use of speech styles that are reminiscent of Robin Lakoff's WL in order to perform a kind of eroticized and powerless femininity which they believe their customers want to buy. Hall has also carried out research among Hindi-speaking hijras (eunuchs): this is another group which uses the gendered meanings of particular language forms to perform gender identity, in the hijras' case switching between masculine and feminine self-constructions (Hall, 1996). There is interest, too, in the institutionalization of gendered norms for using language in communication training for transsexuals seeking gender reassignment: Bucholtz and Hall (1995) report that trainers and their clients are keen readers of, for example, Robin Lakoff and Deborah Tannen!

In these instances the notion of performance has a quasi-literal force, in as much as they are cases of deliberate or self-conscious performance. For that reason they might be seen as marginal cases, shedding little light on the 'ordinary' processes of gender construction. Alternatively, the increased cultural salience of such phenomena as transsexualism, drag and what queer theorists call 'gender fuck' – allegedly subversive play with gender distinctions – might be seen to pose a theoretical challenge to establish feminist ideas, in so far as these phenomena may indicate changes occurring in the forms of (particularly urban and Western) gender relations. What would it mean to answer Simone de Beauvoir's question 'Are there women, really?' by saying 'Yes – but some of them are (biological) men'?

One reason for wanting to explore the 'performativity' thesis in relation to language and gender is that while it acknowledges the constitutive, as opposed to just indexical, role of language using, it also leaves space for the agency and creativity of language users. No feminist can suppose that we are totally free agents, but some researchers have felt considerable dissatisfaction with accounts that imply speakers are automata, programmed from their earliest years to simply repeat the 'appropriate' linguistic behaviour for the gender they have been assigned. It has been pointed out that even the most mainstream and conventional kinds of gender identity can, or even must, be performed in different ways. Kiesling (1997) and Cameron (1997) both explore the range of options for performing masculinity which are drawn on in the linguistic behaviour of straight white men whose ideologies of gender are entirely non-oppositional.

The most serious objection to accounts like Judith Butler's, however, is that in giving subjects a greater degree of agency they imply a degree of freedom that denies the materiality of gender and power relations. As Kotthoff and Wodak (forthcoming) scathingly remark, the apparent belief of some queer theorists that cross dressing (or cross language using) is a revolutionary act capable of overthrowing the gender system as we know it is both trivial and trivializing. As these authors say, it is always necessary to consider the institutional contexts and the power relations within which gender is being enacted. A further problem with 'performativity' is its focus on the *individual* as the agent of performance. Researchers whose main concern is with the construction of gender and power in linguistic *interaction* may well prefer an approach in which social identities and power relations are viewed as 'co-

constructed' or as collaborative 'accomplishments', to use the terminology of CA; that we are not just individual atoms disporting ourselves in a vacuum is particularly evident when the matter under investigation is language, a kind of performance which is inevitably intersubjective. This is one reason why postmodernism has been less attractive to some feminist linguists than the ethnomethodological and symbolic interactionist traditions. These, too, are at least potentially exemplars of Mathieu's 'heterogeneity' paradigm.

Arguably, Judith Butler's early formulations of performativity (see quote earlier) do acknowledge the necessity of attending to questions of power and of intersubjective processes by alluding to the 'rigid regulatory frame' within which bodies are stylized and identities constructed. For social researchers interested in applying the performativity thesis to concrete instances of behaviour, the specifics of this 'frame' and its operations in a particular context will be far more significant considerations than they seem to be in many philosophical discussions. Too often 'gender' in such discussions floats free of the social contexts and activities in which it will always in fact be embedded; it is as if the drag act, a concentrated performance of a generic femininity which is detached for the duration of the performance from any other activity, were the paradigm case of what it is to behave like a woman. This obscures the much greater complexity – not to mention the institutional coerciveness – of most of the social situations in which gender is routinely enacted.

In this connection Kira Hall (1995) notes the paradoxical argument that when telephone sex workers use a 'powerless' form of 'women's language' they are actually 'powerful' in the sense of being autonomous and earning large amounts of money. On one level that might seem to make sense, but ultimately it is naive. Sex work can be seen as offering some women a relatively good economic deal, but this cannot be understood without reference to the gendered (also raced and classed) character of the economy more generally. The deal is only 'good' compared with other deals available to particular groups of women. Furthermore, women's value as sex workers is determined also by a specifically *sexual* economy in which the overwhelming majority of customers are heterosexual men; women in this market may sometimes be the sellers, but they are always the goods. Whatever advantage individual women may derive from deploying a particular kind of language in telephone sex work, the system of meanings on which the marketability of that language depends does not advantage women collectively. By recycling the traditional conjunction of femininity, powerlessness and eroticism, the sex worker's linguistic performance actually reproduces the ideological supports which help maintain women's collective subordination – a point some of Hall's informants themselves recognized. Nor does it alter the underlying material inequalities. Hall's sex workers are not downtrodden victims, but whatever power and agency they manage to acquire are contained within the system: they are not challenging the traffic in women, only the terms of their participation in that traffic.

Drag queens and telephone sex workers could be described as postmodern 'simulacra', copies without originals, in the sense that the femininities they enact are exaggerated stereotypes, fakes. It is significant, though hardly a novel observation, that gender can be faked in this way, precisely because the 'translation' model which takes anatomy as destiny is still so strongly rooted in everyday understandings. Yet for exactly the same reason, 'faking it' changes very little. The power of the fake depends on its perceived relation to the 'real'; analogously, the subversive pleasure claimed for the 'gender fuck' depends on the continued existence, elsewhere, of strict gender norms. Playing with the codes only keeps the codes in play.

It is conceivable that the much-vaunted postmodern 'fluidity' of gender boundaries may function, at the level Susan Gal calls 'ideological-symbolic', to cement particular cultural constructions of gender even more firmly in place. 'Fluidity' means that individual subjects are given licence to cross previously forbidden boundaries; but the gendered meanings and identity choices on offer either side of the line are not at all 'fluid'; on the contrary, they are arguably becoming fossilized in their most exaggerated and dichotomous forms. This may indeed mark a change in the historical forms of gender relations, but from some feminist perspectives it is not obviously a change for the better.

What is interesting (and perhaps alarming) from the perspective of feminist linguistics, however, is the increasingly prominent and self-conscious role which the manipulation of *language* seems to be playing in this process. There is a massive irony in the use of linguistic descriptions whose aim was to *critique* current forms of femininity for the purpose of *codifying* 'women's language' so that individuals such as drag artists and transsexuals can train themselves to be more 'authentic' women! There could hardly be a more pointed demonstration of the dangers, for feminists, of uncritically embracing the ideology of linguistic descriptivism.

The complexity of practice: *is* it gender, really?

In the abstract of a now-classic article titled 'The whole woman', Penelope Eckert addressed her colleagues in the quantitative paradigm of sociolinguistics as follows:

> Speaker's sex has emerged as one of the most important social factors in the quantitative study of phonological variation. However, sex does not have a uniform effect on variables . . . This is because sex is not directly related to linguistic behavior but reflects complex social practice. The correlations of sex with linguistic variables are only a reflection of the effects on linguistic

behavior of gender . . . However, because gender differences involve differences in orientation to other social categories, the effects of gender on
linguistic behavior can show up in *differences within sex groupings*. (1989: 245,
emphasis added)

Eckert does not merely castigate those linguists for whom the division
of a sample into 'men' and 'women' is taken as a self-evident and
sufficient basis on which to generalize about sex or gender differences.
More provocatively, she suggests that the effects of gender may show
up in behavioural differences *between* women, or men. Further, she
explains this by asserting that gender differences 'involve differences in
orientation to other social categories'. Being a woman or a man, from
this perspective, is less about inhabiting some abstract and unitary
category of 'women' or 'men' than it is about living one's other social
identities (such as racial, ethnic, regional, subcultural) in a particular
and gendered way.

Not all feminists would endorse the idea that gender is no more than
an inflection of other social categories, but probably the greatest theoretical change in feminist linguistics over the past twenty years is the
recognition (still in some cases imperfect or confused) that one cannot
easily separate gender from other social divisions when considering its
relation to linguistic behaviour. It is impossible to talk like, or constitute
oneself as, a *generic* woman: 'the whole woman' always also has a class,
an ethnicity, a cultural position. And these will affect both the material
forms of gender relations she experiences (for example, the typical
forms of economic exploitation of women are not identical in different
social classes) and the symbolic representations of femininity and masculinity she has access to or is influenced by (for example, black and
white women may orient to a different range of cultural models for
'feminine' behaviour, attractiveness and so forth). Conversely, one
cannot talk about class or ethnicity without taking account of gender. A
performance of, say, 'white bourgeois' identity is never a genderless
performance.

The theoretical challenge posed by this complexity is to find a model
of the interaction between gender and other social categories which is
not just *additive*. Feminists have long criticized what they call the 'add
women and stir' approach, whereby mainstream disciplines tried to
address critiques of their androcentrism by applying their existing
frameworks to women as well as men. Feminists responded that any
serious consideration of gender would call the original frameworks into
question: you cannot, for example, retain conventional notions of 'the
economy' while taking on board feminist analyses of women's work. A
parallel challenge now faces many feminist scholars, including linguists:
it is widely acknowledged that earlier work was insufficiently concerned with interacting social variables, but in order to redress this
shortcoming we cannot just 'add class/ethnicity and stir'.

Although Eckert uses the term 'gender' and suggests it must be distinguished from 'sex', hers is among the recent work that might lead us to wonder whether 'gender' (like 'women' for Simone de Beauvoir) is itself in need of scrutiny by feminist linguists. When we observe the linguistic behaviour of women and men, are we really observing the effects of *gender* (even where this is conceived as a complex variable, shaped by other social divisions such as those of class and race or ethnicity)? Or is there an intervening variable between social identities and language use?

In fact this is a long-standing question in relation to language and gender. It has often been suggested that what we are really observing in gender differentiated linguistic behaviour are the effects of power (cf. O'Barr and Atkins, 1980). Another candidate for the position of intervening variable, mentioned in Eckert's abstract which I quoted earlier and developed in work by Eckert and McConnell-Ginet (1992), is 'practice'. In other words, it is suggested that our linguistic behaviour arises out of the activities we engage in and the social relations within which we undertake them (Eckert and McConnell-Ginet use the term 'community of practice' to denote the combination of a habitual activity and a set of social relations within which it is embedded). Though it is obvious gender relations (which are also power relations) affect which practices people engage in and under what conditions, the introduction of practice as a variable makes the language–gender relation a mediated one. The potential advantage of this is that it leads away from global statements, and the stereotypical explanations that frequently accompany them, towards a more 'local' kind of account that can accommodate intra- as well as intergroup differences.

Making the difference: demystifying gender

If in this chapter I have problematized the terms in which feminist linguists debate questions of sex and gender, this is not because I feel ready to dispense with such notions altogether. I believe that there are (still) women, really; and that the oppression of women is not a wholly discursive or symbolic construct, but has a material basis in sexual and economic exploitation. Male dominance and female subordination are capable of being articulated in strikingly different ways, but in some form or other they are remarkably pervasive across cultures and through time.

As a feminist *linguist*, however, I do not believe that one can simply derive the forms of social behaviour from an account of the material bases of social inequality. Here, the discursive, or what Susan Gal calls the 'ideological-symbolic', is an important explanatory resource. It is also an arena of power and resistance in its own right. Unfashionable as it might be to say so in these allegedly postmodern times, the function of ideology as it has traditionally been understood is to serve the interests of the powerful by mystifying the sources of their power, making it appear 'natural' and immutable, and inducing us to desire at least some aspects of the status quo even though it disempowers us. Gender differentiation serves this naturalizing and mystifying purpose with respect to male dominance and female subordination, and that is why a feminist cannot be content with a social science which equates studying gender with merely describing the differences. As Penelope Eckert says: 'whatever symbolic means a society develops to elaborate gender differences . . . serve as obfuscation rather than explanation' (1989: 256).

Feminist linguistics precisely deals with one key symbolic means – language – for elaborating gender differences and at the same time, if Eckert's point is taken, obfuscating power relations. Theorizing gender and its relationship to language does not, in itself, dismantle the unequal and unjust social relations which are thereby revealed; one might hope, however, that in revealing them it contributes to the project of demystifying them, denaturalizing them, and so making it less difficult for feminists to change them.

References

Beauvoir, Simone de (1972) *The Second Sex*, trans. H.M. Parshley. Harmondsworth: Penguin.

Bergvall, V., Bing, J. and Freed, A. (eds) (forthcoming) *Rethinking Language and Gender Research*. London: Longman.

Bucholtz, Mary and Hall, Kira (1995) 'Introduction: 20 years after *Language and Woman's Place*', in Kira Hall and Mary Bucholtz (eds), *Gender Articulated: Language and the Socially Constructed Self*. London: Routledge.

Butler, Judith (1990) *Gender Trouble: Feminism and the Subversion of Identity*. New York: Routledge.

Cameron, Deborah (1997) 'Performing gender identity: young men's talk and the construction of heterosexual masculinity', in S. Johnson and U. Meinhof (eds), *Language and Masculinity*. Oxford: Blackwell.

Cameron, Deborah, Frazer, E., Harvey, P., Rampton, B. and Richardson, K. (1992) *Researching Language: Issues of Power and Method*. London: Routledge.

Eckert, Penelope (1989) 'The whole woman: sex and gender differences in variation', *Language Variation and Change*, 1: 245–67.

Eckert, Penelope and McConnell-Ginet, Sally (1992) 'Think practically and look locally: language and gender as community-based practice', *Annual Review of Anthropology*, 21: 461–90.

Gal, Susan (1991) 'Between speech and silence: the problematics of research on language and gender', in Michaela di Leonardi (ed.), *Gender at the Crossroads of Knowledge*. Berkeley, CA: University of California Press.

Gal, Susan (1995) 'Language, gender and power: an anthropological review', in K. Hall and M. Bucholtz (eds), *Gender Articulated: Language and the Socially Constructed Self*. London: Routledge.

Goodwin, Marjorie (1992) *He-Said-She-Said*. Bloomington, IN: Indiana University Press.

Gumperz, John (1982) *Discourse Strategies*. Cambridge: Cambridge University Press.

Hall, Kira (1995) 'Lip service on the fantasy lines', in Kira Hall and Mary Bucholtz (eds), *Gender Articulated: Language and the Socially Constructed Self*. London: Routledge.

Hall, Kira (1996) 'Shifting gender positions among Hindi-speaking Hijras', in V. Bergvall, Javer Bing and Alice Freed (eds), *Rethinking Language and Gender Research*. London: Longman.

Hall, Kira and Bucholtz, Mary (eds) (1995) *Gender Articulated: Language and the Socially Constructed Self*. London: Routledge.

Jespersen, Otto (1922) 'The woman', reprinted in Deborah Cameron (ed.) (1990), *The Feminist Critique of Language: a Reader*. London: Routledge.

Johnson, Sally and Meinhof, Ulrike-Hanna (forthcoming) *Language and Masculinity*. Oxford: Blackwell.

Kappeler, S. (1995) *The Will to Violence*. Cambridge: Polity.

Kiesling, Scott (1997) 'Language and the power of men', in Sally Johnson and Ulrike-Hanna Meinhof (eds), *Language and Masculinity*. Oxford: Blackwell.

Kotthoff, Helga and Wodak, Ruth (eds) (forthcoming) *Communicating Gender in Context*. Amsterdam: John Benjamins.

Lakoff, Robin (1975) *Language and Woman's Place*. New York: Harper & Row.

McConnell-Ginet, Sally (1988) 'Language and gender', in Frederick Newmeyer (ed.), *Linguistics: The Cambridge Survey. Vol. IV: The Sociocultural Context*. Cambridge: Cambridge University Press.

Mathieu, Nicole-Claude (1989) 'Identité sexuelle/sexué/de sexe?', translated and reprinted as 'Sexual, sexed and sex-class identities: three ways of conceptualising the relationship between sex and gender', in Diana Leonard and Lisa Adkins (eds) (1996), *Sex in Question: French Material Feminism*. London: Taylor & Francis.

O'Barr, William and Atkins, Bowman (1980) '"Women's language" or "powerless language"?', in Sally McConnell-Ginet, Ruth Borker and Nelly Furman (eds), *Women and Language in Literature and Society*. New York: Praeger.

Ochs, Elihor (1974) 'Norm-makers, norm-breakers: uses of speech by women in a Malagasy community', in Richard Bauman and Joel Sherzer (eds), *Explorations in the Ethnography of Speaking*. Cambridge: Cambridge University Press.

Sherzer, J. (1987) 'A diversity of voices: women's and men's speech in ethnographic perspective', in Susan U. Phillips, Susan Steel and Christine Tanz (eds), *Language, Gender and Sex in Cross-Cultural Perspective*. Oxford: Oxford University Press.

Tannen, Deborah (1990) *You Just Don't Understand*. New York: Morrow.

Tannen, Deborah (ed.) (1993) *Gender and Conversational Interaction*. Oxford: Oxford University Press.

Tannen, Deborah (1994) *Gender and Discourse*. Oxford: Oxford University Press.

2

GENDER, POWER AND PRACTICE: OR, PUTTING YOUR MONEY (AND YOUR RESEARCH) WHERE YOUR MOUTH IS

Victoria DeFrancisco

This chapter is about resistance. It is about my personal resistance to writing a traditional review of the communication and language literature on gender and power. Instead, I offer a selected review that has helped me and that I hope will help others to clarify important, relevant objectives for feminists as we move forward in the study of communication, language, and gender. I conclude with another act of resistance: that as researchers we focus on the underlying political forces that create not only gender, but race, class, and other experiences of oppression. To make our work further relevant to women, I make two suggestions: that we specifically focus on conceptualizations of power that address violence, and that we focus our analysis on acts of resistance and emancipation. The process and products of such a shift in theory and research will, I hope, move the field to a more central role in the global feminist movement against human rights violations.

To trace my thinking for the reader, I first address why we need a shift in focus on power. I describe my personal journey as a woman, a feminist, a teacher, and a researcher in the study of language and gender; and I assess the limitations of our current dominant approach to the field – gender differences.[1] Second, I address what we as researchers must do to move our field to an emphasis on power and activism. Here, I share what I have found to be useful reconceptualizations of power as emancipation, and I urge researchers to focus on acts of resistance in the face of violent manifestations of power. Third, I outline implications for directions in research methodology and methods.

Charting a path: a personal journey

I have been a disappointed woman.[2] As with many, I came to the study of communication and gender as a result of my personal fascination and frustration in relations with others and owing to a conviction that gender inequalities played a central role in the dynamics of many of these relations. I have made strides in my approach, as have others in the field. We have moved, for example, from an emphasis on amassing statistics of meaningless sex differences in communication style toward the study of gender in context, but I remain frustrated by the barriers we still face.

Much of my frustration stems from the fact that we do know better. Most feminist researchers would concur, for example, that gender dynamics deal with more than mere surface differences in women's and men's speech; they are about power constructions of gender. We need ultimately to transcend gender: to move our research, theory, knowledge, and culture beyond a surface analysis of gender differences and eventually beyond a world organized by oppressive social categories (for example, Bem, 1993). But, *how* to get there remains the difficult part. We are moving into uncharted territory, developing new theories of explanation, and seeking new methods of exploration as we go. Given the limitations of our language, we find it difficult to even talk about gender – masculinity and femininity – without essentializing. Consequently, my research and teaching (and I presume those of others) often fall back to an implicit or explicit emphasis on differences. We can understand this occurrence as the study of differences is what did eventually enable language researchers to reveal male privilege and dominance in day-to-day interaction. The study of predominant feminine socialization tendencies and communication behaviours allowed us to see and appreciate a model for a non-power-based approach to interaction. And, since most previous research has focused on describing gender differences, we have found it difficult to teach a class or write a review article that moves beyond these characterizations.

We researchers have not completely failed to consider the underlying issue of power. In fact, Penelope Eckert and Sally McConnell-Ginet noted that 'power has been the engine driving most research on language and gender, motivated partly by the desire to understand male dominance and partly by the desire to dismantle it (sometimes along with other social inequalities)' (1992: 474). Yet, most research has failed to examine gendered power dynamics beyond who says what to whom. The authors continued: 'gender is constructed in a complex array of social practices within communities, practices that in many cases connect to personal attributes and to power relations but that do so in varied, subtle, and changing ways' (1992: 484). As researchers, we need to examine the layers of cultural and interpersonal context and privilege, and the links between each.

I finally found some direction as to how to move beyond differences, but surprisingly and most notably, it did not come from work within our field. It came from a profound experience in activism: participating in the United Nations Conference on Women in Beijing in the autumn of 1995. There I was challenged to become a true part of an international feminist movement. I had to ask myself what my field of study could bring to this movement faced with violence against women in every facet of society: family, governments, fundamentalist movements, cultural traditions, religion, economics, education, medicine, military, and the environment. What do I say to Sister Mary Soledad who is fighting to save young Thai girls taken into sexual slavery in the Philippines? What do I say to the women who had the guts to speak out against the Iranian government which imprisoned them for such acts of perceived resistance as showing a wisp of hair from under their *hejab* (veil) or protesting the closing of a university? How do I respond to Daphney, a young lesbian from California, who was institutionalized for four years for a 'gender identity disorder', or to the women from Tibet who risked their lives to come to the conference to tell us they have no reproductive rights and little access to other basic health care under Chinese rule?

How do they feel when I tell them I study such things as turn-taking norms in conversation? I know that through applied critical linguistics we can potentially link what I study with the forms and degrees of violence they fight, but *how* do we do that? I believe our field can do much to assist global feminist efforts to fight violence, but we must draw from interdisciplinary resources to do so. We much avoid studying social relations in isolation from useful context information, and we must enlarge the number of methods and approaches we bring to the analysis. To truly become a part of the international feminist movement, we need to move our own research and our applications of others' research beyond that of English speakers (cf. Kotthoff and Wodak, 1997). We need to raise the standards of research accountability so as to do work that emancipates women and girl children. And, consequently, we need to move our analyses beyond a focus on differences.

Instead of the predominant focus on gender differences, I propose that power be placed at the centre of analysis and that gender, race, ethnicity, social class, age, sexual orientation, and other social categories be examined as political tools of oppression. In doing so, we researchers must remain mindful of the risk of glossing over or losing the voices of individual oppressions or presuming one universal power force. I intend, rather, to encourage globally responsible research connected to the oppressions of women and girl children around the world. Many feminists in the field currently do this important work, and I will review examples to provide direction and vision for myself and others.

Gender as difference and/or social power

Reviewers of gender and communication research have typically categorized studies under two predominant frameworks: gender as cross-cultural differences (proponents commonly attributed are Maltz and Borker, 1982; Tannen, 1990) and social power (proponents commonly attributed are Fishman, 1983; West and Zimmerman, 1987).

Although various researchers' interpretations of these two views are not completely dichotomous (cf. Tannen, 1994), general descriptions are helpful for purposes of laying groundwork here. The differences approach posits that communication problems between women and men are parallel to many other cross-cultural misunderstandings: the problems are a result of innocent socialization in different sociolinguistic cultures. Subsequent misunderstandings reflect gender differences in communication styles and are not due to psychological differences, attempts toward domination, or social inequalities (for a more complete review of the differences approach see Cameron, Chapter 1 in this volume; Crawford, 1995; Henley and Kramarae, 1991). Many feminists have criticized this perspective on several counts such as the contribution it makes to over-generalizing gendered behaviour, to further privileging the white middle-class norms on which the generalizations are based, and to maintaining male dominance by failing to address the unequal effects of these differences (for example, see DeFrancisco, 1992; Eckert and McConnell-Ginet, 1992; Henley and Kramarae, 1991; Troemel-Ploetz, 1991; Uchida, 1992).

In contrast, the social power (or dominance) approach allows for the interpretations of communication problems between women and men (and women and women: cf. Houston, 1994, on race) as due to the unequal hierarchical positions they hold in society. Men's speech, for example, becomes an implicit tool of patriarchal power through conscious and less conscious gender-role training where they may learn to dominate a conversation through interruptions, talk time, etc. The theory by itself, however, cannot account for individual differences in behavioural style, context choices in behaviour, or differences among persons of the same sex tied to ethnicity, race, class, or sexual orientation. Failure to account for such variations can lead to overly simplistic links between gender and power.

In suggesting that we put our research focus on power, I am not suggesting that we end the study of cultural differences due to gender. In fact, we need to add to that the study of race, class, ethnicity, age, sexual orientation, and more. As other researchers have pointed out, I am suggesting we conduct our research in a way that recognizes that power and social categories are integrally related (Crawford, 1995; Eckert and McConnell-Ginet, 1992; Gal, 1992; Henley and Kramarae, 1991). The preoccupation with and unquestioning assumptions of differences remain the problem. Instead, more and more feminist scholars in language and communication call for pluralistic approaches to the study of gender with a goal of addressing underlying political inequalities. Eckert and McConnell-Ginet proposed an approach to the study of language and gender that they term 'activist', or 'community based', which calls for abandoning the assumption of gender differences: 'focus on gender content diverts attention from what may ultimately prove the far more interesting question: How does social practice "use" gender differences (seen as central to gender "content") in constructing gender relations and other social relations (and vice versa)?' (1992: 467). They and others (for example, Crawford, 1995; Henley and Kramarae, 1991) proposed that we view gender as a 'dynamic verb' (1992: 462), which helps to reveal gender as a political tool that constructs difference *and* dominance. To put it another way, Sandra Bem (1993) suggested that a focus on differences presumes differences exist and is politically misguided. Instead, she said, researchers should address how under-lying androcentric social institutions transform male/female differences into female disadvantage (1993: 192).

Similarly, Nancy Henley and Cheris Kramarae (1991) called for an approach to studying gender and communication that includes socialization toward differences, social power, psychological differences, and more. In adopting a 'multi-determined social context approach', they still place power in a central role: 'cultural difference does not exist within a political vacuum; rather the strength of difference, the types of difference, the values applied to different forms, the dominance of certain forms – all are shaped by the context of male supremacy and female subordination' (1991: 40). Inherent in the 'multi-determined' approach remains the assumption that power and violence permeate every dimension of social life. I will explore this approach below.

Reconceptualizing power

The magnitude of the concept of power inhibits the ability of any one person or research field to fully capture its essence or to describe all of its manifestations. Its vague pervasiveness provides part of the momen-tum, mystique, and control. Specifically, in studying power, as used against women, Helga Kotthoff and Ruth Wodak explained the diffi-culty: 'male dominance has become naturalized in the institutions of power' (1997: 4) rather than necessarily seen as expression through overt dominance behaviours.

I do not pretend to overcome these problems in one chapter. Instead, I will address issues I see as most pertinent to the study of gender and language and to attempts to make such work activist in nature. First, I will describe some feminist reconceptualizations of power as empower-ment. Second, I offer examples from previous research to illustrate the variety of dominance or power assertions imposed on women and to suggest these are theoretically and practically linked to a culture of violence against women. I conclude this section by proposing that feminist researchers focus on power as manifested in violence and on women's acts of resistance. While I certainly would not claim that all power is violence, I see the focus on violence as most urgent to women.

From power to empowerment to emancipation

As Deborah Cameron et al. (1992) noted, most traditional notions of power have posited an economic view of the construct. That is, while conceptualizations may differ in important ways, power has generally been viewed as a commodity that people have in differing amounts. These conceptualizations reflect the theorists' larger social values. For example, Max Weber (1947), who is still considered the 'father' of modern thought in organizational productivity, regarded power as the ability to impose one's will (such as a supervisor's) on others. Karl Marx (1978), who focused on economically oppressed men, introduced the notion of power as the property of the social economic class with the most resources. His work still viewed power as a commodity; it ignored larger social influences *on* production, and it ignored women's unique oppressions. Steven Lukes (1974) worked from Marx's structural view in his sociological analysis of the times. He suggested that power can also be used unintentionally, but his conceptualization continued to attribute power as the property of authority.

Michel Foucault (1980) disagreed with these tangible, economic views of power. He argued that such views remain far too simplistic and that, instead, power is larger than individuals' actions. They comprise only part of the vehicles of power and thus we experience multiple inter-related structures of power, such as gender, race, and class. Foucault's position of the omnipresence of power seems more consistent with my proposal that we move beyond gender alone to study it through a more encompassing lens focusing on power – a lens that will thus better enable us to identify multiple related oppressions and acts of resistance. However, as Ruth Wodak (1989) pointed out, Foucault seemed to stop short in his assessment of power by focusing on structures and social hierarchies, at the seeming loss of consideration for individual circumstances. He failed to address his own political commitments (see also the feminist critique by Fraser, 1989).

Feminists have predominantly provided the conceptualization of 'empowerment' – which placed emphasis on resisting oppression rather than on exerting power over others. Typically, those using the term 'empowerment' intended to refer to enabling a person or group through strength developed within. Although admirable, this perspective brought its own limitations and questions.

For example, many feminists disagree regarding the level of empowerment sought. In a very simplistic comparison, more liberal feminist interpretations suggested the focus be on individual empowerment (for example, to get a job with pay equal to that of men), whereas more radical feminist perspectives took a structural approach to oppression, viewing the current system as corrupt beyond repair and working to create new alternative systems. Womanist perspectives called for the end of the dual oppressions of race and gender, whereas ecofeminists connected efforts to dominate women with efforts to dominate nature and spirituality and called for a move away from a capitalistic focus on the individual.

In international development work, the focus on empowerment has also had varying responses. Activist women from 'developing countries', such as at the UN Conference in Beijing, or those who have been the object of Western 'developed' countries' research investigations, have rightly cautioned against the ethnocentrism of outsiders attempting to speak for and presuming to empower others through their own outside frame of reference (for example, Mohanty et al., 1991). By giving power to others, empowerment still connotes a controlling agent and can suggest an individualistic, Western emphasis rather than a community focus. Furthermore, as David Corson pointed out, '"Empowerment" as a concept has become completely assimilated into the non-liberationary literature as a hurrah word: it's now seen as the kind of thing that school administrators do to get teachers to do what they (the administrators) want' (personal correspondence, 9 June 1996; also see Corson, 1997). In contrast, the word 'emancipation' appears more consistent with human rights efforts around the world. Further, as Elizabeth Kissling pointed out, empowerment can suggest one fight power with power, such as violence, which is not generally a useful response (personal correspondence, 10 August 1996). Thus, instead of the term 'empowerment', I call for the use of the term 'emancipation' and the objectives it suggests, that 'people decide for themselves what things oppress them and what they value' (Corson, 1997).

Finally, even the objectives of emancipation must be expanded to address nothing less than the reconceptualization of power and its related social structures. Bell hooks, in her classic book *Feminist Theory: From Margin to Center*, noted that before women can reconstruct society, they must reject the false notion that obtaining power in the existing social structure will necessarily lead to the end of sexist oppression (1984: 90). As ecofeminism predicts, work that supports the notions of individual autonomy, achievement, and empowerment will not bring intended social transformation, and will instead help to maintain the status quo with its dualistic notions and focus on control, objectification, and domination (Kramarae, 1990: 352).

Focusing on power as manifested in violence

I suggest we view the reconceptualization of power as a long-term objective. As we attempt to reach this goal, we must examine and make visible current notions and tools of power to which women resist. We need to link commonly recognized serious forms of violent abuse of power, such as rape and other physical assault, with the less consciously recognized forms of harassment and oppression such as street remarks and subtle gender norms; the latter include requests that girl children and women be more polite, smile, take sexist remarks as innocent jokes or flattery, and conform to heterosexual conventions. The examples of oppressive behaviours described here offer only a beginning in the unmasking of the variety and degree to which power as violence against women permeates culture.

Cheris Kramarae (1992) and Elizabeth Arveda Kissling (1991) advanced this perspective by suggesting that we view all forms and degrees of harassment on a violence continuum. This helps lay persons and researchers alike see the theoretical and pragmatic linkage among such behaviours. In general, they proposed that behaviours society commonly portrays as innocent and harmless, such as street remarks and so-called compliments on women's bodies, in actuality serve to harass and to create a context for more overt acts of violence against women. Some of the women in Kissling's study on street remarks viewed men's comments toward them as compliments, 'reward for looking good' (1991: 455), or as harmless male pranks. However, Kramarae argued that acts such as complimenting a woman on her looks, expecting her to behave in a 'ladylike' fashion, or requesting her to smile, all serve to limit women's and girls' actions and self-images. Others in Kissling's study reacted negatively to such behaviours. They described street remarks as invasions of privacy, as inappropriate attention when comments came from strangers, and as an objectification of women. Kissling pointed out that men who make street remarks do so because they can. They have the power of the public street, and society generally sanctions such behaviour. Further, the inability of the receiver to detect whether a man's derogatory comments pose a serious threat adds to the power of his act and helps to maintain an environment of male domination fuelled by the fear of terrorism against women.

Other researchers have made similar connections between verbal behaviours commonly perceived as non-violent and behaviours recognized as physical assault. In a special issue of *Discourse and Society* focusing on the discourse of violence, Teun van Dijk pointed out that contrary to popular belief, discourse and violence are not mutually exclusive, and that in fact 'Discourse may enact, cause, promote, defend, instigate, and legitimate violence' (1995: 307). For example, Charlene Muehlenhard et al. (1991) identified what is considered typical dialogue and non-verbal behaviour as degrees of sexual coercion in many women's and men's sexual relations. Thus coercion is violence – the imposing of one's will on another. In this light, comments such as, 'If you love me, you will have sex with me', 'You don't really mean that, you really want it', 'You're my wife!', or pressing oneself against a woman until she ceases to resist, become more than innocent cultural differences in women's and men's discourse perceptions. These acts of violence help to legitimize more violence.

In groundbreaking research, Sean Gilmore (1995a; 1995b) uncovered on video the violent ways some young men on a US university campus talk to each other about sex with women. The young men portrayed their violent actions and language as if in jest, bragging to each other: 'I did her', 'I dick-slapped her', 'I fucked her until she bled', 'The bitch needed it.' Similarly, in a study of male abusers' talk, Peter Adams et al. (1995) indicated that the men denied their acts of violence through such linguistic devices as reference ambiguity, metaphors, and other indirect assertions about their relational control. The researchers concluded that such devices helped the men to view their assertions as 'natural entitlements' (1995: 401), and that this view, in turn, helped to maintain abusive relations. When we recognize such male behaviours as coexisting in a culture where heterosexuality is compulsory (Rich, 1980), we see how seeming non-violent norms are indeed embedded in violence (see also Buchwald et al., 1993, for descriptions of a variety of other cultural tools which create a culture of rape).

Nancy Henley, in her classic book on gender and non-verbal communication, *Body Politics* (1977), called these types of presumably 'insignificant' behaviours 'micro politics'. Non-verbal behaviours such as taking up more interpersonal space, staring, initiating one-directional touch (as well as socialization to believe that you cannot take up as much space as others, you cannot stare back at others, and you cannot initiate touch) all serve as subtle forms of oppressions and tools of the macro politics of racism, sexism, heterosexism, classism, etc. In fact, Henley pointed out that internalized messages of self-control, not overt physical force, remain the most effective tools of dominance.

Although we must remember that no one behaviour has universal meaning, attempts to make links among verbal and non-verbal behaviour, physical violence, and institutional forms of oppression and violence *are* what we who study gender and communication have to offer the global feminist movement. Thus I suggest, as discussed below, that feminist researchers in this field focus analyses of power both on its manifestations as violence against women and girl children and on women's and girl children's acts of resistance.

Implications for research methodology

The self-reflexive nature of feminist work as inspired by authors such as Audre Lorde (1984) provides a basis as we adopt methods and develop new strategies to study gender and language through the lens of power and resistance. In the following I describe some of the methodological challenges for those of us who study social inequalities in everyday life.

I describe more useful methodological approaches for conducting this type of research, beginning with suggestions from previous studies.

Locating the oppressions (or think globally, act locally)

I begin from a basic feminist premise that to study gender and language we must at a minimum study it in context (for example, Cameron et al., 1992; Eckert and McConnell-Ginet, 1992). We know, for example, that the forms of gender oppression may vary across race, age, ethnicity, sexual orientation, social class, and physical ability, and that social markers of these categories are not static or universal. The question then becomes, what is context? I cannot address all the possible layers of communication context, nor would this be necessarily useful. I will instead point out issues relevant to this discussion.

In the study of language use, context has often been defined quite narrowly, such as a turn at talk, or a conversation. Yet, many feminists have demonstrated the benefits of viewing seemingly innocent context markers, such as geographical location and job opportunities, as politically relevant (for example, Gal, 1994; Nichols, 1983). By considering these types of information we make crucial links among multiple areas and levels of analysis that get to the heart of why I propose we focus our work on power. We must at once study what Henley (1977) called the micro politics of day-to-day routine interaction and the larger cultural and institutional links which feed and are nourished by these (cf. Cicourel, 1992).

Academics credit Jürgen Habermas (1989) most often for recognizing that power structures serve as the sustainable, more far reaching forms of power in society. He wrote that a sole focus on lesser levels of analysis may be misplaced emphasis. His work has influenced a whole linguistic field of critical analysis which, similar to the focus of analysis proposed here, places an emphasis on the study of language used to construct and maintain social inequalities (Wodak, 1995). Consequently, unlike other discourse paradigms, researchers in critical analysis view the study of context as essential to constructing meaning (for example, Fairclough, 1985; Goodwin and Duranti, 1992; Kotthoff and Wodak, 1997; van Dijk, 1995).

Unfortunately, Habermas failed to recognize feminist work that could have informed his own work (see Fraser, 1989). Activist feminists made similar pleas since at least the 1960s – 'the personal is political'. Embedded in these pleas lay the request that in our study of context we focus on emancipatory tools. Nancy Henley (1977), Dale Spender (1985), Cheris Kramarae (1992), Pamela Fishman (1983), and Candace West (for example, West and Zimmerman, 1987) serve as examples of feminist scholars in the field who have argued for research approaches which make visible the ways in which personal experience ties politically to larger social institutions. This type of research contains the makings of consciousness raising. It reveals what societies typically take as natural, innocent differences and turns them on their side: a woman's politeness becomes a strategy of the less powerful, a man's inexpressiveness becomes a privilege to be uncooperative, etc.

These approaches become particularly strong emancipatory tools when the micro analysis does not stop at the descriptive level as do some more traditional linguistic conversational analytic and ethnographic analyses. These feminist researchers make links to other social practices of inequality and assess the impact on the receiver. For example, a study revealing women's efforts to engage heterosexual partners in conversation becomes 'the shitwork of conversation' (Fishman, 1983). By studying conversational attempts in political context, we view women's behaviours much like other unappreciated, unpaid domestic labour of the oppressed, rather than as simply socialized insecurities, as earlier linguists' research suggested (for example, Lakoff, 1975). Many women's struggles are born out of necessity in attempting to have intimate relations with uncooperative partners. At this point, we might question whether an analysis of the impact of oppressive behaviours risks bringing us back to a focus on the oppression rather than on the liberation. However, when women view their behaviours as neither irrational nor insane but rather as realistic responses to others' attempts to control them, they *are* experiencing emancipation.

Working from the inside out

Researchers in discourse have generally barely considered impact beyond the conversational turn, the response a receiver makes to an utterance. And, while we must be cautious of premature judgements and over-generalizations regarding impact, I liken the importance of studying impact in conversation to the study of sexual harassment. The harasser and his or her stated intents do not determine the classification of behaviour as harassment. Rather, the determination rests with the receiver and the effects of the behaviour. Therefore, we must solicit the participants' perspectives whenever possible.

In my own work on white heterosexual marital communication (DeFrancisco, 1989; 1991) I did, however, learn the risk of probing too far. In my reviews with spouses of conversations, each woman described the effect of the conversation as an absence of emotional support from her spouse, similar to Fishman's (1983) study. While any further probing of impact may have risked hurting some women who did not want to question the long-term relationships to which they expressed commitment, explaining these women's pain as due to cross-cultural misunderstandings would have been disrespectful. Identifying and understanding the impact of oppressive behaviours help to illustrate the limitations of using a cross-cultural differences approach in activist research. Further, the study of impact, although risky, can be affirming to the recipients.

When we focus analysis on the abuse of power and its effects, we must also include the power differential between the researcher and the participants. Traditional methods of language research, where the investigator freely imposes her or his 'expert' interpretations (often called descriptions) on the interaction, are inappropriate and woefully incomplete when studying power dynamics. If we adopt an ethical objective to make our research relevant and politically liberating for the participants, respect for the insiders' perspectives is fundamental.[3]

Scholars credit Foucault (1980), perhaps more than any other theorist, for making the observation that power and knowledge are inextricably interrelated. He believed that ultimate social control happens not through overt physical force but through the social control of knowledge and perception. Many feminists have made similar observations (for example, Henley, 1977; Spender, 1985) and several have added an important implication, that research which claims feminist principles should strive to disrupt this power relationship (for example, Alcoff and Potter, 1993; Cameron, 1992; Cameron et al., 1993; 1992; Gal, 1994).

Cameron and associates (1993) proposed a model for the study of language which calls for research that places the participants' perspectives at the centre and that is on, for, and *with* oppressed groups. They clarified, however, that their approach does not reflect a relativist or standpoint theoretical perspective where adherents believe reality exists only in the eyes of the beholder. Rather, they adopted what they called a realist approach – a belief that a social reality exists beyond what the social actors in a given situation can perceive. According to the authors, realism still recognizes that reality may be impossible to fully grasp but holds that it does exist outside and independent of the observers.

In some ways, this approach attracts me because I have faced the dilemma of how to interpret a heterosexual married couple's interaction when the woman did not perceive the man's behaviour as a dominance attempt but I, as the 'expert', did (DeFrancisco, 1989). However, the issue of who can better define that reality now makes me reticent to adopt such a view.

Furthermore, if we adopt the activist position toward research suggested here, any view that leads to a presumption of insider/outsider perspectives may be risky. As Cate Palczewski (personal discussion, 2 May 1996) pointed out, none of us are 'outsiders' when it comes to social oppressions such as racism, classism, and sexism; that is, we either belong to the oppressed group(s), we oppress overtly, and/or we benefit from that oppressive system. None of us stand as outsiders in the study of social interaction. This places feminist researchers in a difficult situation. We may empathize with a woman's perspective, but we cannot presume to be fully inside that situation *or* to have a better vantage point from which to evaluate that situation.

Although earlier perspectives of standpoint theory certainly had limitations (cf. critiques by Cameron et al., 1993; Clough, 1994), there are some basic premises worthy of consideration. One primary premise states that knowledge is socially situated. This seems particularly appropriate for my research proposal because it 'sets the relationship between knowledge and politics at the center' (Harding, 1993: 55–6). Harding (1993) noted another related assumption concerning the activities of those groups at the top (or centre) of the social structure which organize and set boundaries on what persons performing these activities can comprehend about themselves and their world. This implies that research that studies and works with the social members at the bottom (or exterior) of the social structure necessarily provides fuller understanding of the larger society. Their experiences would probably not be evident from the top (or center), but these experiences have implications for the whole society. Thus standpoint theory provides an understanding of why we must consult previously ignored persons and groups as sources of knowledge, and it problematizes seemingly innocent, meaningless events in daily life.

Furthermore, we need not necessarily doom standpoint theory to relativism or the essentialism of women, as some have claimed (Clough, 1994; Henwood and Pidgeon, 1995). For example, several feminists have noted that standpoints at the margins of social life rather than the centre may provide better rather than relative vantage points for learning about the world. Patricia Hill Collins (1990) demonstrated this in her proposal for black feminist thought (or standpoint epistemology) in which communication norms less valued by the predominant white society (such as some black women's and men's use of story telling, riddles, proverbs, and music) serve as acts of resistance and as sites for the construction of knowledge. In discussing another oppressed group, Judith Butler (1990) maintained that knowledge gained from a marginalized group's perspective is relevant to the larger society too. Queer theory suggests homosexuality has nuances for and potentially impacts all interactions, regardless of the participants' sexual orientation. Butler's proposal illustrated the ways in which the inclusion of a marginalized group's experiences has an impact on the larger society. She noted that we need multiple group or 'insider' perspectives in the construction of knowledge.

Content of study: resistance

The issues discussed thus far in this section refer to the process of how we conduct emancipatory research. We need to also consider the crucial related issue of the site or content of study. As noted in the introduction to this chapter, Foucault (1980), hooks (1990), and others have suggested that to truly do liberating research we should study acts of resistance rather than acts of power. Feminists have long understood this concept. In fact, Karlene Faith pointed out the common commitment shared across feminist perspectives: to work against 'invisibility and silence' (1994: 37). However, the predominant focus on gender differences in communication and language research often leads us to place more attention on power assertions over women and to evaluate women's behaviours against presumed masculine norms rather than to focus on the study of resistance.

To say that we will study resistance rather than power still means that we study power at least indirectly because resistance occurs in a context of oppression. But, given the preceding discussions, consider what an emphasis on resistance can do. (1) We include more than individual action in the study of power and oppression; it must include the social structures, networks, customs, norms, etc. that help to give meaning to the resistance. (2) We place the non-dominant resisting groups at the centre of analysis rather than at the margins. (3) We force the researcher out of a position of 'remote objectivity', because as hooks (1990) noted, to resist is to confront pain. Thus, to study it, researchers have to come into contact with it as well, and can no longer hide behind an ethics of objectivity. (4) We make acts of resistance visible and available as examples to others. (5) We move away from tendencies to over-generalize behaviour, as people act in response to a given situation rather than simply exhibiting a socialized behaviour. And (6) we come to better understand the presence of power and the perceptions in that interaction.

As with power, resistance remains multi-faceted and transitory. We can find resistance behaviours to study all around us. In a research review, Marsha Houston and Cheris Kramarae (1991) reported multiple ways women resist, such as: using silence, reclaiming 'trivial' discourse, responding to verbal harassment, telling the truth, utilizing creative code-switching in language, and developing women's presses. As an example of research that focused on acts of resistance, April Chatham-Carpenter and I (1995) conducted a study on the strategies women used across the life-span to build and maintain a positive self-esteem in the face of multiple cultural and interpersonal oppressions which tend to erode many young girls' and women's self-image.

I cannot fully describe the study here. However, relevant to the current discussion, much research has now documented women's struggles with self-esteem, whereas our study focused on solutions as solicited from 21 African-American and 37 Caucasian working-class and middle-class women's perspectives. We found that self-talk which affirmed the individual, offered perspective and helped the individual develop a strong sense of identity became key to protecting one's self-esteem. While the women in the study focused on individual solutions, rather than proposing strategies to change larger oppressive social structures (such as prejudicial images of beauty, sexism in education and careers, or compulsory heterosexuality), several did note resistance strategies that helped them turn social oppressions such as racism, sexism, sexual abuse, and lack of affirmation in the family structure into opportunities for emancipation. They used self-talk (in conjunction with various other strategies) to protect themselves, for example by developing the ability to view racist acts as someone else's problem rather than letting those acts hurt their pride and self-respect.

To further the activist component of this research, another colleague, Karen Mitchell, and her students have facilitated workshops based on our results. They used improvisational theatre techniques to physicalize and address individuals' internal negative messages that create barriers to self-development and acceptance.[4] In this way, personal solutions to unique circumstances become socially relevant.

Putting it all together

Combining the methodological approaches proposed above may help further feminist redefinitions of the commonly sought research 'rigour'. In place of traditional social science connotations of rigour – that it has 'hard', objectifiable data obtained out of context – this redefined rigour places emphasis on the participants' emancipation by linking behaviour to social political institutions, by building on their (and our) perspectives, and by interpreting behaviour in the context of resistance.

This chapter serves foremost as a thought piece, but it does carry specific suggestions for research methods. First, it proposes a more thorough examination of the layers of context to include multiple descriptions and insider reactions to those layers. This will require researcher innovations in what have traditionally been viewed as the perimeters of study, so that the world becomes our laboratory and we draw more freely from other disciplines, the mass media, current events, etc. Second, the call for insiders' perspectives suggests we need greater collaboration from the inception of a project. Thus, we may use more grounded, non-directional approaches to render participants a hand in determining the focus. Researchers must make greater attempts to review interactions with the participants, where, for example, the participants control the tape recorder and locate what *they* consider important in a previously recorded interaction. And, third, the call for a focus on resistance suggests we move away from an emphasis on describing victimization to an emphasis on problem-solving.

Research which follows these guidelines is likely to find results similar to what Susan Gal (1994) found in her review of cross-cultural studies on gender, language use, and resistance. There was no evidence of a separate women's culture as might be predicted from a 'cultural differences' research approach. She found 'rather linguistic practices that are more ambiguous, often contradictory, differing among women of different classes and ethnic groups and ranging from accommodation to opposition, subversion, rejection, or autonomous reconstructions of reigning cultural definitions' (1994: 409). Such observations seem ripe for an advancement of this field of study toward a more central contribution to and with global feminist movements.

Conclusions

Yes, I have been a disappointed woman attempting to be a part of the field of gender, language, and communication research, and I assume that I am not alone. My work and thinking about the issues discussed above and those of other researchers in the field *have* certainly progressed, but now when I engage in research and teaching on this topic, I have the eyes upon me of Sister Mary Soledad fighting sex trafficking in the Philippines; Daphney, the young lesbian from the US, who raised international consciousness to see that homophobic acts are human rights violations; the women who live in exile from patriarchal rule in Iran; and other women from around the world resisting oppression and serving as role-models in feminist activism. How will my work enhance theirs, and what will I say to them about the work in which I engage? These issues have directed my critical analysis of gender, power, and practice.

In response, I have called for approaches to the study of gender and communication which do the following: place power and resistance at the centre of analysis; define power as multi-faceted; place an emphasis on revealing violence against women; draw from interdisciplinary resources in methods and methodology; allow us to make links among local acts of oppression and global feminist movements; and truly emancipate the oppressed.

In sum, I actually do not make such a radical request: that we consider our work on gender and language as part of a global human rights campaign, that we recognize and make visible to others violence against women of all forms as violations of human rights – the universal rights of equality, security, liberty, integrity, and dignity for all (Schuler, 1995). Human rights include the ability to cross a street without comments from others, to have mutually consenting sex with whom you choose, to engage in a conversation on an equal footing with other participants, to be evaluated on your contributions rather than your social identity, and to be free to conceive of linguistic communities which are not based on competition, oppression, autonomy, and consumption. Research which continues to limit analyses of these types of experiences to the realm of gender differences alone does a great disservice. It not only lets the social institutions involved off the hook and makes it more difficult to link the injustices to other forms of human rights violations, but it helps to maintain the status quo.

Perhaps I am premature to envision a world where individual and group worth do not depend on gender, ethnicity, race, social class, or sexual orientation, but why can we not have more feminist language and communication researchers at the forefront as social change agents? Why are micro analyses of language not playing a role in grass-roots efforts and in the efforts of official governments? Imagine the next international women's conference where, rather than serving merely as consultants on translation matters, we play a more integral role in charting the future.

Notes

1. I use the term 'gender' here to remind the reader that we are talking about more than biological sex. As has been established by other feminist scholars, persons 'do' gender, that is, we learn and enact it in our daily lives. This distinction becomes essential because most of the earlier researchers of gender and communication actually studied differences according to sex, rather than emergent power inequalities in the construction of gender. However, when I use the term 'gender', I also note that clear distinctions between sex and gender are not possible, nor are they desirable. I refer the reader to Eckert and McConnell-Ginet's excellent discussion, where they clarified that 'Bodies and biological processes are inextricably part of cultural histories, affected by human interventions' (1992: 463).

2. Lucy Stone, a leader in the US suffragist movement, was the first to use this phrase. She was speaking at a national women's rights convention in 1855. 'The last speaker alluded to this movement as being that of a few disappointed women. From the first year to which my memory stretches, I have been a disappointed woman . . . In education, in marriage, in religion, in everything, disappointment is the lot of woman' (Stanton et al., 1881: 165).

3. I do note that there are socially imposed perimeters which make a completely collaborative research process next to impossible, such as the standards of individual scholarship for dissertations and promotion, time limitations, and the lack of compensatory funds for participants.

4. The theatre techniques are from Augusto Boal's *Theatre of the Oppressed* (1985).

References

Adams, Peter, Towns, Alison and Gavey, Nicola (1995) 'Dominance and entitlement: the rhetoric men use to discuss their violence towards women', *Discourse and Society* 6(3): 387–406.

Alcoff, Linda and Potter, Elizabeth (eds) (1993) *Feminist Epistemologies*. New York: Routledge.

Bem, S.L. (1993) *The Lenses of Gender: Transforming the Debate on Sexual Inequality*. New Haven, CT: Yale University Press.

Boal, Augusto (1985) *Theatre of the Oppressed*, trans. Charles A. Leal McBride and Maria-Odilia Leal McBride. New York: Theatre Communication Group.

Buchwald, Emilie, Fletcher, Pamela R. and Roth, Martha (eds) (1993) *Transforming a Rape Culture*. Minneapolis, MN: Milkweed Editions.

Butler, Judith (1990) *Gender Trouble: Feminism and the Subversion of Identity*. New York: Routledge.

Cameron, Deborah (1992) 'New arrivals: the feminist challenge in language study', in George Wolf (ed.), *New Departures in Linguistics*. New York: Garland. pp. 213–29.

Cameron, Deborah, Frazer, Elizabeth, Harvey, Penelope, Rampton, Ben and Richardson, Kay (1992) *Researching Language: Issues of Power and Method*. London: Routledge.

Cameron, Deborah, Frazer, Elizabeth, Harvey, Penelope, Rampton, Ben and Richardson, Kay (1993) 'Ethics, advocacy and empowerment: issues of method in researching language', *Language and Communication*, 13(2): 81-94.

Chatham-Carpenter, April and DeFrancisco, Victoria (1995) 'Pulling yourself up again: women's choices and strategies for recovering and maintaining self-esteem'. Paper presented at the Organization for the Study of Communication, Language, and Gender National Conference, St Paul, MN.

Cicourel, Aaron, V. (1992) 'The interpenetration of communicative contexts: examples from medical interviews', in Charles Goodwin and Alessandro Duranti (eds), *Rethinking Context: Language as an Interactive Phenomenon*. Cambridge: Cambridge University Press. pp. 291-310.

Clough, Patricia T. (1994) *Feminist Thought: Desire, Power, and Academic Discourse*. Oxford: Blackwell.

Collins, Patricia Hill (1990) *Black Feminist Thought: Knowledge, Consciousness and the Politics of Empowerment*. New York: Routledge.

Corson, David (1997) 'Critical realism: an emancipatory philosophy for applied linguistics?', *Applied Linguistics*, 18(2): 166-88.

Crawford, Mary (1995) *Talking Difference: On Gender and Language*. London: Sage.

DeFrancisco, Victoria (1989) 'Marital communication: a feminist qualitative analysis'. PhD dissertation, University of Illinois, Champaign/Urbana, IL.

DeFrancisco, Victoria (1991) 'The sounds of silence: how men silence women in marital relations', *Discourse and Society*, 2(4): 413-24.

DeFrancisco, Victoria (1992) 'Book review: *You just don't understand: women and men in conversation*', *Language in Society*, 21(2): 319-24.

Eckert, Penelope and McConnell-Ginet, Sally (1992) 'Think practically and look locally: language and gender as community-based practice', *Annual Review of Anthropology*, 21: 461-90.

Fairclough, Norman (1985) 'Critical and descriptive goals in discourse analysis', *Journal of Pragmatics*, 9: 739-63.

Faith, Karlene (1994) 'Resistance: lessons from Foucault and feminism', in H. Lorraine Radtke and Henderikus J. Stam (eds), *Power/Gender: Social Relations in Theory and Practice*. London: Sage. pp. 36-66.

Fishman, Pamela (1983) 'Interaction: the work women do', in Barrie Thorne, Cheris Kramarae and Nancy Henley (eds), *Language, Gender and Society*. Rowley, MA: Newbury House. pp. 89-102.

Foucault, Michel (1980) *Power/Knowledge: Selected Interviews and Other Writings*, ed. C. Gordon. Brighton: Harvester. pp. 1972-7.

Fraser, Nancy (1989) *Unruly Practices: Power, Discourse, and Gender in Contemporary Social Theory*. Minneapolis, MN: University of Minnesota Press.

Gal, Susan (1992) 'Language, gender, and power: an anthropological view', in Kira Hall, Mary Bucholtz and Birch Moonwomon (eds), *Locating Power:*

Proceedings of the Second Berkeley Woman and Language Conference, vol. 1. Berkeley, CA: Berkeley Women and Language Group, University of California–Berkeley. pp. 153–61.

Gal, Susan (1994) 'Between speech and silence: the problematics of research on language and gender', in Camille Roman, Suzanne Juhasz and Christanne Miller (eds), *The Women and Language Debate: a Sourcebook*. New Brunswick, NJ: Rutgers University Press. pp. 407–31.

Gilmore, Sean (1995a) 'Sports sex: a theory of sexual aggression', in Helen Sterk and Lynn Turner (eds), *Difference That Makes a Difference: Examining Research Assumptions in Gender Issues*. Westport, CA: Greenwood.

Gilmore, Sean (1995b) 'Behind closed doors: men's conquest sex talk'. PhD dissertation, University of Illinois, Urbana/Champaign, IL.

Goodwin, Charles and Duranti, Alessandro (1992) 'Rethinking context: an introduction', in Alessandro Duranti and Charles Goodwin (eds), *Rethinking Context: Language as an Interactive Phenomenon*. Cambridge: Cambridge University Press. pp. 1–10.

Habermas, Jürgen (1989) *Theory of Communicative Action. Vol. 2: Lifeworld and System: a Critique of Functionalist Reason*. trans. Thomas McCarthy. Boston, MA: Beacon.

Harding, Sandra (1993) 'Rethinking standpoint epistemology: what is "strong objectivity"?', in Linda Alcoff and Elizabeth Potter (eds), *Feminist Epistemologies*. New York: Routledge. pp. 49–82.

Henley, Nancy (1977) *Body Politics: Power, Sex, and Nonverbal Communication*. Englewood Cliffs, NJ: Prentice-Hall.

Henley, Nancy and Kramarae, Cheris (1991) 'Gender, power, and miscommunication', in Nikolas Coupland, Howard Giles and John M. Wiemann (eds), *'Miscommunication' and Problematic Talk*. Newbury Park, CA: Sage. pp. 18–43.

Henwood, Karen and Pidgeon, Nick (1995) 'Remaking and link: qualitative research and feminist standpoint theory', *Feminism & Psychology*, 5(1): 7–30.

hooks, bell (1984) *Feminist Theory: from Margin to Center*. Boston, MA: South End Press.

hooks, bell (1990) *Yearning: Race, Gender and Cultural Politics*. Boston, MA: South End Press.

Houston, Marsha (1994) 'When black women talk with white women: why dialogues are difficult', in Alberto Gonzalez, Marsha Houston and Victoria Chen (eds), *Our Voices: Essays in Culture, Ethnicity and Communication: An Intercultural Anthology*. Los Angeles, CA: Roxbury. pp. 133–9.

Houston, Marsha and Kramarae, Cheris (1991) 'Speaking from silence: methods of silencing and of resistance', *Discourse and Society*, 2(4): 387–400.

Kissling, Elizabeth A. (1991) 'Street harassment: the language of sexual terrorism', *Discourse & Society*, 2(4): 451–60.

Kotthoff, Helga and Wodak, Ruth (1997) 'Gender issues in language and communication', in Helga Kotthoff and Ruth Wodak (eds), *Communicating Gender in Context*. Amsterdam: Benjamin.

Kramarae, Cheris (1990) 'Changing the complexion of gender in language research', in Howard Giles and Peter Robinson (eds), *Handbook of Language and Social Psychology*. Chichester: Wiley. pp. 345–61.

Kramarae, Cheris (1992) 'Harassment and everyday life', in Lana Rakow (ed.), *Women Making Meaning: New Feminist Directions in Communication*. New York: Routledge. pp. 100–20.

Lakoff, Robin (1975) *Language and Woman's Place*. New York: Harper & Row.

Lorde, Audre (1984) 'The master's tools will never dismantle the master's house', in Cherrie Moraga and Gloria Anzaldua (eds), *This Bridge Called My Back: Writings by Radical Women of Color*. New York: Kitchen Table, Women of Color Press. pp. 98–101.

Lukes, Steven (1974) *Power: A Radical View*. Basingstoke: BSA/Macmillan.

Maltz, Daniel N. and Borker, Ruth A. (1982) 'A cultural approach to male–female miscommunication', in John Gumperz (ed.), *Language and Social Identity*. Cambridge: Cambridge University Press. pp. 195–216.

Marx, Karl (1978) 'Preface to *A Contribution to the Critique of Political Economy*', in Robert Tacker (ed.), *The Marx Engels Reader*. New York: Norton. p. 4.

Mohanty, Chandra Talpade, Russo, Ann and Torres, Lordes (eds) (1991) *Third World Women and the Politics of Feminism*. Bloomington, IN: Indiana University Press.

Muehlenhard, Charlene L., Goggins, Mary F., Jones, Jayne M. and Satterfield, Arthur T. (1991) 'Sexual violence and coercion in close relationships', in Kathleen McKinney and Susan Sprecher (eds), *Sexuality in Close Relationships*. Hillsdale, NJ: Lawrence Erlbaum. pp. 155–76.

Nichols, Patricia C. (1983) 'Linguistic options and choices for black women in the rural South', in Barry Thorne, Cheris Kramarae and Nancy Henley (eds), *Language, Gender, and Society*. Rowley, MA: Newbury House. pp. 54–68.

Rich, Adrienne (1980) 'Compulsory heterosexuality and lesbian existence', *Signs*, 5(summer): 631–60.

Schuler, Margaret A. (1995) *From Basic Needs to Basic Rights: Women's Claim to Human Rights*. Washington, DC: Women, Law and Development International.

Spender, Dale (1985) *Man Made Language*. London: Routledge & Kegan Paul.

Stanton, Elizabeth Cady, Anthony, Susan B. and Gage, Matilda Joslyn (eds) (1881) *History of Woman Suffrage*, vol. I. Rochester, NY: Susan B. Anthony. p. 165.

Tannen, Deborah (1990) *You Just Don't Understand: Women and Men in Conversation*. New York: Ballantine.

Tannen, Deborah (1994) *Talking from 9 to 5: How Women's and Men's Conversational Styles Affect Who Gets Heard, Who Gets Credit, and What Gets Done at Work*. New York: William Morrow.

Troemel-Ploetz, Senta (1991) 'Review essays: selling the apolitical', *Discourse and Society*, 2(4): 489–502.

Uchida, Aki (1992) 'When "difference" is "dominance": a critique of the "anti-power-based" cultural approach to sex differences', *Language and Society*, 21: 547–58.

van Dijk, Teun A. (1995) 'Editorial: the violence of text and talk', *Discourse and Society*, 6(3): 307–8.

Weber, Max (1947) *The Theory of Social and Economic Organizations*, trans. A.M. Henderson and Talcott Parsons. New York: Oxford University Press.

West, Candace and Zimmerman, Donald H. (1987) 'Doing gender', *Gender and Society*. 1: 125–51.

Wodak, Ruth (1989) 'The irrationality of power', in James A. Anderson (ed.), *Communication Yearbook*, vol. 12. Newbury Park, CA: Sage. pp. 76–94.

Wodak, Ruth (1995) 'Critical linguistics and critical discourse analysis', in Jef Verschueren, Jan-Ola Ostman and Jan Blommaert (eds), *Handbook of Pragmatics Manual*. Amsterdam: Benjamins. pp. 204–10.

3

GENDER AND RACISM IN DISCOURSE

Nora Räthzel

> Indeed, at times the process of analysis is largely based around critically interrogating one's own taken-for-granted assumptions and expectations.
>
> (Wetherell and Potter, 1992: 103)

Often discourse analysis targets the way in which reality is constructed. In this sense, discourse analysis belongs within a social constructivist framework (see Potter and Wetherell, 1987; Wetherell and Potter, 1992; Edwards and Potter, 1992). Insight into the general question of how reality is constructed can be found in many different ways. It is possible to examine: the constitution of the subject; the way it is oppressed by hierarchies; and dominant sexist (for example) discourses (for example, Lovering, 1995: 27). Kitzinger and Thomas look at the discursive strategies through which 'sexual harassment' is made 'invisible or non-existent' (1995: 46). Their analysis aims to refute positivistic research attempting to 'devise watertight definitions of "sexual harassment"' (1995: 46). They instead argue for the necessity of developing a more sophisticated understanding of the 'complexities within which the definition and discursive management of "sexual harassment" is enmeshed' (1995: 47). Discourse analysis is utilized to illuminate the specific mechanisms through which dominance/subordination – elements which structure society as a whole – are produced in daily life. In such discussions, the focus is on these mechanisms and their effect on those who are the object of subordination/oppression. The goal is to develop more effective means against persecution.

Taking New Zealand as an example, Wetherell and Potter (1992) set out to analyse the discourse of racism by looking at 'the language of racism' within a theoretical framework that reformulates questions of 'reality', 'society' and 'identity' in a social constructionist way. The work challenges the 'representational analysis' that looks at the way discourses represent or misrepresent reality. They address the social effects of racist discourses and explore the social agency of those engaged in racist discourses. In reference to the question of identity, they ask if discourse should 'be read for signs of subjectivity' and whether or not 'it is useful to think of [a person within their sample expressing racist views] as the author of his discourse and to look to the author for an explanation of the form of his work' (1992: 8). Wetherell and Potter's work seeks not only to identify the language of racism at a given time and place, but in doing so, to discuss some general epistemological questions of theorizing. The authors view racist discourses as ever-changing ways of constructing the 'other' and the 'self' in a way that devaluates this other and justifies his/her exploitation. Ruth Wodak (1995) examines the way in which discourses about 'others' – in this case Eastern Europeans – have changed in Austria since the dissolution of the state-socialist systems. In the context of Austrian exclusionary policies, her focus is on strategies by which negative images of those excluded are constructed and thus legitimize such politics of exclusion. Teun van Dijk (1987; 1991; 1993; 1996) has examined extensively the discursive strategies and mechanisms through which people are constructed as inferior. He analyses racism as a discourse which legitimizes and sustains domination of white people over black.

Placing my own views in the context of these varied approaches, I would like to emphasize one element these different accounts share. All deal with the way in which sexist or racist discourses function in order to ensure the oppression of those who are the objects of these discourses. Against the background of this work and based on its findings I find it possible to focus on those who take part in racist discourses without these participants actually being the main source of the discourse. In this chapter I will not examine politicians (whose racist discourses may have their origins in specific political interests). Furthermore I am not concerned with members of racist and fascist groups or racist and fascist individuals, or with the media, who either support certain politics or hope to sell their products and therefore engage in racist arguments. This selectivity is not because I consider any of these social actors to be unimportant, but because I think that if we want to understand how racism functions, we also need to examine those who appear to play a minor role in its success. This chapter studies images of migrant populations (Turks in Germany) held by young women who consider themselves to be anti-racist. My aim is not to refute their self-perception, but to show how such perceptions are part and parcel of discourses of exclusion and inferiorization. Because the specific group I am focusing on in my research differs somewhat from those cited above, I do not concentrate my attention on the way these discourses of the other are racist and exclusionary and legitimize oppression. Given the large body of work on the effects and mech-anisms of racisms, and given that the images I analyse do not differ significantly from those which have been analysed elsewhere, I can assume that the exclusionary character of such images is known, regardless of whether or not they are defined as racist, neo-racist, hostility towards foreigners, or part of the discourses of orientalism and exoticism (Lutz, 1989; 1992). My interest is focused on those who have such images. As Wodak has argued, 'discourse about Others is always connected with one's own identity, that is to say, with the question "how do we see ourselves?" The construction of identity is a process of differentiation, a description of one's own group and simultaneously a separation from the "others"' (1995: 126). My question then is: how do women see themselves through the images they construct of the other? Because women and, moreover, anti-racist women are the subject of my attention, I want to formulate the question more specifically: how do women position themselves within structures of domination by positioning the other? Although racist discourses legitimize and sustain the oppression of those who are its objects, I argue that whenever oppressed groups take part in such discourses – consciously or unconsciously – they also reproduce and entrench their own subordination. My thesis is that racisms, or more generally, exclusionary constructions of the other, are forms of a *rebellious self-subordination*. Such an understanding could be a point of departure for an anti-racist strategy towards some everyday racisms. In this chapter, I will address the effect of images of the other on those who have such conceptions through the analysis of empirical material. Moreover, in what I call the analysis of the analysis I attempt to discuss the concepts, the theoretical assumptions and the understanding of discourse implied in my way of looking at the data. In order to avoid a long introduction before considering the material itself, I shall discuss only some of the most general assumptions in the following section. Most of the theoretical concepts will be discussed in the course of interpreting the empirical data.

Some theoretical assumptions

Racism and sexism are social structures of oppression rather than individual opinions about others; however, social structures would not exist if they were not constantly produced and reproduced by individuals in daily life. Avtar Brah asks how the 'racialized "Other"' is constituted in the psychic domain: 'How do the "symbolic order" and the social order articulate in the formation of the subject? In other words, how is the link between social and psychic reality to be theorized?' (1992: 142). Hall points to a similar problem in defining 'identity':

> I use identity to refer to the meeting point, the point of suture, between on the one hand the discourse and practices which attempt to 'interpellate', speak to us or hail us into place as the social subjects of particular discourses, and on the other hand, the processes which produce subjectivities, which construct us as subjects which can be 'spoken'. Identities are thus points of temporary

attachment to the subject positions which discursive practices construct for us.
(1996: 5f)

In the framework of my analysis, I will look at the interface of general discourses and individual positionings. A discourse can only 'hail us into place' if we speak it. In defining others, we experience ourselves as the autonomous subjects of the discourse. That we simultaneously construct ourselves and are constructed by the effect of our own discourse escapes our knowledge. As a member of the majority – those who are defined as belonging to the nation – I consider my main goal to be to deal with this group. To analyse those who are the objects of racism would imply the danger of reproducing the power relations one wants to overcome. 'It has been shown repeatedly that Black informants are reticent about discussing their experiences of White racism with a White interviewer' (Essed, 1991: 67). I have only undertaken such analysis when invited by members of minority groups to do so (see, for example, Räthzel, 1995).

While feminist research in Germany focuses on the binary construction of gender and sees women as the other of a dominantly male society (for example, List, 1993), research on racism concentrates on the construction of ethnic groups as the other minorities (see Gümen, 1995). The following analysis looks at the ways in which what I would call the 'belonging other' (women defined as members of the nation-state)[1] constructs the 'alien other' (those who are defined as people of an illegitimate presence, such as migrant populations, ethnic minorities, 'other races'). I will examine how those who are themselves the object of marginalization see other marginalized groups. This is because I am concerned with the possibilities and impediments of alliances between different marginalized groups. I am interested in the way in which patriarchal, racist and sexist structures are intertwined. Such structures are partly reproduced through what I call ideologies. This term has been – to a certain extent justifiably so – devalued over the last ten years. It is a concept which seems to have as many meanings as people who use it. I therefore consider it necessary to spend some time discussing my own interpretation of the concept and the reason I use it. To analyse discourse as ideological seems odd, as Foucault meant to substitute the term 'ideology' by the term 'discourse' (see below). The following reflections should clarify why I think it possible and even useful to use the concept within a critical discourse analysis which does not assume that individuals have a 'false consciousness'.

Defending the concept of ideology

Barrett (1991) reconstructs the numerous discussions on the concept of ideology, with the issue of truth dominating the debate. The struggle between a critical concept of ideology ('false or distorted consciousness' etc.) and a concept that depicts ideology as the consciousness of certain classes (ideology of the working class, of the Communist Party) has structured the discussions. Both concepts have been challenged successfully enough, in Barrett's opinion, to discredit the concept of ideology within Marxist theory:

> The retrievable core of meaning of the term ideology is precisely this: discursive and significatory mechanisms that may occlude, legitimate, naturalize, or universalize in a variety of different ways but can all be said to mystify. In such a usage, the term ideology is clearly a general term referring to mystification. (1991: 167)

Barrett's proposal for the use of the term 'ideology' does not live up to the criticisms she herself has most sophisticatedly argued for in her book. 'Ideology' becomes again a term to describe 'false consciousness' (who has 'correct consciousness'?). If (according to Barrett) ideology is a process of mystification, can we conclude that a demystification would produce the real object – 'the truth'? Because she goes on to propose that we might better use concepts like 'a partial truth' or 'a naturalized understanding or a universalistic discourse' instead of ideology, Barrett herself seems unsatisfied with her solution: 'Better, perhaps, that we oblige ourselves to think with new and more precise concepts, rather than mobilizing the dubious resonances of the old' (1991: 168). I do not agree with this proposal either as I believe the term 'ideology' can define a much more precise constellation than the term 'a partial truth' which does stay within the 'false–correct' dichotomy.

Haug (1984) insists that Marx's concept of ideology cannot in any way be understood as a theory of consciousness. It is instead a theory of the 'Rekonstruktion des (abgehobenen) Bewußtseinsdiskurses als "Sprache des wirklichen Lebens" in bestimmten gesellschaftlich-politischen Verhältnissen' (1984: 25); in other words, a theory that 'reconstructs a discourse of consciousness, which has lost contact with the real world as a "language of the real world" within specific social and political relations'. It is a theory of how individuals are societalized within societies structured through domination, through repressive and ideological state apparatuses. By acting within these institutions, within these 'spaces of practice', individuals learn how society is structured.

In this interpretation, Marxist theory of ideology begins with the assumption that in modern capitalist societies the division between manual and mental labour has led to the expropriation of human faculties (that is, the ability to collectively control one's own life and social conditions; see also Holzkamp, 1983). These abilities to regulate have been appropriated by the state and its institutions. Individuals are thus left with the necessity to gain (partial) competence within (wider) structures of incompetence. The method through which the state regulates societal contradictions and antagonisms is by transforming opposing interests into the language of given eternal values that are valid for all members of the society: 'Rich and poor alike are forbidden to sleep under bridges.' In the non-ironical version, employees and employers are social partners and neither should try to gain advantage over the other. If workers have the right to go on strike, justice demands that the owners of the plants must have the right to close them.

With the division between rulers and ruled emerges a group of people who earn their living through the production of ideas. Their belief that ideas rule the world is a conceptualization and 'eternalization' of their way of living. Because state institutions function 'from the top down', they produce a similar image of society and life in general. For example, a judge who applies legal codes is likely to see the law as the ultimate motor of society. The difference between such a concept of ideology and a concept which views ideology as a 'false consciousness' or mystification seems to be negligible. Both state that the way we perceive things is not the way they are. What we perceive is mystified in the first version, while in the second it is 'upside-down'. The second version views individuals not as fools filled with erroneous ideas, but as people thinking according to the way their existence is structured. The notable difference is that in the first version we are asked to examine the way in which people think and then possibly asked to alter this thinking, to educate. In the second version we focus our attention on the social structures within which people act *and* on the way in which they act and think. We are entreated to investigate social structures *together with* people's activities and ideas as a complex set of relationships mutually influencing each other. It is possible to read this request as a demand to deduce ideologies from economic structures and to assign ideologies to classes. The larger strand of Marxist thinking has chosen this path which has consequently proved to be a dead end.

To say that a certain way of thinking is linked to a certain way of living and acting is not the same as to say that economic structures *determine* the way in which people think. People have different experiences and live in different kinds of institutions and within different structures at the same time. When Marx suggests that the 'ruling ideas are always the ideas of the rulers' this is not to imply that other ideas do not exist, that there are no practices of resistance and no competing ideas. One could otherwise not explain how a critique of these structures is possible.

The suggestion to analyse the ways in which people think within the context of their experiences and activities can also be interpreted in a postmodern or poststructuralist way. Donna Haraway (1991) has made a strong point of speaking of 'situated knowledges' as opposed to 'objective truth'. She defines the problem as how to have *simultaneously* an account of radical historical contingency for all knowledge claims and knowing subjects, a critical practice for recognizing our 'semiotic technologies' for making meanings, *and* a no-nonsense commitment to faithful accounts of a 'real' world, one that can be partially shared and friendly to earth-wide projects of finite freedom, adequate material abundance, modest meaning in suffering, and limited happiness. (1991: 187, emphasis in the original)

Her proposal is a 'doctrine of embodied objectivity that accommodates paradoxical and critical feminist science projects: feminist objectivity means quite simply *situated knowledges*' (1991: 188, emphasis in the original). Haraway reformulates objectivity as being 'about particular and specific embodiment, and definitely not about the false vision promising transcendence of all limits and responsibility. The moral is simply: only partial perspectives promise objective vision . . . Feminist objectivity is about limited location and situated knowledge, not about transcendence and splitting of subject and object' (1991: 190). This is another reason why Barrett's proposal to replace ideology with a term like 'partial truth' seems less persuasive. It assumes the possibility that a total truth exists. Given our limitations, we can always only have 'partial truths'.

While all truth is partial, not all partial truths are ideological. Returning to Haug's reading of Marx's theory of ideology, I believe an ideology can be defined as a knowledge that does not account for the spatial and historical conditions of its insights. It is to the extent that people make sense of their experience by referring to given, eternal values that they argue in an *ideological form*. If one views *ideology in general* as a form of societalization from above and *specific ideologies* as a set of ideas which change over time and reproduce and legitimize this form of societalization, one can tell the difference between ideology and theory. This understanding is to be had not by claiming that one is true and the other false, but by analysing the *form* of the respective statements. Does the form appear to deduce statements from some pre-given values, or does it try to analyse social processes, conflicting interests, existing power relations? In short, does it argue in a way that is open to contradiction, doubt and counter-proof? Does it acknowledge its own historical and spatial limitations? Examples of ideological thinking will be analysed later in the chapter.

Interests versus values: political aims of discourse analysis

This way of understanding knowledge as situated, and ideology precisely as a form of knowledge that denies its being situated, makes it possible to depart from the 'false–correct' dichotomy in a different way than suggested by Wetherell and Potter:

It may seem to many that if we abandon a view of discourse as merely faithfully reflecting or failing to reflect reality, we are also abandoning some of the best weapons of anti-racist practices. The contrasting of racist claims with 'the real facts' has been and will probably continue to be extremely important in establishing the moral and scientific authority of anti-racism . . . The argument that 'truth' needs to be created as well as 'discovered', and our stress on the active and 'interested' nature of discourse and scientific description, does not absolve the social and biological scientist from ethical and political commitments. (1992: 68)

I would suggest that 'correcting' racist images by saying how those depicted in them 'really are' is a form of anti-racism that remains entirely within the framework that constitutes power relations between those who are defined as belonging and those who are not. The nominating power remains on the side of those who are defined as belonging – only now they tell the unprejudiced truth about those defined as not belonging. The correction also assumes that images of the other are what the discourse is about. Instead, as I shall try to prove, images of the other are more about the self than about this other.

Referring to political commitments does not solve the problem of perspectives. These commitments are exterior to discourse analysis, to the discourses and to those who construct the discourses and are constituted by them. The same holds true for Rosalind Gill's proposal: 'What is needed is a kind of relativism or epistemological skepticism which does not eschew or efface the question of values' (1995: 182).

Here I would rather take Marx's position. He insisted that science should not be accommodated to any exterior standpoint. Referring to values would mean to remain within an ideological discourse which, to my understanding, infers perspectives from given values. While this might be necessary for political struggles, the aim of discourse analysis should be a different one. It should not try to replace one set of values with another, but rather should try to construct a discourse around the interest of self-determination. Instead of any moral appeals, the deconstructive strategy of discourse analysis might be more successful if it appeals to what it finds – to interests instead of morals. The viability of such a strategy is dependent upon the ability of the analysis to uncover the goal of people's interests. It is dependent on the ability to discover, as Marx said, something that people already dream of and which they only have to comprehend in order to appropriate (1970: 346). The aim of the following discourse analysis is therefore to find out what kinds of dreams, interests and desires are encapsulated in images of the other.

Empirical analysis

Collecting and categorizing the data

In 1994 I gave a seminar entitled 'Images of "foreigners" in the media'. Before starting to outline the course, I asked students to write down what they associated with the following terms: German women,

Turkish women, German men, Turkish men. The question was part of a teaching strategy: I wanted to discuss the students' answers in relation to the media images (newspapers, documentaries, films) to be analysed. In previous seminars I had made similar inquiries, asking students to write down what they thought when hearing the term *Ausländer* (foreigners). One of the results had been that the term 'foreigner' is associated with Turks – mainly with men from Turkey. This time I decided to ask directly about Turkish men and women.

My inquiry resulted in a rich variety of descriptions of the four groups of people. In the following, I will use only the answers given by the female students, as I was particularly interested in the way women constructed the other. When speaking about 'the students', I refer to the 20 female students of German origin of which my sample consisted.

These data differ in one significant way from the data that usually form the base of discourse analysis. In all the cases I know, the material is drawn from longer interviews which makes it possible to analyse conversational strategies and the conversational functions of certain expressions. For several reasons I chose to content myself with spontaneous associations written down anonymously. In every instance, the context in which I gathered the material was a teaching situation. One part of the seminar consisted in teaching theories of racism, ideology and culture. To discuss the ways in which general ideologies are reworked and transformed in everyday thinking it was useful to rely on material provided by the students themselves. It had the advantage of combining teaching and learning for both the students and myself.

I view this method of collecting data and discussing and analysing them together with those from whom they are collected as one possible way of practising what Dorothy Smith has called a sociology from the standpoint of women:

> Here, I am concerned with the problem of methods of thinking which will realize the project of a sociology for women; that is, a sociology which does not transform those it studies into objects but preserves in its analytic procedures the presence of the subject as actor and experiencer. Subject then is that knower, whose grasp of the world may be enlarged by the work of the sociologist. (1981: 1)

I think no method can avoid transforming those who are studied into objects. The question is whether this object status is reified or, in giving back one's findings to those studied, one can reverse the relation and the analyst can now become the object of inquiry and analysis. In the best case scenario, the commonly developed findings can be useful to both.

One could argue that such spontaneous associations are unimportant because they are not what people would 'truly' think given time to reflect. I think Billig's conviction – that one cannot classify individuals' statements into some that are truer than others – is equally valid in this case (1991: 126). Those images which come into an individual's mind first because they are so broadly disseminated throughout society (via the media, scientific work, novels, films, etc.) do influence the way in which those considered as not belonging to the nation are treated. Those half-conscious images do influence our ways of perceiving others and even more so if they are not taken seriously and worked through. We experience the world through language and such conceptions are part of our perceptive frames.

My first step in dealing with the material was to sort it into categories. The categories chosen were deduced from German critical psychology – a theory about the way in which individuals societalize themselves and are societalized. Human beings are defined as having to ensure the reproduction of the human species, their material needs and their bodily existence by collectively controlling their life conditions (see Holzkamp, 1983). This assumption led me to sort the material under the following headings: (1) family, paid work, body practices (forms in which reproduction of the species and of material needs are conducted); (2) politics, state institutions, structures of dominance and gender relations, forms of resistance (forms in which people exercise control over their life conditions or are controlled by others); (3) social position, leisure time, character features. The third set of headings emerged from the material itself, which revealed statements that could not easily be subsumed under the previous headings. In analysing their meaning, I related them to the first two sets of categories.

Analysing the data

Victims and agents

In the student's images, both German and Turkish women are pictured as similar. Both appear most frequently in a family context and more often than German and Turkish men. German women are connected with family 16 times, Turkish women 21 times. German men are mentioned 5 times in connection with family, Turkish men 13 times. This picture already shows the similarity's limits. Turkish women are mentioned much more often within family and Turkish men almost as often as German women. Ethnic ascriptions almost override gender ones. Let us now look at the specific vocabulary used in describing Turkish and German women within the family and also in connection with gender relations more generally. German women

> have their families and households to provide for, their ideal is the family, older generations of women are mainly within families, [German women] accept their role, they are fixed on their roles, they are obsequious, oriented towards men, make themselves beautiful for men, [they are] too powerless, tamed, without will, conformists, mere supporters (*Mitläufer*).

Turkish women

> look overworked at a young age (if they have children), sacrifice them-
> selves for their families, [they are women] standing behind their men, they
> are dependent, outside the men's community, dominated, oppressed, have
> to subordinate themselves to their men, arrange themselves within certain
> limits, but in the end have to accept the decisions made by their husbands,
> they are surrounded by small children [are] often pregnant, from being
> dependent on their fathers they change to being dependent on their
> husbands, [the question is always their] honour.

Although both groups of women are seen as being subordinated within
the family and in their relation towards men, their ways of subordination are opposed to each other. German women are seen as subordinating themselves actively, while Turkish women are depicted as being
the victims of men, of their nature (they are often pregnant) and of
ideologies (honour).

One might initially think that German women are seen more negatively, as they are described as being responsible for their subordination. While this might be the case, it is precisely this critique that makes
them more human. If somebody is criticized for being a mere supporter,
it is at least assumed that she could also swim against the current. In
contrast, the pitiful description as victims leaves Turkish women no
possibility to alter their situation.

We can recognize this dichotomy between activity and passivity as
the one which is used to characterize men and women. As Sandra
Harding has shown, Western philosophy divided the world into binary
oppositions where the negative side was ascribed to women, the
positive to men: 'Western philosophy problematizes the relationship
between subject and object, mind and body, inner and outer, reason
and sense: but these relationships would not need to be problematic for
anyone were the core Self not always defined exclusively against
women' (1986: 152). In this dominant view, women are also the passive
victims whereas men are the active conquerors of the world.

The description of German women as active and Turkish women as
passive victims uses this dichotomy and transforms it. German women
are seen as active, but also as the agent of their own subordination. This
places them above the Turkish victims, but it does not transform them
into 'conquerors of the world'. The dichotomy between activity and
passivity is reproduced while at the same time its meaning is shifted.
Because both groups of women are pictured as having a subordinated
position within the family and in relationship to men, the superior
position assigned to the active German women is ambivalent. Activity is
articulated with subordination rather than self-determination. This leads
us to some reflections on the way in which dominant discourses are
reworked in everyday life and how they assume an ideological form.

Reproduction as transformation   One might reformulate van Dijk's suggestion that 'social actors implement and reproduce ideologies in/by their discourses and other social practices' (1996: 8). Social actors do not just implement and reproduce ideologies; in using dominant ideological constructions in daily life they also shift the meanings of those ideologies. It is these specific meanings that are significant because they help explain why these dominant ideologies are used and what kinds of conflicts are reworked in this usage.

Deconstructing and reconstructing meaning   In the above analysis, the meaning which I discover (so to say) is engendered in the confrontation between the descriptions of the two groups of women: German women are said to 'accept their roles', while Turkish women 'have to accept the decisions of their husbands in the end'. This small variance between 'to accept' and 'having to accept' marks the difference between active self-subordination and being subordinated. The comparison exemplifies the fruitfulness of a deconstructive approach. The relationship between the signifiers and what they are meant to signify is deconstructed. Instead the relationships between the signifiers themselves and thus the way in which this relationship produces meaning are studied. My claim that German women are seen as subordinated but at the same time superior to Turkish women rests on the assumption that activity and passivity have positive and negative connotations, respectively, in the dominant discourse.

Dominant discourse and the mundane   This reference to the dominant discourse could be criticized as an instance of reducing people's statements to abstract ideologies. Such charges have been made against a great deal of discourse analysis. One critic, Sue Widdicombe, calls this a 'tendency towards ascriptivism' (1995: 108). She has criticized an author for describing a statement as a 'discourse of permissive sexuality' without giving sufficient attention to the specific meaning of this statement within the process of interaction: 'The point is that by elevating their own political agendas as the pre-established frame, researchers may actually undermine the practical and political utility of the analysis they undertake' (1995: 111). In her own analysis Widdicombe is at pains to understand the specific way in which her respondents (young people belonging to different subcultures) understand the political dimension of their subculture:

> However, in affirming the political dimension of the subculture, respondents must also address certain problematic inferences thereby made available . . . in particular they employ a variety of descriptive strategies through which they avoid the potential inference that political activity is merely informed by their membership of the subculture. (1995: 123)

They do so, Widdicombe goes on to explain, because:

> if the basis of political action is seen to lie in collective identification, then this may constitute a threat to individual integrity and the authenticity of their action . . . Given, that people do have a strong sense of themselves as individuals . . . the most effective way of marketing particular political claims is likely to be through appealing to personal choices and decisions rather than by appealing to collective identities or shared oppression. (1995: 123f)

I think Widdicombe makes an important point in emphasizing the necessity of listening to what people say rather than recognizing a political discourse one is already familiar with in any specific statement. As Althusser warned, 'reconnaissance est méconnaissance'. Despite the argument's strengths, Widdicombe's distinction between specific interaction and general political discourse does not convince me. In claiming that respondents want to protect their 'individual integrity' in preference to 'collective identification', that they 'have a strong sense for themselves as individuals', she fails to see that those notions of 'individual integrity' or of 'personal choice' are no less elements of a more general political (in fact, ideological) discourse than the concept of 'permissive sexuality' – the (superficial) use of which she criticizes at the beginning of her article. Specific interaction and general political discourse cannot be opposed in the sense Widdicombe does. The mundane, as Widdicombe calls it, does not exist outside general dominant discourses and their counter-discourses.

But only elements of the dominant ideology are reworked in daily life. Ideological effects are also the result of specific ways of using theories to construct images of self and other.

Ideological effects of theoretical usage In their descriptions of German and Turkish women, the students constructed a binary opposition between these two groups by using (consciously or not) two opposing theories of women's subordination for the respective groups. The theory of human agency is applied in the case of German women. In the case of Turkish women, the theory of women being victims of oppression is used.[2]

Whether these theories have 'trickled down' or 'trickled up' is unclear in this case.[3] What is interesting is the outcome of this usage. In separating social structures and individual agency a double transformation takes place. Social structures are transformed into 'Turkish culture' – something that exists only somewhere else. In the case of the German women, social structures have totally disappeared and women's subordination is reduced to shortcomings in women's characters. Social structures are thus legitimized by simply disappearing from sight. In the case of the Turkish women they are criticized, but at the same time naturalized and reified. As a result, there seems to be no possibility to change them. Women are described as having to yield in the end.

The separation of individual agency, the social relations within which this agency takes place and the relegation of these relations to different ethnic groups transforms the message of 'agency theory' – that social relations can be altered because they are also a result of individual actions – into the demand to alter one's character in order to liberate oneself from oppression. The image of German women subordinating themselves can be read as reproducing a central ideological figure of modern and, even more so, of postmodern/neo-liberal capitalism – the figure of the meritocratic society: 'life is what you make of it.'

Why is this statement ideological? It does not refer to subordination to the state but rather refers to the contrary. It is an interpellation constructing the individual as the agent of her/his own fate. Indeed, it depends on the context whether or not this statement forms part of an ideology. If it is used in a way that serves to isolate the individual's activity from its social context, it becomes a value meant to guide actions. It is consequently assumed that if an individual does not make the best out of his or her life, he or she is the only one to be blamed. In essence, this legitimizes power relations as they fall out of sight. On the other hand, if this statement is situated in a context where the 'making of one's life' is part of a collective activity dealing with changing power relations and with improving the individual and ways of life in general, then it becomes a 'partial truth' which can help to transcend concepts of victimization.

The next section continues the analysis of the empirical data, looking at forms of resistance in the descriptions of German and Turkish women.

Forms of resistance: collectivity and individuality

Descriptions referring to German women dominated the resistance category. Neither Turkish nor German men appeared and only a few statements described Turkish women. Turkish women were said to form a

> women's community, that is, they stick closer together than German women, women help women, [they form] unity. [Those] who break with their role as women are very self-confident.

German women were depicted as

> having a fighting spirit, breaking out, emancipated (6), politically and socially committed, self-determined, they do not want to confine themselves anymore, they are slowly becoming more self-confident, they are partly becoming more self-confident, they demand a great deal of themselves, they rebel and this scares men. [They take part in the] women's movement (2).[4]

The few remarks concerning Turkish women that could be interpreted as forms of resistance refer to a collectivity (with the exception of self-confidence). Most of those concerning German women depict them as struggling individually. This coincides with the way they were perceived within the family and in gender relations. Just as they consented to their submission individually, they also rebel individually. The words describing this rebellious attitude are such that the point of departure remains as opaque as their final destination. The words describing subordination were related to political or family structures or to gender relations. Resistance is only associated with politics in three cases: 'women's movement', 'politically and socially committed', and, maybe, 'emancipation'. The other elements could describe an individual's competitive behaviour geared towards asserting oneself against others as well as a struggle against relations of subordination.

Interrelations of gender and ethnicity

If we look at some of the categories depicting Turkish men, we find similarities with views of Turkish women. In their leisure time Turkish men are described as

> sitting in teahouses for Turkish men, having their own cafés where they play cards together, drinking tea (4), sitting together in a café, sitting all in front of the Turkish shop, [walking in] men's groups on the streets, [being] sociable amongst themselves, [forming a] men's society.

Turkish men as well as Turkish women are seen as being more social than German women (and men); however, Turkish men are described as doing pleasurable things together, whereas the women's collective has the aim of supporting women. These descriptions show how gender relations and ethnic relations are articulated. To both Turkish men and women, the trait of sociability is ascribed. This reflects inversely the process of individualization for which Western industrialized societies are known. Turkish men and women are associated with more social ways of behaviour – a behaviour which is viewed as premodern in the dominant Western discourse. At the same time, the image of Turkish women as victims of oppression leads to a description of women's communities as institutions for support. They are not seen to spend time together for pleasure.

On the one hand, the ability of Turkish women to support each other is ascribed to their nationality (as social behaviour is equally ascribed to Turkish men). On the other hand, it is ascribed to them as being women – women who are the victims of social subordination. Because the creation of women's communities is ethnicized and depoliticized, they do not appear as a form of resistance which could serve as a model for

other women. An element of self-criticism shining through the statement 'Turkish women stick closer together than German women'
remains a yearning without consequences.

Patriarchy and class relations

The most astonishing result, for myself and the students, was their
description of German men. I would like to share the great variety and
– in spite of that – homogeneity of these descriptions with the readers.
My German female students described German men as:

> Often little sensitive, smug, exploitative, weak, hungry for power, loud,
> lusting for a career, money is important; it is always the other who is
> 'mean', no self-criticism, subtle, but the more crass egocentrics; you have
> to become someone, ambitious, submissive towards authorities, primi-
> tive, dependent on others; intolerant, narrow-minded, damaged by TV,
> damaged by alcohol, bigmouth, ranging from the absolute big macho to
> the soft guy; they prefer to hear compliments, instead of making them;
> they are afraid of emancipated women, they depend on women, failed
> patriarchs, they want to be reassured; make their name at the cost of
> women, 'chauvis' [chauvinists] (2), little dictators, not emancipated; either
> father types, or chauvis, or dominating types; machos, violent, abuse,
> violence against women, preference for Thai women, 100,000 to 200,000
> rapes every year, the same number of child abuses; body-builder types,
> muscles, weight-lifting, pub, beer drinker, playboy reader, 'Tutti-Frutti'
> [television sex show] watchers; car is the symbol of status, car lover, car
> fanatic, hobbies, football (2), tennis, watching TV, playing cards, the
> tabloid press, do not know what to do with their leisure; insecure, insecure
> concerning their role towards women, at odds with themselves; they want
> to be employed, they learn to dance the tango, likeable.

For the sake of comparison, let us turn to the descriptions of Turkish
men:

> Hordes of men, exclusion of women from public space, power of decision,
> strict with their daughters, dominant in public space, women walk behind
> them, 10 metres in front of the women, head of family (3), educated to be
> machos, separate themselves from women, pasha; violence, threat,
> chauvis (2), machos (3), abuse (2), awkward abuse, dominating (2), often
> macho types, patriarchs, let themselves be served, angst, swing their
> swords; speak German badly, drive Opel or Ford, act as a clique; Turkish
> café, teahouses, men have their own cafés to play cards, men's group on
> the street, sitting together in a café, sitting all in front of the Turkish shop,
> [walking in] men's groups on the streets, sociable amongst themselves,
> men's society, they always have a chain in their hand, prayer chain, they
> play tavla, and backgammon, drinking raki; are extroverted, autocratic,
> narcissistic, egocentric, snobbery, truthfulness, pride, helpful, friendship
> with men (tenderness).

At first glance, both Turkish and German men are constructed as dominant, as patriarchs. At second glance, one detects that the image of the dominating German man is cracking: they are called *'failed* patriarchs' and *'little* dictators'. They are also 'soft' and 'insecure'. Reading all the descriptions, one can feel anger and ridicule being transmitted at the same time. Contrary to the patriarchal (successfully so) images of Turkish men, the words do not express anxiety on the part of those who write. Why should this be so?

A closer look at those descriptions that do not deal with men's relations to women might give us a clue. They refer mostly to men's activities during leisure and show an image of men that tends to be associated with the 'lower classes' – a lack of education (watching too much TV, drinking too much, identifying mainly with cars, watching sex shows, reading the tabloid press, etc.). The argument that I introduced to the students was that they were describing a behaviour which they thought to be typical of working-class men. That is, they constructed German men as an other not only in gender terms, but in class terms as well. Some students found this explanation convincing, others opposed it. They interpreted their descriptions as a kind of self-hatred, identifying themselves with the ethnic aspect of the term 'German men'. The kind of male domination that is criticized in the students' images of German men is the direct, brutal and visible one. Men's dominant positions in society and the more subtle forms of sexism are left out. In picturing men this way, students refer to some forms of male domination, but at the same time position themselves as superior – as intellectuals challenging those who only care for cars, their bodies and exploitative forms of sexuality. This diminishes the power of men and thus the weight of their domination. At the same time, it distracts from social structures of domination and men's positions within them. Those placed in lower positions are seen as powerful. While this may perhaps make domination less threatening, at the same time it could impede some sort of alliances that could become necessary at times.

Constructions of the other as rebellious self-subordination

As we have seen, categories that are part of dominant Western ideologies are used and reworked to construct images of (alien) others. The main binary constructions determining the images of Turkish and German women were those of *passivity* opposing *activity* and of *individuality* opposing *collectivity*. Turkish women stood for passivity and collectivity (the latter together with Turkish men). German men were described along the extremes of *mind* and *body*, orienting them around physical activities. This can be considered as one way in which racisms and sexisms interrelate: the dominant dichotomic structures are used to construct different sets of power relations. Those who are constructing the other are positioning themselves on the positive pole of the dichotomy. In doing so they exercise power over the others.

As most clearly expressed in the last phase of his work, Foucault has analysed the ways in which power is produced and reproduced throughout society at large:

> Die Macht wird nicht besessen, sie wirkt in der ganzen Dicke und auf der ganzen Oberfläche des sozialen Feldes gemäß einem System von Relais, Konnexionen, Transmissionen, Distributionen etc. Die Macht wirkt durch kleinste Elemente: die Familie, die sexuellen Beziehungen, aber auch: Wohnverhältnisse, Nachbarschaft etc. [Power is not owned, it works through the whole thickness and on the whole surface of the social field like a system of relays, connections, transmissions, distributions, etc. Power works through smallest entities: family, sexual relations, but also housing relations, neighbourhoods, etc.] (1976: 114, my translation of the German translation)

Foucault admits that within a social field there is 'one class' which strategically holds a privileged position, but he insists that nobody, including the state, either owns or possesses power:

> Der Staatsapparat ist eine konzentrierte Form – eine Hilfsstruktur – das Instrument eines Systems von Mächten, die weit darüber hinausgehen, so daß praktisch gesehen weder die Kontrolle noch die Zerstörung des Staatsapparates ausreichen können, um einen bestimmten Machttypus zum Verschwinden oder zur Veränderung zu bringen. [The state apparatus is a concentrated form – an auxiliary structure – the instrument of a system of powers, which go far beyond this form. Therefore, in practice, neither control nor destruction of the state apparatus would be sufficient to make a certain type of power disappear or to bring change about.] (1976: 115, my translation of the German translation)

While this is an important point which contradicts the rather simple idea that by destroying the state or by taking it over one can do away with power relations, it fails to see the specific relations between the different powers at work: the power within the state is reinforced (and can only exist) through the power exercised within society at large by individuals who are, in subordinating others, simultaneously subordinating themselves. This is the case because, as our example shows, power over others is not exercised arbitrarily in daily life. Individuals make use of dominant ideologies. While the women in our sample put themselves in a favourable position in relation to Turkish men and women and also in relation to German men, they reinforced the dominating dichotomies by taking them for granted. The power structures of society at large are transformed into individual ways of perceiving self and other. It is by gaining power that dominant power structures are internalized and become part of the individual's view of the world. The dominant position these German women created for themselves (or for the group they are assigned to) was an ambivalent one. They saw German women as active individuals, but their activity was self-subordination. They viewed them as being resistant, but their resistance was seen as an individual activity. One could say that the micro-physics of power work to reinforce the macro-physics of power.

I would argue that it is not the belief that women or Turkish women are passive victims alone that is problematic. It is the binary structure of thinking itself that is the problem. I do not agree with Harding's statement quoted above – that the binary relationships in Western philosophy 'would not need to be problematic for anyone were the core Self not always defined exclusively against women' (1986: 152). It is precisely the framing of a complex, contradictory reality in binary structures that recreates the dominant power relations on the everyday level. The opposing poles of such structures take the form of eternal values from which actions are deduced. It is in this sense that I would call this way of structuring reality, ideological.

Billig makes an important point when he says, 'one should not expect that the themes of an ideology or pattern of beliefs should be internally consistent' (1991: 147). I have tried to show that the connotations that come to mind when thinking of Turkish and German men and women are inconsistent. Yet the story does not end here. On a more abstract level, there is a consistency – namely that of constructing the world in binary oppositions. In my opinion, this consistent *form* of argumentation is important to analyse along with its inconsistent *contents*. If we want to change the way in which we subordinate ourselves by reproducing ideological world-views, it is not only the contents that are at stake, but the form in which we structure them.

To clarify this point it is useful to look once again at the images of German women in comparison to the other three images. One important aspect of this comparison was that there are similarities on 'ethnic' as well as on 'gender' grounds. German and Turkish women share their connection to the family just as German and Turkish men share patriarchal features. Turkish men and women are both seen as being more social. What do German men and women share? Determining this is more complicated because it can only be detected in the more general structure of the descriptions. The students said that German women 'make themselves beautiful for men, use make-up (2), are slim, obsessed with dieting'. This is similar to the image of German men as 'body-builder types'. In both cases, people are seen as being obsessed by disciplining their bodies, shaping them according to certain norms. This attitude towards the body does not exist in the images depicting Turkish men or women. In addition, both German men and women are seen as individualistic. The similarities between German men and women that distance them from Turkish men and women is their *form of societalization*.

In other words, the other is constituted as the mirror image of different, problematic aspects of the self, such as the conflicting processes of societalization. The other is a victim, where the self is an agent. The other lives collectively where the self is individualized. The other has a 'natural relationship' with the body while the self shapes the body according to societal norms, etc. We can see how these oppositions reflect those forms of societalization which cut individuals off from their desires and thus subordinate them to existing power relations. I would therefore argue that racism is not only a form of subordination, but a form of rebellious subordination. Individuals rebel against their subservient role, but by using the dominant dichotomies to subordinate others their rebellion ends in subordinating themselves as well. In psychoanalytic terms this structure has already been analysed as 'the return of the repressed'. The reason for not using this concept is my reluctance to conceptualize subordination merely as repression. I prefer Foucault's thesis that power is creative: it creates power relations and thereby constitutes the subject in a specific way. It does not merely suppress people's liberating powers, it transforms them.

The homogenous other and the complex self

Returning to our empirical data, we can observe a major difference between images of the other and images of the self. Examining all the characteristics ascribed to German women, we can see that they cover a wide range of social positions, behaviours and traits. German women are 'subordinated' as well as 'emancipated'; they work in 'badly paid jobs' (like Turkish women) but have also a 'tendency toward upward mobility'; they are 'housewives' but also 'single' and 'having children is not a priority'; they are 'not political' but also 'politically committed'.

We cannot assume that through these images the female students in the sample described themselves, but it is striking that this group (to which they are defined as belonging) is the only one that is pictured in a variety of aspects, in a contradictory, non-homogenous way. This emphasizes my point that one crucial problem with images of the other is the structure of thinking – the dichotomic structure that freezes the other (and the self) into her/his place. Theories of racist images assume that they constitute the counter-image of the self. The image of the other enables the self to define itself as the reversed mirror image of the negative features assigned to the other. As Balibar (1988) has pointed out, no nation consists of one ethnic group. To construct a national unity, a 'fictional ethnicity' has to be invented. One way of doing this is to define the national self in opposition to the non-national other (1988: 70f).

Considering our results, the idea that discourses of the other produce two homogenous images might have to be rethought. Discourses seem to have two different effects: while the other is constituted as homogenous, the self is constituted as flexible and heterogeneous. The findings of this single inquiry are not sufficient for a definite answer, but they are useful to formulate questions for further research.

The construction of a fictitious, homogeneous ethnic group as the basis for the nation seems to be primarily the aim of political and public discourses. In everyday discourses, however, something else seems to happen. Internal contradictions are accounted for and influence the ways in which the other is constructed. For instance, in our sample German men were seen as even more alien than Turkish women.

Conclusions

Political perspectives of discourse analysis: possibilities and limitations

I would argue that discourses of the other are one way in which individuals internalize the 'social order'. As such, they are vital to the cohesion of societies and therefore difficult to grasp firmly.

The strength of these discourses can turn into their weakness. In order to achieve an imaginary subject position, the discourses about the other must contain elements of criticism and longings for self-determination, as the data above have shown. By discovering the elements of criticism and liberation that are enclosed within those discourses (for example, the longing for collectivity and the aspiration to activity and to individual freedom in our sample) one might set them free. My assumption is that if people engage in realizing their expectations and aspirations, if they begin to develop the ability to change their conditions of life, they do not 'need' to think in binary oppositions of self and other in order to reconcile themselves with structures of domination. Of course, this must be taken as a theoretical formulation rather than as a description of any empirical reality. Empirically, there is no 'before' and 'after' subordination. We are always consenting and resisting to domination, making reasonable as well as opportunistic compromises, etc. The importance lies in first learning to understand stereotyped images of the other as indicators for a social/personal/political conflict which finds an imaginary 'solution' through the production of such images and then searching for solutions to this conflict rather than for solutions to the 'problem' of the other.

This implies the reconstruction of a discourse articulating the discontent of the individuals with the ways in which they live. This discontent and the desires encapsulated within the discourse of the other should be positioned as the crucial forces for producing change in the new discourse. In other words, the question should be: can a discourse be constructed that has the effect of producing not subordination but resistance and self-determination? It cannot be an interpellation to 'be nice to strangers' or to construct positive images rather than negative ones. All such appeals would stay within an ideological, moral discourse. It would have to be a framework within which the individuals position themselves as handling and embracing conflicts and contradictions as a means to regulate the conditions under which they live.

Deconstruction as reconstruction

In the context of discourse analysis, such a political perspective could be called a deconstruction which is simultaneously a reconstruction. I agree with Laclau's suggestion in one of his earlier works:

> Le discours marxiste ne peut donc pas se limiter à interpréter la réalité, il doit aussi la constituer. Mais alors, le discours marxiste perd son privilège de représenter la transparance d'une science qui nous montrerait le mouvement extra-discursif de la réalité; il devient au contraire une partie de cette réalité, une façon de la constituer discursivement. (Laclau, 1981)

Translation

> *Marxist discourse therefore cannot restrict itself to interpreting reality; it must also constitute it. However, Marxist discourse then loses the distinction of representing the clarity of a science that can show us the way reality moves outside discourse; on the contrary, it becomes part of that reality, a way to constitute it discursively.*

The same would apply to a feminist anti-racist discourse. This is also a solution to the problem of objectivity. In order to become a part of the world, the feminist anti-racist discourse has to struggle for recognition and conviction. Only to the extent that individuals are convinced by it can the discourse win hegemony, and thereby become 'true', a 'partial truth'.

One has to make an effort not to see this reconstruction as sufficient. Derrida has warned:

> I've never thought or hoped (especially not hoped!) that a deconstructive practice (as such) would invade the entire field and occupy a dominant position fit for transforming the existence of a party, not to speak of all the rest. It is absolutely indispensable that other types of practices – scientific or otherwise – be pursued. But the idea that a deconstructive discourse might come to command and replace other practices, discursive or not, is a kind of madness or comedy that doesn't interest me in the least. (1993: 229)

In our context I consider this to mean that deconstructing images of the other and reconstructing them into discourses of resistance and self-determination can only be one of the conditions that are necessary to initiate a change in the social structures which produce subordination, exploitation, racisms and sexisms. In order to transform power relations it is not enough for individuals to reposition themselves as agents of social change and deconstruct their images of the other; however, in not doing this, the attempt to get rid of racism and sexism might merely reproduce them in a more subtle way.

Notes

I am grateful to Ruth Wodak, Frigga Haug and Karen Rosenberg for their very substantial and helpful comments.

1. This expression is intended to illustrate the process by which 'ethnic minorities', 'foreigners', etc. are constructed. To be, or not to be, defined as belonging to the nation-state has nothing to do with having or not having the 'right' passport, being a native or of migrant origin. See, for example, the positions of Turkish migrants, so-called ethnic Germans and Jews in Germany.

2. A condensed account of theories of oppression versus theories of agency can be found in Davis (1995).

3. Wetherell and Potter (1992) discuss the relation between social sciences and common sense. Some theorists, such as Moscovici, claim that social science is 'a resource plundered by common sense', while others, like Baudrillard, suggest that 'academic theories and intellectual labor always feed off the currency of ideas *already* available in a society' (1992: 168). As Wetherell and Potter argue, there is no need to choose between either of these accounts for both processes are likely to work and to intertwine with one another.

4. Numbers in parentheses indicate how often a word was mentioned.

References

Balibar, Etienne (1988) 'Racisme et nationalisme', in Etienne Balibar and Immanuel Wallerstein (eds), *Race, nation, classe: les identités ambiguës*. Paris: la Decouverte. pp. 54–92.

Barrett, Michèle (1991) *The Politics of Truth: from Marx to Foucault*. London: Polity.

Billig, Michael (1991) *Ideology and Opinions*. London: Sage.

Brah, Avtar (1992) 'Difference, diversity and differentiation', in James Donald and Ali Rattansi (eds), *'Race', Culture and Difference*. London: Sage. pp. 126–50.

Davis, Kathy (1995) *Reshaping the Female Body: the Dilemma of Cosmetic Surgery*. London: Routledge.

Derrida, Jean (1993) 'Politics and friendship', in Ann Kaplan and Michel Sprinkler (eds), *The Althusserian Legacy*. London: Verso.

Edwards, Derek and Potter, Jonathan (1992) *Discursive Psychology*. London: Sage.

Essed, Philomena (1991) *Understanding Everyday Racism*. London: Sage.

Foucault, Michel (1976) *Microphysik der Macht*. Berlin: Merve-Verlag.

Gill, Rosalind (1995) 'Relativism, reflexivity and politics: interrogating discourse analysis from a feminist perspective', in Sue Wilkinson and Celia Kitzinger (eds), *Feminism and Discourse: Psychological Perspectives*. London, Thousand Oaks, New Delhi: Sage. pp. 165–86.

Gümen, Sedef (1995) 'Geschlechterverhältnisse und Ethnisierung im Alltagsleben und in der Sozialstruktur. Ein theoretischer und empirischer Beitrag zur sozialen Konstruktion von Differenz. Exposé zur Habilitation'. Unpublished manuscript.

Hall, Stuart (1996) 'Who needs identity?', in Stuart Hall and Paul du Gay (eds), *Questions of Cultural Identity*. London: Sage. pp. 1–17.

Haraway, Donna (1991) 'Situated knowledges: the science question in feminism and the privilege of partial perspective', in Donna Haraway, *Simians, Cyborgs, and Women*. London: Free Association Books. pp. 183–201.

Harding, Sandra (1986) *The Science Question in Feminism*. Ithaca, NY: Cornell University Press.

Haug, Wolfgang Fritz (1984) *Die Camera Obscura des Bewußtseins: Kritik der Subjekt/Objekt-Artikulation im Marxismus*. Berlin: Argument-Verlag.

Holzkamp, Klaus (1983) *Grundlegung der Psychologie*. Frankfurt am Main: Campus.

Kitzinger, Celia and Thomas, Alison (1995) 'Sexual harassment: a discursive approach', in Sue Wilkinson and Celia Kitzinger (eds), *Feminism and Discourse: Psychological Perspectives*. London, Thousand Oaks, New Delhi: Sage. pp. 32–40.

Laclau, Ernesto (1981) 'La politique comme construction de l'impensable', in B. Conein et al. (eds), *Matérialités discursives*. Lille. pp. 65–74.

List, Elisabeth (1993) *Die Präsenz des Anderen: Theorie und Geschlechterpolitik*. Frankfurt am Main: Suhrkamp.

Lovering, Kathryn Matthews (1995) 'The bleeding body: adolescents talk about menstruation', in Sue Wilkinson and Celia Kitzinger (eds), *Feminism and Discourse: Psychological Perspectives*. London, Thousand Oaks, New Delhi: Sage. pp. 10–31.

Lutz, Helma (1989) 'Unsichtbare Schatten? Die 'orientalische Frau in westlichen Diskursen – Zur Konzeptualisierung einer Opferfigur', *Peripherie*, 37: 51–65.

Lutz, Helma (1992) *Welten verbinden, Türkische Sozialarbeiterinnen in den Niederlanden und der Bundesrepublik Deutschland*. Frankfurt am Main: IKO.

Marx, Karl (1970) 'Briefe aus den "deutsch-französischen Jahrbüchern"', in Karl Marx, *Friedrich Engels: Werke*, vol. I. Berlin: Dietz-Verlag. pp. 337–46.

Potter, Jonathan and Wetherell, Margaret (1987) *Discourse and Social Psychology*. London: Sage.

Räthzel, Nora (1995) 'Images of Heimat and images of "Ausländer"', in Aleksandra Åslund and Raoul Granqvist (eds), *Negotiating Identities*. Amsterdam. pp. 45–68.

Smith, Dorothy (1981) 'The experienced world as problematic: a feminist method'. Sorokin Lecture no. 12. Saskatoon: University of Saskatchewan.

van Dijk, Teun (1987) *Communicating Racism: Ethnic Prejudice in Thought and Talk*. London: Sage.

van Dijk, Teun (1991) *Racism and the Press*. London: Routledge.

van Dijk, Teun (1993) *Elite Discourse and Racism*. London: Sage.

van Dijk, Teun (1996) *Discourse, Racism and Ideology*. La Laguna: RCEI Ediciones.

Wetherell, Margaret and Potter, Jonathan (1992) *Mapping the Language of Racism*. New York: Columbia University Press.

Widdicombe, Sue (1995) 'Identity, politics and talk: a case for the mundane and the everyday', in Sue Wilkinson and Celia Kitzinger (eds), *Feminism and Discourse: Psychological Perspectives*. London: Sage. pp. 106–27.

Wodak, Ruth (1995) 'The genesis of racist discourse in Austria since 1989', in Carmen Rosa Caldas-Coulthard and Malcom Coulthard (eds), *Reading in Critical Discourse Analysis*. London: Routledge. pp. 107–28.

4

GENDER AND LANGUAGE IN THE WORKPLACE

Shari Kendall and Deborah Tannen

Interaction in the workplace is characterized by a unique constellation of constraints: an institutional structure in which individuals are hierarchically ranked; a history of greater male participation in most work settings, especially at the higher ranking levels; a still existing, though recently permeated, pattern of participation along gender lines; periodic external evaluation in the form of raises, promotions, task assignments, and performance reviews; and a situation in which participants are required to interact regularly with others who are neither kin nor chosen affiliates. The workplace thus provides a special challenge to gender and language researchers as well as an opportunity to observe interaction in the context of these constraints.

Research on language in the workplace has focused primarily on task-related talk among professionals and lay persons. The majority of research on gender and language in the workplace has retained this focus, with a handful of studies branching out to examine talk among co-workers and among professionals. In addition, a few studies have considered the use and importance of non-task-related talk in the workplace. For example, Tannen (1994a) notes the importance of informal talk to getting work done and receiving opportunities needed for advancement. Bates (1988) finds that informal use of military, athletic, and sexual language in the workplace produces a subtle separation between women and men, and alienates those who do not participate in the use of sexual language from the informal power structure in the organization.

These studies notwithstanding, the research on gender and language in the workplace falls primarily into two categories, based on the work roles of, and relationships among, speakers. In the first category are studies that address how women and men interact with each other at work. In the second are studies that focus on how women and men enact authority in professional positions. A third area of investigation, addressed in many of the studies in the two preceding categories, is the effect of women's and men's language use on how they are evaluated and reacted to.

In the present chapter, we will review representative sources in each of these areas and then suggest that the theoretical and methodological approach of framing is a particularly useful one for understanding the interrelation of gender and power in the workplace. This claim is supported by reference to the authors' research.

Pioneering work on gender and language stems from the feminist movement of the 1960s and 1970s, reflecting notions of social roles that were current then (Lakoff, 1975; Thorne and Henley, 1975; McConnell-Ginet et al., 1980). As attention turned to the investigation of gender itself (see Cameron, 1997), discourse and gender research shifted to a 'social construction' paradigm. Recent volumes that advocate this position are Crawford (1995), Hall and Bucholtz (1995), and Johnson and Meinhof (1997). In this paradigm, gendered identities – and other aspects of social identity – are maintained and (re-)created through social practices, including language practices. Individuals are active producers of gendered identities rather than passive reproducers of socialized gender behaviour. The framing approach advocated in this chapter provides a powerful theoretical and methodological approach that accounts for, and explicates, how language practices and gendered identities are dynamically linked in interaction.

Women and men actively choose ways of framing to accomplish specific ends within particular interaction. These choices are drawn, in part, from sociocultural norms for how women and men are expected to accomplish such actions through talk. Individuals' language choices, in the local interaction, invoke these gendered norms and, thus, perform gendered identities as well. Gendered ways of framing are, in this sense, resources for accomplishing the speakers' purpose. This model accounts for the observation that many women and men do not construct gendered identities in ways consistent with gender-related cultural norms. Likewise, it accounts for the fact that behaviour that transgresses such norms may be perceived in respect to these norms, which provide a 'rigid regulatory frame' for women's and men's behaviour (Cameron 1997: 49). As Bem (1993) describes, gender norms include a lens of 'gender polarization' – the ideology that women's and men's behaviour is dichotomous. When viewed through this lens, women and men who diverge from gender norms may be perceived as speaking and behaving 'like the other sex'. Furthermore, if women and men do speak in similar ways, they are likely to be evaluated differently (Tannen, 1994a; West, 1995). Norms for gendered language use are, therefore, constraints as well as resources (Cameron, 1997; Hall and Bucholtz, 1995; Johnson, 1997; Ochs, 1992; Tannen, 1994a; 1994b; West and Zimmerman, 1987). As Erickson (1995) puts it, 'There is human agency, but it can only be exercised in a world of social gravity.'

How women and men interact in groups

Research on how women and men interact with each other at work has tended to focus on amount of participation and influence. The research suggests that, in groups, men tend to get and keep the floor more often than women, talk more often and for longer, interrupt more, and make different kinds of contributions, using language strategies that challenge, create and maintain status distinctions (i.e. they create and maintain asymmetrical alignments between themselves and interlocutors). Women, according to this research, tend to get and keep the floor less frequently and for less time, interrupt less, and use language strategies that are more supportive and that minimize status distinctions.

A sense of this research may be gleaned by considering the phenomenon of interruption, one of the most widely investigated language behaviours in general as well as in the gender and language literature. Despite the highly complex nature of determining when an interruption occurred, and the equally if not more complex nature of determining its intention and effect (these are discussed in Tannen, 1994c), most studies simply count interruptions and make the overly simplified conclusion that the 'interrupted' is disadvantaged. James and Clarke (1993) review the literature that appeared between 1965 and 1991 on gender differences in interruption and note radical differences in definitions, and hence identifications, of interruption. They conclude, nonetheless, that most research has found no significant difference between the genders in number of interruptions initiated, in either cross-sex or same-sex interaction, even when taking into account the content of the interruption relative to the interrupted's talk, whether the interruption occurs in unstructured conversations or conversations in seminars or work groups, and whether the researcher differentiates between supportive or disruptive interruptions. Keeping Tannen (1994c) and James and Clarke (1993) in mind as cautionary tales, we nonetheless can observe that a review of research on gender and workplace interaction suggests some potential, albeit inconclusive, patterns. Workplace studies (some of which are reviewed below) that compare the frequency of men's and women's interruptions in mixed-sex groups suggest that men may interrupt women more frequently in these contexts, although the results vary. Studies (reviewed below) comparing how often professional women and men interrupt, or are interrupted by, lay persons suggest that men professionals may interrupt clients more frequently, and that women professionals may be interrupted more often than men in the same position. Similarly, in a study of the conversational interaction of women and men managers working in groups of ten at a management school, Case (1985; 1988) finds that the men managers tend to interrupt more than the women managers.

Two classic studies set the stage for investigations of how women and men tend to interact with each other in groups in the workplace. Eakins and Eakins (1976) analysed seven university faculty meetings, and found that the men spoke more often and for longer than the women, and that each of the men in the faculty meetings interrupted more often than each of the women, even when taking into account the total number of turns taken. Edelsky ([1981] 1993) analysed five university faculty meetings and found that during the more structured segments, there were few interruptions but men took longer turns than the women.

More recent studies examine the *nature* of turns. Case (1985; 1988), for example, found that women and men managers tend to make different types of contributions in groups. She assessed the frequency of 34 gender-related speech variables in each of the managers' speeches, creating a speech profile for each manager. Then, using statistical analysis, she identified two predominant speech styles that correlated with sex. Based on the types of strategies used in these styles, she characterized the style used primarily by women as a facilitative, personal style, and the style used primarily by men as an assertive, authoritative style. She found that the men tended to use more strategies of display such as joking, swearing, using slang, and talking about competition and aggression, as well as more of the strategies that appeal to authority and maintain status distinctions, such as appealing to objectivity instead of personal experience and giving direct commands. (See Goodwin, 1990, for a discussion of boys' use of commands and how this type of directive creates and maintains status distinctions.) The women tended to use more strategies that engaged others and minimized status differences, such as backchannelling, adding to others' comments to shift topics, and using modal constructions rather than imperatives.

These results are similar to those that Tannen (1994a) describes for interactions that she observed and analysed in several large corporations. She found that some men were more likely to speak in ways that claimed attention and got credit for their contributions, whereas women were more likely to preface statements with a disclaimer, speak at a lower volume, and try to be succinct so as not to take up more speaking time than necessary, especially at meetings. Tannen found that women and men tended to make different kinds of contributions as well, based, in part, on having different conventionalized ways of exploring ideas. More men than women used an oppositional format to accomplish a range of interactional goals, including the discussion of ideas. According to Tannen, those who use this style view challenge and debate as necessary for developing and strengthening ideas. Many women who do not engage in ritual opposition may take such challenges literally, as indication of weaknesses in their ideas, or as personal attacks; moreover, they may find it impossible to do their best in what they perceive as a contentious environment.

Case (1994) and Tannen (1994a) argue that when women and men interact in groups, a mismatch in the styles that they typically use is likely to produce unbalanced participation, so that those who end up having proportionately more influence in groups and appearing more competent and capable (and hence wielding more authority) are more likely to be men. Tannen suggests that when one speaker approaches a discussion through an oppositional format and the other approaches it in ways that maintain the appearance of equality, the latter (who is more likely to be female) is at a disadvantage. Likewise, Case argues that men's interactional styles in organizations currently work to their advantage by leading to domination of talk and increased influence in decision-making in groups. Tannen also points out that women begin with a disadvantage in workplaces that have previously had men in positions of power because these workplaces already have established male-style interaction as the norm.

The insight that styles of interaction more common among men have become the workplace norm again builds on the pioneering study of Edelsky ([1981] 1993). In the faculty committee meetings Edelsky taped, the women participated more equally in unstructured and informal parts of the meeting – portions that are not institutionalized and do not carry as much authority in the organization. In a review of the literature that appeared between 1951 and 1991 on gender differences in amount of talk, James and Drakich (1993) found a pattern that alludes to the connection between institutionalized interaction in the workplace and male norms of interaction. The studies they reviewed suggest that men talk more in formal task-oriented contexts or other formally structured contexts – a description that applies to key workplace settings – whereas women are likely to talk as much or more in informal contexts.

Some studies have investigated the interaction of women in all-women groups, revealing some interesting comparisons with the patterns found in groups of women and men. Linde (1991) examined how two women who are equal partners in a design firm managed the agenda in one face-to-face meeting and in three telephone meetings. Linde notes that the women negotiated the topics equally even though there was no formal prior agenda and no specified chair for the meeting. She found that, in the meetings, the women 'are careful to negotiate closings which are agreed to by both parties and are not abrupt. Pre-closings are extensive, which assures that both participants have had their say, before a current topic is concluded. Similarly, the introduction of new topics is negotiated, rather than unilaterally announced or begun' (1991: 310). Although Linde does not discuss gender as a potential influence on how these women negotiated topics, their topic shifts are similar to the reciprocal shifts that Ainsworth-Vaughn (1992) found women doctors tended to use with their patients, which contrasted with the unilateral shifts that the men doctors used more often.

In summary, studies that address how women and men interact with each other at work suggest that men tend to get and keep the floor more often and for longer than do women in formal task-oriented contexts, and that women and men tend to use language strategies that perform different interactional functions and create different alignments between themselves and other participants.

How women and men enact professional authority

Many of the studies reviewed above take as their starting point that workplace norms are masculine norms, owing to the historically greater participation of men in these professions, the current numerical predominance of men at higher levels, and/or the cultural interpretations of given types of work that dictate who is thought to be best suited for that work. (See McElhinny, 1993, for a discussion of the cultural interpretations of types of work that result in one or the other gender being regarded as being best suited for a given type.) This research focus is motivated, in part, by discussions of the links between language, gender, and power. For example, Lakoff explains that the norms of men's discourse styles are institutionalized, that they are seen not only as 'the better way to talk but as the only way' (1990: 210). Gal argues that men's discourse styles are institutionalized as ways of speaking with authority, that institutions are 'organized to define, demonstrate, and enforce the legitimacy and authority of linguistic strategies used by one gender – or men of one class or ethnic group – while denying the power of others' (1991: 188).

Given these findings, it is not surprising that many studies have focused on women in professions in which women have not traditionally been significantly represented. In particular, numerous studies have addressed the question of whether women and men enact authority in these professions in ways similar to their male counterparts. The majority of studies conclude that women adopt some of the practices associated with the profession that have been established by men while adapting others. For example, McElhinny found that the women police officers she observed project a 'police officer' identity by adopting discourse management techniques that portray 'facelessness in face-to-face interaction' (1995: 236). But they also adapt interactional norms of policing by projecting a more middle-class image of a police officer who is rational, efficient, and professional, rather than the working-class image of the police officer that is centred on displays of physical force and emotional aggression (1995: 219–20).

West (1984; 1990), Pizzini (1991), Ainsworth-Vaughn (1992), and Fisher (1993) consider how women and men physicians interact with patients. West (1984) finds that, although doctors generally interrupt patients more frequently than the reverse, when women doctors see men patients, it is the doctors who are interrupted more often. West (1990) analysed directive–response sequences in medical encounters.

She found that men doctors tended to give aggravated directives that explicitly establish status differences, whereas women doctors tended to mitigate their commands, using directive forms that minimize status distinctions between themselves and their patients. West concludes that women are constituting the role of physician in a way that exercises less interactional power than men physicians typically exercise.

Pizzini (1991) compares women and men gynaecologists' use of humour in gynaecological exams. She found that both the women and the men used humour to interrupt their patients, but the men interrupted their patients more frequently. Furthermore, the men tended to use interrupting humour to reestablish their scientific authority, whereas the women did so to discontinue discussions they considered unnecessary.

Ainsworth-Vaughn (1992) found that women doctors she observed downplayed status differences by using reciprocal topic shifts that share interactional power between doctor and patient, whereas men doctors tended to shift topics unilaterally, without waiting for patient agreement. She concludes that men and women physicians realize greater interactional power *vis-à-vis* their patients than do women physicians, and predicts that 'the ways women constitute being a woman physician will surely affect social and sociolinguistic norms for the role and for the encounter' (1992: 424).

Fisher (1993) contrasts the medical consultation of a (woman) nurse practitioner with the consultation of a (man) doctor to assess whether nurse practitioners, who claim to bring caring to the practice of medicine, minimize the asymmetry in the provider–patient relationship. She concludes that the doctor recreates his status as medical expert by asking narrowly focused questions and by moving rapidly to diagnostic closure. The nurse practitioner, in contrast, simultaneously reinforces her authority and 'distances herself from it, minimizing her professional status' (1993: 102) by establishing and maintaining a gender-based solidarity, asking open-ended questions, and not moving rapidly toward diagnostic closure. In this way, the nurse practitioner refrains from imposing her medical expertise and her definition of the situation, and legitimates the patient's feelings.

In each of these studies, women physicians speak in ways that minimize status differences and downplay their own authority. These findings make a significant contribution to the language and workplace literature, much of which focuses on interactional asymmetries in interactions between professionals and lay persons. Based on the research presented in their collection, Drew and Heritage conclude that 'In many forms of institutional discourse . . . there is a direct relationship between status and role, on the one hand, and discursive rights and obligations, on the other' (1992: 49). The linguistic behaviour of the women physicians reported in the studies described above suggest that, although a connection between status/role and discursive rights and obligation exists, this relationship is mediated by gender-related patterns as well.

Those studies that mentioned effectiveness found that the women's strategies were actually more effective in these contexts. In Fisher (1993), the doctor and his patient never reached agreement on the cause of or treatment for her condition, but the nurse practitioner and her patient reached a compromise agreement. West (1990) found that more 'polite' directives produced more compliant responses and, since women doctors used more of the polite directives, they had a greater rate of compliance from patients overall.

Researchers have also focused on how women and men enact authority in managerial positions. Tannen (1994a), Horikawa et al. (1991), and Tracy and Eisenberg (1990/1991) investigate how superiors give orders to subordinates. Patterning much as physicians were shown to speak with their patients, the men superiors in these studies tended to speak in ways that maintain or maximize status differences, whereas the women superiors tended to speak in ways that minimize status differences.

In her analysis of women and men in corporations, Tannen (1994a) notes that the women she observed in positions of authority tended to give directives to subordinates in ways that saved face for the subordinate, whereas many men in similar positions tended not to give directives in this way. However, Tannen cautions against assuming that talking in an indirect way necessarily reveals powerlessness, lack of self-confidence, or anything else about the internal state of the speaker. Indirectness, she notes, is a fundamental element in human communication and one that varies significantly from one culture to another. Although women in her study were more likely to be indirect when telling others what to do, she suggests that their motivation may be to save face for their interlocutors, especially subordinate interlocutors. Men were also often indirect, but in different situations and in different ways. For example, many men tended to be indirect when revealing weaknesses, problems, or errors, and when expressing emotions other than anger (1994a: 90). Tannen explains that those who would not use indirectness in a particular way often misjudge those who use it in that way. Those who expend effort to save face for a subordinate – including indirect approaches – can be seen as being manipulative or somehow less than honest.

Using an experimental design, Horikawa et al. (1991) investigate the effects of request legitimacy on the directness and politeness of women and men managers' compliance-gaining tactics. They asked women and men managers to report what they would say if they had to cancel a subordinate's vacation in one of two scenarios. In one scenario, the manager had no formal right to request that the subordinate cancel the vacation, so the manager needed to gain the compliance of the subordinate; in the other scenario, company policy gave the manager the right to cancel the vacation and, therefore, the manager did not need to gain the subordinate's compliance. Horikawa et al. found that the strategies that both women and men managers said they would use were less direct and more polite when they needed to gain the subordinate's compliance. However, when the managers did not need to gain the subordinate's compliance, the women managers used less direct and more polite requests than the men; in other words, if these managers would actually speak the way they said they would, the women would expend linguistic effort to protect the face of the subordinate even when the subordinate is obligated to comply.

Tracy and Eisenberg (1990/1991) conducted a role-play experiment which suggests that women in positions of authority expend linguistic effort to save face for their subordinates. Twenty-four dyads of college students, all of whom had work experience, were asked to orally criticize letters written by another. In one situation, the student role-played a supervisor giving feedback to an employee; in the other, the student role-played a subordinate giving feedback to a superior. Naive judges completed questionnaires rating each of the speakers in terms of the degree to which their criticism was concerned with clarity and attention to face. Strategies rated high in attention to face included positive initial statements prefacing negative comments, positive endings, and explanations for the criticisms. Strategies rated as low in attention to face included statements magnifying the size of the problem and blatant face attacks such as name-calling, unqualified statements about the worthlessness of the work, and strong reprimands for minor errors. Tracy and Eisenberg note that the women were significantly more concerned about the other's face when they were in the superior role than when they were in the subordinate role.

Nelson (1988) demonstrates a similar pattern in which a higher status woman supports women of lower status. She describes the interaction between herself (a professor) and graduate teaching assistants in small groups intended to discuss and improve the assistants' teaching. Nelson reports that she 'tried to minimize authoritarian behavior' by modelling ways of phrasing criticism that avoided 'making light of any writer or her work' and by herself using the strategies that she wanted to encourage: praising others, focusing attention on others' strengths, being emotionally open in revealing weaknesses, and involving others in decision-making (1988: 202, 201).

All of these studies indicate that how women and men in positions of authority speak – and how women and men claim that they would speak in these situations – is influenced by both gender and status. Woods (1989) examines the patterns of interruption in triads of higher ranking and lower ranking women and men colleagues to determine the relative influences of gender and occupational status on patterns of interruption. (She does not specify the context in which she tape-recorded but does note that the conversations were naturally occurring and surreptitiously taped with consent to use them given after.) The men subordinates in her study interrupted higher status women more often than the reverse, and the subordinate men interrupted higher status women more often than they interrupted higher status men. In addition, the men succeeded in gaining the floor by this means 85% of the time, compared with 52% for the women. She concludes that, in these interactions, gender-based patterns of interruption overrode status variables.

In an analysis of how three headmistresses speak in committee meetings, Wodak (1995) examines women in another type of 'managerial' position, that of the head of a school. (A headmistress is the Austrian equivalent of the principal in US schools.) She finds that the headmistresses speak in ways that 'disguise' their 'power and authority' (1995: 46). For example, in one meeting, one headmistress announced that she was limiting her accessibility in a way that overtly maintained her emphasis on cooperation and openness. She suggested that the change would enable her to 'be there for everyone' even though, as Wodak points out, she was actually restricting their access to her. Another headmistress, in her report at the beginning of a meeting, downplayed her criticism of the teachers' lack of discipline in their classrooms by providing possible reasons (such as 'children are like that'), by using a rhetorical question, and by praising the teachers. The third headmistress, in a committee meeting with parents, indirectly criticized the parents for not being prepared by embedding the statement, that they should 'think about what they need or what they want' beforehand, in her description of the committee's purposes.

The language behaviour of the headmistresses, as described by Wodak, is consistent with the other studies discussed in this section in that the headmistresses enact their authority by using language strategies that overtly appeal to equality and consensus, and thereby overtly minimize status differences. Her description of these women's language strategies underscores two important points that are explained by Tannen (1994a) and suggested by the research of Case (1985; 1988), West (1990), Ainsworth-Vaughn (1992), and Fisher (1993). First, the strategies used by the women described in this section to lead and to interact with subordinates and lay persons are authoritative strategies even though they overtly minimize status differences. Wodak suggests that the headmistresses' strategies are 'controlling and authoritarian strategies' used 'to achieve their aims' (1995: 54). However, these leadership strategies differ from those traditionally used by men in these roles and circumstances, so they are not as readily associated with these roles and, consequently, are less recognizable as authoritative. Nonetheless, these strategies are effective, especially when used with others who share this style. Wodak argues that the headmistresses' leadership styles, although different from each other, all draw on authoritative strategies of motherhood. She suggests that, because 'the pattern of maternity was shared by all those involved in the institution of the school', the women's strategies were accepted by teachers and parents and were 'not seen as an uncomfortable exercising of power' (1995: 54).

In summary, studies that focus on how women and men enact authority in professional positions suggest that women tend to expend linguistic effort to minimize status differences between themselves and their subordinates or patients (or, as Tannen puts it, save face for them), whereas men tend to use strategies that reinforce status differences. Thus, the women and men in these studies tend to create and maintain different alignments between themselves and their subordinates or patients. The women exercise their authority by using language strategies that create a symmetrical alignment (that is, they downplay their authority). The men use language strategies that create and maintain an asymmetrical alignment, the alignment that is traditionally associated with authority.

Evaluations of women and men based on their verbal behaviour

Research suggests that institutional identities such as 'manager' and 'physician' are socioculturally associated with one or the other sex and with the interactional styles typically used in these positions. In other words, the predominance of one sex in institutional positions creates and maintains gender-related expectations for how someone in that position *should* speak. Such associations simultaneously are produced by, and serve to reproduce, gender ideologies: socioculturally defined expectations for how women and men should speak and behave. In addition, interactional styles traditionally used by individuals in authoritative positions become authoritative themselves and come to be seen as 'speaking with authority'. The result of these combined processes is that expectations for how individuals in positions of authority should speak to subordinates are similar to expectations for how men should speak and interact. In this section, we examine these associations and the implications they have for how women and men are evaluated in the workplace, based on their ways of speaking.

Lakoff questions whether that 'mythic golden mean' between aggression and deference – assertion – is possible for women, or 'whether, too often, assertive behavior is misidentified as aggression' (1990: 207). Three experimental matched guise studies demonstrate that assertive language is not evaluated in the same way when it is used by women and by men. Carli (1990) assessed how college students perceived a persuasive message performed by a woman or a man who spoke assertively or tentatively (which in her study was characterized by the presence of disclaimers, tags, and hedges). She found that women who spoke more assertively were perceived as more competent and knowledgeable than women who spoke tentatively, but they influenced men less, and were perceived as less likeable by women. Men were judged as more influential, knowledgeable, competent, and likeable regardless of how they spoke.

Crawford (1988) found that women who spoke more assertively – for example by telling a boss to discontinue calling them demeaning names – received lower likeability ratings than men in the same situation, especially from older male raters. Crawford (1995: 65) notes that this may have significant ramifications in workplaces in which older men are in power. Sterling and Owen (1982) conducted a study in which college students heard police officers persuading a student to relinquish an alcoholic beverage that the student was consuming in public. The officers spoke in either a demanding, 'assertive' style (using imperatives and direct orders) or a 'reasoning' style (expressing empathy and requesting compliance). Women using a demanding style were rated as less feminine, but evaluation, of men officers' masculinity were not influenced by their speech style.

In each of these studies, the ratings that women received for competence, likeability, and/or femininity depended on their language behaviour and the sex of the rater, but the ratings the men received did not. Assertive women were perceived as more competent but less likeable, less influential or less feminine. These studies suggest that women must choose between being 'assertive' or being likeable and feminine. Wiley and Crittenden (1992) highlight this opposition. They surveyed 128 tenured men professors in a matched guise experiment to discover how these professors perceived the kinds of accounts that women and men academics give for publishing success. They find that, in the eyes of these senior colleagues, the modest accounts of success that are typically given by women academics enhance femininity but detract from professionalism, whereas the causal explanations typically offered by academic men support a positive professional identity and confirm a masculine gender identity as well.

A growing body of research, then, demonstrates that women in authority face a 'double bind' regarding professionalism and femininity. Lakoff describes the double bind this way:

> When a woman is placed in a position in which being assertive and forceful is necessary, she is faced with a paradox; she can be a good woman but a bad executive or professional, or vice versa. To do both is impossible. (1990: 206)

One of the sources for women's inability to be perceived as being both a good authority figure and a good woman is that, as Tannen puts it, the 'very notion of authority is associated with maleness' (1994a: 167). This phenomenon, which Tannen demonstrates at length on the basis of observation, is supported by experimental studies examining the link between what it means to be a man and what it means to be a manager.

In two classic studies, Schein (1973; 1975) found a significant resemblance between terms describing 'men' and 'managers' and a near zero, non-significant resemblance between descriptions of 'women' and 'managers', based on questionnaires completed by 300 men and 167 women managers. In 1989, Heilman et al., Brenner et al., and Schein et al. replicated Schein's earlier work; the studies that included women and men raters found an intriguing change from the earlier studies. Heilman et al. (1989) surveyed 268 men managers and found the same resemblance between 'men' and 'managers'. Brenner et al. (1989) surveyed 420 men and 173 women managers and found the same pattern among the men surveyed, but not the women. Among the women managers, there was a significant resemblance between the ratings of 'men' and 'managers', but there was also a similar resemblance between the ratings of 'women' and 'managers'. Schein et al. (1989) surveyed 145 men and 83 women management students, and found the same discrepancy between the attitudes of the men and women surveyed. The men perceived a link between 'men' and 'managers' but not between 'women' and 'managers', whereas the women saw a resemblance between 'managers' on the one hand and both 'women' and 'men' on the other. According to Schein (1994), similar patterns were found in studies conducted in the United Kingdom, Germany, China, and Japan.

Based on these results, Schein (1994) concludes that, as women have moved into management, managerial sex typing has diminished among women, but men have 'continued to see women in ways that are not complimentary *vis-à-vis* succeeding in positions of authority and influence'. Nieva and Gutek (1980) review a large number of studies in which evaluators were given descriptions of hypothetical persons who were identical except for sex. They found that, given identical qualifications of performance, there is a general tendency to give men more favourable evaluations than women. This bias is particularly strong in situations that, until the present, have been predominantly male domains. However, as Williams (1995[1992]) points out, such discrimination cannot be solely the result of 'tokenism', which Kanter (1977) described as the pattern in which members of under-represented groups will be subject to predictable forms of discrimination. Williams found that 'token' men in the 'female professions' (nursing, librarianship, elementary school teaching, and social work) *are* discriminated against, but with a twist: Whereas women often encounter a 'glass ceiling' that prevents them from advancing upward in male-dominated professions, men encounter a 'glass escalator' that prevents them from remaining in lower-level positions. As Williams puts it, 'As if on a moving escalator, they must work to stay in place' (1995[1992]: 197).

Women who attempt to resolve the double bind by using interactional strategies associated with men find that women (and men) who speak in ways expected of the other sex may be judged harshly. In her study of women and men managers interacting in groups, Case (1985; 1988; 1993) finds that two of the most influential members of the groups were a woman and a man whose styles combine ways of speaking expected of the two sexes. However, these two individuals were not pleased with the receptions they got in the group, and the woman fared worse; she was widely disliked and provoked openly hostile comments from others in the group. As Tannen (1994a) notes, this study suggests that women and men who do not conform to expectations for their gender may not be liked.

Evidence for this pattern is found in Edelsky and Adams's (1990) comparison of turn-taking and topic violations in six political debates. A woman in the Arizona gubernatorial debate who was a long-time party insider, spoke in ways similar to how the men spoke in this and other debates: she took full turns that were out of turn, inserting some of these turns into otherwise orderly episodes, and she was the only woman to make a demeaning move and to engage in friendly repartee with moderators. The authors note that by speaking in these ways, she was able to make the debate an equal forum; however, she was later lampooned in political cartoons and on local call-in talk shows for being 'mannish' (1990: 185). Because she spoke in ways that were common in political debates but more typically associated with men, she was evaluated negatively in a way that the men were not.

Some researchers suggest that language strategies that women use to downplay their authority are drawing on the resources available to them. Tannen notes that our 'primary images of female authority come from motherhood' (1994a: 161). Wodak observes that three school headmistresses drew on strategies associated with the role of mothers because 'The exercise of power within the parameters of the traditional mother role is considered socially legitimate' (1995: 45). It is likely, then, that women who downplay their authority or draw on the resource of mother for an authoritative style are attempting to resolve the double bind between professionalism and femininity.

Women in the workplace

Despite such evidence for negative perceptions of women in authority at work, research does not support the idea that the ways many women speak are powerless interactional strategies or necessarily the result of insecurity or other psychological states. Instead, the findings suggest that the strategies that many women tend to use are designed for specific ends and, in many cases, are effective for getting others to do things and getting work done.

Case draws on studies of management to argue that the ways that many women speak in the workplace are suited for 'current organizational realities' (1994: 160). Parker and Fagenson argue, in a review of research on the trends of women in management worldwide, that organizations are finding that a diverse workforce is not just useful, but a 'demographic imperative' (1994: 12). In addition, some research on management suggests that women are fostering a type of power which, as Case notes, 'involves the ability to accomplish goals and to help others achieve their goals as well' (1994: 162). For example, Astin and Leland (1991) find, in a cross-generational study of 77 women leaders, that these women use collaborative, participative communication and demonstrate a leadership style based on empowerment and collective action.

A great deal of research on language and gender in the workplace suggests that the ways that many women speak may have other benefits as well. Holmes argues, based on her extensive research in New Zealand, that 'the interactive strategies which are typically found in the talk of women appear to be the kinds of strategies that encourage high quality exploratory talk' (1995: 212). Coates (1995), comparing women and men speaking in law, medicine, and education, argues that women in these professions maintain a more cooperative discourse style rather than adopting the more adversarial style that is typically used and valued in these professions. If this is the case, women's increasing participation in the workplace may help to alleviate some of the problems that result from asymmetrical interactions between professionals and lay persons that have been reported in the language and workplace literature.

A framing approach to gender and language at work

As the preceding literature review makes clear, one of the most striking aspects of the workplace context is the hierarchical nature of relations among speakers. In the remainder of this chapter, we will draw on our own research to suggest that the most fruitful theoretical framework for understanding how gender-related patterns interact with the influence of hierarchical relations, as well as other issues of gender and of workplace communication, is a framing approach. Rather than counting up features such as interruption and then assigning totals to females and males, the researcher needs to ask what alignment each speaker is establishing in relation to interlocutors and to the subject of talk or task at hand. In other words, what persona is being created, and how are linguistic strategies functioning to create that alignment?

The usefulness of a framing approach can be seen in the literature on ways women and men tend to create their authority, as reviewed above. As Tannen (1994a; 1994b) has argued elsewhere, the differences in how women and men enact authority may best be understood as differences in the alignments that women and men tend to take up in relation to their interlocutors. In interpreting her own observations as well as results of studies by others, the women, Tannen suggests, tended to downplay their own authority both to avoid appearing 'bossy' – to be what they consider a good manager and a good person – and to save face for others by taking a ritual (not literal) one-down position. The view of their behaviour as intended to save face for the subordinate is key to understanding the behaviour. This contrasts with a psychological approach that would see such ways of speaking as evidencing lack of self-esteem or powerlessness. A framing approach allows us to see that women who talk this way are not evidencing a lack of authority but rather enacting their authority in a different way.

This perspective emerges as well in a study by Kendall (1993) conducted in a radio station control room. Kendall describes how a (woman) technical director of a radio news/talk show instructed a (man) substitute soundboard operator in a way that saved face for him. The director arrived at the recording room early to make sure that the substitute operator had the information he needed to operate the soundboard. She knew that he had a thorough technical knowledge of the equipment but was unfamiliar with the routines of this show and inexperienced in this role. When she entered the room, he was visibly nervous. The director could have run through a list of information about what to do and what not to do, issuing direct commands right up until airtime; instead, she phrased information in a way that implied that what she was saying was not general technical knowledge (which he should have) but information particular to that show (which he could not be expected to have). For example, instead of saying 'Don't forget that tapes have a one-second lead-in,' she said, 'On this show everything has that one-second dead roll.' She avoided giving direct orders by saying, for example, 'Probably we will want to re-cue the switch' when obviously it was he who had to re-cue the switch. After making sure that he had all the information he needed, she engaged him in small talk about personal computers, positioning herself as a novice in a domain in which he had expertise. Although he had been visibly agitated at the beginning of the conversation, the small talk allowed him to sit back with his feet up and discuss a subject in which he felt competent. By the time the show began, he was visibly relaxed. There were no errors during the live broadcast that day. Kendall suggests that, in this interaction, the director enacted her authority by speaking in ways that saved his face because, by so doing, she built his confidence to enable him to do his job, and thus accomplished her job as well.

The power of a framing approach is also exemplified in a study by Kuhn (1992) examining the classroom discourse of university professors, although she does not use that term. Kuhn noticed that the American women professors she observed were more assertive in giving students direct orders at the beginning of the term than were the men she observed. This initially surprised her, but she concluded that it was because they spoke of 'the requirements' of the course as if these were handed down directly from the institution, and then told the students how they could fulfil the requirements. For example, one American woman professor said, 'We are going to talk about the requirements.' Kuhn contrasts this with the men professors in her study who also handed out lists of requirements in the form of syllabuses but made it explicit that the syllabuses represented decisions they personally had made. For example, one man said, 'I have two midterms and a final. And I added this first midterm rather early to get you going on reading, uh, discussions, so that you will not fall behind.' A simple counting approach would have yielded the results that the women professors were more assertive than the men. This could have been presented as results that fail to confirm the findings of earlier studies, and left at that. Noting, however, that the women were talking about the syllabus as if it were handed down by the institution explains why they might feel comfortable describing the requirements in more assertive terms than the men who put 'on record' the fact that they are describing requirements they themselves have set. Thus the 'framing' approach, which asks what alignment the speaker is taking to the subject of talk and to interlocutors, allows a much more meaningful understanding of ways of speaking.

Tannen (1994b) proposes a framework for understanding the relationship among gender, power, and workplace communication that combines a framing approach with a new theoretical construct of power and solidarity. According to Tannen, researchers must ask not only about power, but also about how power and solidarity (in her terms, status and connection) interact, taking into account the conventionalized nature of many linguistic strategies. What is conventionalized, in other words, is not simply a way of exercising power but ways of balancing the simultaneous but conflicting needs for status and connection.

The framing approach that Tannen proposes draws on Goffman (1977) to point out that the relationship between gender and language is 'sex-class linked' in the sense that ways of speaking are not necessarily identified with every individual man or woman but rather are associated with women as a class or men as a class in a given society. By talking in ways that are associated with one or the other sex class, individuals signal their alignment with that sex class.

The remainder of this chapter lays out this framework by summarizing the argument and examples in Tannen (1994b). Building on the sociolinguistic concept of power and solidarity, Tannen substitutes the term 'connection' for 'solidarity', and sees these two dynamics as intertwined and both ambiguous (for example, calling someone by first name can show either closeness or lack of respect) and polysemous (it can signal both at once). She proposes that these be conceptualized on a multidimensional grid as shown.

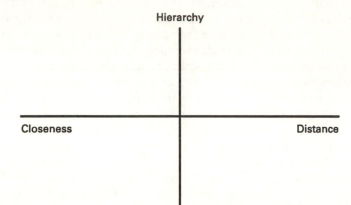

This grid illustrates that hierarchy/equality is one axis, and closeness/distance another. Americans seem to conceptualize relationships along an axis that runs from the upper right to the lower left: from hierarchical and distant to equal and close. We put business relations in the upper right quadrant, and family and close friendship in the lower left, as shown.

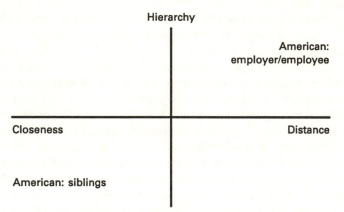

In contrast, other cultures, such as Japanese, Chinese, and Javanese, tend to conceptualize relationships along an axis that runs from the upper left to the lower right: from hierarchical and close to equal and distant. The archetype of a close, hierarchical relationship for members of these cultures is the mother–child constellation, which is the basis for conceptualizing hierarchical relationships at work as well. In this cultural view, equal relationships are not typically close but rather distant, such as business associates at similar levels in their organizations.

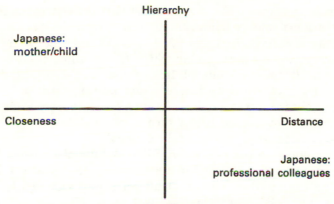

In analysing workplace discourse, then, the analyst must ask how the linguistic strategies used balance the needs for connection (or solidarity) and status (or power), and the answer to that question can be gleaned by asking what alignment a speaker is taking to others, to the task at hand, and to the material under discussion. Finally, one can ask whether the ways of speaking observed are associated with one or the other sex class, regardless of whether the speaker is a member of that sex class.

Tannen (1994b) presents two examples of workplace interaction – one among men and the other among women – in order to illustrate how the speakers balance both status and connection, and to suggest that their ways of speaking are best understood through a theory of framing.

The first example is from a conversation taped by Lena Gavruseva (1995) that took place in the office of a local newspaper between John, the editor-in-chief, and Dan, a recently hired writer. Dan was walking past John's office, spied him sitting at his desk with his door open, and stepped into the office to engage in friendly chat, which he initiated by asking, 'What are you scowling at, John?' In response, John began talking about problems involving another staff member's computer, in the course of which he referred to Dan's computer as 'that little shitburner of an XT'. Dan responded by saying that his computer 'sucks'. In response to this remark, John began asking Dan what was wrong with his computer and offering to repair it.

During playback, Dan told Gavruseva that he intended his remark 'It sucks' as a ritual exchange of woes in the service of solidarity. In choosing the vulgar verb 'sucks', he took his cue from John's use of the term 'shitburner'. Because he intended his remark in this spirit, he averred, he was taken aback when John treated his remark as a literal complaint about his computer and offered to remedy the situation. Because of the paralinguistic and prosodic quality of John's offers – fast-paced and overbearing, from Dan's point of view – Dan became increasingly uncomfortable, a discomfort that peaked when John proclaimed that he could fix Dan's computer in 25 seconds. It is also possible (though this is purely speculative) that John felt obligated, as the boss, to do something about a problem brought to his attention, regardless of the spirit in which it was mentioned. In any case, Dan told Gavruseva that he felt John was 'showing him up' and putting him 'on the spot'. Gavruseva observed that John was framing Dan as a supplicant. In other words, connection-focused banter turned into a statusful (and stressful) interchange because of hierarchical relations.

At this point, Dan restored balance by playfully challenging his boss, and the boss agreed to the shift in alignment by playing along. I suggest that in the excerpt that follows, Dan's reframing signalled to his boss that he had stepped over a line, and that John tacitly agreed to redress the imbalance of power by bonding with Dan as two men who can talk indelicately, and can align themselves in opposition to women.

Knowing that John had been suffering from an intestinal ailment, Dan shifted the topic to John's health by asking, 'How are you feeling today, John?' John responded:

> um Actually my guts started grinding and I thought, 'Hey, it's back,' but I had like a heavy night last night. I mean I went to bed at six, and only came out to like piss and drink water, and eat a can of tuna fish. I mean it was bad. I get a gastro-intestinal thing at both ends. It was it was spewing. It was violent.

Dan responded, 'Not simultaneously. Please tell me no.' John reassured him, 'No no no but it was intense. And it made me so glad that there was no girlfriend around, nobody could take care of me. There's only one fucking thing I hate it's being sick and somebody wants to take care of me.'

With his query about John's health, Dan redirected the conversation away from one that framed Dan as subordinate (both because he needed to report his problems to John and because John declared himself able to fix in 25 seconds a problem that Dan was unable to fix) in favour of a conversation that framed John as potentially one-down (a sufferer of embarrassing physical ailments). John went along with the reframing by recounting the symptoms of his intestinal distress. By talking explicitly about body functions gone awry, he seems to be positioning Dan as an equal: they are now two men who can talk openly about topics such as these, which they might not do if women were present. John then goes further toward aligning himself with Dan, man to man, by referring to how annoying women can be. Moreover, the very act of choosing the topic and having John accede to it reframes Dan as higher in status than he was in the preceding interchange. At the same time, however, as Gavruseva pointed out to me, John is still framing himself as someone who does not need help. In this example, then, Dan and John reflect and negotiate their relative status while apparently engaging in office small talk.

Contrast this with the following segment that was taped by Janice Hornyak (in preparation) in connection with her study of discourse in an all-woman office. Tina had been telling a story when June, the mail clerk, entered the office to deliver mail. Tina stopped her narrative and invited June into the room, and into the interaction, by commenting on her clothing. The other women joined in:

June:	Hii.
Tina:	Hey! Ah, we gotta see this getup. Come on in.
Heather:	C'mere June!
Tina:	She she she's uh . . . that's cute.
Heather:	Lo:ve that beau:tiful blou:se!
Janice:	Hey, high fashion today.
Tina:	Cool.
June:	Hi . . . I had the blouse /?/ and didn't know what to wear it with. And I just took the tag off and /?/ said /?/ I'm gonna wear it with a vest.
Tina:	And that hair too.
Janice:	Oh that's neat.
Heather:	Is that your Mom's? [Tina laughs.]
June:	No I got this from uh /?/
Tina:	What is it?
June:	/It's from/ Stylo.
Tina:	I've heard of it.
June:	The one in Trader Plaza that has all that wild stuff.
Heather:	What'd you do to your hair?
June:	Added /?/. Judith said you just are bored, you have to do something. [All laugh.]

At first glance, this too is an instance of office small talk. Nonetheless, relative status is a pervasive influence on this interaction as well. The complimenting ritual is initiated by Tina, who is the manager of the office as well as the daughter of the company's owner. She is the highest status person in the interaction. June, the mail clerk (and also the intruder into the office), who is the object of the complimenting, is the lowest status person present. Complimenting June on her clothing was a conventionalized, sex-class linked resource by which Tina could include June in the conversation, even though she did not want to include her in the narrative event she interrupted, as Tina might have done if a status equal and/or friend had entered unexpectedly. Importantly, one could not imagine their alignment reversed: June would be less likely to have entered with the mail and called out to Tina regarding her clothing. As with John in the computer-fixing segment, the highest status person controlled the framing of the interaction.

There are many aspects of the preceding small talk examples that differ along lines of gender, such as the use of profanity by the men and the ritual complimenting among the women. By examining the alignments that the speakers take up to each other and to the topics of talk, however, we are able to glean a deeper understanding of what they are trying to accomplish: both the men and the women negotiate their relative status while simultaneously reinforcing the connection between them, though the ostensible focus is more explicitly on connection among the women.

We suggest, then, that examining discourse in the workplace through a framing approach allows deeper insight into how gender interplays with hierarchical relations – in other words, issues of gender and power.

References

Ainsworth-Vaughn, Nancy (1992) 'Topic transitions in physician–patient interviews: power, gender, and discourse change', *Language in Society*, 21: 409–26.

Astin, Helen S. and Leland, Carole (1991) *Women of Influence, Women of Vision: a Cross-Generational Study of Leaders and Social Change*. San Francisco: Jossey-Bass.

Bates, Barbara (1988) *Communication and the Sexes*. New York: Harper & Row.

Bem, Sandra Lipsitz (1993) *The Lenses of Gender: Transforming the Debate on Sexual Inequality*. New Haven and London: Yale University Press.

Brenner, O., Tomkiewicz, J. and Schein, V.E. (1989) 'The relationship between sex role stereotypes and requisite management characteristics revisited', *Academy of Management Journal*, 32(3): 662–9.

Cameron, Deborah (1997) 'Performing gender identity: young men's talk and the construction of heterosexual masculinity', in Sally Johnson and Ulrike-Hanna Meinhof (eds), *Language and Masculinity*. Oxford and Cambridge: Blackwell.

Carli, Linda L. (1990) 'Gender, language, and influence', *Journal of Personality and Social Psychology*, 59(5): 941–51.

Case, Susan S. (1985) 'A sociolinguistic analysis of the language of gender relations, deviance and influence in managerial groups'. PhD dissertation, State University of New York at Buffalo.

Case, Susan S. (1988) 'Cultural differences, not deficiencies: an analysis of managerial women's language', in Laurie Larwood and Suzanne Rose (eds), *Women's Careers: Pathways and Pitfalls*. New York: Praeger.

Case, Susan S. (1993) 'Wide-verbal-repertoire speech: gender, language, and managerial influence', *Women's Studies International Forum*, 16(3): 271–90.

Case, Susan S. (1994) 'Gender differences in communication and behaviour in organizations', in Marylin J. Davidson and Ronald J. Burke (eds), *Women in Management: Current Research Issues*. London: Paul Chapman.

Coates, Jennifer (1995) 'Language, gender and career', in Sara Mills (ed.), *Language and Gender: Interdisciplinary Perspectives*. London and New York: Longman.

Crawford, Mary (1988) 'Gender, age, and the social evaluation of assertion', *Behavior Modification*, 12: 549–64.

Crawford, Mary (1995) *Talking Difference: on Gender and Language*. London: Sage.

Crittenden, Kathleen and Wiley, Mary G. (1985) 'When egotism is normative: self-presentational norms guiding attributions', *Social Psychology Quarterly*, 48: 360–5.

Drew, Paul and Heritage, John (1992) 'Analyzing talk at work: an introduction', in Paul Drew and John Heritage (eds), *Talk at Work: Interaction in Institutional Settings*. Cambridge: Cambridge University Press.

Eakins, Barbara W. and Eakins, R.G. (1976) 'Verbal turn-taking and exchanges in faculty dialogue', in Betty L. Dubois and Isabel Crouch (eds), *The Sociology of the Languages of American Women*. San Antonio, TX: Trinity University.

Eckert, Penelope and McConnell-Ginet, Sally (1992) 'Communities of practice: where language, gender, and power all live', in Kira Hall, Mary Bucholtz, and Birch Moonwomon (eds), *Locating Power: Proceedings of the Second Berkeley Women and Language Conference*. Berkeley, CA: Berkeley Women and Language Group.

Edelsky, Carole ([1981] 1993) 'Who's got the floor?', in Deborah Tannen (ed.), *Gender and Conversational Interaction*. New York and Oxford: Oxford University Press.

Edelsky, Carole and Adams, Karen (1990) 'Creating inequality: breaking the rules in debates', *Journal of Language and Social Psychology*, 9(3): 171–90.

Erickson, Frederick (1995) 'Discourse analysis as a communication chunnel: how feasible is a linkage between Continental and Anglo-American approaches'. Presented at GLS 1995: Developments in Discourse Analysis, 19 February, Washington DC.

Fisher, Sue (1993) 'Gender, power, resistance: is care the remedy?', in Sue Fisher and Kathy Davis (eds), *Negotiating at the Margins: the Gendered Discourse of Power and Resistance*. New Brunswick, NJ: Rutgers University Press.

Gal, Susan (1991) 'Between speech and silence: the problematics of research on language and gender', in Michaela di Leonardo (ed.), *Gender at the Crossroads of Knowledge: Feminist Anthropology in the Postmodern Era*. Berkeley, CA: University of California Press.

Gavruseva, Lena (1995) 'Constructing interactional asymmetry in employer–employee discourse'. Paper presented at the Annual Meeting of the Linguistic Society of America, New Orleans, 5 January 1995.

Goffman, Erving (1977) 'The arrangement between the sexes', *Theory and Society*, 4(3): 301–31.

Goodwin, Marjorie H. (1990) *He-Said-She-Said: Talk as Social Organization among Black Children*. Bloomington, IN: Indiana University Press.

Hall, Kira and Bucholtz, Mary (1995) 'Introduction: twenty years after *Language and Woman's Place*', in Kira Hall and Mary Bucholtz (eds), *Gender Articulated: Language and the Socially Constructed Self*. New York and London: Routledge.

Heilman, Madeline E., Block, Caryn, Martell, Richard and Simon, Michael (1989) 'Has anything changed? current characteristics of men, women and managers', *Journal of Applied Psychology*, 74(6): 935–42.

Holmes, Janet (1995) *Women, Men and Politeness*. London and New York: Longman.

Horikawa, Randy Y., Mickey, Jeffrey and Miura, Steven (1991) 'Effects of request legitimacy on the compliance-gaining tactics of male and female managers', *Communication Monographs*, 58(4): 421–36.

Hornyak, Janice (in preparation) 'Shifting between personal and professional frames in office discourse'. PhD dissertation, Georgetown University.

James, Deborah and Clarke, Sandra (1993) 'Women, men, and interruptions: a critical review', in Deborah Tannen (ed.), *Gender and Conversational Interaction*. New York and Oxford: Oxford University Press.

James, Deborah and Drakich, Janice (1993) 'Understanding gender differences in amount of talk: a critical review of research', in Deborah Tannen (ed.), *Gender and Conversational Interaction*. New York and Oxford: Oxford University Press.

Johnson, Sally (1997) 'Theorizing language and masculinity: a feminist perspective', in Sally Johnson and Ulrike-Hanna Meinhof (eds), *Language and Masculinity*. Oxford and Cambridge: Blackwell.

Johnson, Sally and Meinhof, Ulrike-Hanna (1997) 'Introduction', in Sally Johnson and Ulrike-Hanna Meinhof (eds), *Language and Masculinity*. Oxford and Cambridge: Blackwell.

Kanter, Rosabeth Moss (1977) *Men and Women of the Corporation*. New York: Basic Books.

Kendall, Shari (1993) 'Constructing competence: gender and mitigation at a radio network'. Presented at Annual Meeting of the American Association for Applied Linguistics, 7 March 1994, Baltimore, Maryland.

Kuhn, Elisabeth D. (1992) 'Playing down authority while getting things done: women professors get help from the institution', in Kira Hall, Mary Bucholtz and Birch Moonwomon (eds), *Locating Power: Proceedings of the Second Berkeley Women and Language Conference*, vol. 2. Berkeley: Berkeley Women and Language Group, University of California–Berkeley.

Lakoff, Robin (1975) *Language and Woman's Place*. New York: Harper and Row.

Lakoff, Robin T. (1990) 'Why can't a woman be less like a man?', in *Talking Power: the Politics of Language*. San Francisco: Basic Books.

Linde, Charlotte (1991) 'What's next? The social and technological management of meetings', *Pragmatics*, 1(3): 297–317.

McConnell-Ginet, Sally, Borker, Ruth and Furman, Nelly (eds) (1980) *Women and Language in Literature and Society*. New York: Praeger.

McElhinny, Bonnie (1993) 'We all wear the blue: language, gender and police work'. PhD dissertation, Stanford University.

McElhinny, Bonnie (1995) 'Challenging hegemonic masculinities: female and male police officers handling domestic violence', in Kira Hall and Mary Bucholtz (eds), *Gender Articulated: Language and the Socially Constructed Self*. New York and London: Routledge.

Nelson, Marie W. (1988) 'Women's ways: interactive patterns in predominantly female research teams', in B. Bate and A. Taylor (eds), *Women Communicating: Studies of Women's Talk*. Norwood, NJ: Ablex.

Nieva, Veronica and Gutek, Barbara (1980) 'Sex effects on evaluation', *Academy of Management Review*, 5(2): 267–76.

Ochs, Elinor (1992) 'Indexing gender', in Alesandro Duranti and Charles Goodwin (eds), *Rethinking Context: Language as an Interactive Phenomenon*. Cambridge: Cambridge University Press.

Parker, Barbara and Fagenson, Ellen A. (1994) 'An introductory overview of women in corporate management', in Marylin J. Davidson and Ronald J. Burke (eds), *Women in Management: Current Research Issues*. London: Paul Chapman.

Pizzini, Franca (1991) 'Communication hierarchies in humour: gender differences in the obstetrical/gynaecological setting', *Discourse and Society*, 2(4): 477–88.

Schein, Virginia E. (1973) 'The relationship between sex role stereotypes and requisite management characteristics', *Journal of Applied Psychology*, 57(2): 95–100.

Schein, Virginia E. (1975) 'The relationship between sex role stereotypes and requisite management characteristics among female managers', *Journal of Applied Psychology*, 60(3): 340–4.

Schein, Virginia E. (1994) 'Managerial sex typing: a persistent and pervasive barrier to women's opportunities', in M.J. Davidson and R.J. Burke (eds), *Women in Management: Current Research Issues*. London: Paul Chapman.

Schein, Virginia E., Mueller, R. and Jacobson, C. (1989) 'The relationship between sex role stereotypes and requisite management characteristics among college students', *Sex Roles*, 20(1/2): 103–10.

Sterling, Bruce S. and Owen, John W. (1982) 'Perceptions of demanding versus reasoning male and female police officers', *Personality and Social Psychology Bulletin*, 8: 336–40.

Tannen, Deborah (1994a) *Talking from 9 to 5: Women and Men in the Workplace: Language, Sex and Power*. New York: Avon.

Tannen, Deborah (1994b) 'The sex-class linked framing of talk at work', in Deborah Tannen, *Gender and Discourse*. New York and Oxford: Oxford University Press.

Tannen, Deborah (1994c) 'The relativity of linguistic strategies', in Deborah Tannen, *Gender and Discourse*. New York and Oxford: Oxford University Press.

Thorne, Barrie and Henley, Nancy (eds) (1975) *Language and Sex: Difference and Dominance*. Rowley, MA: Newbury House.

Tracy, Karen and Eisenberg, Eric (1990/1991) 'Giving criticism: a multiple goals case study', *Research on Language and Social Interaction*, 24: 37–70.

West, Candace (1984) *Routine Complications: Troubles with Talk between Doctors and Patients*. Bloomington, IN: Indiana University Press.

West, Candace (1990) 'Not just "doctor's orders": directive–response sequences in patients' visits to women and men physicians', *Discourse and Society*, 1(1): 85–112.

West, Candace (1995) 'Women's competence in conversation', *Discourse and Society*, 6(1): 107–31.

West, Candace and Zimmerman, Don H. (1987) 'Doing gender', *Gender and Society*, 1: 125–51.

Wiley, Mary G. and Crittenden, Kathleen S. (1992) 'By your attributions you shall be known: consequences of attributional accounts for professional and gender identities', *Sex Roles*, 27(5/6): 259–76.

Williams, Christine L. (1995 [1992]) 'The glass escalator: hidden advantages for men in the "female" professions', in Michael S. Kimmel and Michael A. Messner (eds), *Men's Lives*, 3rd edition. Needham Heights, MA: Allyn & Bacon.

Wodak, Ruth (1995) 'Power, discourse, and styles of female leadership in school committee meetings', in David Corson (ed.), *Discourse and Power in Educational Organizations*. Cresskill, NJ: Hampton.

Woods, Nicola (1989) 'Talking shop: sex and status as determinants of floor apportionment in a work setting', in Jennifer Coates and Deborah Cameron (eds), *Women in their Speech Communities: New Perspectives on Language and Sex*. Essex: Longman.

5

IDEOLOGIES OF PUBLIC AND PRIVATE LANGUAGE IN SOCIOLINGUISTICS

Bonnie McElhinny

The early stages of feminist thought in a discipline are typically associated with filling in gaps: correcting sexist biases in the existing literature and creating new topics out of women's experience. In feminist sociolinguistics examples of such research include the study of gossip (for example, Harding, 1975), of sexist language (Lakoff, 1975), and of women's consciousness-raising groups (Kalčik, 1974). However, as Thorne and Stacey note, as feminist work proceeds in a discipline 'feminists discover that many gaps were there for a reason, i.e. that existing paradigms systematically ignore or erase the significance of women's experiences and the organization of gender' (1993: 168). The task of feminist scholars thus goes beyond adding discussions of women to address the broader goal of the transformation of existing conceptual schemes in their disciplines. For example, in history, feminist and other radical scholars have challenged the assumption that history is primarily about politics, public policy and famous individuals. The inclusion of women has even led to a rethinking of the notion of historical periodization itself, since historical turning points are not necessarily the same for women as for men (Kelly-Gadol, 1977). Scholars have also turned to thinking about gender as a 'primary field within which or by means of which power is articulated . . . for concepts of power, though they may build on gender, are not always literally about gender itself' (Scott, 1986: 1069). In art, scholars turned from a search for the great women artists to an understanding of how the training practices for artists had denied women access to crucial materials, mentors and examples. In literature, feminist scholars have extended their project from the critique of texts by male authors and the recovery of texts written by female authors to asking questions about how literary periods and notions of dominant aesthetic modes are established, and thus how certain writers, texts and genres become valued as central or canonical (see, for example, Feldman and Kelley, 1995). In anthropology, feminist scholars and others have questioned the value of that traditional analytic category 'culture', arguing that this notion smooths over contradictions and conflicts of interest within (and perhaps even between) cultures in ways that may be particularly likely to obscure the lives of women and other disadvantaged cultural members (Abu-Lughod, 1993). They've also asked questions about how the canon of anthropological thought gets constructed (Behar and Gordan, 1996).[1]

Feminist sociolinguists and linguistic anthropologists are also increasingly asking questions about fundamental analytic concepts in sociolinguistics that must be revalued when gender is taken seriously. The definition of hypercorrection (Cameron and Coates, 1988), of standard and vernacular language (Morgan, 1994a; 1994b), of women's language (Inoue, 1994) and even theories about the way language marks social identity (Eckert and McConnell-Ginet, 1992; Ochs, 1992) have all been critiqued by feminist sociolinguists.

This chapter constitutes a contribution to the ongoing feminist re-evaluation of fundamental assumptions in disciplines by focusing on, and deconstructing, a dichotomy used in sociolinguistics, the dichotomy of 'ordinary' and 'institutional' language.[2] This dichotomy is implicitly informed by liberal political and neoclassical economic theory, and with these theories shares three problems: (1) an emphasis on the separation rather than the interpenetration of spheres; (2) a theory of social identity that focuses on abstract individualism; and (3) the idealization of fraternal interactions. The dichotomy, that is, encodes a theory of the social world in terms of a model of the relevant social spheres, with a specific picture of personhood, and with a specific picture of the paradigmatic form of social relations. Because of spatial constraints, I'll focus on the first of these problems in this chapter.[3] As with other research standpoints, this dichotomy is one from which 'certain features of reality come into prominence and from which others are obscured' (Jaggar, 1983: 382). The dichotomy's flaw is not in its inevitably partial vision, but rather in a failure to acknowledge its position and what these categories reveal and obscure. This dichotomy, I argue, is most useful for understanding American middle-class lives, and among them, most useful for understanding the lives of American middle-class men. With Michelle Rosaldo I want to argue that

> ways of thinking about language and about human agency and personhood are intimately linked: our theoretical attempts to understand how language works ... inevitably tend to reflect locally prevalent views about the given nature of those human persons by whom language is used. (1982: 203)

However, unlike her, I'm not focusing on cross-cultural comparisons of linguistic ideologies, but rather considering how a hegemonic Western linguistic ideology may distort our understandings of how interactions, especially among or with those in less powerful positions, occur in the West. In this sense, the dichotomy is ideological. It is contestable, socially positioned, and linked to particular social interests.[4] The assumption of difference between ordinary and institutional language obscures the fact that the possibility of insisting on such a difference is a privilege associated with one's economic and social status within a society. In particular, poor people (and women, especially minority women, are disproportionately poor) who must rely on state aid are forced to open themselves up to state scrutiny in ways that collapse this distinction. In addition, as a result of an emphasis on the separation rather than the interpenetration of spheres, relationships between occupations (including mothering) and gendered styles have been ignored, and discussions of family interaction have been conducted outside political economic contexts. Obscuring the politics of families is particularly detrimental for women and children. The recalcitrance of this dichotomy to critique may lie in its deep affiliation with hegemonic Western norms as expressed in liberal political and neoclassical economic thought. This chapter argues that the terms 'ordinary' and 'institutional' are ideological labels rather than designations of structures, interactions, or spheres.[5] As such the use of these labels is always already a theory of the social world. The labels, and the representation of the social world they represent, must be understood as contested, instead of assumed.

Linguistic studies of ideology

The topic of ideology has experienced a surge of interest in European sociolinguistics and North American linguistic anthropology recently (see, for instance, Fairclough, 1989; 1992; 1995; Friedrich, 1989; Gal, 1989; Hill and Mannheim, 1992; Kroskrity et al., 1992; Wodak, 1989; Wodak and Matouschek, 1993; Woolard and Schieffelin, 1994; van Dijk, 1993). Studying language ideology is a

> much-needed bridge between linguistic and social theory, because it relates the microculture of communicative action to political economic considerations of power and social inequality, confronting macrosocial constraints on language and behavior. (Woolard and Schieffelin, 1994: 72)

This area is ripe for study, since many social theorists holding a 'language as ideology' view do not adequately theorize notions of language, ideology and social control, while many linguists fail to explore the political implications of linguistic choices (Gal, 1989: 359–60). Susan Philips points out that

> language has become relevant in the study of ideology because of its widely recognized involvement both in thought and in social action and for some because of its concreteness or materiality. Language is central to the creation, promulgation and maintenance of ideologies. We experience the world through human interaction that is constituted by discourse and much of the

ideational content of human dealings is expressed and mentally experienced through language. (1992: 377)

In the European-centred tradition of critical discourse analysis, the importance of studying ideology is often linked to understanding non-violent means of exercising power over others (see Wodak and Matouschek, 1993: 227, for a useful summary). For instance, van Dijk argues that '"modern" and often more effective power is mostly cognitive, and enacted by persuasion, dissimulation or manipulation . . . managing the mind of others is essentially a function of text and talk' (1993: 254). This explains, argues Fairclough (1993), why ideology has received such emphasis in twentieth century social theory. Under these sociohistorical circumstances, discourse analysis is particularly important because of its 'distinctive . . . role in the constitution and reproduction of power relations and social identities' (1993: 139).[6]

The responsibility of linguists is not, however, simply to contribute to studies of ideology, but is also to reflect upon ideologies about language, including and especially our own linguistic ideologies. Woolard and Schieffelin (1994) describe some of the ways linguists' analytic categories have been ethnocentric, nationalist and bourgeois. Ethnographic critiques of speech act theory have pointed out how its underlying assumptions are rooted in 'an English language ideology, a privatized view of language emphasizing the psychological state of the speaker while downplaying the social consequences of speech' (1994: 59). Nineteenth century philology and the emerging discipline of linguistics contributed to religious, class and/or nationalist projects, while the idealism of twentieth century formal linguistics has contributed to class-linked and class-perpetuating norms of prescriptivism. Critics of linguistic relativism have pointed out how it works to assuage bourgeois guilt over the destruction of native Americans. Smitherman-Donaldson (1988) considers the reproduction of racism in academic discourse on African-American speech. Studies of ideologies promulgated in linguistic studies have thus pointed to the ways that such ideologies have reified and obscured a wide range of social inequalities.

Notably absent from this list, however, is the way linguists' ideologies might have supported gender bias, or gender bias as it interacts with other forms of bias. My critique of the ordinary/institutional distinction thus simultaneously participates in an ongoing feminist reanalysis of fundamental terms in sociolinguistics as well as the ongoing examination of linguists' linguistic ideologies. I'll begin by describing the definitions of institutional and ordinary language currently in use, and then demonstrate their connection to public–private dichotomies widely critiqued by feminist scholars. I'll then show how these discourse spheres, though posited as separate, actually interpenetrate, and the ways that the interpenetrations are most marked for those who are least privileged.

Defining institutional and ordinary language

The focus on 'ordinary' conversation and everyday cognition and social practice was originally articulated in sociology as a challenge to the Parsonian structural-functionalist focus on systemic analysis, and to the notion of social actors as structural dopes (Goodwin and Heritage, 1990: 284–5). The focus on 'ordinary' language in sociolinguistics can also be understood as part of a wider strategy that celebrates non-standard or everyday speech patterns as a challenge to official language norms that are disadvantageous for many speakers (see Gumperz, 1982; Labov, 1972). The political effectiveness of this opposition lies in its celebration of the ordinary; its limitations and political liabilities also lie in this.[7] The problem with the strategy of inverting the values is that this reform fails to critique structuralist sociology's distinction between public and private spheres (Gamarnikow and Purvis, 1983; 2).

'Ordinary conversation' is defined by Levinson as 'that familiar predominant kind of talk in which two or more participants freely alternate in speaking which generally occurs outside specific institutional settings like religious services, law courts, classrooms and the like' (1983: 284). By contrast, 'institutional' language is often characterized by an orientation to some core goal, task or identity associated with an institution, and constraints on what participants can relevantly say (Drew and Heritage, 1992: 22).[8] Formally, institutional language may be realized by reductions of the range of possibilities for participation that are found in ordinary conversation, in the form of restrictions on turn-taking, the use of specialized vocabularies, asymmetrical question–answer sequences, and special opening and closing sequences (Drew and Heritage, 1992; Goodwin and Heritage, 1990).

Scholars generally offer two kinds of arguments (one formal, and the other social) for positing ordinary conversation as the basic interactional mode.[9] First, the notion of an unmarked communicative context is said to be essential to pragmatic explanations of deixis and discourse explanations of turn-taking (Levinson, 1992; Sacks et al., 1974).[10] Second, conversation is taken to be the prototypical kind of interaction since it is the form in which people are first exposed to language and thus serves as the matrix of language acquisition (Goodwin and Heritage, 1990: 289; Levinson, 1983: 284; Schegloff, 1987):

> Ordinary conversation is the predominant medium of interaction in the social world. It is also the primary form of interaction to which, with whatever simplifications, the child is initially exposed and through which socialization proceeds. Thus, the basic forms of mundane talk constitute a kind of benchmark against which other more formal or 'institutional' types of interaction are recognized or experienced . . . The study of ordinary conversation, preferably casual conversation between peers, may thus offer a principled approach to determining what is distinctive about interactions involving, for example, the specialism of the school or the hospital or the asymmetries of status, gender and ethnicity, etc. (Drew and Heritage, 1992: 19)

Whether or not it is possible to establish a formally unmarked communicative context, the logic which moves from arguing that ordinary
conversation is formally unmarked to socially prototypical is problematic. In Drew and Heritage's argument ordinary conversation moves
from being defined as a mode of interaction contrasted with institutional or formal talk to a default mode of interaction among peers
who share the same status, and indeed the same identity. They move
from positing face-to-face interaction as the 'primordial site of sociality'
(Schegloff, 1987: 208) into a more culturally specific notion of conversation as egalitarian exchanges among peers. This is an empirical claim,
and yet it is here treated as a first principle. This definition already
assumes the distinction of institutional and ordinary language, and the
spheres in which they are spoken, when in fact what counts as institutional talk (such as political or ritual talk) may be precisely what a
scholar must discern (see, for example, essays in Brenneis and Myers,
1984, on political talk in egalitarian societies). Furthermore, some
cultures and some subcultures value and orient towards a certain kind
of institutional talk, rather than peer interaction, as the prototype of
conversational exchange (see Duranti, 1993, and Kroskrity, 1992, for
examples). This may in turn influence behaviour in 'ordinary' conversation. Finally, the invocation of a felt difference between ordinary and
institutional talk remains silent about who feels this difference: might
this difference be experienced differently by people positioned differently within society?

The separation of public and private spheres as ideology

Like other false dichotomies, the ordinary/institutional dichotomy
obscures differences within categories, assumes that differences
between the categories is as great (or greater) than differences within
them, and ignores interpenetrations between them (Butler, 1990; Scott,
1990). Before I turn to some examples, I'll consider some of the extensive feminist work on a similar distinction, that of public and private
spheres, and argue that the ordinary/institutional distinction is a
linguistic version of this ideological distinction. The construction of the
ideology of complementary and distinct public and private spheres is
one of the dichotomies most intensively studied by Western feminists
(for example, Cancian, 1989; Dahlerup, 1987; Hurtado, 1989; Jaggar,
1983; Pateman, 1989; Rosaldo, 1974; 1980; Strathern, 1988; Yanagisako
and Collier, 1987).[11] Indeed, this study has been intensive and extended
enough that in a recent book review one feminist scholar even dubbed
the theoretical debate on private versus public spheres as 'rather stale'
(Valverde, 1994; 210). A dismissal of continuing investigations of how
this division perpetuates itself seems to underestimate how deep-rooted
these ideological principles are in Western life and thought. The very

centrality of these principles is linked to their recalcitrance to change. This centrality motivates the need to expand political critique into new disciplines and political arenas, as well as regularly renew it in scholarly and public forums where the critique has already been offered. Dismissing the need for further such studies also assumes that the private and public split has the same meaning everywhere, when in fact part of the classificatory power of the distinction may be in lumping together dissimilar situations (as, for instance, the distinctions 'women' and 'men' often do). Pateman has noted that 'The term "ideology" is appropriate here, because the profound ambiguity of the liberal conception of the private and public obscures and mystifies the social reality it helps constitute' (1989: 120).

What social reality is mystified by the public–private distinction? Numerous historians (see, for example, Cancian, 1989; Smith-Rosenberg, 1985) have remarked that the sharp ideological distinction between private and public social spheres in the West can be tied to the industrial revolution. As commodity production moved outside households, work and family were increasingly distinguished. Households became defined as homes, refuges from the heartless competitive world of early capitalism. These distinctions were, of course, ideological, not actual. They best described and describe the lives of middle-class households, but even there the distinction was troubled. The private–public distinction is not necessarily relevant to the lives of poor women and women of colour whose every act is subjected to a kind of public scrutiny (Hurtado, 1989) or applicable to immigrant households shaped by other cultural distinctions (Yanagisako, 1987).[12] The economic distinctions between home and work also became encoded in the political theory – liberalism – which arose alongside industrial capitalism. The distinction between public and private is covertly normative in liberal economic theory, but in liberal political theory it is overtly normative: the private is the realm in which the state may not act in liberal political theory (Jaggar, 1983: 144).

Contrasts between the political and the personal, the economic and the domestic, the institutional and the ordinary depoliticize the domains contrasted with the political, the economic, the institutional. To do this is to 'shield such matters from generalized contestation and from widely disseminated conflicts of interpretation; and, as a result, [to] entrench as authoritative certain specific interpretations of needs', in particular those which tend on the whole to advantage dominant groups and individuals and disadvantage their subordinates (Fraser, 1989: 168). Issues such as wife battering, women's unpaid work in households, and the need for community and institutional child care, are bracketed off as non-political. 'Leaks' between these categories are signs of social and structural shifts; promoting the visibility of, and alternative interpretations of, such leaks is part of the political work of social movements.

The interpenetration of ordinary and institutional language

Occasionally the ordinary/institutional distinction is explicitly mapped onto private/public language (see Fabian, 1986: 139–41). More often, however, this mapping is implicit. Like the notion of public/private, the ordinary/institutional dichotomy works not simply as a descriptive distinction but as a normative one that obscures the interpenetration of spheres. There are institutionalized inequities in families linked to larger social and political-economic forces that are ignored by seeing families as egalitarian contexts. There are also personalized interactions that disguise institutional power by modelling themselves on these idealized families. Drew and Heritage dismiss a large body of sociological, anthropological and feminist research which defines families as institutions (cf. Hartmann, 1981a; 1981b; Ochs and Taylor, 1992; Thorne with Yalom, 1992) in a footnote: 'Notwithstanding the standard sociological usage within which the family is also a social institution, we will avoid using the term to describe activities that would be glossed as family dinners, picnics, and the like' (1992: 59, n. 1). By assuming rather than demonstrating that the family is not like other institutions, Drew and Heritage thereby violate their own ethnomethodological principles – and end up reinscribing an idealized notion of families familiar from liberal political and economic theory, where, as Jaggar points out, 'If home is [viewed] as a haven from the heartless world . . . [and] the sphere in which people exercise natural human affections, these will be degraded if subjected to the impersonal scrutiny of the law' (1983: 144). Though the cultural centrality of 'ordinary' conversation is partly said to be established because of its importance in language socialization, the ways that children are simultaneously exposed to interactional asymmetries in families – between adults and children, between older and younger children, between women and men – are all obscured in the idealization of families (see Ochs and Schieffelin, 1984, and Wodak and Schulz, 1986, for descriptions of variations in language socialization practices).

Indeed, the construction of people as ordinary can itself be a political move for someone working within an institution. In her ethnography of a centre for Jewish senior citizens living in an urban ghetto, Barbara Myerhoff (1978: 88–9) describes a ritual graduation ceremony designed by a new teacher of Yiddish history whose hope is to revitalize the centre, and draw its members (and himself) to the attention of the world and their own children. Throughout the ceremony the teacher underlines how the centre's members, humble and uneducated, have been disgracefully ignored and forgotten. Some members of the audience grumble: '"I, for one, would appreciate it if he wouldn't make us out to be quite so humble," Hannah whispered.' However the teacher goes on to have a poem read for the graduates:

You are
Silent and humble

Who weave their lives in a hidden way
Modest in thought and deed, unheralded,
Unsparing in speech and rich in beauty
Hidden is your fine spirit.

Hannah grumbles again about hearing more about how we are humble. A man sitting near her says, 'Humble, maybe, but silent, not so much.' Both are shushed loudly by other members of the audience. By painting these senior citizens as silenced, the teacher tries to take credit for revealing them to the world, for returning their voices to them. The senior citizens contest this portrait of themselves. The example highlights the importance of discerning from whose perspective the label *ordinary*, or *humble*, or *silent*, is being applied, and for what purposes.

In addition to seeing how the imposition of the label 'ordinary' can be a political act, we can consider how 'institutional' language attempts to use 'ordinary' language to effect its own ends. Impersonal market relations are personalized with the use of 'ordinary' talk based on 'real' feelings and 'private' experiences in the commodity of country music (Fox, 1992) and in the growth of the phone sex industry (Hall, 1995). Fairclough (1989; 1993) points to the 'synthetic personalization' (that is, the tendency to treat people handled as masses as individuals, or with simulated solidarity) found in bureaucratic forms, letters and interactions, a process he understand as 'the appropriation of private domain practices by the public domain' (1993: 140). See also Hochschild (1983) on flight attendants' routinized performance of positive affect. Advertising discourse, often using these personalizing devices, penetrates into homes through television, radio and print media. The widespread use of mass-produced greeting cards (di Leonardo, 1992; Papson, 1986) is a commodification of the work of communication with kin and friends. Numerous kinds of bureaucratic and professional interventions, interviews and interactions (Cicourel, 1992; Cunningham, 1992; Fairclough, 1989; Gumperz, 1982; Leach, 1972; Schiffrin, 1994) and many kinds of therapeutic talk (Fairclough, 1989) also exemplify the interpenetration of 'institutional' and 'ordinary' language.[13]

Some occupational identities, as Marxist scholars have long noted, are powerful enough to shape world view and behaviour in a variety of realms, including 'ordinary' interactions. There are a variety of stereotypes about elementary school teachers speaking in 'inappropriately' simple and cheerful ways that suggest this, including this anecdote recounted by anthropologist Michael Dorris:

Adam's first-grade teacher was Alice Hendrick, a woman of many years' experience, of utter patience and optimism and understated skill. She had taught six-year-olds for so long that even when speaking to adults, she clearly enunciated each word and gave frequent, supportive, rather unnerving compliments. 'What nice shiny shoes you're wearing,' she once said when I attended a PTA meeting. 'And you arrived right on time!' (1989: 103)

In my fieldwork with police officers, I found that many police officers said that once they were hired, interactions with friends and family often came to be oriented around their occupational identities.[14] For instance Naisha, an African-American female police officer, stated that the job had taken away her freedom to act like herself.

> You go to a party, they're all like this. 'Shhhh, her comes Naisha.' What am I gonna do, arrest my family? Even my mother she'll be introducing us, 'This is my son John, William, and my daughter Naisha, she's a cop.' Why didn't she say, 'This is my son John, He's an accountant'? Right away people are starting to tell me, 'Yeah, I had this cop stop me once.' Why would she do that? [81B-540]

Police officers regularly described other ways that the institutionalized interactional style that they were socialized into on the job changed their interactions with spouses and children (that is, 'ordinary' conversation). Many police officers, male and female, described adopting an authoritative style with their children. One officer reported having his wife tell him to 'stop ordering our kids around'. Another reported acting according to the advice he gives to men involved in domestic disputes ('just take a walk – let things cool down') when he argued with his wife. She responded with anger at his refusal to engage in discussion with her. He acknowledged that perhaps advice useful for a dispute so severe as to require police attention may not be the best for all disputes with his wife. Many police officers believed that the high rate of divorce among police officers is in part a result of their taking their interactional style home.

These examples suggest that interactional styles at work and with friends and family are not independent and distinct. The notion of individuals' involvement in different communities of practice offers an alternative way of talking about variations in communicative contexts:

> Speakers develop linguistic patterns as they act in their various communities in which they participate . . . in practice, social meaning, social identity, community membership and the symbolic value of linguistic form are constantly and mutually constructed. (Eckert and McConnell-Ginet, 1992: 473)

The notions of interpenetration, intertexuality, interdiscursivity and heteroglossia all can also be used to demonstrate that

> even the apparently most homogeneous or self-contained text exhibits, at a close analysis, elements that link it to other texts, with different contexts, different norms and different voices . . . In all kinds of social situations, verbal and kinesic conventions interpenetrate one another to form complex messages, with multiple points of view and different voices . . . To be a competent member of a given speech community means to be an active consumer and producer of texts that exploit heteroglossia and at the same time reproduce at least the appearance of an overall encompassing system. (Duranti, 1994: 5–6)[15]

Investigating the ways that different members of an interaction are using different genres thus allows one to see how people 'are busy producing orders and oppositions that can be assessed and played against legitimate expectations' (1994: 6). Interpenetration, then, can be one sign of conflict between different groups or ideologies in a given interaction (1994: 106). I turn to examples of just such conflict in the following section.

The interpenetration of public/private spheres in welfare, legal and medical contexts

One of the defining characteristics of institutional language is said to be that it exhibits constraints on what participants can relevantly say (Drew and Heritage, 1992). However, because conversational analysts do not assume that one can decide if talk is institutional simply by virtue of the setting, but rather hold that institutional talk is that in which professional identities are made relevant (1992: 3–4), we will see that institutional representatives have considerable latitude in designating what counts as institutionally 'relevant'. The interpenetrations that result in the United States are particularly significant for women, especially poor women and women of colour, since they are more likely to need institutional aid because women's work often pays less, because they often have custody of children, because they are often working as caregivers for the elderly, because they have fewer opportunities to work as casual labourers than men and because the control of reproduction is culturally construed as women's responsibility (Fraser, 1989: 147–8; Golden, 1992: 29). Poor men and men of colour are also disproportionately affected. This section reviews studies of 'institutional' talk in welfare, legal and medical contexts to illustrate the range and kinds of these interpenetrations.[16] Each of these studies problematizes the definition of institutional and ordinary talk, the separation of public and private spheres of talk. In some cases the original analysts themselves make a version of this point; where this is true it is so noted. In many cases, however, I am reanalysing the data in order to make this point.

State welfare contexts

Since I've outlined the ways that liberal political theory specifically legislates against state interference in people's private lives, it seems appropriate to begin by looking at the cases where the state does feel justified in so interfering. I'll begin, then, with a consideration of interactions in a social welfare office. Although the other examples below are drawn from American institutional contexts, this first example is drawn from a Swedish context, largely because I am unaware of any sociolinguistic studies of interaction in American welfare offices (a lacuna perhaps revealing, in and of itself, of how 'institutional' has been defined in American sociolinguistics).[17] Linell and Fredin (1995: 302) note that the state distinguishes between those who are 'legitimately' poor (that is, poor because of illness or involuntary unemployment) and those who are 'illegitimately' poor because of laziness or substance abuse). Because of this distinction social workers in a welfare office are licensed to determine the legitimacy and credibility of clients' requests for assistance by asking probing questions about the applicant's use of time, attempts to seek work, and living arrangements, including the intimacy of his/her relationship with the person s/he may be living with. The level of financial aid often therefore turns out to be a peripheral topic, while the clients' moral characters are central. The social workers then make judgements about clients (in at least the sense of deciding how to award money) based on the intelligibility of their answers to the state. A woman who lived in a collective (rather than as a boarder or a single renter), a man who lived with a woman who was not a sexual partner, and a man whose trip to another city to try to settle the affairs of a failed business led to a failure to register at a local employment office, all presented life and household circumstances which did not fit the norms of the social welfare office, and led to further and sometimes repeated questions about the client's life. For instance, the first man had to respond to repeated questions about whether his apartment mate was a girlfriend or mistress. He needed, that is, to repeatedly state that they shared a household and not a bed. For poor people, then, the realm of what is institutional often includes a much wider range of what is 'ordinary' or 'private' for wealthier people.

Institutional representatives do not, of course, unthinkingly reflect state-based ideologies. Often they have chosen to work with particular populations because of their empathy or political alignment with those groups. Linell and Fredin's study adopts a subtle and, I think, sympathetic approach to the analysis of the social workers' behaviour.[18] They present a Bakhtinian analysis of social workers' discourse strategies to show how social workers often develop polyvocal monologues in which they are adopting the client's perspective as well as that of the social welfare system (1995: 316). This polyvocality itself questions the clarity of the ordinary/institutional distinction.

Differences in how ordinary/institutional boundaries are drawn for social groups accorded more or less social privilege is also evident in a study done by sociologist Prudence Rains and described and further analysed in Fraser (1989). The study considers black teenagers' reception of instruction in pre-natal care, schooling and counselling from a municipal social worker. The teenagers drew on the health services, while resisting the psychotherapeutic aspects of the programme. The following is Fraser's description:

> The young black women resisted the terms of the psychiatric discourse and the language game of question-and-answer employed in the counseling

sessions. They disliked the social worker's stance of nondirectiveness and moral neutrality – her unwillingness to say what *she* thought – and they resented what they considered her intrusive, overly personal questions. These girls did not acknowledge her right to question them in this fashion, given that they could not ask 'personal' questions of her in turn. Rather, they construed 'personal questioning' as a privilege reserved to close friends and intimates under conditions of reciprocity. (1989: 179)

Here there is an active contest between recipients of state services, and the state representative, about what is 'private' and 'relevant'. Houghton's (1995) work on adolescent Latinas who are institutionalized after being labelled as school truants, or as inhabitants of crowded or unsanitary homes, arrives at similar findings. Once institutionalized these women found that

> personal freedoms and choices [that] are often taken for granted by citizens who comply with mainstream values are contingent upon attendance and success in therapy. These freedoms often include the 'privilege' of parenting one's children, for instance, or of reuniting with family members . . . Social workers relocate individuals geographically and thereby prevent them from interacting in community, family and peer groups that potentially subvert mainstream values. Residents are often denied visitations with family because such visits are deemed likely to undermine 'therapeutic progress'. (1995: 129)

The women were asked to submit to therapy to address their resistance to dominant values which emphasize work and material acquisition, to address contraceptive 'problems' and a perceived reliance upon the welfare state. Like the African-American women described in Rains's study, these young Latina women also resisted therapeutic attempts, in this case by mimicking almost to the point of parody therapists' linguistic strategies, and by introducing a genre of talk they called *girl talk*, used in free-time periods, into the therapeutic encounters. Their use of 'ordinary' talk in 'institutional' settings was a form of resistance.

Legal contexts

Evidence that a strict boundary between public and private spheres, and between topics which are institutionally relevant and those which are not, is a class privilege does not only arise in welfare offices. It also arises in interactions with representatives of other state bureaucracies, including legal aid lawyers and police officers. Indeed, Sarat found that the welfare poor did not distinguish between those agencies which regulated their access to welfare benefits and those which were supposedly more clearly their advocates, like legal aid services (1990: 351). He cites comments from Spencer, a 35-year-old man on public assistance whom he talked to in a legal services office:

> You know it's all pretty much the same. I'm just a welfare recipient whether I'm here or talking to someone over in the welfare office. It's all welfare, you

know, and it seems alike to me. I wish it was different but I've got to live with
it this way. They're all the same. Welfare, legal services, it's all the Man.

Not only are no distinctions drawn between bureaucratic contexts by
these recipients, but also distinctions between legal and ordinary interactions are collapsed for most of them:

> The legal consciousness of the welfare poor is . . . substantively different from
> other groups in society for whom law is a less immediate and visible presence.
> Law is, for people on welfare, repeatedly encountered in the most ordinary
> transactions and events of their lives. Legal rules and practices are implicated
> in determining whether and how welfare recipients will be able to meet some
> of their most pressing needs. Law is immediate and powerful because being on
> welfare means having a significant part of one's life organized by a regime of
> legal rules invoked by officials to claim jurisdiction over choices and decisions
> which those not on welfare would regard as personal and private. (1990: 344)

Being a welfare recipient with the need for legal assistance is being a
person who must deal with the rules of welfare, many of which seem to
clients more like confinement by the state than protection by it (1990:
345, citing White). The clients of legal aid offices cannot assume a
private space in their lives, but instead must struggle for it: '[The
welfare poor's] recognition that ". . . the law is all over" expresses, in
spatial terms, the experience of power and domination; resistance
involves efforts to avoid further "spatialization" or establish unreach-
able spaces of personal identity and integrity' (1990: 347). Interestingly
enough, the strategies for resistance used by legal aid clients also
collapse the public/private distinction, but rather than collapsing it all
into an impersonal/institutional domain, they collapse it into a private/
personalized domain, and understand many of the problems they
experience with the welfare/legal bureaucracy as personal attacks. Sarat
provides a cogent analysis of this strategy:

> [A client who interprets his problem as a personal attack] denied the bureau-
> cratic legitimacy which accompanies claims that decisions are impersonal and
> resisted efforts to clothe power in the rhetoric of rules. This tendency to see
> problems with welfare as personal attacks is quite consistent with views of law
> as driven by assessments of character or by who, not what, you know. (1990:
> 360)

The welfare poor thus challenge bureaucracies' presentations of themselves as neutral, objective and professional. Interactions which institutional representatives might perceive as 'institutional' are thus shown to
be 'personal' and paternalistic in the eyes of clients.

My analysis of an interaction between a male African-American
police officer (PO) and an African-American homeless women (C) who
wants to report a burglary further supports the idea that the definition
of 'institutional' and 'personal' may not be self-evident, given different

participants' strategies for understanding an interaction (see McElhinny, 1996a). In this interaction one of the woman's best friends from a homeless shelter has taken some of her belongings. The alleged thief turns out to be known to the officer, who has arrested her in the past for prostitution, drug use and child neglect. This interaction is notable in a number of ways for challenging the institutional/ordinary distinction. For instance, this officer tends to use familiar and vernacular language. Police officers, like other professionals, must use a specific vocabulary that marks, as it establishes, their orientation towards policing institutional norms. Sometimes this may include a technical register (*homicide* for 'murder', or *minor* for 'kid' or 'child') but, unlike other professionals, for police officers the professional knowledge deemed most relevant is not classroom knowledge but 'street' knowledge. The police officer's use of terms like *rockhead* (for 'crack user'), *jug* (for 'alcohol'), his use of vernacular language, and even his use of the address terms *baby*, *girl* and *girlfriend* all work to establish this orientation. Perhaps more noteworthy and egregious, however, are the discourse sequences that the officer uses to establish that he has a certain amount of 'knowledge' about the two women, as well as to determine if the victim is telling the truth. In Example 1 he displays his 'knowledge' about Emily, the alleged thief, by asking a leading question (note the use of street lexical items like *ho* for 'whore' in lines 1, 3 and 5, the use of informal address forms like *girl* in line 9).[19]

Example 1
```
 1  PO:  Emily hoing ever- any more?
 2  C:   Huh?
 3  PO:  Emily ever ho any more?
 4  C:   Hole?
 5  PO:  Hoing!
 6  C:   I don't
 7  C:   [xxxxxxx]
 8       [<police radio>]
 9  PO:  See you doing it to me again girl.
10  C:   I DON'T KNOW.
11       I'm telling the truth.
12       I don't know.
```

In Example 2 the officer treats the victim like a suspect, asking her questions about prostitution and drug use. This example also illustrates (see line 15) that part of the complainant's reaction to the officer's increasingly familiar probing is to use formal address forms like *sir* and *officer*.

Example 2
```
 1  PO:  What about you?
 2  C:   I don't ho.
```

```
 3        (2.0)
 4   PO:  Did you stop?
 5   C:   I never di::d.
 6        (3.0)
 7   PO:  Then how did you get money for drugs?
 8   C:   What you mean [how'd I get money for dr-]
 9   PO:                 [How'd you get money to get] high?
10   C:   When I used to get high?
11   PO:  Yeah.
12   C:   I had a welfare check.
13   PO:  That don't go nowhere.
14        You can't get no mileage out of that.
15   C:   I never did it like that officer.
16        I never did- sold my body for no drugs.
17        If I didn't have it
18        I just didn't have it.
19   PO:  Okay.
20        (9.0)
```

Despite the claim by Drew and Heritage (1992: 27) that institutional interactions are perceived as 'unusual, irksome or discomforting' because the restrictions on contributions, asymmetries and positions of relative ignorance for clients compare unfavourably with the relative equality and equal knowledge states of speakers in 'ordinary' conversation, the complainant's attentiveness to 'legally enforceable norms' are a resource for her resistance of the police officer here. At the points where she invokes the officer's formal identity with the use of *sir* or *officer*, he typically discontinues his current line of questioning.

Now, it is well established that the way that responsibility for actions is differentially assigned to different groups in a society reflects certain notions about personhood, so that for instance in the American legal system minors and the mentally insane are understood as less responsible for their actions than other people, and they are also understood as something less than full people (Hill and Irvine, 1993: 20–1). This encounter suggests how greater responsibility for forestalling crime is assigned to those who regularly inhabit the environments where criminal activity most frequently occurs, irrespective of what actual knowledge they have, by virtue of the greater knowledge they are supposed to have about how to forestall it. The same connection between familiarity and responsibility often works in assessment of date rape and domestic violence (see Ehrlich and King, 1996; Drew, 1992). This more rigorous standard of proof makes it more difficult for these victims to get their rights as citizens recognized. It also opens them up to the kind of intrusive institutional and personal questioning exemplified here.

Medical contexts

In medical interactions, discourse analysts have carefully documented a variety of ways in which diagnoses seem to be based on physicians' stereotypes about women (with different stereotypes applied to different groups of women) rather than on medically available facts. Often, such stereotypes mean physicians resort to questions about, and explanations based on ideas about, women's home or family life, rather than the immediate medical problem. These examples show how boundaries between public and private, institutional and ordinary, talk are redrawn depending upon the client and stereotypes about such clients.

Paget (1983) describes a series of medical encounters between a male physician and a female patient in which a physician arrives at an assessment that the woman's basic health is good and that the problem is 'her nerves', or hypochondria. The woman, a postoperative cancer patient concerned about the possible spread of her cancer, is subsequently diagnosed by another physician with cancer of the spine. Paget notes a number of different kinds of topical and discursive discontinuities in the encounters, partly explicable by the physician's ignoring the woman's comments or questions. The physician is eager to shift discussion away from the physical problems the woman has had since her most recent cancer operation to problems in the woman's marriage before the operation: 'Do you have any problems in your home with your husband or your marriage or is that . . .?' (1983: 64).[20]

Fisher's (1983) study of how the treatment of women with abnormal Pap smears is negotiated in two clinics shows how, even within similar institutional contexts, what constitutes private and public talk can be defined differently for different populations. In a faculty clinic staffed by physicians, no women received hysterectomies, while in a community clinic staffed by residents and serving a population of older, poor and/or Mexican or Mexican-American women with many children, over 50% of the women received hysterectomies. In the faculty clinic, Fisher notes that the 'physical layout honored the humanness of patients. There was a separation of public and private space. The waiting room was separated from the backstage medical area. Examining rooms were separated from consulting offices' (1983: 153). In the community clinic, however,

> there was no separation of public and private space. There was no waiting room. Patients sat in the hall outside of the examining room overhearing medical talk that frightened them. There were also no consulting offices. All talk with patients occurred either in the halls (in the presence of other patients) or in the examining rooms . . . it is a very different experience to sit across the desk from a doctor, fully clothed, discussing your medical problem from having a similar discussion with a resident while you are sitting undressed on the examining table. (1983: 153)

Finally, Borges's (1986) discussion of the medicalization of non-medical problems shows how distinctions between institutional and ordinary problems are collapsed into the category of the institutional in ways that feed the increasing power of certain institutions in contemporary society. She describes one physician–patient interaction in which a woman who is currently undergoing a divorce and living in an area without any friends or family nearby reveals to an internal medicine specialist that she is eating little (just 'salads and I drink my glass of wine and uh I eat strawberries'), smoking, drinking more heavily, and taking contraceptives because they make her feel less depressed. The physician arranges a further appointment, seemingly to check on her emotional health and determine if a therapeutic group or medication might be warranted. Borges wonders:

> Is this medical help? I wonder. In theory a clergyman, a social worker, or even a friend could have provided this function. Looking back on this encounter one striking element is the extent to which the medical encounter deals with the private issue of this woman's life and the lack of any sort of critique of the social relationships that seem to be the cause of her depression. There is a remarkable absence of a critical analysis of the distressing social patterns within her family and little mention of strategies for structural change (except therapeutic intervention). (1986: 31–2)

Although it's possible to imagine a kind of medicine in which the professional's responsibility is precisely this kind of therapeutic role, the professional in this case seems to be stepping in in the absence of any other support network for the patient.[21] Borges underlines that traditional medicine, when so practised, may work to defuse socially caused distress, and thus works as a conservative social force.

In a second interaction examined in the same paper a woman new to a neighbourhood describes herself as exhausted, achey and nervous. She also mentions that she's undertaken an extraordinary amount of entertaining and community work recently but resists a physician's suggestion that the solution to her stress is to take on less (1986: 47). In the end, despite the doctor's naming her problem as 'suburban syndrome', he provides the woman with a renewable prescription for a tranquillizer. Again, Borges's analysis is useful. The encounters demonstrate, she writes, that 'the general tendency to rely on technical solutions (at least quasi ones) for personal problems that would otherwise involve matters of individual responsibility and choice leads to a depoliticization of the individual and society' (1986: 34). She concludes that in both cases

> Not only do these women shift the responsibility for understanding themselves upon their doctors . . . but because of the false expectations they nurture, they in turn create a growing market for technical experts and their products (tranquilizers, birth control pills, etc.). The human needs for intimacy – family, friendship, and community – are transferred onto the mystique of the physician, a technical expert. (1986: 34)

Here the collapse of ordinary and institutional talk into the institutional feeds the importance of the medical institution – but does not enable asking questions about political and economic institutions that make treatment necessary. As static, structuralist categories, 'ordinary' and 'institutional' talk do not permit historical understandings (or interrogations) of the constructions of these categories.

Explanations for interpenetrations

One way of understanding some of these interactions could be that the institutional representative overstepped professional boundaries. This explanation is a common one in sociolinguistic studies:

> Research on interaction in conversation, classroom, medical settings and so forth tends overwhelmingly to present exchanges in terms of single sets of shared rules and understandings, and the orderliness they produce. Disorders . . . are almost automatically seen as failures or breakdowns not to be accounted for within the system. (Pratt, 1987: 51)

From this viewpoint, the problem is precisely that there has been some interpenetration of ordinary and institutional discursive spheres, and therefore the solution is their separation. This view presupposes that professionalism is the norm, and that institutional representatives who are intrusive are individuals working outside institutional boundaries. This view also assumes that what it means to speak on behalf of the institution and on one's own behalf is rather straightforwardly determined (see Drew and Heritage, 1992: 3–4). This explanation leaves us with the niggling question of why certain classes of people (the poor, women, certain minority groups) seem to more frequently end up with such aberrant institutional representatives – and perhaps even why it's been relatively easy for sociolinguists to find and record such interactions, if they are in fact aberrations from typical practice.

Another way, however, of understanding these interactions is that the institutional representatives are behaving precisely as the institution would have them act. First, let's consider how institutional concerns would shape the welfare interactions. Because Americans live in a limited welfare state where benefits are only given to those who qualify for such assistance (those who are 'entitled' to it), people must continually prove that they are poor, sick, disabled or old enough to qualify for state aid. All applicants are continually suspected of being freeloaders. To need aid is thus to be forced to open oneself up to state scrutiny. The explanation for why certain groups of people are more subject to scrutiny lies in this. As Aida Hurtado points out,

> the public/private distinction is relevant only for the white middle and upper classes since historically the American state has intervened constantly in the private lives and domestic arrangements of the working class. Women of Color have not had the benefit of the economic conditions that underlie the public/private distinction. Instead the political consciousness of women of Color

stems from an awareness that the public is *personally* political . . . There is no such thing as a private sphere for people of Color except that which they manage to create and protect in an otherwise hostile environment. (1989: 849)

The ambivalence about the provision of assistance that is part of the structure of the American welfare system, the unofficial mandate of relief agencies to refuse aid rather than grant it, leads to certain kinds of bureaucratic behaviours that make aid difficult to obtain, or unattractive. Golden notes that, 'Even before the Reagan administration began to attack the relief system, the agencies were always under fire for giving too much to people who were undeserving. Relief officials were in a sense forced to degrade their clients because "the general public requires it"' (1992: 61–2). Some of the 'rituals of degradation' to which relief-seekers are subject include endless waiting in anterooms, impolite or indifferent behaviour from case workers, wading through numerous appeal processes to get benefits, having benefits abruptly terminated without explanation, lack of knowledge about their rights, and even paying in supermarkets with food stamps. These rituals of degradation work in precisely the same way as did eighteenth century paupers' badges (1992: 61).[22] We've seen some of the discursive construction of indifference and 'impoliteness' above.

Now, not all the institutional clients described here are seeking welfare benefits. Some are seeking legal assistance which is much less controversially supposed to be available for all American citizens, yet they are still subjected to a ritual of degradation. Others are seeking medical assistance. This suggests that the categories used for sorting citizens that influence the welfare bureaucracy also influence other kinds of bureaucratic behaviour. This is not surprising if one considers the place of these categories in shoring up larger socioeconomic systems:

What has to be understood, however, is that the loathing of 'reliefers' is not an accidental feature of American culture. It has deep roots in the two main tenets of market ideology: the economic system is open, and economic success is a matter of individual merit (and sometimes luck); those who fail – the very poor – are therefore morally or personally defective . . . the ritual degradation of a pariah class . . . serves to mark the boundary between the appropriately motivated and the inappropriately motivated, between the virtuous and the defective. The point is, then, that relief practices are not a mere reflection of market ideology; they are an agent in nurturing and reinforcing that ideology. (Piven and Cloward, 1993: 149)

Paradoxically to many Americans who have grown markedly mistrustful of the state precisely because 'a government that does little is unlikely to generate confidence, affection or loyalty' (1993: 448), a partial solution may be to extend the state in certain ways. This is one way, though not the only way, to create the economic conditions that Hurtado notes would be required to undergird the public–private, and institutional–ordinary, distinction for the poor. Extending the state need not mean extending institutional scrutiny to all citizens if extension simply means that the state straightforwardly assures legal, medical and other services to all citizens without regard to 'legitimacy' of need. It has been argued that bureaucratic interactions are by nature depersonalizing and intrusive (Ferguson, 1984). However, studies by Nordic scholars suggest that in countries with more comprehensive welfare states, that is, states which provide a basic level of social security as citizens entitlements, rather than those like the US which provide poor relief after means testing (see Piven and Cloward, 1993: 409–10), all citizens are treated as customers of the state rather than having some citizens singled out as charity cases. This marks the 'fundamental difference between being dependent as consumers of public services or being dependent as clients on social welfare. The status as clients is often associated with economic dependency, control and social stigmatization' (Borchorst and Siim, 1987: 146).[23]

This difference in treatment of citizens, depending upon whether they are understood as consumers or as clients, is also evident within the United States in the ways applicants for different kinds of state aid are served. In the labour-market-based programmes like unemployment insurance which tend to serve more men than women, beneficiaries are required to do less work in order to qualify and remain eligible, they are less subject to intrusive controls and surveillance, and they are more likely to receive cash rather than 'in kind' benefits. Thus, beneficiaries of these programmes are 'positioned as *purchasing consumers*' (Fraser, 1989: 151, her emphasis). Beneficiaries of 'relief' programmes such as Aid to Families with Dependent Children, food stamps and Medicaid – programmes which overwhelmingly serve (or served) families (especially female-headed families) – are continually suspected of making fraudulent claims, and are subjected to various kinds of administrative humiliation, including surveillance, and reception of 'in kind' benefits (like food stamps) or money which is designated for specific purposes. These beneficiaries are thus '*clients*, a subject-position that carries far less power and dignity in capitalist societies than does the alternative position of purchaser' (1989: 152, her emphasis).

The extension of the state is only a partial solution because, as Fraser (1989) points out, in both subsystems of the welfare state people are positioned in ways that are not empowering, since their problems are treated as individual cases in ways that erect barriers against collective identification. The state

> imposes monological, administrative definitions of situation and need and so preempts dialogically achieved self-definition and self-determination. It positions its subjects as passive client or consumer recipients and not as active co-participants involved in shaping their life conditions. Lastly it construes experienced discontent with these arrangements as material for adjustment-oriented, usually sexist therapy and not as material for empowering processes or consciousness-raising. (1989: 155)

This leave feminists in the complex position of opposing cuts to social welfare, but trying to oppose the ways welfare systems reinforce, instead of challenge, structural inequalities.

Conclusion

As literary critic and queer theorist Eve Sedgwick has stated, one of the most important epistemological contributions of feminist thought to contemporary social analysis is pointing out how 'categories of gender and, hence, oppressions of gender can have a structuring force for nodes of thought and axes of cultural discrimination whose thematic subject isn't explicitly gendered at all' (1990: 34). In particular, she notes that dichotomies – such as, culture versus nature, mind versus body, rational versus emotional, active versus passive – have been particularly fruitful sites for feminists to unearth the masked, and therefore perhaps all the more insidious, construction of gender hierarchies (1990: 34).

The critique of dichotomies is not only part of a feminist scholarly tradition, however. Indeed, one way of understanding the history of sociolinguistics and linguistic anthropology is as a systematic attempt to dismantle structuralist dichotomies that have oversimplified or distorted our understandings of language as social life. As Gal (1989: 346) has noted, challenges to the dichotomies of *langue* and *parole*, social and individual, and synchrony and diachrony constituted the founding moments of American sociolinguistics (see Hymes, 1974; Labov, 1966; Weinreich et al., 1968). Later scholarship successfully deconstructed other dichotomies, including literary/poetic and ordinary language (Fox, 1992; Labov, 1972; Pratt, 1977; Williams, 1977), emotional and referential language (Besnier, 1990), formal and informal language (Irvine, 1979), oral and written language (Chafe and Tannen, 1987; Tannen, 1982) and idealist and materialist conceptions of language (Friedrich, 1989; Gal, 1989; Williams, 1977; Woolard, 1985).

In this chapter I've critiqued a dichotomous contrast between ordinary and institutional language which I've argued masks gender hierarchies, as well as class and ethnic ones. I've argued that the dichotomy assumes Western bourgeois cultural and gender norms. Postulating ordinary and institutional interactions as separate obscures contexts in institutional settings, especially those serving women, the poor and minorities, over what is legitimately institutional. It also obscures interactional inequalities in putatively ordinary interactions (such as families), and the ways that people's interactions in work settings can shape interactional styles elsewhere. Use of the terms as if they mark already defined spheres is actually part of the reification of those spheres. Instead, 'institutional' and 'ordinary', like the terms 'public' and 'private' are best understood not as designations of structures, spheres, or things, but rather as cultural classifications and ideological labels that are differently applied in different social situations by different people.[24]

These problems are more than isolated and unrelated problems in sociolinguistic thought. They are linked to a bourgeois model of social life that underpins a liberal political and economic system. The division between public and private life, of which the institutional/ordinary distinction is one example, obscures interpenetrations and relationships between home and work, home and state. The dichotomous contrast is problematic because it is simultaneously too broad and too narrow. It is too broad in that it overgeneralizes across differences within the categories of 'ordinary' and 'institutional', and because the seeming comprehensiveness of the two categories makes it more difficult to bring interpenetrations of contexts into focus. It is too narrow because it does not see the economic conditions that underlie the possibility of the distinction, and the way they are shaped by and reflect a liberal political theory that speaks from a bourgeois point of view.

Notes

The work upon which this chapter is based was supported by the Mellon Foundation, the National Science Foundation, Stanford University, the University of Toronto, Washington University, the Wenner–Gren Foundation for Anthropological Research and the Women's Studies Program at the University of Pittsburgh. I'd like to thank Ruth Wodak for her comments, questions and support. I also thank the participants in the seminar 'Language and gender' at the University of Toronto (Susan Ehrlich, Robin Oakley, Jack Sidnell, Claudia Schumann, Leena Tomi, Kelly Welch), all of whom helped me think through this chapter in a series of rich discussions around these issues. Finally, my appreciation to Lisa Freeman and Gayle Haberman, whose comments on sections of this chapter helped tighten up several key points.

1. Although, as I'll note below, feminist sociolinguists have begun to question fundamental analytic categories, we have yet to question the construction of the sociolinguistic canon, namely that body of works which is regularly taught in undergraduate and graduate classes, and which is understood as obligatory knowledge for qualifying as a sociolinguistic scholar (though see McElhinny, 1994c, for a description of how the work of an eighteenth century woman linguist, Hester Lynch Thrale, was overshadowed by her friend Samuel Johnson). This is a rich area for further inquiry.

2. This dichotomy is central to the analytic tradition of conversational analysis. To focus on this dichotomy might thus seem to single out conversational analysis for perpetuating a particular ideological tradition. There are, however, related dichotomies in other sociolinguistic traditions (ritual versus ordinary talk in the ethnography of speaking, standard versus vernacular language in variationist sociolinguistics) that can be deconstructed in similar ways. See Duranti (1994) for a deconstruction of the ritual/ordinary distinction, and Haeri (1991) and McElhinny (1993a) for a deconstruction of the standard/vernacular distinction. The point here, as I argue more fully below, is that Western

sociolinguistics does not stand apart from deeply rooted Western conceptual dichotomies.

3. The other two problems are more fully reviewed in McElhinny (1997). There I consider the ways the use of this dichotomy draws upon a notion of personhood, abstract individualism, that has been most extensively elaborated in the liberal economic theory that undergirds, and describes, capitalist relations. I also consider how a focus on fraternal interactions implicitly suggests that egalitarian relations are most successfully undertaken among people who are more alike than different, and thus occasions problems for considering what egalitarian relationships might look like when one takes gender, age, ethnicity, and other aspects of social diversity and identity fully into account.

4. The term 'ideology' has been used with a wide range of meanings (see Eagleton, 1991, and Woolard, 1992, for two useful reviews). Some argue that ideology is necessarily false, deceptive, mystifying or distorting, while others are agnostic about the truth of ideologies, focusing on seeing them as socially positioned. Those that focus on social positioning sometimes argue that ideology is used by socially dominant groups to promote their interests, while others argue that ideology can be found in all social groups. Finally, some definitions of ideology pick out ideas and beliefs which are simply used as symbols by a group, while others pick out those which are involved in social contests. It is important, I believe, to retain some notion of ideology which distinguishes between true and false beliefs (or, more cautiously, more false and less false beliefs), since 'if we extend the term ideology to include oppositional political movements, then radicals at least would want to hold that many of their utterances, while ideological in the sense of promoting their power-interests, are nonetheless true' (Eagleton, 1991: 26). Feminists, Marxists, and anti-racists all have ideologies too. However, it is also important to point out, as Eagleton (1991: 15–16, 19) does, that ideas may not be false but may still promote or legitimate the interests of dominant groups (for example, through false generalization), and that it seems appropriate to retain the term 'ideology' for those cases as well. This is precisely the sense in which the ordinary/institutional distinction is ideological. I therefore follow Fairclough (and Gramsci) in focusing primarily on the social effects of ideology, rather than truth value (1995: 76).

5. I borrow this formulation from Fraser's (1989: 166) discussion of the putative boundaries separating political, economic and domestic dimensions of life.

6. For a more extensive review of language and ideology as used in critical discourse analysis, see Fairclough (1995: 70–84) and Wodak (1989).

7. The strengths and limitations of this strategy parallel the political uses and liabilities of other kinds of essentializing identity politics. For a discussion of the implications of this for feminism see Butler (1990) and Jaggar (1983), for feminist sociolinguistics see McElhinny (1993a; 1996b), and for anti-racist practice see hooks (1990).

8. Michael Agar provides a slightly different definition of institutional and ordinary talk. Institutional talk is that, he says, in which 'one person – a citizen of a modern nation/state – comes into contact with another – a representative of one of its institutions' while 'natural conversation' is characterized by 'symmetrical social relations, unconstrained topic flow, and informality of style' (1985: 147). Note that there is some mixing of criteria here for defining the two forms of talk: whether the speaker is speaking on her/his own behalf or that of an

institution, how egalitarian the interaction is, formality, and topic control. The discussion below applies equally well to this definition.

9. Not every commentator places equal weight upon both of these. For example, Drew and Heritage (1992: 21) are careful to point out that they are less interested in specifying the features which define ordinary or institutional talk than in designating some 'family resemblances' among cases of institutional talk and some reasons for them.

10. I do not have the space to review the formal evidence here, though I will briefly note that the idea and portrait of a universal basic turn-taking system as biased towards two-party conversation without preallocation of turns has been challenged as ethnocentric. In particular, the predisposition towards free alternation of speakers (rather than, say, simultaneous talk) doesn't seem to be required by human processing constraints, nor does it seem to be the conversational norm in all cultures (Reisman, 1974; Morgan, 1996). In addition, turn-taking rules are construed in this model as 'a sharing device, an "economy" operating over a scarce resource' (Levinson, 1983: 297) where that resource is the conversational floor. But there are speaker situations, and possibly even cultures, where the floor is not necessarily seen as a valued good (Bauman, 1989), but rather the production of silence is. An even more radical critique of the notion of turn-taking would not simply point out that silence, as well as the floor, can be a valuable good, but would question instead the free-market economic metaphor implicit in talking about conversation as a 'speech exchange system', replacing this metaphor with, say, a metaphor of 'conversation as collective' (see, for example, Kalčik, 1974).

11. Feminist critiques of the ideological force of the public/private distinction have used two distinct definitions of private and public (Dahrlerup, 1987; Pateman, 1989). One sense is the distinction of domestic life (the *family*) from the political (the *state*) critiqued by, for example, radical feminists who extended the realm of the political into the realm of the home and family with the slogan 'personal is political', thus enabling them to bring issues of domestic violence, incest, and marital inequalities into greater visibility (Koedt et al., 1971). The other is the distinction of the *family* from the *economy/workplace* used by, for example, socialist feminists who argued that the distinction (as used by both Marxists in terms of production/reproduction and liberal theorists in the division between private and public) obscured the work done by women in household settings (motherwork, domestic tasks, administration, financial planning) and overinflated the importance of work done in the public sphere (Ferguson and Folbre, 1981; Hartmann, 1981a; 1981b; Jaggar, 1983: 212–3). 'Institutional' talk provides a covering rubric for both workplace and state interactions.

12. The meanings of the distinctions are also far from uniform, even in European and North American contexts: East European feminists currently point out that the construction of a private sphere was more liberating for women in oppressive states than was participation in the public sphere, though the political strategies of Western feminists have suggested the opposite (see Funk and Mueller, 1993).

13. A rather different example suggests the ways people can resist the intrusion of commodity capitalism into spaces they designate as 'private'. In the summer of 1996 the University of Toronto installed metal frames for advertising in bathroom stalls, positioned on doors directly opposite toilets. The frames contain rotating ads for cars, alcohol and other commodities meant to appeal to

an undergraduate student population. Resistance to the intrusions of commodity capitalism into this space quickly appeared as responses, some in the form of graffiti on the ads, others in the form of formal protests issued by university groups (including the faculty association). That there is not similar resistance to ads appearing elsewhere in the university suggests that the institution, and the stall users, have different ideas about the relative privacy that toilet stalls accord users. Such struggles are useful for denaturalizing what is designated as institutional and non-institutional.

14. All discussions of police officers in this chapter draw on fieldwork with the Pittsburgh Police Department in 1991–2 (also described in McElhinny 1993a; 1993b; 1994a; 1994b; 1995a; 1995b).

15. For further discussion of interdiscursivity see Fairclough (1993: 137).

16. Fraser (1989: 185) critiques Foucault for his focus on the discourses of traditional institutions (legal, medical, etc.) in ways that ignore, for instance, the discourses of social movements. She argues that this rather traditional approach thus misses out on a possibility for discussing contestations of some of these institutional discourses. Sociolinguistic investigations of institutions could be critiqued in similar ways. Assumptions about what counts as institutional talk have largely led sociolinguists to ignore a number of alternative institutional discourses, including the discourse of collectives (versus that of corporations), the discourse of midwives and nurse practitioners (versus that of physicians), the discourse of the welfare rights movement (versus that of state organizations), interactions in the offices of non-profit organizations and headquarters for social movements, among others.

17. There are of course philosophical, sociological and ethnographic descriptions of such interactions in, for example, Fraser (1989), Golden (1992), and Piven and Cloward (1993).

18. Nonetheless, Linell and Fredin's (1995) analysis sometimes falls into the trap of using the welfare system's categories of analysis for understanding the clients (see Pratt, 1987, for a similar critique of Cicourel, 1982). For instance, they claim that the exact relations of this man and his apartment mate never become clear. This is certainly the social worker's belief, as evidenced by her repeatedly returning to this question. However, the client's responses are consistent on this point. Further, Linell and Fredin describe disagreements between welfare workers and clients as clashes between the everyday, personal rationalities of the clients and the state's norms (1995: 311, 313). This explanation simply suggests that the problem is a sort of cultural conflict, and thus the solution would be acquainting each with the concerns of the other. The problem with this understanding however, as with some other dual-culture understandings of social problems, is that it suggests that the problem is a misunderstanding rather than disagreement. The focus on different communities with different rationalities fails to look at ongoing relations of dominance, or at processes of appropriation, penetration and cooptation and how to distinguish among them. See Goodwin (1994), Pateman (1989), and Pratt (1987) for similar arguments on slightly different issues.

19. *Hoing* is *whoring*, with a vocalized /r/, that is, an /r/ that has become a vowel. The phonological process of /r/-vocalization is widely found in African-American speech, though this process is largely lexicalized in this word now. The complainant displays innocence by not initially understanding the slang/African-American Vernacular English term used by the police officer (line 2). When the

police officer repeats his question, the complainant treats the missing phone as an /l/ that is vocalized (line 4), a phonological process that is also widely found in African-American Vernacular English, as well as in the regional dialect of Pittsburghers (see McElhinny, 1993a: 242–58). By misunderstanding the word, the complainant resists the officer's insinuations and displays innocence about the activity.

20. The patient described by Paget does not refuse to answer the physician's questions. It's possible to interpret this as the patient's cooperation with the physician's construction of what counts as institutional, but as Woolard (1985) has pointed out, speakers' cooperation with hegemonic norms does not indicate whether or not they concede the legitimacy of those norms. Pratt (1987: 53) also points out that many sociolinguistic analyses of institutional interaction have difficulty distinguishing cooperation from coercion, compliance or some other complex response. In this case, the fact that the patient sought medical advice elsewhere suggests she has not adopted the physician's way of viewing her.

21. The appropriateness of this strategy of moving from a narrow focus on disease to looking more broadly at a patient's lifestyle is not necessarily being questioned here. Practitioners of holistic medicine regularly and systematically make broad inquiries into all aspects of patients' lives as an important part of their attempts to restore health. The patients who seek such medical practitioners are, however, licensing them to ask such questions – and in turn may be given the opportunity to discuss their problems in ways quite different from traditional medical interviews (see Fairclough, 1992: 138–49, for a comparison of a traditional medical interview and an interaction with an alternative (homoeopathic) practitioner).

22. Piven and Cloward point out that another target (they claim it is the principal target) of such spectacles of degradation, particularly in moments of welfare state contraction, is the able-bodied poor who remain in the labour market: 'Harsh relief practices serve to enforce work . . . some few of the very young, the old, or the disabled are allowed on the rolls even during periods of political stability. But once there, they are systematically punished and degraded, made into object lessons for other poor people to observe and shun, their own station raised by contrast' (1993: 147).

23. The metaphor of citizens as consumers (rather than, say, workers) has its own problems. It applies a commodity logic to state services rather than more comprehensively attacking the pervasiveness of such logic.

24. I am inspired here by Fraser's (1989: 166) description of how the terms 'public' and 'private' are terms of political contest.

References

Abu-Lughod, Lila (1993) *Writing Women's Worlds: Bedouin Stories.* Berkeley, CA: University of California Press.

Agar, Michael (1985) 'Institutional discourse', *Text*, 5(3): 147–68.

Bauman, Richard (1989) 'Speaking in the light: the role of the Quaker minister', in Richard Bauman and Joel Sherzer (eds), *Explorations in the Ethnography of Speaking.* Cambridge: Cambridge University Press. pp. 144–62.

Behar, R. and Gordan, D. (eds) (1996) *Women Writing Culture.* Berkeley, CA: University of California Press.

Besnier, Niko (1990) 'Language and affect', *Annual Review of Anthropology*, 19: 419–51.

Borchorst, A. and Siim, B. (1987) 'Women and the advanced welfare state: a new kind of patriarchal power?', in A. Sassoon (ed.), *Women and the State: the Shifting Boundaries of Public and Private*. New York: Routledge. pp. 158–90.

Borges, Stefanie (1986) 'A feminist critique of scientific ideology: an analysis of two doctor–patient encounters', in Sue Fisher and Alexandra Todd (eds), *Discourse and Institutional Authority: Medicine, Education and Law*. Norwood, NJ: Ablex. pp. 26–48.

Brenneis, Donald and Myers, Fred (eds) (1984) *Dangerous Words: Language and Politics in the Pacific*. New York: New York University Press.

Butler, Judith (1990) *Gender Trouble: Feminism and the Subversion of Identity*. New York: Routledge.

Cameron, Deborah and Coates, Jennifer (1988) 'Some problems in the sociolinguistic explanation of sex difference', in D. Cameron and J. Coates (eds), *Women in Their Speech Communities*. London: Longman. pp. 13–26.

Cancian, Frances (1989) 'Love and the rise of capitalism', in B. Risman and P. Schwartz (eds), *Gender and Intimate Relationships*. Belmont, CA: Wadsworth. pp. 12–23.

Chafe, Wallace and Tannen, Deborah (1987) 'The relation between written and spoken language', *Annual Review of Anthropology*, 16: 383–407.

Cicourel, Aaron (1982) 'Language and belief in a medical setting', in Heidi Byrnes (ed.), *Contemporary Perceptions of Language: Interdisciplinary Dimensions*. Washington, DC: Georgetown University Round Table. pp. 48–78.

Cicourel, Aaron (1992) 'The interpenetration of communicative contexts: examples from medical encounters', in Alessandro Duranti and Charles Goodwin (eds), *Rethinking Context: Language as an Interactive Phenomenon*. Cambridge: Cambridge University Press. pp. 291–310.

Cunningham, Clark (1992) 'The lawyer as translator, representation as text: towards an ethnography of legal discourse', *Cornell Law Review*, 77: 1298–1387.

Dahlerup, D. (1987) 'Confusing concepts – confusing reality: a theoretical discussion of the patriarchal state', in A. Sassoon (ed.), *Women and the State*. London: Routledge. pp. 93–127.

Di Leonardo, Michael (1992) 'The female world of cards and holidays: women, families and the work of kinship', in Barrie Thorne with Marilyn Yalom (eds), *Rethinking the Family: Some Feminist Questions*. Boston: Northeastern University Press. pp. 246–62.

Dorris, Michael (1989) *The Broken Cord*. New York: Harper Perennial.

Drew, Paul (1992) 'Contested evidence in courtroom cross-examination: the case of a trial for rape', in Paul Drew and John Heritage (eds), *Talk at Work: Interaction in Institutional Settings*. Cambridge: Cambridge University Press. pp. 470–520.

Drew, Paul and Heritage, John (1992) 'Analyzing talk at work: an introduction', in Paul Drew and John Heritage (eds), *Talk at Work: Interaction in Institutional Settings*. Cambridge: Cambridge University Press. pp. 3–65.

Duranti, Alessandro (1993) 'Intentions, self and responsibility: an essay in Samoan ethnopragmatics', in Jane Hill and Judith Irvine (eds), *Responsibility and Evidence in Oral Discourse*. Cambridge: Cambridge University Press. pp. 24–47.

Duranti, A. (1994) *From Grammar to Politics: Linguistic Anthropology in a Western Samoan Village*. Berkeley, CA: University of California Press.

Eagleton, Terry (1991) *Ideology: an Introduction*. London: Verso.

Eckert, Penny and McConnell-Ginet, Sally (1992) 'Think practically and look locally: language and gender as community-based practice', *Annual Review of Anthropology*, 21: 461–90.

Ehrlich, Susan and King, Ruth (1996) 'Consensual sex or sexual harassment: negotiating meaning', in Victoria Bergvall, Janet Bing and Alice Freed (eds), *Rethinking Language and Gender Research: Theory and Practice*. Longman: London.

Fabian, Johannes (1986) *Language and Colonial Power: the Appropriation of Swahili in the Former Belgian Congo 1880–1938*. Berkeley, CA: University of California Press.

Fairclough, Norman (1989) *Language and Power*. London: Longman.

Fairclough, Norman (1992) *Discourse and Social Change*. Cambridge: Polity.

Fairclough, Norman (1993) 'Critical discourse analysis and the marketization of public discourse: the universities', *Discourse and Society*, 4(2): 133–68.

Fairclough, Norman (1995) *Critical Discourse Analysis: the Critical Study of Language*. London: Longman.

Feldman, P. and Kelley, T. (eds) (1995) *Romantic Women Writers: Voices/Countervoices*. Hanover University Press.

Ferguson, A. and Folbre, N. (1981) 'The unhappy marriage of patriarchy and capitalism', in L. Sargent (ed.), *Women and Revolution*. Boston: South End Press. pp. 313–38.

Ferguson, Kathy (1984) *The Feminist Case against Bureaucracy*. Philadelphia: Temple University Press.

Fisher, Sue (1983) 'Doctor talk/patient talk: how treatment decisions are negotiated in doctor–patient communication', in Alexandra Todd (ed.), *The Social Organization of Doctor–Patient Communication*. Norwood, NJ: Ablex. pp. 135–57.

Fox, A. (1992) 'The jukebox of history: narratives of loss and desire in the discourse of country music', *Popular Music*, 11(1): 53–72.

Fraser, Nancy (1989) *Unruly Practices: Power, Discourse and Gender in Contemporary Social Theory*. Minneapolis: University of Minnesota Press.

Friedrich, Paul (1989) 'Language, ideology and political economy', *American Anthropologist*, 91(2): 295–312.

Funk, N. and Mueller, M. (eds) (1993) *Gender Politics and Post-Communism: Reflections from Eastern Europe and the Former Soviet Union*. New York: Routledge.

Gal, Susan (1989) 'Language and political economy', *Annual Review of Anthropology*, 18: 345–67.

Gamarnikow, E. and Purvis, J. (1983) 'Introduction', in E. Gamarnikow, D. Morgan, J. Purvis, and D. Taylorson (eds), *The Public and the Private*. London: Heinemann. pp. 1–6.

Golden, S. (1992) *The Women Outside: Meanings and Myths of Homelessness*. Berkeley, CA: University of California Press.

Goodwin, Charles (1994) 'Professional vision', *American Anthropologist*, 96(3): 606–33.

Goodwin, Charles and Heritage, John (1990) 'Conversation analysis', *Annual Review of Anthropology*, 19: 283–307.

Gumperz, John (ed.) (1982) *Language and Social Identity*. Cambridge: Cambridge University Press.

Haeri, N. (1991) 'Sociolinguistic variation in Cairene Arabic: palatalization and the Qaf in the speech of men and women'. PhD dissertation, University of Pennsylvania.

Hall, Kira (1995) 'Lip service on the fantasy lines', in Kira Hall and Mary Bucholtz (eds), *Gender Articulated: Language and the Socially Constructed Self*. New York: Routledge. pp. 183–216.

Harding, Susan (1975) 'Women and words in a Spanish village', in Rayna Reiter (ed.), *Toward an Anthropology of Women*. New York: Monthly Review Press. pp. 283–308.

Hartmann, Heidi (1981a) 'The family as the locus of gender, class and political struggle: the example of housework', *Signs*, 6(3): 366–94.

Hartmann, Heidi (1981b) 'The unhappy marriage of Marxism and feminism: towards a more progressive union', in Lydia Sargent (ed.), *Women and Revolution*. Boston: South End Press. pp. 1–42.

Hill, Jane and Irvine, Judith (1993) 'Introduction', in J. Hill and J. Irvine (eds), *Responsibility and Evidence in Oral Discourse*. Cambridge: Cambridge University Press. pp. 1–23.

Hill, Jane and Mannheim, Bruce (1992) 'Language and world-view', *Annual Review of Anthropology*, 21: 381–406.

Hochschild, Alice (1983) *The Managed Heart: the Commercialization of Human Feeling*. Berkeley, CA: University of California Press.

hooks, b. (1990) *Yearning: Race, Gender and Cultural Politics*. Boston: South End Press.

Houghton, Catherine (1995) 'Managing the body of labor: the treatment of reproduction and sexuality in a therapeutic institution', in Kira Hall and Mary Bucholtz (eds), *Gender Articulated: Language and the Socially Constructed Self*. New York: Routledge. pp. 121–41.

Hurtado, Aida (1989) 'Relating to privilege: seduction and rejection in the subordination of white women and women of color', *Signs*, 14(4): 833–55.

Hymes, Dell (1974) *Foundations in Sociolinguistics*. Philadelphia: University of Pennsylvania Press.

Inoue, Miyako (1994) 'Gender and linguistic modernization: historicizing Japanese women's language', in Mary Bucholtz, Anita C. Liang, Laurel Sutton and Caitlin Hines (eds), *Cultural Performances: Proceedings of the Third Berkeley Women and Language Conference*. Berkeley, CA: Berkeley Women and Language Group, University of California–Berkeley. pp. 322–33.

Irvine, Judith (1979) 'Formality and informality in communicative events', *American Anthropologist*, 81: 773–90.

Jaggar, Alison (1983) *Feminist Politics and Human Nature*. Totowa, NJ: Rowman & Allanheld.

Kalčik, S. (1974) '. . . like Ann's gynecologist or the time I was almost raped', in C. Farrer (ed.), *Women and Folklore*. Austin, TX: University of Texas Press. pp. 3–11.

Kelly-Gadol, J. (1977) 'Did women have a renaissance?', in R. Bridenthal and C. Koonz (eds), *Becoming Visible: Women in European History*. Boston: Houghton-Mifflin. pp. 139–63.

Koedt, A., Levine, E. and Rapone, A. (eds) (1971) *Radical Feminism*. New York Times: Quadrangle.

Kroskrity, Paul (1992) 'Arizona Tewa Kiva speech as a manifestation of linguistic ideology', *Pragmatics*, 2(3): 296–310.

Kroskrity, P., Schieffelin, B. and Woolard, K. (eds) (1992) *Language Ideologies*, special issue of *Pragmatics*, 2(3).

Labov, William (1966) *The Social Stratification of English in New York City*. Washington, DC: Center for Applied Linguistics.

Labov, William (1972) *Language in the Inner City*. Philadelphia: University of Pennsylvania Press.

Lakoff, Robin (1975) *Language and Woman's Place*. New York: Harper & Row.

Leach, E. (1972) 'The influence of cultural context on non-verbal communication in man', in R. Hinde (ed.), *Non-Verbal Communication*. Cambridge: Cambridge University Press. pp. 315–47.

Levinson, Stephen (1983) *Pragmatics*. Cambridge: Cambridge University Press.

Levinson, Stephen (1992) 'Activity types and language', in Paul Drew and John Heritage (eds), *Talk at Work: Interaction in Institutional Settings*. Cambridge: Cambridge University Press. pp. 66–100.

Linell, Per and Fredin, Eric (1995) 'Negotiating terms in social welfare office talk', in Alan Firth (ed.), *The Discourse of Negotiation: Studies of Language in the Workplace*. Oxford: Pergamon. pp. 299–308.

McElhinny, Bonnie (1993a) 'We all wear the blue: language, gender and police work', PhD dissertation, Stanford University.

McElhinny, Bonnie (1993b) '"I don't smile much anymore": gender, affect and the discourse of Pittsburgh police officers', in Kira Hall, Mary Bucholtz and Birch Moonwomon (eds), *Locating Power: Proceedings of the Second Berkeley Conference on Women and Language*, vol. II. Berkeley, CA: Berkeley Women and Language Group, University of California–Berkeley. pp. 386–403.

McElhinny, Bonnie (1994a) 'An economy of affect: objectivity, masculinity and the gendering of police work', in Andrea Cornwall and Nancy Lindisfarne (eds), *Dislocating Masculinity: Comparative Ethnographies*. London: Routledge. pp. 159–71.

McElhinny, Bonnie (1994b) 'Discourses of rights and responsibility: police officers and complainants negotiate the meaning of assault'. Paper presented at the University of Toronto, January 1994.

McElhinny, Bonnie (1994c) 'Gender, "familiar" conversation and eighteenth century linguistics'. Paper presented at the Third Berkeley Conference on Women and Language, April 1994.

McElhinny, Bonnie (1995a) 'Challenging hegemonic masculinities: female and male police officers handling domestic violence', in Kira Hall and Mary Bucholtz (eds), *Gender Articulated: Language and the Socially Constructed Self*. New York: Routledge. pp. 217–43.

McElhinny, Bonnie (1995b) 'How to make a homeless woman look illogical and inconsistent: the fragmentation of identity in institutional encounters'. Paper presented at the Annual Meeting of the American Anthropology Association, invited session on 'Towards a postmodern linguistic anthropology'.

McElhinny, Bonnie (1996a) 'When a homeless woman reports a burglary: challenging ideologies of public and private language in sociolinguistics'. Manuscript.

McElhinny, Bonnie (1996b) 'Strategic essentialism in sociolinguistic studies of gender', in *Gender and Belief Systems: Proceedings of the Fourth Berkeley*

Conference on Women and Language. Berkeley, CA: Berkeley Women and Language Group, University of California–Berkeley.

McElhinny, Bonnie (1997) 'Policing gender'. Manuscript.

Morgan, M. (1994a) 'Theories and politics in African American English', *Annual Review of Anthropology*, 23: 325–45.

Morgan, M. (1994b) 'No woman, no cry: the linguistic representation of African American women', in M. Bucholtz, A.C. Liang, L. Sutton and C. Hines (eds), *Cultural Performances: Proceedings of the Third Berkeley Women and Language Conference*. Berkeley, CA: Berkeley Women and Language Group, University of California–Berkeley. pp. 525–41.

Morgan, M. (1996) 'Women's narratives in the English speaking African diaspora: identity and memory'. Paper presented at AAAL 1996, Chicago.

Myerhoff, Barbara (1978) *Number Our Days*. New York: E.P. Dutton.

Ochs, Elinor (1992) 'Indexing gender', in Alessandro Duranti and Charles Goodwin (eds), *Rethinking Context*. Cambridge: Cambridge University Press. pp. 335–58.

Ochs, Elinor and Schieffelin, Bambi (1984) 'Language acquisition and socialization: three developmental stories and their implications', in Richard Shweder and Robert LeVine (eds), *Culture Theory: Essays on Mind, Self and Emotion*. Cambridge: Cambridge University Press. pp. 276–322.

Ochs, Elinor and Taylor, Carolyn (1992) 'Family narrative as political activity', *Discourse and Society*, 3(3): 301–40.

Paget, Marianne (1983) 'On the work of talk: studies in misunderstandings' in Alexandra Todd (ed.), *The Social Organization of Doctor–Patient Communication*. Norwood, NJ: Ablex. pp. 135–57.

Papson, Stephen (1986) 'From symbolic exchange to bureaucratic discourse: the Hallmark greeting card', *Theory, Culture and Society*, 3(2): 99–111.

Pateman, Charles (1989) *The Disorder of Women: Democracy, Feminism and Social Theory*. Stanford: Stanford University Press.

Philips, Susan (1992) 'A Marx-influenced approach to language and ideology', *Pragmatics*, 2(3): 377–86.

Piven, F. and Cloward, R. (1993) *Regulating the Poor: the Functions of Public Welfare*, 2nd edn. New York: Vintage.

Pratt, Mary (1977) *Toward a Speech Act Theory of Literary Discourse*. Bloomington, IN: Indiana University Press.

Pratt, Mary (1987) 'Linguistic utopias', in N. Fabb, D. Attridge, A. Durant and C. MacCabe (eds), *The Linguistics of Writing: Arguments between Language and Literature*. New York: Methuen. pp. 48–66.

Reisman, Karl (1974) 'Contrapuntal conversations in a Antiguan village', in Richard Bauman and Joel Sherzer (eds), *Explorations in the Ethnography of Communication*. Cambridge: Cambridge University Press. pp. 110–24.

Rosaldo, Michelle (1974) 'Woman, culture and society: a theoretical overview', in Michelle Rosaldo and Louise Lamphere (eds), *Woman, Culture and Society*. Stanford: Stanford University Press. pp. 17–42.

Rosaldo, Michelle (1980) 'The use and abuse of anthropology: reflections on feminism and cross-cultural understanding', *Signs*, 5(3): 389–417.

Rosaldo, Michelle (1982) 'The things we do with words: Ilongot speech acts and speech act theory in philosophy', *Language and Society*, 11: 203–37.

Sacks, H., Schegloff, E. and Jefferson, G. (1974) 'A simplest systematics for the organization of turn-taking for conversation', *Language*, 50: 696–735.

Sarat, A. (1990) '". . . The law is all over": power, resistance and the legal consciousness of the welfare poor', *Yale Journal of Law and the Humanities*, 2: 343–79.

Schegloff, E. (1987) 'Between micro and macro: contexts and other connections', in J. Alexander, B. Giesen, R. Munch and N. Smelser (eds), *The Micro–Macro Link*. Berkeley, CA: University of California Press. pp. 207–36.

Schiffrin, Deborah (1994) *Approaches to Discourse Analysis*. Cambridge: Cambridge University Press.

Scott, Joan (1986) 'Gender: a useful category of historical analysis', *American Historical Review*, 91(5): 1053–75.

Scott, Joan (1990) 'Deconstructing equality-vs-difference; or, the uses of post-structuralist theory for feminism', in M. Hirsch and E. Fox Keller (eds), *Conflicts in Feminism*. New York: Routledge. pp. 134–48.

Sedgwick, Eve (1990) *Epistemology of the Closet*. Berkeley, CA: University of California Press.

Smith-Rosenberg, C. (1985) *Disorderly Conduct: Visions of Gender in Victorian America*. New York: Oxford University Press.

Smitherman-Donaldson, Geneva (1988) 'Discriminatory discourse on Afro-American speech', in G. Smitherman-Donaldson and Teun van Dijk (eds), *Discourse and Discrimination*. Detroit: Wayne University Press. pp. 144–75.

Strathern, Marilyn (1988) *The Gender of the Gift*. Berkeley, CA: University of California Press.

Tannen, Deborah (1982) 'The oral/literate continuum in discourse', in Deborah Tannen (ed.), *Spoken and Written Language: Exploring Orality and Literacy*. Norwood, NJ: Ablex. pp. 1–16.

Thorne, B. and Stacey, J. (1993) 'The missing feminist revolution in sociology', in L. Kauffman (ed.), *American Feminist Thought at Century's End*. Cambridge, MA: Blackwell.

Thorne, Barrie with Yalom, Marilyn (eds) (1992) *Rethinking the Family: Some Feminist Questions*. Boston: Northeastern University Press.

Valverde, M. (1994) 'Review of *Maternity and Gender Policies: Women and the Rise of the European Welfare State, 1880s–1950s'* (eds Gisela Bock and Pat Thane); *Poor and Pregnant in Paris: Strategies for Survival in the Nineteenth Century* (Rachel Fuchs); *The House of Eugenics: Race, Gender and Nation in Latin America* (Nancy Leys Stepan); *Wake Up Little Susie: Single Pregnancy and Race before Roe v. Wade* (Rickie Solinger); *The Politics of the Body in Weimar Germany* (Cornelia Usborne)', *Signs*, 20(1): 209–15.

van Dijk, Teun (1993) 'Principles of critical discourse analysis', *Discourse and Society*, 4(2): 249–83.

Weinreich, U., Labov, W. and Herzog, M. (1968) 'Empirical foundations for a theory of language change', in W.P. Lehmann and Y. Malkiel (eds), *Directions for Historical Linguistics*. Austin, TX: University of Texas Press. pp. 97–195.

Williams, Raymond (1977) *Marxism and Literature*. Oxford: Oxford University Press.

Wodak, Ruth (ed.) (1989) *Language, Power and Ideology*. Amsterdam: Benjamins.

Wodak, Ruth and Matouschek, B. (1993) '"We are dealing with people whose origins one can clearly tell just by looking": critical discourse analysis and the study of neo-racism in contemporary Austria', *Discourse and Society*, 4(2): 225–48.

Wodak, Ruth and Schulz, Muriel (1986) *The Language of Love and Guilt: Mother–*

Daughter Relationships from a Cross-cultural Perspective. Amsterdam: Benjamins.

Woolard, Katherine (1985) 'Language variation and cultural hegemony: toward an integration of sociolinguistic and social theory', *American Ethnologist*, 12: 738–48.

Woolard, Katherine (1992) 'Language ideology: issues and approaches', *Pragmatics*, 2(3): 235–49.

Woolard, Katherine and Schieffelin, Bambi (1994) 'Language ideology', *Annual Review of Anthropology*, 23: 55–82.

Yanagisako, Sylvia (1987) 'Mixed metaphors: native and anthropological models of gender and kinship models', in Jane Collier and Sylvia Yanagisako (eds), *Gender and Kinship: Essays toward a Unified Analysis*. Stanford: Stanford University Press. pp. 86–118.

Yanagisako, Sylvia and Collier, Jane F. (1987) 'Toward a unified analysis of gender and kinship', in J. Collier and S. Yanagisako (eds), *Gender and Kinship: Essays toward a Unified Analysis*. Stanford: Stanford University Press. pp. 14–52.

6

GENDER, DISCOURSE AND SENIOR EDUCATION: LIGATURES FOR GIRLS, OPTIONS FOR BOYS?

David Corson

This chapter links its discussion of gendered discursive practices in schooling to a discussion of the important differences in 'life chances' that education can confer upon its graduates. Education usually gives people two types of life chances: additional 'options' in their lives, which means a greater range of choices in their future; and stronger 'ligatures', which means the bonds between individuals and groups that develop as a result of people's experiences in education. I suggest that there are sex differences in access to options and ligatures that relate directly to gendered discursive practices and norms that the institution of education helps to reproduce and reinforce.

Life chances: options and ligatures

Strong evidence from many countries confirms that cultural and class groups develop very different needs and interests which have to be addressed with different social and education policy solutions. In trying to understand the nature of these differences, I find value in two concepts introduced by Ralph Dahrendorf in his book *Life Chances* (1978). He speaks of 'options' and 'ligatures' as the two distinguishing kinds of 'life chances' that societies offer to their members. I am focusing my discussion in this chapter from 'societies' to 'education within societies'.

Put simply, options in education are the range of choices that people receive as a result of their education. The wider the range of options, the greater the future life chances that individuals possess. Ligatures are life chances of a very different kind. These are the bonds between people established as a result of their membership in society, or, in this discussion, their participation in that society's education.[1]

Western people, living in the midst of capitalist social relations, have little difficulty acknowledging the role that 'options' have in offering increased life chances to those who possess them. But many Western people do have difficulty acknowledging the role that 'ligatures' have in offering increased life chances to people. This may be because the value of 'ligatures' has become hidden for Westerners in their rush to develop and extend capitalist economic options. Perhaps an example here will help to explain what I mean.

In a newspaper article, David Suzuki talks about the imposition of Western-style capitalist options on Papua New Guinean communities. This recent process has undermined the work of thousands of years building up community ligatures which in many ways gave these people life chances well beyond any possible quality of life that the options of global economics can now offer. Suzuki quotes a local social scientist, Nick Faraclas:

> 'Imagine a society where there is no hunger, homelessness or unemployment, and where in times of need, individuals can rest assured that their community will make available to them every resource at its disposal. Imagine a society where the decision makers rule only when the need arises, and then only by consultation, consensus and the consent of the community. Imagine a society where women have control over their means of production and reproduction, where housework is minimal and childcare is available 24 hours a day on demand.
> 'Imagine a society where there is no or little crime and where community conflicts are settled by sophisticated resolution procedures based on compensation to aggrieved parties for damages, with no recourse to concepts of guilt or punishment. Imagine a society . . . in which the mere fact that a person exists is cause for celebration and a deep sense of responsibility to maintain and share the existence.'
> Such a place is not fiction, says Faraclas: 'When the first colonizers came to the island of New Guinea, they did not find one society that exactly fit the above description. Instead they found more than 1000 distinct language groups and many more distinct societies, the majority of which approximated closely to the above description, but each in its own way.' (1995: B8)

While these were hardly perfect societies, they did provide life chances that are very important for the human condition. Yet within 100 years of the introduction of Western options, nearly all of the real gains in life chances have been seriously eroded. The ligatures that bound these people to one another, and to their cultures, were traded for options that have destroyed communal values built up over 40,000 years.

The Harvard Project on Human Potential borrows Dahrendorf's ideas to suggest a gendered dimension to the distribution of options and ligatures. It offers the example of Third World women, who seem poor in options and rich in ligatures. But because ligatures provide some of the most important benefits in life, namely support, structure, and motivation, and a sense of respect and continuity, it is altogether likely that women in some Third World settings experience their lives as highly satisfying even though Western observers might think that they could not do so (Levine and White, 1986: 203).

In some societies and among some cultural groups, ligatures are seen as positive ends in themselves to be deliberately cultivated as a goal in life, and not as the instruments to other ends that people from capitalist economies sometimes hold them to be. I am thinking of the Maori of New Zealand, the Aborigines of Australia, and the Navajo, the Cree, and the Inuit of North America, for example (Corson, 1993). Even in the midst of the rich options their countries extend to their citizens, it is often the ligatures that mean much more to these peoples, even when that valuing of ligatures leads to a reduction in options.

Most education systems in capitalist countries are quite strong in providing students with options but very weak in providing them with ligatures. Yet in English-speaking countries in particular, many of the clients of contemporary education come from ethnic communities where ligatures are prized. For some, such as the thousands of refugees from Indo-China or the Balkans, ligatures of one kind or another may be all that remain to them. For others, such as the ancestral peoples mentioned above, there is a cultural continuity reinforcing the preservation of ligatures that remains largely outside the understanding of people from outside those cultures.

In this chapter I am looking at differences in the life chances that male and female students get from their schooling, especially life chances affected by the highly specialized discursive practices that schools engage in. I suggest that girls derive much more in the way of ligatures from the discursive practices of their education than boys do. Boys seem to derive more options for themselves, partly because of their greater readiness to monopolize the discursive practices of schooling and to capitalize on the competitive bias inherent in those practices. Moreover boys from dominant family backgrounds also manage to develop a limited set of ligatures through their education, from their contacts with other similarly privileged males (the 'old school tie' and the 'old boy network'). They are able to convert these 'ligatures of reciprocity' into life chances that become powerful options for later use.

I begin discussion in the next two sections by considering the different discourse norms that research suggests are more typical of one sex than the other. By laying out this evidence, I am not implying that these different norms are much more than trends that are a little more characteristic of one sex than the other. But they are ideological trends that get reproduced, rather uncritically, in discourse from one generation to another, and they do seem to carry weighty implications for the life chances of males and females.

Linking gendered discourse norms with access to power

Across societies, power is the great variable that separates men and women from one another. Routine female exclusion from public spheres of action also often excludes them from access to the creation, maintenance, and elaboration of dominant ideologies and the sign systems used to express them. All the many societies and cultures examined in Philips et al. (1987) display key political and public-speaking roles and speech genres in which women participate rarely, or not at all. Rarely are they direct participants in shaping the shared conceptual frameworks of dominant groups, which are applied in characterizing and evaluating actions, events, and other phenomena. But in the same societies, men are not notably excluded from the key activities that women dominate.

In short, men in these societies have greater command of the discourses of power than women. Men are able to define the activities that attract status. From her ethnographic studies in Papua New Guinea, Bambi Schieffelin (1987) suggests that it is the activities engaged in by women compared with the activities engaged in by men, rather than gender itself, that associate with the linguistic choices that are made: men engaging in women's activities tend to use language in much the same way as the women would. Again the key variable in this is differential access to power. When men place themselves in relatively powerless situations, identified by the activities that they are engaged in, their language tends to be indistinguishable from that of women in the same activities. If women themselves are under-valued in that society, then the activities that they engage in and the language used by them will be under-valued. The social solidarity of people doing these same activities, regardless of their sex, is expressed through the language that they use.

As the complexity of the domain of research into language and gender becomes more apparent, the role of power immanent in wider structural arrangements is becoming even more important. Early research such as Lakoff's (1975) was based on explicit and straightforward linguistic features discovered in the speech of women that contrast with those of men. But as discussion so far suggests, these individual features are often artefacts of overall interactional differences in style between women and men that are reinforced by sociocultural practices and values quite removed from any obvious connection with language.

For example, women and men usually belong to rather different subcultures which themselves have their own methods for empowering agents in their actions within wider social structures. The differences in language use that are often identified between men and women are largely a product of different modes of socialization that arise within enduring sociocultural boundaries and structural constraints: men and women have internalized different norms for interaction within the sexes, in much the same way as the members of different cultures, living in the same social space, have different norms for interaction and often misunderstand one another accordingly. But there is more than cultural difference in play here.

In the same way as forced immersion in a majority culture can constrain the discursive practices of the members of a minority culture living in the same social space (Corson, 1993), structural arrangements reflecting the archaic values of dominant male social groups often constrain the discursive practices of contemporary women, even though they are far removed in time for those archaic values. In much the same way as a minority culture group gets few opportunities to influence the discourse of the dominant group because of prevailing structures of power, women as a group also get relatively few opportunities to reform discursive practices that reach much beyond surface forms of language. Why does this happen?

I have already mentioned the prevalent factor in all this. Women in most cultural contexts are clearly an oppressed group when compared with men as a group. It follows that almost any sex differences in discourse are interpretable with respect to this clear difference in power between men and women.[2] But even this difference in power between men and women has a discursive dimension to it, an insight that we owe to Foucault. Indeed any exercise of power by human actors is affected by the discursive nature of power itself (Foucault, 1972; 1977; 1980): rather than a privilege that is ascribed to the individual, power itself is a network of relations constantly in tension and ever present in activity; rather than possessed and localized in individual hands, power is exercised through the production, accumulation and functioning of various discourses; rather than the mere verbalization of conflicts of domination, power is the very object of human conflict; and rather than concerned with conscious intention or decision, the study of power is best located at the point where any intentions of the powerful are invested in real and effective practices.

As Foucault observes, history constantly teaches us 'that discourse is not simply that which translates struggles or systems of domination, but is the thing for which and by which there is struggle, discourse is the power which is to be seized' (1984: 110). This carries a strong message for any group seeking to emancipate itself, and a message for women in particular: to change the imbalances in discursive power and to get recognition for the discursive norms and practices that they prefer, women have to get more control over the dominant discourses, since that is the power that has to be seized. And this raises several contradictions for women, which is a point I return to below.

This kind of explanation for differences in discursive practices, based on the effects of sociocultural dominance, is a necessary balance to add to a simple sociocultural explanation of difference, if only because subcultures of women are themselves plainly susceptible to wider power forces within cultures. At the same time, of course, women usually have their own discourse norms that are not necessarily defined in reference to dominant male norms, or determined by historically dominant male values. For example, in societies where there is a high level of formal education, the models of language regarded as prestigious by many women may be drawn from the class of educated women elites, whose own preferred norms may vary considerably from their male peers. So the context or setting of discourse, including the class, gender, and cultural interests of all the participants, heavily influences discourse practice.

Cooperative and competitive discursive practices among adults

A developing aim of research into language and gender is to understand the differences that appear in discourse in capitalist societies where unequal power relations traditionally prevail. A key example is in the setting of the home, where women have to work harder than men to maintain conversations, asking more questions, supporting and encouraging male responses (Fishman, 1983). In their turn, men in the home tend to respond less frequently to women's attempts at interaction. Pamela Fishman concludes that men control the content and rhythm of conversation in this way. They establish their right to define what the interaction will be about. And they determine when and where interaction will occur. In an extension of Fishman's study, DeFrancisco (1991) recorded heterosexual married couples and also interviewed her participants after the events. Her research confirms that women do more of the conversational work in marital relations, but are more often silenced by the men's behaviour, especially by what they describe as men's 'patronizing', 'put-down' and 'teachy' behaviour.

Also in Fishman's research, the number of statements made by men matches the number of questions asked by women. While men make twice as many statements, women ask more than twice as many questions to which the men often decline to respond, although the women almost always respond to male statements. So what is going on here? Does the exercise of latent or explicit power explain this pattern of differences? I believe that it does largely explain it. As part of their socialization into gendered discursive ideologies, men more often concentrate on keeping control of discourse, while women often have quite different purposes, to do with creating affiliationary bonds with other interactants. Since the sexes develop these trends in interaction through socialization and enculturation, it is possible to explain the observed differences by reference to power relations that are long established or legitimated as norms for interaction within the structures, the archaic values, the socialization practices and the discourse arrangements of societies.

The influence of unequal power relations is evident too in the patterns of interruptions and silences recorded in male–female conversations. This second set of patterns suggests that men from Western capitalist backgrounds tend to exercise rigorous topic control in their conversations (Fasold, 1990). On the one hand, they often interrupt in such a way as to breach conventions about when to speak and when to remain silent. But on the other hand, they decline to support the topics that women are developing. This marked tendency is consistent with another finding that it is women who initiate conversational topics, but it is men who control their development by their minimally responsive behaviour (Klann-Delius, 1987). Again, these different patterns of interaction are much more than mere linguistic trends. Rather, they reflect the conventional levels of respect that dominant members of societies have shown over time for the thoughts, interests, views, activities, and rights of women.

So far, I have mentioned two sets of patterns that show up in male–female conversational contexts. Paula Treichler and Cheris Kramarae (1983) summarize several other characteristically male practices that contrast with female practices: males more often interpret questions as requests for information; they often ignore the comments of previous speakers; they more frequently make declarations of fact and opinion; and they talk more often, and at greater length. Men also use taboo expressions in their speech much more often (Smith, 1985). Separate research studies from Sweden, Brazil, and the USA report that women use far less profanity and obscenity than men, a pattern that occurs in girls' and boys' speech as well.

Other research also emphasizes this cooperative versus competitive dimension that appears in men's and women's interaction styles in Western capitalist settings. While many men shift topics rapidly, hearing other people's problems as requests for solutions, many women prefer to use questions as part of conversational maintenance rather than as the requests for information that men tend to use them for. Women also tend to acknowledge any previous contributions that are made to the discussion. They tend to interpret verbal aggression as personal, negative, and disruptive. For many women, this male competitive style of interacting prevents conversation from being used to show care and responsibility: to negotiate and express a relationship; to support and cooperate; and to establish a sharing, engaging, and communal exchange (Maltz and Borker, 1983).

Interpreting this evidence in a different way, Deborah Cameron (1985) questions whether women really are more cooperative in their talk than men. She wonders if their observed willingness to adopt a cooperative style might not be an artefact of feminist gatherings, where participants are urged not to interrupt, or raise their voices, or show deviance from solidarity. Less attractive interactive functions can be served in this way, such as binding conversational partners to a specific attitude for political purposes and constraining genuine criticism. However, Diane Reay (1991) observes a similar consensual pattern among British girls as young as seven years of age who also avoid strategies of questioning and challenging one another's ideas when working in a single-sex group (see below). Reay suggests that acting consensually in this way is not the same as being democratic, since democratic interaction always allows the possibility of conflict, which is something the girls in the single-sex group in her study try to avoid in much the same way as adult women may do, on the evidence and according to Cameron's account. This strategic use of 'cooperative' discourse by women, then, seems far removed from an ideal kind of speech situation, but it is certainly no more distant from it than the competitive discourse practices often adopted by men.

On the evidence, there is not much to admire in the informal competitive talk of Western males in many contexts of interaction. Men's talk resembles a form of display, involving joke telling, boasting, ribbing, and verbal aggression. It is very largely a matter of getting control of the interaction and keeping it. Men tend to take longer turns at talk and have a greater rate of controlling pauses filled with vocalizations, like 'um' and 'ah', while women smile more often and direct their gaze longer at their conversational partners. While women give many nods and responses such as 'yes' and 'mmm' to signal that they are listening attentively, men often give barely minimal responses to the talk of others, or they give none at all (Maltz and Borker, 1983).

These many contrasting trends in male–female discourse obviously leave room for misunderstandings to arise in mixed-sex conversations. This occurs especially when women are trying to manage affiliative goals, but have to do so within domains of interaction that are controlled by men whose attention is on the outcome of the interaction, not on its processes. This discursive quandary has a major impact in Western societies, where the process of winning access to positions of institutional power often depends on possessing the kinds of verbal skills needed to function successfully in roles created to meet the historical values and language norms of dominant Western males.

When women take on gendered administrative roles and have to conform to discursive norms that are not their own, even if only temporarily, they risk being misperceived as pseudo-male. At the same time during their occupancy of these gendered roles, they often lose the personal satisfaction that comes from achieving their own affiliative goals in interaction through a use of their own preferred discourse styles. On the other hand, when women do hold administrative posts under conditions that allow them to shape the roles and discursive norms of the posts according to their own preferences, they tend to succeed very well in exercising leadership (Shakeshaft and Perry, 1995; Wodak, 1995). This may be because the cooperative set of conversational properties that women more often tend to possess (Troemel-Ploetz, 1994) allows them to develop a greater range of effective leadership strategies, like sharing power with others rather than struggling over it, or constructing equality rather than conversational asymmetry, or protecting face rather than winning empty victories.

This is not to say, however, that the preferred styles of women can be characterized as 'women's language', or that there are 'two cultures' interacting when mixed-sex groups converse. Indeed any differences that research uncovers are always limited in their range of reference to the precise sociocultural group from which they were drawn, and to the social context in which the differences were observed (see Freeman, 1997). Lack of concern for the context of situation, including the cultural identities of the interactants, was a frequent weakness in the early research on sex and language.

Lakoff's exploration of 'women's language' was critically extended by O'Barr and Atkins (1980), who also based their research on the observed frequency of different features of language. After examining more than 150 hours of courtroom testimony by women and men, they suggest that a better name for the language more often used by women, and sometimes called 'women's language', would be 'powerless language'. They argue that the tendency of women to use 'powerless language' more often than men is due to the greater tendency of women to occupy relatively powerless positions in certain social contexts. Men are just as likely to use this language if they are placed in positions of disempowerment, or in situations where they lack the expertise necessary to control the interaction. In other words, social status and/or expertise in specific contexts is reflected in the discourse behaviour adopted by those doing the interacting.

But other research modifies this conclusion somewhat. In fact, in situations where women possess the *de facto* power that comes from having genuine expertise, that power is not always enough to outweigh structural and historical differences in power that are linked to sex. The literature offers many examples that underline this tendency: when female experts are in discussion with male non-experts (Smith, 1985), the expert females are perceived as less dominant and less in control even than the non-expert males. Valerie Walkerdine (1987) reports a study where two four-year-old boys refuse to assume the role of powerless objects in their teacher's discourse, and instead with her consent recast her as the powerless 'woman as sex object' of their own discourse. Elsewhere speakers of either sex are more polite with male ticket sellers than they are with female ticket sellers in a railway station (Brouwer, 1982); and in professional–client interaction in a legal-aid setting, the level of authoritarian or participatory interaction varies according to the sex of the client and the professional (Bogoch, 1994).

Others find women using more 'women's style' across a range of contexts: in laboratory conversations, in interactions with police in a police station, and in requesting information (Crosby and Nyquist, 1977). Pointedly, however, women and men in this study are both much more hesitant and indirect than are the police officials themselves in the police station setting; and in the railway station study 'all of the kinds of utterances that women are characteristically supposed to use more often than men – utterances indicating insecurity and politeness – were used more often by both women and men when speaking to the male ticket seller' (Brouwer et al., 1979: 47).

It seems that where sex differences in speech do emerge, they are strongly influenced by the particular discourse context, including the sex and perceived power of the addressee. Different inequalities that exist in power, dominance, expertise, and status intersect with gender, class and cultural differences and receive expression in different forms of discourse in different discourse settings. But it is important to stress that these coercive expressions of power are rarely overwhelming influences. Free agents will always try to find ways to counter structural forms of determination. Indeed efforts to resist dominant discourse structures are often observed; and they go on all around us.

Yet the effects of widespread and prevailing ideologies of gendered interaction, reinforced through enculturation and socialization, are so great that they are simply taken for granted for much of the time by most people. So the patterns of interaction get reproduced from generation to generation. In response to the more competitive male patterns of interaction, women as less dominant members of societies seem to collaborate in their own discursive oppression, usually accepting the hegemonic relationship in a naturalizing rather than a critical way. Instead of modifying the male discursive practices that are often unlike their own, females adopt more cooperative practices that tend to reinforce males in their belief that their own practices are acceptable and normal.

These different norms, some more competitive and some more cooperative, become ideological impositions that females accept in taken for granted ways, as do males. Parents model and pass on these discursive patterns to boys and girls in early childhood, and as I suggest below, the same patterns are already established in the discursive norms of school age children well before they enter their first school. The norms become sex-specific cultural interests that males and females feel disposed to defend, and these norms or tendencies distinguish male from female discourse practices. So from early childhood onwards, most males and females seem to manifest and develop a broadly different understanding of the form and the purpose of conversational interactions.

In short, while girls and women from some cultures tend to see conversation more as a cooperative activity, men and boys tend to see it more often as a competitive exchange. Moreover when children continually witness a model of communication in which the male competitive approach consistently prevails, then they tend to regard it as naturalistically necessary: not just as the way things are, but as the way things should be. This in turn reinforces the positions of dominance that males occupy in social systems, since their competitive norms are reinforced even by those who have neither the wish nor the disposition to adopt those norms themselves. So while research largely confirms the popular view that women and girls are good at interpersonal skills such as sympathetic listening, careful questioning, and sustaining flagging conversations (Cheshire and Jenkins, 1991), these skills may derive from imbalances of power in the social world that force women and girls to make a cooperative virtue out of an asymmetrical necessity.

Education plays a key role in all this, because of the dominant role that it has in the secondary socialization of most children. At different stages, it rewards boys and girls in subtle and also blatant ways for modelling their own gendered norms of interaction and behaviour. Also the research evidence suggests that, especially at its senior levels in English-speaking and other countries, education places an unequal value on competitive discursive practices at the expense of cooperative discursive practices and the ligatures that they build. This means that the cooperative discursive practices, into which girls rather than boys are socialized in their early lives, attract less and less value as children progress through schools.

Boys, on the other hand, grow up in schools that are still modelled on discursive practices that had their historical roots in the competitive values of dominant males more than a century ago. So almost inevitably, conventional schools give more value to the gendered discursive practices of boys, and many boys tend to get more options from their schooling as a result.

Cooperative and competitive discursive practices among children

Compared with studies of adult sex differences, studies of boys' and girls' language that are not predicated on assumed inherited differences are still few, and most of them can be summarized briefly. Firstly, those studies that examine cooperation and competition in conversations between boys and girls have found the same patterns of male dominance, even among children aged three to four years, as exist among adults (Esposito, 1979; Klann-Delius, 1987).

For example, in conversations observed between boy–girl pairs, the boys interrupt twice as often as the girls (Esposito, 1979). Yet this pattern of dominance through interruptions does not appear when boys have conversations with older people. In these settings, boys tend to give even more listener responses than girls to adult speakers (Dittmann, 1977). Again structures of dominance seem influential in this pattern: the need to recognize and conform to power relationships, based on age in this instance, seems to influence the discourse of boys who in turn reflect the pattern by reversing it in their discourse with girls. Moreover, these patterns of dominance seem to correlate with the behaviour of parents and teachers when they interact with girls and boys (Klann-

Delius, 1987). These significant adults make more listener responses and fewer interruptions when boys are talking than when girls are talking.

Significant sex differences also appear among older children in oral English examinations in England and Wales, where mixed groups of adolescent boys and girls are asked to show their proficiency in collaborative discussion (Jenkins and Cheshire, 1990; Cheshire and Jenkins, 1991). While boys and girls in these formal conversational activities offer a similar number of minimal responses to other inter-actants such as 'yeah' or 'mmm', the responses serve very different purposes for the girls than they do for the boys. For girls the responses usually signal conversational support. For boys they are used to gain a foothold in the conversation. Also in this formal oral examination setting, boys seem to make many more inappropriate remarks that close down discussions than do girls. In respect to both these findings, it is hard to escape the conclusion that it is socialization into the norms for interaction in single-sex male or female groups which influences the conversational behaviour of both boys and girls in this formal setting. Indeed there seems to be strong support for this inference in other studies looking at single-sex group interaction. So how do the sexes differ in their own single-sex interactions?

Girls and boys in Western capitalist countries do have very different modes and methods of interaction in their single-sex groups (Thorne, 1986) and these norms are often reinforced by careful segregation of the sexes in many social settings. In their recreational activities, girls tend to be less public than boys. They engage with one another in small groups or in friendship pairs, in locations where confidences can be exchanged in strict privacy. Other sign systems reinforce this tendency, especially the different messages given to children by the different forms of recreation that the sexes enjoy. For example, girls' play tends to be more cooperative than boys'. It involves collaborative rather than competitive pastimes. The turn-taking that is a feature of girls' play is also a feature of their conversations with other girls. As a result, sticking to the rules of turn-taking is treated more seriously by girls than by boys. When disagreements occur in girls' groups, speakers tend to express the disagreements indirectly by using fewer direct impera-tives and more phrases that solicit engagement and promote a sense of groupness.

So through their membership of single-sex groups, boys and girls seem to acquire different rules for creating and interpreting discourse. In summary, I think we can infer that these rules are themselves modelled on male or female adult roles. Children then proceed to reapply their single-sex group rules of discourse in mixed contexts, often doing so in dysfunctional ways, as they continue to do as adults. The cycle of communication and miscommunication continues when the rules are reproduced in mixed-sex and single-sex adult interactions, producing the gendered type of practices that I summarized in the previous section.

Research certainly suggests that these informal but influential rules do in fact carry over into adulthood and inform the kinds of communication that single-sex adult groups develop (Maltz and Borker, 1983). These differences, preserved in the discourse conventions of the two sexes, often produce that significant degree of miscommunication between women and men in general that I have already noted. Typically in their turn very young boys and girls reproduce the differences, modelling and learning the behaviour of adult males and females, who were once small boys and girls themselves. Indeed the ideologies associated with these conventional rules become habitual when adults encourage young children to be acquiescent and uncritical of the world around them. So they readily become socialized into reproducing these discursive patterns themselves.

While I should stress again that there are always obvious attempts at resistance to this kind of discursive reproduction, much of this process has an automatic character to it, since the ideologies are far from explicit and they go unrecognized at the time of their transfer. For much of the time they are transferred unconsciously in the models offered by adults who themselves take the rules for granted. So it would be wrong to say that schools are manipulating the behaviour of boys and girls, or that children are intentionally indoctrinated into acquiring male or female discourse conventions. This is not the purpose of schools. But it is often their function.

Cooperative and competitive discursive practices in schools

Much has been written arguing that schools are competitive agencies of social control. And I find it hard to mount an argument against this view. In almost everything schools do, they are comparing and sorting children, evaluating their performances against one another, or against some arbitrary norm that disadvantages some at the same time as it advantages others. And frankly there is only a modicum of fairness and social justice in the way that schools go about doing all of this (Corson, 1993; 1995a). These same institutions are also powerful agencies of social control in other respects (Corson, 1995b) because of the discursive power that they exercise and because of their place in an established hierarchy of social formations which can always be oppressive, even in the most benign of political arrangements. I want to concentrate in this section on the ways in which classroom practices, in particular, reinforce and reward the competitive discursive tendencies of children while marginalizing cooperative tendencies. Classrooms do this in ways that obviously give certain options to the many boys who have spent all their lives learning to use and practise competitive forms of interaction.

In all the countries studied in Alison Kelly's (1988) review of sex differences in teacher–pupil interaction, there are strong general indications that female and male teachers tend to pay less attention to girls than to boys at all ages, in various socio-economic and ethnic groupings, and in all subjects. This review looked at 81 quantitative studies of primary and secondary schools, across all ages, school levels, subjects, and socio-economic and ethnic groupings. Also girls receive less behavioural criticism, fewer instructional contacts, fewer high-level questions and academic criticism, and slightly less praise than boys. While girls volunteer to answer questions as often as boys, they are less likely to call answers out. This pattern continues in more recent studies. Kelly's analysis also indicated that male teachers give slightly more attention to boys than to girls. While girls volunteer to answer questions as often as boys, they are less likely to initiate contact with teachers. The boys initiate more contact with teachers in classroom talk, while girls tend to contact the teacher outside this context (see Bjerrum Nielsen and Davies, 1997).

Teachers read and respond to the behaviour of boys and girls quite differently. According to Scandinavian studies cited by Bjerrum Nielsen and Davies (1997), a typical discourse unit in a primary school class-room goes as follows:

1   The teacher asks a question.
2   A girl raises her hand and is appointed to answer.
3   The girl does so briefly and her answer is usually correct.
4   A boy interrupts with an interesting comment on the topic.
5   The teacher leaves the girl and engages in an exchange with the boy.
6   Other boys then join the discussion.
7   The girls silently wait for the next question or may use the time to whisper together.

These studies also indicate that teachers tend to respond to the form of girls' contributions, and to the content of boys' contributions. Another study reported by Bjerrum Nielsen and Davies (1997) found that level of academic achievement, which often corresponds to socio-economic and ethnic background, differentiates boys more than girls. In other words, low-achieving boys get more behavioural criticism, while the high-achieving boys 'receive the best of everything'. In the same study, low-achieving girls came out as the group in the classroom talk that gets the least teacher attention. Still other studies have found this to be the case for high-achieving girls (Kelly, 1988).

These patterns also appear in non-English-speaking contexts. In Quebec, Baudoux and Noircent (1993) look at interactional differences between francophone girls, boys, and teachers during the last year of high school. The girls seem to keep themselves back from whole-class interactions. They allot themselves a subordinate role both physically and intellectually in the classroom. At the same time, they adopt strategies to compensate for these differences in power, strategies that allow them to meet their own personal goals.

Moreover it is well attested that all these many differences in interaction occur despite teachers' assertions that they do not treat or wish to treat girls and boys differently (Sadker and Sadker, 1985) and teachers are often unaware of their differential treatment of girls and boys. For example, teachers in one United States study routinely gave boys greater opportunities to use science instruments and equipment than girls. Another American study reports cultural bias in teachers' treatment of immigrant students in science classes, with immigrant girls at the bottom in respect and treatment (Corson, 1997). So in rather straightforward ways, the ideologies that teachers embrace as their core professional practices continually reward the competitive norms of many majority culture boys.

Other research on finer aspects of teacher–pupil discourse is also appearing. This looks for example at variations in the types of questions asked by teachers, and at the allocation of turns in interaction. There are reports that teachers direct more open-ended questions at boys in the early years of schooling, and more yes/no questions at girls (Fichtelius et al., 1980). Consistent with other studies, this apparent expectation from teachers that boys 'might have more to say than girls' could in turn encourage some girls to think that they have less to say that might interest teachers. In fact the anecdotal evidence suggests exactly this.

There is evidence in Michelle Stanworth's (1983) study that male and female British pupils in late adolescence experience the classroom as a place where boys are the focus of teacher–pupil interactions, while girls are on the margins. Even teachers describe themselves as more interested in the boys, and they are seen by their pupils as more concerned with the boys. They are also more aware of the identities of boys, and they are more willing to allow the boys to upstage the girls in interaction. In the same study, many of the girls who are not admired by their female classmates manifest interactional features that are more characteristic of boys, even though these are the very features that the same girls admire the boys for possessing. In other words, in their perceptions of one another, the girls pillory the use of discourse practices that could allow them to compete with the boys, thereby to this extent collaborating in their own oppression.

It seems that by giving less prestige to girls' contributions, teachers are reinforcing the cycle of injustice that begins long before schooling in the adult-to-child socialization practices of early childhood. The distinctive linguistic capital that older girls at least bring into mixed-gender classrooms is not often recognized as relevant to those settings. At the same time, the dispositions for viewing the world that many girls acquire in their own socialization discourages them from placing an adequately high value on a use of more competitive language norms that might allow them to compete equally. How does all this impact on their behaviour and their attitudes to the real-life options extended to them in classrooms?

Bjerrum Neilsen and Davies (1997) provide a comprehensive summary of the effects of years of differential treatment on adolescent girls. Although girls are often praised in the primary school, perform better, and are more satisfied with school, their satisfaction with school (and the satisfaction of teachers with them) falls in secondary school. Apart from the serious decrease in self-esteem that girls often manifest from the onset of puberty, for them speaking up in class becomes a time of anxiety. Some girls manage to adopt the more 'masculine' approach that they see valued in school. Others respond to boys' more competitive displays by becoming silent or oppositional. Although they get better marks than boys, girls' classroom participation seems to change for the worse in adolescence. They become less compliant to the will of teachers, less self-confident, and less interested in taking part in classroom discussions.

Scandinavian studies also suggest that in adolescence, girls are neither taken seriously in regard to the male norms of school curriculum and classroom discourse, nor given possibilities to develop their personal and social orientation. In other words, girls meet the explicit demands of obedient behaviour but still lose because the more inventive and individualistic behaviour of the boys matches the implicit and real norms for success. Early in their school careers, Scandinavian girls are 'the putty of the classroom' (Bjerrum Neilsen and Davies, 1977). Their primary schools exploit the greater orientation that girls have for the interpersonal in order to make classrooms function. Later however, in adolescence, when a public space for communication has been established for academic encounters by the boys with the teacher and with each other, the girls are 'left over' as uninteresting students. And this cycle of reproductive differential treatment does its work from generation to generation of students. So what kind of practices might begin to change all this?

Towards reform in school and classroom practices

It seems that by giving less prestige to girls' contributions, teachers are reinforcing the cycle of injustice that begins long before schooling in the adult-to-child socialization practices of early childhood. The distinctive linguistic capital that older girls at least bring into mixed-gender classrooms is not often recognized as relevant to those settings. At the same time, the dispositions for viewing the world that many girls acquire in their own socialization discourages them from placing an adequately high value on the use of more competitive language norms that might allow them to compete equally. But again this communication of adult practical ideologies has an automatic character to it. Many studies do confirm that teachers are unaware of the fact that they treat boys differently from girls, and even disbelieve the evidence when confronted with it. Indeed, it is common for both male and female teachers to defend their actual practices with the sincere disclaimer that 'we treat them all the same, here' (Biggs and Edwards, 1991; Fennema and Peterson, 1985; Morse and Handley, 1985). So school-wide programmes of professional development, aimed at changing teachers' behaviours and then their attitudes, do seem to be fundamental to reform (Corson, 1997).

Oral language activities are still under-used as pedagogies in schools. There is no doubt that at all levels of schooling they are important for mastering the curriculum and for intellectual development itself. But they are also important for developing the ligatures that schools, especially senior schools in English-speaking countries, seem to be bypassing at present. They are also important for giving girls a greater measure of pedagogical equality in classrooms. Yet even here, the tendency for boys to dominate is still observed. Earlier discussion already mentions the tendency even young boys have to control mixed-sex interactions, when adults are not directly involved. This same pattern seems to translate to classroom pupil–pupil interaction.

For example, while girls act cooperatively in single-sex groups and competitively if necessary when working in mixed-sex groups, boys are competitive all the time, regardless of the context (Whyte, 1983). At the same time, girls clearly have a greater preference for approaching their classwork through peer and group activities. In a study of six senior schools in New Zealand (Burns et al., 1991), many more girls than boys in mixed-sex and mixed-ability chemistry classes want to consult other students about their work, and they try to do so when given the chance. While the girls enjoy discussing their work with friends, and go out of their way to promote discussion even outside school hours, most of the boys in the same study say that they do not and would not consult other students under any circumstances.

The sex difference in preferences about groupwork among older students is consistent with the differences in preferences and in interaction patterns that already begin to appear by seven years. But while the girls in her British study enjoy groupwork much more than the boys, Diane Reay (1991) also reports that the girls are far more likely to go along with the suggestions of others in the group. She says that this is consistent with girls giving a higher priority to achieving consensus than boys. In contrast, boys tend to work at their group tasks using hierarchies of control, direct imperatives, and direct questions that challenge each other's ideas. Reay's findings that seven-year-old girls enjoy group sessions much more than the boys seems very important. I believe that the girls' preference for groupwork here is early but consistent evidence that collaborative discursive interests and norms are more widely distributed among young girls than young boys. Indeed this conclusion is underlined by several other findings in the same study: these seven-year-old girls already report a sense of oppression in mixed-sex groups; they sense a devaluation of female experience; they are already aware of the different value systems that girls and boys have; and they believe that the boys' values are more highly regarded in the classroom.

Sex also seems to interact with the other variables of class and culture to intensify the trends in classroom interaction that I am highlighting (for the evidence to date see Corson, 1997). Grazyna Baran is an experienced secondary science teacher who talks about the many pupils in her London girls' school:

> Girls, particularly working class and immigrant girls, lack confidence in themselves and their abilities, especially in unfamiliar areas. Having spent a lot of time watching them, I have noticed that girls exert pressures on each other which reinforce this lack of confidence. There is pressure not to brag, 'show yourself up' or make a fuss; otherwise you may be labelled 'big-headed'. Discretion and modesty are valued, while outspokenness and self-assertion are suspect, if not 'punished' by the group (unless they express anti-authoritarianism).
>
> Imagine a girl attempting to formulate a question in a science lesson under such pressures. She is likely to expose her vulnerability in two ways. First, she risks the censure of the whole group. Second, she almost certainly risks being dismissed and thus unintentionally ridiculed by the teacher for failing to pose the question in a sufficiently abstract frame of reference to be recognized by that teacher. In such a context, girls may readily reject scientific knowledge wholesale as being at odds with their own experiences. (1987: 91)

The pressure of peer group values that Baran describes here is similar to the structural contradictions that minority cultural values create for some children. And their impact on interaction in the conventional classroom is similar: those affected are reluctant to play the school's game by revealing expertise, interest, or even self-doubt in their interactions with the teacher.

This compounding effect, produced when sociocultural background interacts with sex in classroom discourse, receives only incidental attention in the research to date, and mainly in studies addressing ethnic rather than sex differences in interaction. Even so, there are clear indications of sex differences in the studies. In Sarah Michaels's (1981) research, young African-American children use a 'topic-associating' style more often in 'sharing time' activities and it is usually the girls who do so. In replication studies, Michaels and Courtney Cazden (1986) confirm that the children's narratives which favour a topic-associating style are perceived more negatively and they find that African-American girls use the episodic style more often.

Other patterns suggesting that there is interactive incompatibility between teachers and minority children appear in British, American,

Canadian, and New Zealand research. For example, the kind of relationships that Afro-Caribbean children experience when interacting with their teachers in England is very similar for both boys and girls, but it is different from that experienced by majority culture children (Wright, 1987). Not only do all the minority children see themselves as being 'picked on' by teachers, but the proportion of the teachers' time that they enjoy is also very different from other student groups. Beth Goldstein (1988) also reports clear gender biases in the presentations of teachers to Hmong refugee girls in the United States. Rezai-Rashti (1994) looks at minority female students in some Canadian schools where racism and sexism are regarded as systemic. Here the relationships between the students and the school personnel are framed in what the author calls 'colonial discourse': the pressure to assimilate often leads the girls to reject their first language and culture and to replace it with the superficial trappings of a capitalist consumer culture in order to fit in with dominant Canadian norms.

Also examining classroom interaction, but in a New Zealand girls' high school, Alison Jones (1987) reports that working class girls from immigrant Pacific Island families receive only rare moments of teacher interaction, while middle class majority culture girls enjoy most of the teachers' attention. She sees at least two effects coming from this imbalance: the minority girls, as a result, do not receive equal opportunities to learn school knowledge; and the same girls learn different things about the process of learning, becoming more passive receivers of knowledge and so fitting the image that their teachers create for them.

Finally, in their study of new entrant Panjabi-speaking children in Britain, Netta Biggs and Viv Edwards (1991) report only slight differences in the patterns of interaction that culturally different girls and boys initiate with their teachers. But they also find that teachers themselves initiate significantly fewer moments of interaction with the minority girls. The researchers argue that because different amounts of time and different kinds of teacher interaction are associated with different groups of children, then it must be the teachers themselves who are reluctant to interact with the minority girls. So are schools finding ways to moderate these differences?

By varying the context of interaction, including the sociocultural background of participants, worthwhile change may come about. There are some indications, in senior classrooms for example, that changes in the topic and the nature of the class activity can produce sharp differences in pupil-initiated contacts with teachers. Studies of girls and boys in six senior schools in New Zealand, working in mixed-sex and mixed-ability chemistry laboratories, suggest that different patterns of interaction can develop with teachers in this type of setting (Burns et al., 1991; Burns and Bird, 1987). More girls seek discussion with the teacher in dealing with their learning problems, while it is mainly the boys who admit that they are afraid of revealing any incompetence by approaching teachers. Perhaps pupil laboratory sessions of this type can promote marked contrasts in interactive patterns, since the large sex differences found in more formal activities where teachers control interaction seem to disappear in less formal or practical sessions.

Broadly consistent with the above studies, there is evidence that girls in early adolescence who are engaged in craft, design and technology courses in England have more contacts with the teacher than boys, and they are also longer contacts. The girls interrupt more, and they make more unsuccessful attempts to initiate contact. In short, they are more competitive in their interaction. These practical sessions also tend to reverse the usual ratio of teacher-to-pupil contacts found in formal classes, where teachers usually control interaction (Randall, 1987). But there are other factors at work in the same school setting that help to explain these differences: the teacher, the head teacher, and the local authority were all strongly committed to providing equal opportunities for girls. As a result, projects of equal interest to the sexes were available, and there was minimal gender stereotyping in the way that lessons were handled. It seems that in this positive context of female empowerment, where teachers value the interests of girls and boys, girls receive a more just distribution of interactive opportunities and more control over the discourse. For more specific and detailed structural and pedagogical reforms, see Corson (1997), Blackmore and Kenway (1995), and Gaskell et al. (1995).

In summary, the growing number of studies to date that outline sex differences in school settings now offer more than preliminary indications of patterns of interaction that may exist more generally. When coupled with other evidence about adult discursive practices and about the norms for interaction that children in single-sex groups adopt, there are adequate grounds here to suggest two developmental trends in discourse practices as girls and boys reach towards maturity.

Firstly, in mixed-group and whole-class contexts, throughout their school careers, girls as a group continue to use the cooperative interactional patterns that they are accustomed to using in their own groups. Boys as a group tend to shed these patterns as a result of the more competitive discursive norms met and acquired in their single-sex interactions, which are ultimately modelled on adult single-sex behaviour and increasingly influenced by it as boys mature. Secondly, as a result of their own socialization within single-sex groups whose interaction is also modelled on the adult pattern, girls as a group continue to develop competence and interest in a more conversational and cooperative approach to their classwork; while boys as a group thrive more on a competitive and individualist approach to the curriculum because they are increasingly socialized in ways compatible with that approach, and also because schooling itself, at its more senior levels, still does little to reward and reinforce the use of cooperative interactional patterns that would be more consistent with girls' acquired cultural interests.

Conclusion: converting ligatures into options

My general point is that girls in the more traditional forms of schooling in English-speaking countries could be systematically excluded from genuine participation in the kinds of intellectually developing activities that are appropriate to their acquired discursive interests, because of the interactional styles and the classroom techniques that schools traditionally use and which teachers adopt, often against their will. But the observed willingness of girls to work cooperatively at senior school level in interactive activities offers an attractive opportunity for teachers. This conclusion licenses a greater use of oral language work with many girls, and probably with many boys too in the senior school. It also supports a recommendation that after consulting their preferences, girls should be allowed to approach the curriculum in this way, if their real interests are to be served.

Indeed if schools everywhere placed greater emphasis on cooperative work, especially at the senior levels, then greater prestige would attach to these ligature-building practices in societies more generally. This is because the senior levels of education remain the more prestigious levels in most people's minds, and the practices they endorse take on that prestige. In short, they become high-status sociocultural practices outside schools because of the institutional privileging that schools give them, just as the practice of giving public lectures once had great prestige, on the analogy with its now slightly diminished place in higher education.

So I am suggesting as part of this process that the many ligatures people already create with one another would become more socially valued, more in line with their real importance. Their actual status in social life would increase and they would be pursued by males and females alike as acquisitions worth having. This is not to suggest at all that they are not worth having. On the contrary, in getting access to many of the more worthwhile life chances that the world offers to people, girls and women in some cultures are already immensely advantaged by the ligatures they develop, inside and outside schools. In other words, girls tend to get more ligatures from their school experience than boys, because the cooperative discursive practices that they tend to favour bring them closer to other individuals and groups through their formal and informal interactions in and around schools. These ligatures then become options, because girls more often than boys are ready to put their interactive skills to work, developing and maintaining ligatures in all the many life and work situations where these skills are valued and necessary (Wodak, 1995; Waite, 1997).

Girls also get options from their schooling, of course, that are similar to those of boys. But in the more traditional approaches to education, they do not get as many. This is because the discursive practices that girls derive from their enculturation and socialization increasingly put them at a disadvantage in the more male competitive setting of traditional senior schools, even though traditional senior schools are not very like real-world human communities at all. But in a few places, girls now enjoy higher success rates in senior school education than boys.[3] This is happening even in those areas of the curriculum where boys have traditionally been dominant, like the sciences and mathematics. In these places, educationists have given more attention in recent years to the use of 'ligature-building' interactive pedagogies in high school education, especially groupwork and team approaches to assessment. The latter are being used more often to replace the external, solitary, and norm-referenced forms of assessment that encourage competition and individual performance, thus discouraging the very forms of cooperative learning that involve interaction with peers.

If social institutions in other places began to place a higher value on ligatures, to match the central importance that ligatures have for the human condition, girls would more readily be able to convert their richer resource of ligatures into options, and would also be able to maximize the value of the options that they do receive. This would give girls life chances that many boys and men living in Western capitalist countries are systematically denied, because of their competitive discursive socialization and because of forms of education that reinforce and reproduce those discursive practices. I believe that boys have always been the real losers, and the world loses because of it.

Notes

My thanks to Victoria DeFrancisco at the University of Iowa, and to Deborah Tannen at Georgetown University, for their helpful comments on an earlier draft of this chapter.

1. Deborah Tannen sees a close conceptual link between 'ligatures' and her own term 'connections'. There is certainly a lot of overlap. But the way that Dahrendorf uses 'ligatures' suggests a much richer connotation than just connections. People who have ligatures benefit considerably from having them, not just in the material sense. In other words their 'life chances' go up because ligatures give them more support, structure, motivation, and a sense of respect and continuity in their lives. Dahrendorf's term also covers cultural bonds of all kinds between people, not just interactive bonds.

2. Except in those circumstances where women are institutionally empowered, and where very interesting variations do occur (see Wodak, 1995; Waite, 1997).

3. Notably in England and Wales, in Australia, and in Ontario (Corson and Lemay, 1996; Corson, 1997), but apparently not in the United States (AAUW Report, 1995).

References

AAUW Report (1995) *How Schools Shortchange Girls: A Study of Major Findings on Girls and Education*. New York: Marlowe.

Baran, G. (1987) 'Teaching girls science', in M. NcNeil (ed.), *Gender and Expertise*. London: Free Association Books.

Baudoux, C. and Noircent, A. (1993) 'Rapports sociaux de sexe dans les classes du collégial québécois', *Revue canadienne de l'éducation*, 18: 150–67.

Biggs, N. and Edwards, V. (1991) '"I treat them all the same": teacher–pupil talk in multi-ethnic classrooms', *Language and Education*, 5: 161–76.

Bjerrum Nielsen, H. and Davies, B. (1997) 'The construction of gendered identity through classroom talk', in B. Davies and D. Corson (eds), *Oral Discourse and Education*. Boston: Kluwer.

Blackmore, J. and Kenway, J. (1995) 'Changing schools, teachers, and curriculum: but what about the girls?', in D. Corson (ed.), *Discourse and Power in Educational Organizations*. Cresskill, NJ: Hampton. pp. 233–56.

Bogoch, B. (1994) 'Power, distance and solidarity: models of professional–client interaction in an Israeli legal aid setting', *Discourse and Society*, 5: 65–88.

Brouwer, D. (1982) 'The influence of the addressee's sex on politeness in language use', *Linguistics*, 20: 697–711.

Brouwer, D., Gerritsen, M. and De Haan, D. (1979) 'Speech differences between women and men: on the wrong track?', *Language in Society*, 8: 33–50.

Burns, J. and Bird, L. (1987) 'Girls' cooperation and boys' isolation in achieving understanding in chemistry', in *GASAT Conference Proceedings*. Victoria University of Wellington, New Zealand.

Burns, J., Clift, C. and Duncan, J. (1991) 'Understanding of understanding: implications for learning and teaching', *British Journal of Educational Psychology*, 61: 276–89.

Cameron, Deborah (1985) *Feminism and Linguistic Theory*. London: Macmillan.

Cheshire, J. and Jenkins, N. (1991) 'Gender differences in the GCSE Oral English Examination: Part 2', *Language and Education*, 5: 19–40.

Corson, David (1993) *Language, Minority Education and Gender*. Clevedon, Avon: Multilingual Matters.

Corson, David (1995a) *Using English Words*. Boston: Kluwer.

Corson, David (ed.) (1995b) *Discourse and Power in Educational Organizations*. Cresskill, NJ: Hampton.

Corson, David (1997) 'Changing the education of girls from immigrant cultures', in D. Corson, *Changing Education for Diversity*. London: Open University Press.

Corson, David and Lemay, S. (1996) *Social Justice and Language Policy in Education*. Toronto: University of Toronto Press.

Crosby, F. and Nyqiust, L. (1977) 'The female register: an empirical study of Lakoff's hypotheses', *Language in Society*, 6: 313–22.

Dahrendorf, R. (1978) *Life Chances*. Chicago: University of Chicago Press.

DeFrancisco, Victoria (1991) 'The sounds of silence: how men silence women in marital relations', *Discourse and Society*, 2: 413–23.

Dittmann, A. (1977) 'Developmental factors in conversational behaviour', *Journal of Communication*, 22: 404–23.

Esposito, A. (1979) 'Sex differences in children's conversation', *Language and Speech*, 22: 213–20.

Fasold, Ralph (1990) *The Sociolinguistics of Language*. Oxford: Basil Blackwell.

Fennema, E. and Peterson, P. (1985) 'Autonomous learning behaviour: a possible explanation of gender-related differences in mathematics', in L. Wilkinson and C. Marrett (eds), *Gender Influences in Classroom Interaction*. Orlando, FL: Academic Press.

Fichtelius, A., Johansson, I. and Nordin, K. (1980) 'Three investigations of sex-associated speech variation in day school', *Women's Studies International Quarterly*, 3: 219–25.

Fishman, Pamela (1983) 'Interaction: the work women do', in Barrie Thorne, Cheris Kramarae and Nancy Henley (eds), *Language, Gender and Society*, Rowley, MA: Newbury House.

Foucault, Michel (1972) *The Archaeology of Knowledge*. London: Tavistock.

Foucault, Michel (1977) *Discipline and Punish: the Birth of the Prison*. New York: Pantheon.

Foucault, Michel (1980) *Power/Knowledge: Selected Interviews and Other Writings 1971–1977*. New York: Pantheon.

Foucault, Michel (1984) 'The order of discourse', in M. Shapiro (ed.), *Language and Politics*. London: Blackwell.

Freeman, R. (1997) 'Researching gender in language acquisition and use', in N. Hornberger and D. Corson (eds), *Research Methods in Language and Education*. Boston: Kluwer.

Gaskell, J., McLaren, A. and Novogrodsky, M. (1995) 'What is worth knowing? Defining the feminist curriculum', in E. Nelson and B. Robinson (eds), *Gender in the 1990s: Images, Realities, and Issues*. Toronto: Nelson. pp. 100–18.

Goldstein, B. (1988) 'In search of survival: the education and integration of Hmong refugee girls', *The Journal of Ethnic Studies*, 16: 1–27.

Jenkins, N. and Cheshire, J. (1990) 'Gender issues in the GCSE Oral English Examination: Part 1', *Language and Education*, 4: 261–92.

Jones, A. (1987) 'Which girls are "learning to lose"?', in S. Middleton (ed.), *Women and Education in Aotearoa*. Wellington: Allen & Unwin.

Kelly, A. (1988) 'Gender differences in teacher–pupil interactions: a meta-analytic review', *Research in Education*, 39: 1–23.

Klann-Delius, Gisela (1987) 'Sex and language', in Ulrich Ammon, Norbert Dittmar and Kurt Mattheier (eds), *Sociolinguistics*, Berlin: de Gruyter.

Lakoff, Robin (1975) *Language and Women's Place*. New York: Harper & Row.

Levine, R. and White, M. (1986) *Human Conditions: the Cultural Basis of Educational Development*. New York: Routledge & Kegan Paul.

Maltz, Deborah and Borker, Ruth (1983) 'A cultural approach to male–female miscommunication', in John Gumperz (ed.), *Language and Social Identity*. Cambridge: Cambridge University Press.

Michaels, S. (1981) '"Sharing time": children's narratives styles and differential access to literacy', *Language in Society*, 10: 423–42.

Michaels, S. and Cazden, C. (1986) 'Teacher/child collaboration as oral preparation for literacy', in B. Schieffelin and P. Gilmore (eds), *The Acquisition of Literacy: Ethnographic Perspectives*. Norwood, NJ: Ablex.

Morse, L. and Handley, H. (1985) 'Listening to adolescents: gender differences in science class interaction', in L. Wilkinson and C. Marrett (eds), *Gender Influences in Classroom Interaction*. Orlando, FL: Academic Press.

O'Barr, W. and Atkins, B. (1980) '"Women's language" or "powerless language?"', in S. McConnell-Ginet, R. Borker and N. Furman (eds), *Women and Language in Literature and Society*. New York: Praeger.

Philips, S., Steele, S. and Tanz, C. (eds) (1987) *Language, Gender, and Sex in Comparative Perspective*. Cambridge: Cambridge University Press.

Randall, G. (1987) 'Gender differences in pupil–teacher interaction in workshops and laboratories', in G. Weiner and M. Arnot (eds), *Gender under Scrutiny*. London: Hutchinson.

Reay, D. (1991) 'Intersections of gender, race and class in the primary school', *British Journal of Sociology of Education*, 12: 163–82.

Rezai-Rashti, G. (1994) 'The dilemma of working with minority female students in Canadian high schools', *Canadian Woman's Studies/Les cahiers de la femme*, 14(2): 76–82.

Sadker, M. and Sadker, D. (1985) 'Sexism in the schoolroom of the '80s', *Psychology Today*, March: 54–7.

Schieffelin, B. (1987) 'Do different worlds mean different words? An example from Papua New Guinea', in S. Philips, S. Steele and C. Tanz (eds), *Language Gender, and Sex in Comparative Perspective*. Cambridge: Cambridge University Press.

Shakeshaft, C. and Perry, A. (1995) 'The language of power vs the language of empowerment: gender differences in administrative communication', in D. Corson (ed.), *Discourse and Power in Educational Organizations*. Cresskill, NJ: Hampton. pp. 17–30.

Smith, P. (1985) *Languages, the Sexes and Society*. Oxford: Blackwell.

Stanworth, M. (1983) *Gender and Schooling: a Study of Sexual Divisions in the Classroom*. London: Hutchinson.

Suzuki, D. (1995) 'The hubris of global economics', *The Toronto Star*, 29 July: B8.

Tannen, Deborah (1984) *Conversational Style: Analyzing Talk among Friends*. Norwood, NJ: Ablex.

Thorne, B. (1986) 'Girls and boys together . . . but mostly apart: gender arrangements in elementary schools', in W. Hartup and Z. Rubin (eds), *Relationships and Development*. Hillsdale, NJ: Lawrence Erlbaum.

Treichler, Paula and Kramarae, Cheris (1983) 'Women's talk in the ivory tower', *Communication Quarterly*, 31: 118–32.

Troemel-Ploetz, S. (1994) '"Let me put it this way, John": conversational strategies of women in leadership positions', *Journal of Pragmatics*, 22: 199–209.

Waite, David (1997) 'Language, power and teacher–administrator discourse', in Ruth Wodak and David Corson (eds), *Language Policy and Political Issues in Education*. Boston: Kluwer.

Walkerdine, V. (1987) 'Sex, power and pedagogy', in M. Arnot and G. Weiner (eds), *Gender and the Politics of Schooling*. London: Unwin Hyman.

Whyte, J. (1983) *Beyond the Wendy House: Sex Role Stereotyping in the Primary School*. York: Longmans.

Wodak, Ruth (1995) 'Power, discourse, and styles of female leadership in school committee meetings', in David Corson (ed.), *Discourse and Power in Educational Organizations*. Cresskill, NJ: Hampton. pp. 31–54.

Wright, C. (1987) 'The relations between teachers and Afro-Caribbean pupils: observing multiracial classrooms', in G. Weiner and M. Arnot (eds), *Gender under Scrutiny*. London: Hutchinson.

7

DIFFERENCE WITHOUT DIVERSITY: SEMANTIC ORIENTATION AND IDEOLOGY IN COMPETING WOMEN'S MAGAZINES

Suzanne Eggins and Rick Iedema

Exploring the function of difference

Ever since the emergence of second wave feminism, often dated from the 1963 publication of Frieden's *The Feminine Mystique*, feminists have questioned the role of women's glossy magazines in presenting and maintaining patriarchal definitions of femininity. More than 30 years later, although the rhetoric of feminist academics has shifted from expressing 'concern' that women continue to read these magazines to one expressing 'respect' for the pleasure the magazines give (Hermes, 1995), feminist analysts of popular culture are still perplexed by two questions, summarized by Macdonald:

> Why do out-of-date myths of femininity still continue to exert a magnetic pull over us, and why is it easier to criticize those media that target us than to explain their fascination? (1995: 11)

Not only do glossy women's magazines continue to thrive in the 1990s, but in some markets (such as Australia) we have seen over recent years a proliferation of new titles, targeting women in the 25–40 age group. Proliferation suggests diversity: more choice would indicate that a greater range of different femininities are on offer. This suggests that in order to understand the continuing attraction of these magazines, we need to ask: what is the function of difference between women's magazines?

This chapter does two things. First, it reports on a commissioned research project which uses social semiotic techniques of analysis to investigate differences between two closely related Australian women's magazines, *New Woman (NW)* and *SHE*. This part establishes the nature and extent of the differences between the publications. Second, the chapter places these analytical outcomes within a broader socio-semantic framework such as proposed by Basil Bernstein (1975; 1990; 1996).

Based on our analysis of both verbal and visual patterns across all major sections of the magazines, we argue that each magazine offers readers a different but largely internally consistent ideology of femininity. We relate these differences to Bernstein's notion of coding orientation, suggesting that *New Woman* instantiates semantic orientations typical of an elaborating code while *SHE* instantiates the semantic orientation of a restricted code. We then explore the internal contradictions which typify *NW*'s editorial style, and relate these to contradictions which more generally attach to the ideologies and social relations of elaborated coding orientations. Finally, we suggest that rather than being a function of social background, difference becomes a resource used to naturalize an ideology and create consumer choice.

Background to the research

In the cut-throat world of magazine publishing, it is becoming increasingly evident that demographic studies, which constitute most if not all of the industry's significant investment in market research, are becoming unreliable as indicators of audience characteristics and preferences. Previously invaluable indicators such as income and education level are no longer able to differentiate adequately between audiences for each of the larger number of competing publications.

In an attempt to overcome the limitations of quantitative demographic research, the publishing industry is now exploring more reflexive forms of research: rather than looking at the audience, researchers now look instead at the magazines. Thus, for example, the German linguists Erbring and Shabedoth (1993) used linguistic analysis to identify editorial differences among four German women's magazines with ostensibly similar readerships. Their analysis brought out significant differences in the ways the magazines conceived and realized audience preferences and interests. Importantly, Erbring and Shabedoth's work inverts the focus of publishing research. Attention is not on interviewing buyers, mapping their buying habits against their socio-economic backgrounds, and extrapolating from the several thousand interviewees across the millions of readers nationwide. Instead, the analysis centres on the magazine as a semiotic construct and reveals the working assumptions of (predominantly women) writers and editors as crucial in the positioning of their audiences. This shift from observing the market to analysing the texts as a means of articulating a magazine's market position signals an inchoate but crucial move from the view of the media as transparent reflector of 'what goes on out there' to a recognition of the text as the semiotic product of an institution with its own priorities, interests, and assumptions, all of which come together in a product which offers particular discourse(s) on femininity.

While our research was inspired by Erbring and Shabedoth's work, our method of analysis derives from social semiotic approaches to text. Following Halliday's social semiotic theory (for example, Halliday, 1978; Halliday and Hasan, 1985; Halliday, 1994)[1] we assume that semiosis (that is, the process of meaning making) does not merely construe *representational* reality (its ideational function), but also enacts *social* relations (its interpersonal function). Since we are dealing with a semiotic system and not with a transparently representative set of meanings organized and ordered by 'other realities', semiosis also requires an enabling or *textual* function, through which ideational and interpersonal meanings are textured into coherent, cohesive, and thus 'recognizable' text. These are functions that operate always and simultaneously: they are, in fact, *metafunctions* (that is, functions that intrinsically shape the language, not functions which language users can freely turn on or off).

Moreover, Halliday (1978) posits a link between these semiotic metafunctions and the social context of discursive events: the stratum of social context *is realized by* the stratum of language.[2] This metafunction–context hookup suggests that the meanings made by the magazines are not arbitrarily, or accidentally, related to the contexts in which those magazines are produced, or to those in which they tend to be consumed. Instead, the meaning making (or discursive) practices which operate behind and those which are publicized by the magazines are redundant[3] to a greater or lesser extent with the ways in which particular audiences (would like to) position themselves. In other words, there is likely to be a 'degree of fit' between the meanings instantiated in the magazines, the habituses of their producers, and the habituses of their readerships (cf. Bourdieu and Wacquant, 1992: 129).[4] This issue will be further addressed in the discussion later in this chapter.

Methodology of textual analyses

Our research compared and contrasted editorial style in *New Woman* (*NW*) and *SHE*, two glossy monthly magazines both targeted (by two different publishers) at women in the 25–40 age group.[5] Following a pilot study of one issue of each magazine, we formulated three principles for our analysis of editorial style:

1   Analysis is quantitative. 'Editorial style' is rarely a matter of *always* using or *never* using a particular linguistic feature. It is, rather, a matter of the *more frequent* use of one pattern and the *less frequent* choice of another.
2   Analysis is cumulative. Interestingly and surprisingly, the expression of editorial style is not confined to just one part of the magazine (such as the editorial or the main feature). Rather, editorial style is realized prosodically or recurrently throughout a magazine: language and image patterns on the cover tend to be reinforced and developed

in the table of contents and through the editorial statement, and are reflected in the letters published, the kinds of features and the ways they are written and illustrated, the type of fiction published, and even the way the horoscopes are written and presented.[6]

3   Analysis deals with visual as well as verbal patterns. We are dealing with magazines as multi-modal semiotic constructs. As will be shown below, a great deal of redundancy and coherence exists between each magazine's use of images and its use of language.[7]

We surveyed six issues of each magazine, from September 1994 to February 1995. In each issue we focused on the more/less frequent linguistic and visual patterns expressed in what we considered to be the six key sections of the magazines: cover, table of contents, letters to the editor, expert/advice columns, horoscopes, and main features.[8]

In the following sections we will first touch on some of the similarities noted in the literature. Then we will detail the differences we found in each of the six main sections of the magazines. In the final section of the chapter we will amalgamate these analyses to summarize the different socio-cultural orientations of the magazines.

Similarities between the magazines

Women's magazines are generally seen as part of the network of discourses which maintain capitalist-patriarchal definitions of femininity (for example, Gilbert and Taylor, 1991; McCracken, 1993; Macdonald, 1995). Like romance fiction and soap operas, mainstream women's magazines have been critiqued for offering women very constrained sets of meanings about femininity. Although, as our later analysis will show, researchers need to carefully distinguish various magazine products, our analysis of *NW* and *SHE* produced ample evidence to support the claims that women's magazines maintain the following key elements of the code of femininity.

Orientation to appearance   Both *New Woman* and *SHE* urge women to work on their bodies and to consume beauty-enhancing goods (cosmetics, clothes etc.) to appear attractive to men. Women are portrayed predominantly in portrait shots, that is, passively displaying themselves for the onlooker rather than engaging in action of any kind. The major proportion of revenue for these magazines comes from advertising, underlining the point made by Gilbert and Taylor that 'consumption has come to be seen as a way of completing the ideal feminine identity' (1991: 12–13) and thus achieving what McCracken identifies as a major function of these magazines: 'women's magazines repeatedly succeed in linking desire to consumerism' (1993: 301).

Responsible heterosexuality   Both *NW* and *SHE* urge women to desire and pursue heterosexual relationships and to take interpersonal responsibility for the success or failure of such relationships. This is seen in the almost total absence of articles presenting successful or sanctioned non-heterosexual relations. For example, *SHE* presents deviant sexual relationships as unacceptable (*Female transvestites who drive women wild, When you find out your husband is gay, My brother is my lover, Fathers who steal their own children*). There are also frequent articles about managing relations with men (*How to talk to a naked man* (*SHE*); *The truth about Aussie blokes, Love works: essential traits of couples who thrive* (*NW*) and how to do heterosexual sex better (*Brain sex: how to use your head in bed, Love or lust: what's best in bed* (*NW*); *How to have hot sex again* (*SHE*).

In the letters and advice columns of the magazines we found evidence to support Macdonald's claim that: 'the problem pages in women's monthly magazines reinforce the mythology that relationships are women's work, and that women have to take the initiative if improvements are to be achieved. The individualistic nature of the letter and answer format prohibits any consideration of the wider implications of feminist campaigns for personal equality' (1995: 175). This links up with the third major similarity between the magazines, as follows.

Desocialization   Both *NW* and *SHE* efface all issues of difference other than that of binary sex/gender. Thus, social division separates the world into 'men' and 'women', but differences in social class, economic or educational background, and ethnicity are not explicitly mentioned. This is seen visually in that images are predominantly of individuals placed within an indeterminate or idealized social setting, rather than of groups. Images are also predominantly socially intimate (medium close-up or close-up shots), effacing broader social contexts.

Personalization   Both magazines construct a confiding personal relationship with the individual reader, encouraging her to identify with the feminine community. The magazines excel at making the reader believe she is an autonomous individual, a voluntary member of a classless community of beautiful and successful women. McCracken suggests that: 'women, at the magazines' luring, experience a sometimes real and sometimes utopian sense of community while reading these texts, confident of participating in normal, expected feminine culture' (1993: 299). This appeal also contributes to the desocialization of women, preventing the reader from becoming aware of herself as a socio-historical subject, who is being actively positioned by the texts she reads.

Multi-modal similarities   In addition to the ideational and interpersonal similarities identified so far, we also note that the magazines in question are produced and sold in similar ways. Both are colourful glossies. The two magazines look, feel, and even smell similar (when perfume samples are included). Both offer regular give-aways; both use a variety of coloured fonts on the covers, and they contain similar advertisements. The magazines are sold in the same sections of the same outlets, usually right next to each other. Both seem to offer the same promise of a light read and an enjoyable sensual experience.

These similarities are fundamental and constitutive of the genre, screaming out to the reader that both magazines are doing something similar. However, when looking at the magazines in detail we become aware of patterns of difference which perpetuate traditional views of femininity (*SHE*) and which subtly neutralize alternative (feminist) women's positionings (*NW*).

Research findings

We will now review the differences between the magazines in the six main sections studied: covers, tables of contents, letters to the editor, expert/advice columns, horoscopes, and features.

Magazine covers

The analysis presented in Table 7.1 summarizes the patterns displayed on the covers. Examples of covers from each magazine have been included in Figures 7.1 and 7.2.

Table 7.1 shows that *NW* and *SHE* differ linguistically in all three semantic functions. Ideationally, the cover patterns reveal the different semantic domains that are the main concern of the magazines. While *NW* covers a range of domains, suggesting that the new woman's life is varied and diverse, *SHE* reveals a fairly tight concentration on topics to do with sexual dilemmas.

Interpersonally, by selecting a range of different clause types, and particularly interrogatives (*Is climbing the corporate ladder killing you? You love him, but can you live with him?*), *NW* seeks to directly interact with its readers. This direct interaction is backed up by the use of the pronoun *you* to directly interrogate the reader. This contrasts with *SHE*, where most of the headlines are not clauses at all but noun phrases or nominal groups (*The 20 biggest beauty lies, Women who hunt men for marriage*). A nominal group is a static linguistic structure, which represents reality as 'things' rather than as 'doings'. A nominal group offers only limited ways to include reference to the reader (for example as the possessor *Your personal A–Z kilojoule and fat counter*).

Textually, a clear contrast appears between striving for what is new and showing the familiar. The positioning of the cover titles in *NW* indicates that 'what we're telling you is news' (see Figure 7.1). Their

Table 7.1 *Summarizing linguistic patterns of* New Woman *and* SHE *covers*

Pattern	New Woman	SHE
Ideational	− Tight semantic focus: power; beauty; sex; jobs; + Mental verbs + Material/action verbs − Locations	+ Tight semantic focus: kinship; taboos; secrets; + Being verbs + Exotic/foreign locations (Middle East, Asia)
Interpersonal	+ Range of clause types: interrogatives, declaratives, imperatives − Complex noun phrases + 'You' (reader) as subject, goal or addressee + Positive lexis (can, will, success, happiness, achieve) + Idiomatic expressions	− Range of clause types + Complex noun phrases − 'You' + Negative lexis (can't, don't forced, dead) − Idiomatic expressions
Textual	+ Writing on right-hand side ('news') + Specific reference ('you', named celebrities) as single individuals	+ Writing on left-hand side ('given', familiar) − Specific reference (women, men)

+ Text displays comparatively *frequent* use of a feature.
− Text displays comparatively *infrequent* use of a feature.
= Text displays *moderate* use of a feature.
\# Text displays *variable* use of a feature (pattern unclear).

position in *SHE* indicates a familiarity: 'what we're telling you is what you already know' (see Figure 7.2). A further important difference is in the kind of participants featured in the cover titles. In *NW*, participants are often specific individuals, a first expression of the strongly individualistic focus of the magazine. In *SHE*, participants are generic groups (*men, women*) or unnamed, non-celebrity individuals whose individual identity is not important (*A mother on death row*). This is a first sign of *SHE*'s concern to subordinate individual identity to the primacy of readers' location within traditional sexual/social groupings, that is its concern to maintain boundaries between categories of people (cf. Sacks, 1972).

Interestingly, these verbal patterns are supported by, or enact, the magazines' titles: *NW* connotes, along with 'newness', active participation in rebirth, dynamic change, openness, and liberation, while *SHE* connotes a static, distant, observation of women's estate, without any hint of challenge or change. Further evidence of these contrasts is found in the visual analysis of the magazine covers, summarized in Table 7.2.

The models on the covers of *NW* often appear at an angle, thereby creating the impression of movement and action (Arnheim, 1982). *SHE*

New Woman

JAN 1995

MIDLIFE OASIS
The older you are,
the better life gets

New Zip-out Guide
Our pick of the
very best beauty
products around

**IS IT SAFE
TO FLIRT
AT WORK?**

Bumper Horoscope Special

The 'no kids' option:
What you must know

$4.20
INZ $5.95 (INCL GST)

NEW YEAR, NEW MEN
Who's hot (and who's not) in '95

12 pages of no-fail energy boosters for body and soul

Never Feel Tired Again!

Figure 7.1   *Cover from* New Woman *magazine, January 1995* (© New Woman (Australia) Magazine – January 1995)

Figure 7.2   *Cover from* SHE *magazine, February 1995* (© SHE Magazine (Australia) – February 1995)

Table 7.2 *Visual patterns in magazine covers*

Pattern	*New Woman*	*SHE*
Ideational	Faces at angles creating vectors, hair in disarray, faces off-centre (either left or right of centre); photos often 100% detailed Casual clothing styles	Conceptual images, flat insubstantial backgrounds, linguistic elements inside picture space, degrees of abstraction (shoulders blurry; only face in focus) Traditional clothing styles
Interpersonal	Medium close-ups or close-ups; all smiles; high modality (strong colours, contrasts, many primary colours)	Medium close-ups of models; no smiles; frontal gaze (inclusions; 'demands'), level with viewer; high modality (strong colours, contrasts, although many pastels and secondary colours)
Textual	Model's face either theme or new with sell-lines in opposite position; colours more contrastive; font size 80+	Sell-lines colour-rhyme with *SHE*, but strength of colours never consolidated through colour contrast; models centred with text wrapped around, new/ideal emptyish, new/real filled with sell-lines and shoulder; model as centre of triptych mediating theme sell-lines and empty space, new sell-lines; eyes consistently just above centre

models, by contrast, often appear static and centred, or otherwise distant (long shot) and side-on. Whereas *NW* models will have 'young' clothes and hairstyles (that is, they are seemingly less rigidly and stylishly groomed), *SHE* models will have a more 'classical' appearance. Thus, if *NW* attempts to emulate a kind of 'down-to-earth' youthful casualness, *SHE* aims for stylish finesse.

Interpersonally, the *SHE* model maintains a rigid social distance, while the *NW* model generates the impression of possible contact. For example, the model on the front of the January 1995 issue of *NW* is at an angle to the camera (see Figure 7.1). Her body leans marginally towards us. Her hair is wind-swept. She smiles. This is quite unlike the serious, constrained posture of the *SHE* cover model on its February 1995 issue (see Figure 7.2) – a cover which is quite typical of that magazine's covers in general. *NW* adopts a more playful approach – of photographer to model, of designer to audience, and of model to viewer. In short, *NW* covers are less ordered, less predictable than *SHE* covers. The definite, rigid boundaries that are apparent in *SHE* (reflecting negatively on social contact) are weakened in *NW* (allowing engagement).[9]

Textually, the page and image layout of the *SHE* cover tends to centre the face of the model, and more specifically, centre the (almost smiling) mouth. The image is spherical (wholistic) rather than geometric (perspectival), to use Arnheim's (1982: 73) terms. The model figures not in a logical, rational world, but in a centred, spiritual world.[10] Further, she appears to us peering through a window whose frame is constituted of variously coloured lines of text. She is thus positioned as being 'on the other side of (or beyond) the magazine's content', in a world of her own.

The models on *NW* covers take up a more interactive and playful role; they tend to be positioned as if on their way 'through' the window frame of the magazine (the diagonal vectors suggesting movement: Arnheim, 1982: 107). Either the cover titles are positioned as given (on the left) and the model as new (on the right), or the other way around. Since *NW* thereby positions its cover models as being 'at the same level of (visual) reality' as the other elements which appear on the cover, *NW* appears to construe a more practical and engaged attitude, less distant than *SHE*.

Tables of contents

The patterns revealed in the cover pages are largely reinforced by those in the tables of contents pages. Figures 7.3 and 7.4 are examples. Table 7.3 summarizes their verbal patterns in *NW* and *SHE*.

There is an initial contrast in simply the types of columns which constitute each magazine. While *NW* has fewer features, it lists a large number of regular columns. In *SHE* we find more features, and fewer regular columns. This is an initial indication of the higher 'newsiness' of *SHE*, that is, its concern to report on (and judge) events in a 'factual' there-and-then world rather than deal with the 'interpersonal' here-and-now world of readers.

Ideationally, we see that *NW*'s contents typically span diverse lexical domains, including fashion, beauty, health, the workplace, relationships, and contemporary issues. However, these different domains are permeated by themes focusing on change and development, with a recurrent reference to positive moral virtues. *SHE*, on the other hand, covers a more restricted range of fields, all tightly related to sexual taboos. A further difference discernible from the contents page is that *NW* contains texts more oriented to offering instructions: texts in the 'how-to', or instructional, genre. While *SHE* has some of these, it favours texts which explain rather than instruct. There is a significant difference also in tense, with *NW* contents being predominantly present tense, but with *SHE*'s contents written in the past tense: this of course correlates with the forward/dynamic/subjective (*NW*) versus traditional/static/objective (*SHE*) distinction already seen as obtaining between the two magazines.

The contents pages also make evident a key interpersonal opposition which obtains throughout the magazines: that which contrasts the

New Woman

CONTENTS

JANUARY 1995

fresh faces... our hottest list ever

28

On the Cover

Other Features

56

midlife oasis

82 free your mind

66

heavenly bodies:
star guide for '95

Figure 7.3   *Table of contents from* New Woman, *January 1995* (© New Woman (Australia) Magazine – January 1995)

SHE

Top: feast on the many exotic flavours from Asia, page 150.
Above: Australians are getting fatter, but all is not lost. Turn to page 98 for everything you need to know to win the diet war.

Above: treat yourself to a life of luxury in the most beautiful lingerie, page 24.
Bottom: sample the wonderful lifestyle in the Mediterranean – its culture, food and decor, page 134.

Photograph of Mandy Cameron by James Calderaro. Hair and make-up by Robert Snow for Republic Workshop. Recreate Mandy's look using make-up from Yardley. Complete Performance Oil-free Make-up in Milkwood SPF12 foundation; Point to Point Eyeshadow Trio; Blackbird Waterproof Mascara; Hazelnut Kohl Definer Pencil; Hazelnut Brow Definer Pencil; Butterscotch Blusher; Hot Chocolate Moisturising Lipstick. Gingernut Lip Definer Pencil. Howard Showers single-breasted jacket. O'Connor cotton shirt. Baubridge and Kay Jacquard tie. Diamond earrings from Michal Design Jewellers.

FEBRUARY 1995

Figure 7.4   *Table of contents from* SHE, *February 1995* (© SHE Magazine (Australia) – February 1995)

Table 7.3 *Verbal patterns in tables of contents*

Pattern	New Woman	SHE
Genres	− Features (average 11)	+ Features (average 16)
		= Fashion, beauty, health
	+ Regulars (average 15)	− Regulars (average 10)
Ideational	+ Diverse lexical domains	− Diverse domains
	= Fashion, beauty, health Change; risk taking; newness, improvement; excitement; virtues	+ Food and home; sexual behaviour; secrets Unusual, perverted; vices, crimes
	+ Circumstances of manner (how to do things)	+ Circumstances of cause (why things happened)
	+ Present tense	+ Past tense
Interpersonal	+ Positives: purr lexis; assertive clauses	+ Negatives; snarl lexis; negated clauses
	+ Declaratives	+ Non-finite clauses
	+ Interrogatives	
	− Possibility (and certainty)	+ Possibility
	+ Idioms/colloquialisms	− Idioms
	+ Prestige lexis	− Prestige lexis
	+ Intensification	
Textual	− Matchability between cover and table of contents	+ Matchability (lots of verbal links between cover and table of contents)
	+ Additional text	− Additional text
	+ Lengthy (2 pp.)	+ Brief (1 p.)

Note For key see Table 7.1.

essentially positive outlook of *NW* with the essentially negative one of *SHE*. This is seen through types of purr lexis (*NW: love, long-lasting, improvement, ideal*) versus snarl lexis (*SHE: cult, battle, goodbye, scandalous, betrayal*). This difference is also evident in clauses, between affirmations (*NW: Help is at hand*) and negations (*SHE: Don't take the pain laying down*). The frequent use of both interrogatives and declaratives in *NW* construes interaction with the reader, whereas the use of various forms of dependent clauses (*Why your partner shouldn't be your best friend*) in *SHE* avoids such engagement.

These are continuations of patterns set up on the cover. *SHE*'s contents reveal possibility and doubt; yet the magazine sticks with neutral, not formal, language. *NW*, on the other hand, is assertive and certain in its contents, further contributing to its positive outlook. *NW* is also more idiomatic, frequently drawing on colloquialisms and intensifications to create an air of casual conversation. In an apparently peculiar mix of levels, however, *NW* also contains items of a prestigious lexis (*podiums, biogenetic boundaries*), which appear to signal an assumed educational level in readers (see discussion later). So if *SHE* combines distance,

Table 7.4   *Visual patterns in tables of contents*

Pattern	New Woman	SHE
Ideational	Mix of portraits and action shots	Top left (ideal, new) typically a woman (long shot) creating vectors, then (middle) a home/food/furniture shot, then (bottom; often) more women in action shots
Interpersonal	High modality (colours in photos)	High modality (colours in photos)
Textual	Unpredictable layout: contents generally listed on the left (thematic), but right (new) varied in terms of page numbering, font size (mid-group/clause changes), photo topic/type, colour; two pages (left and following right); photos of varying sizes arranged in zig-zag from top right to bottom right	Predictable layout: at left, cover repeat (100% detail) and listing of contributors to photo; at centre, rigid contents presentation; at right, photographic 'orientation'; contents positioned as 'mediator' between cover (promise) and contents (fulfilled); strong boundaries (separate categories; discrete ordered photos); and (right) page

neutrality, negativity, and probability, *NW* combines closeness, relaxedness, positivity, and certainty.

Textually, it is difficult to match the entries in the table of contents in *NW* with the items mentioned on the cover: the cover descriptions are often transformed, not only making it necessary for readers to search through the contents (and perhaps the magazine) to find the articles of interest, but also reinforcing an impression of flexibility and casualness. In *SHE* the degree of matchability is very high, with the contents page reproducing virtually verbatim the titles from the cover. *NW* adds to the relaxed confusion by providing quite lengthy glosses to its contents headings, while *SHE* provides very little text additional to the cover titles. This may also explain why *NW*'s contents page runs to two pages, while that of *SHE* is only one page. Table 7.4 shows the visual patterns in the *NW* and *SHE* tables of contents.

The table highlights the following patterns. Ideationally, *NW*'s table of contents tends to mix portraits and action shots (frequently men though, not women). *SHE*'s table of contents features mainly portraits, alternated with shots of the home, furniture, or food. *SHE*'s preference for portraits again underlines its concern with stasis.

Both magazines use strong colours, thereby construing their 'closeness to (interpersonal, *NW*; social, *SHE*) reality' (see Kress and van Leeuwen, 1990: 51, on 'colour modality'). Textually speaking, *NW*'s tables of contents have relatively unpredictable layouts. Sometimes page numbers are blown up, different colours are used, and often text blends/overlaps with images which point towards (that is, contain vectors pointing towards) the relevant article. *SHE*'s contents is very ordered, very straight (see Figure 7.4). There are strong boundaries between topics, and between text and images. This strong sense of separation parallels, as a principle, the lack of social engagement suggested by the magazine's front cover and its stasis. Thus, where *NW* again construes its layout *as if* breaking through rigid conventions and boundaries, *SHE* construes it in terms of conformity, distance, and immobility.

We judged that, following the table of contents, the next (in sequence) most important section of the magazines was the editorial. This, after all, is explicitly signed by the editor and could therefore be considered a major indicator of editorial style. Only *NW* in fact has an editorial, so no comparison is possible. The absence of an editorial in *SHE* is itself suggestive of a lesser concern to establish contact and solidarity with readers.

Letters to the editor

We move on now to consider the letters to the editor sections of the magazines. The letters to the editor section is an important site for the expression of stylistic differences as (even if we accept that the letters are written by readers and not composed by editorial staff) the process of selection of letters for publication offers the editorial team a clear opportunity to reflect back to readers their image of the desired/ assumed reader and their attitude towards readers, and to indicate which concerns are relevant to the magazine. Table 7.5 summarizes the main differences.

The table shows the following patterns. There are differences in the preferred or most frequently published genres of the letters in each magazine. In *NW*, the preferred genre is that of the exposition: a structured argument, working through the stages of stating a thesis (*Women don't want bad guys*), offering evidence in support of the thesis (*most women want healthy and harmonious relationships and you can't achieve that with a nasty man*), usually followed by a dismissal of counter-evidence (*not all men are bastards*), and ending with a summary and reiteration of the thesis (*These are the men with whom you should be angry*). The expository genre is the genre of literate, often tertiary educated writers: it draws on a range of sophisticated linguistic resources (conjunction, lexical abstraction, textual staging: Martin, 1985). The types of expositions found in *NW* are generally hortatory expositions; that is, they do not merely present evidence to support a point, but call upon us to act or react in some way in regard to the thesis (*Don't blame feminists for causing a rift between men and women*).

In *SHE*, on the other hand, the preferred genre is that of the exemplum (Plum, 1988; Martin, 1992), the text type which uses an event to exemplify a moral truism. Letters are mostly in the vein of

Table 7.5 *Summary of linguistic patterns in letters to the editor*

Pattern	New Woman	SHE
Genre	+ Exposition: mostly hortatory, some analytical	+ Exemplum, mostly of readers' own life experiences
Ideational	+ Issues, abstracts (nominalizations) Type of articles published: relationships; women's issues + Mental/intellectual focus (what readers thought/feel)	+ Particulars of readers' negative experiences: trauma, taboos etc.
Interpersonal	+ Critical + Positive exhortations (let's get out there and do something) + Objective, generalized response ('we') + Requests for readers to change + Occasional editorial response	+ Congratulatory + Negative attitudes (my life is an example of why this must not happen) + Subjective, personal response ('I') + Requests re editorial content − Editorial response
Textual	+ Reactive to magazine's editorial policy + Letters foregrounded + Letter of the month + Prestige language (carefully composed)	+ Reactive to points in prior articles + Letters foregrounded + Letter of the month − Prestige language (idiomatic, ambiguous)

Note For key see Table 7.1.

agreeing with articles published, and of offering an incident from the letter writer's own life to justify the point (*I shed long-repressed tears after reading 'My father's revenge' . . . From the time I was three, my mother subjected me to the same type of psychological repression*). The exemplum is not an argument, but a recount which is given moral significance. It is relatively static (not demanding any response from the reader), and is confirming ('these are our values') rather than challenging ('this is what they/you should do'). We can see how the genre choices here are reinforcing patterns already suggested in earlier sections of the magazines: *NW* challenges and renews: *SHE* reaffirms and immobilizes.

One interesting textual difference here is that whereas *NW* letters are often written in response to editorial decisions (*the hypocrisy of NW's publishing articles on East Timor while presenting fashion shots filmed in Indonesia*), in *SHE* letters are often responses to particular points in specific articles (*As a former anorexic, I was disappointed by* [what Fay Weldon had to say]). The *NW* pattern seems to indicate the orientation towards abstraction, as writers comment on the policy implications behind an article, whereas *SHE* writers focus on particular details within articles. This follows in part from the genre preferences in each

Table 7.6 *Summary of patterns in expert columns*

Pattern	New Woman	SHE
Genre	Very limited explicit advice columns + Agony aunt (psychologist) + 'Hip solutions to social dilemmas' (early issues)	Almost no explicit advice columns − Agony aunt + Limited (average 2)expert columns as 'problem and solution'
Ideational	Personal failings: shyness, feeling trapped, inability to express self	Your child Relationships: you and other
Interpersonal	Female experts Positive: achievement, overcoming	Male experts Negative: avoidance
Textual	Specific advice	Generic advice

Note For key see Table 7.1.

magazine, and is also related to the prestige/formal/written language preferred by *NW* letter writers compared with the more vernacular/ informal/spoken language of *SHE* letter writers.

Interestingly, both magazines give salience to their letter columns, publishing them early in the magazines, giving plenty of space, and awarding a prize to the letter of the month. Although this apparently indicates a similar desire to establish an interactive relationship with the readers, the points made above indicate that substantial differences are identifiable within the content of the letter columns. There are no significant visual differences between the presentations of letters to the editor in *SHE* and *NW*, however.

Expert columns

The main differences between the *NW* and *SHE* expert and agony columns across the six issues are summarized in Table 7.6.

Consistent with its empowered and solidary tenor, *NW* contains very few explicit expert advice columns. There is an agony aunt (a clinical psychologist, 'Amanda'), who responds in the traditional way to readers' letters. For a while there was also a second expert column, 'Hip solutions to social dilemmas'. This was written in letter form: a reader's letter constituted the problem, and the expert's letter offered a solution, working through the stages of redefining the problem and suggesting a course of action. Thus, while expert advice is limited, it is given in interreactive, dialogic genres.

In *SHE* we find similarly restricted expert advice columns. Interestingly, there is no agony aunt, but there are generally two expert columns dealing with 'Your child' and 'Relationships'. These are monologic rather than in reaction to letters. The absence of an agony aunt column (which cannot be achieved except through the interactive letter genre) and the presence of these two monologic expert genres reinforces *SHE*'s concern with both authoritative knowledge and lack of direct engagement with readers, seen also in other aspects of the magazine.

Ideationally, *NW*'s agony aunt deals with the types of problems likely to impede the ambitious working woman: shyness, the inability to express oneself, and feelings of being trapped. These are problems experienced by the individual alone. In *SHE*, the ideational domains covered by experts have to do with readers in their relationships with key kinship members: children or lovers/spouses. This woman-as-individual versus woman-as-role opposition is now a recognizable theme differentiating the two magazines.

Interestingly, the magazines construe the interpersonal relationship of authority as follows: experts in *NW* are female, while those in *SHE* are male. This again suggests a more pro-women stance of *NW*, and a more traditional-patriarchal position of *SHE*. The positive/negative contrast reappears here: solutions to *NW* problems are positive, with over-coming and achievement emphasized; in *SHE*, the advice tends to be how to avoid negative situations from occurring. Another now familiar textual opposition arises here as well: the advice offered in *NW* is specific, in response to particular individual problems; in *SHE* the advice is generic and generalized, being offered to all members of a particular kinship group and assumed relevant to all.

Horoscopes

Horoscopes are useful texts for stylistic analysis, as not only do both magazines contain them, but they encode in a very distilled form the resident astrologer's judgement of readers' interests and needs, and thus positioning. Table 7.7 summarizes the oppositions.

NW's horoscopes put emphasis on readers' attributes and qualities: who you are, in terms of what qualities you possess. Naturally, these attributes are extremely flattering ones: readers invariably are intel-ligent and have good taste. Their fears are also profiled, as is their financial situation and the kinds of pleasures they enjoy. The readers are further constructed as intelligent and sensitive through the use of mental process verbs of cognition (thinking) and affection (liking).

In *SHE*, on the other hand, the horoscope focuses on activities rather than attributes: on what readers will be doing, generally centring around having encounters with men. Where attributes are mentioned, these are attributes not of the reader herself, but of elements of her world (*A man who is resourceful, good looking or born around November, a charming man, your apologetic actions*).

NW continues its more highbrow orientation by using nominalizations to talk about generalities rather than specificities. In contrast, *SHE* keeps to unnominalized language, focusing on particular events and

Table 7.7 *Summary of linguistic features of horoscopes*

Pattern	New Woman	SHE
Ideational	What you have/are: i.e. your qualities, intelligence, taste; your fears; finance; pleasure; your mental activity	What you will be doing: dating, meeting What things happening to you are like: helpful, good looking, straightforward attributes of your world
	Packed pre-things + Nominalizations − Non-contingent predictions Very limited astrological technicality (explained)	Packed post-things − Nominalizations + Contingent predictions: if single . . . then . . . No astrological technicality
Interpersonal	'You' alone + Certainty + Positives/flattery (win, fascinating, intelligence) Female astrologer: doesn't refer to self	'You' in relation to a man + Possibility + Negatives (avoid, startle, reconciliation) Female astrologer: doesn't refer to self
Textual	+ End of magazine + Lengthy (2 pp. and extra-long New Year section) + Featured month on left-hand page	+ Beginning of magazine + Brief (left-hand page only) + Featured month at bottom of left-hand page

Note For key see Table 7.1.

actions. Interestingly, the predictions in *SHE* are heavily contingent on readers' situating themselves within traditional social groupings: for example, *if single* then one lot of predictions apply, whereas *if married*, others operate (see our comments on membership categories above). As we would expect from earlier patterns, *NW* does not make predictions dependent on social groupings.

Interpersonally, *NW* discusses the reader separately from other people, reinforcing the individualistic orientation of the magazine. In *SHE*, the 'you' of the horoscopes is frequently talked about in relation to a man. Whereas *NW*'s predictions are assertive and certain, *SHE*'s predictions are tempered by expressions of possibility. The positives of the *NW* horoscope echo the positives of the previous sections, while the negatives and maybes in *SHE*'s horoscopes have similar reverberations with the rest of its content.

These linguistic patterns are further complemented by the visual patterns. *NW*'s horoscopes are rather more artful that *SHE*'s: a whole page is spent on the star sign of the month, with an apparently symbolically meaningful photo or image accompanying the predictions. This 'arty' page leaves a lot of white space, again suggesting openness, possibility, absence of constraints. *SHE*'s horoscopes are far more packed in; there is no open space. Predicting the future does not allow too much openness, too much space, or too many possibilities.

NW's horoscopes cover two pages: the future is important, although the section appears late in the magazine. *SHE*'s horoscopes are generally only one (left) page, and therefore less important, yet they come early on in the magazine. While *NW*'s horoscopes are positioned as what the reader will take away from the magazine (that is its 'news'; suggesting the 'closeness' between magazine and readers and reinforcing its immediacy and relevance), *SHE*'s early horoscopes are its 'given', they set the tone for what is to come within the scope of the magazine. The ordered, constrained nature of *SHE*'s horoscopes, with the future as 'given', and the more 'creative' nature of *NW*'s horoscopes, construing the future as 'news', both parallel the respective patterns so far discussed.

Features

We have left discussion of features until this point as they are the most varied and most complex component of the magazines. However, despite apparently wide variation in topics, authors and approaches, we have found that the visual and verbal choices in features continue to reinforce the same stylistic patterns identified in the shorter and more constrained sections of the magazines, as discussed above. In this section we will summarize major patterns in features, and then discuss how several specific feature articles illustrate these patterns. Table 7.8 summarizes the main oppositions.

Bearing in mind that we are generalizing across a wide range of different articles, the table suggests the following patterns. *NW* includes frequent first-person features by well-known writers or celebrities. These fictionalized pieces tend to be either embroidered recounts (for example, of single fathers coping with children) or personal assessments of particular issues. Third-person features (such as by staff journalists) are usually 'macro-genres': this means that the feature article is in fact a combination (either embedding or chaining) of different genres (Martin, 1994). Usually the main article is a descriptive report (giving information about something), but there are often boxed-off sections of procedures (how to deal with something raised in the report), and sometimes exemplums (short profiles of people who have experienced the issue). There is a general drift towards procedural-oriented texts, that is the giving of advice, in 'how-to' structures such as 'problem and solution'.

In contrast, in *SHE* most of the features are third-person articles, usually interviews or descriptive reports. They are usually single genres, with a preference for the rather static descriptive report (this is how things are). The contrast between action through procedural features (*NW*) and immobility through report features (*SHE*) re-

Table 7.8 *Summary of linguistic features of feature articles*

Pattern	New Woman	SHE
Genre	+ Personal assessment/report: many first-person features by well-known writers or celebrities, e.g. Kathy Lette + Macro-genres + Advice genres: procedures	+ Descriptive reports: third-person articles, interviews or descriptive accounts + Single genres
Ideational: overall message	Positive/successful transgressive gender-role behaviours (e.g. sensitive single fathers, empowered prostitutes; what women can learn from wearing a penis)	Negative/unsuccessful transgressive sex-role behaviours (e.g. disillusioned male sex slave; female transvestites; women alcoholics; wife shopping)
preferred topics of reports	Instructions on how to enter a man's world (how to flirt at work, how to surf) Rewards/benefits of behaving 'unnaturally' Male/female emotions; self-development; workplace behaviour	Interviews with women as innocent victims (women dying of AIDS, or forced to have abortions) Penalties/costs of behaving 'unnaturally' Sex gone wrong
Preferred locations	Everyday; familiar; urban Australia	Exotic, unfamiliar (Asia, Middle East, Hollywood) or seedy urban areas (King's Cross, Sydney)
Celebrity interviews	Individual up-coming thirtyish film stars Celebrity interviews support positive-transgressive focus	Only groups of celebrities, written about not interviewed Reports support negative transgressive focus (stars whose lives have gone wrong)
Interpersonal	+ 'I': told from an 'insider's' perspective + Positive orientation: you can do it! + Purr lexis: rewards	+ 'They': from an outsider's perspective + Negative orientation: why you can't do it; + Snarl lexis: punishments
Textual	− Focal feature − Specific participants/ individuals + Short features + Carefully constructed pieces	+ Two focal pieces: report and the big issue + Generic participants/ individuals + Long features − Carefully constructed pieces

Note For key see Table 7.1.

emerges. There is also a marked difference in the overall ideational messages being expressed. In *NW*, the overall message of the features seems to be that *gender*-transgressive behaviour (for example, women becoming more assertive/masculine, men becoming more sensitive/feminine) is rewarded. The procedural genres reinforce this message by providing instructions on how to get into a man's world. In *SHE*, on the other hand, the message is that *sexually* transgressive behaviours (such as having sex with tabooed kin or against standard morality) will have negative outcomes. This message is reinforced by the interview and report texts, which focus on women as largely innocent victims of transgressive behaviours.

At a more specific level, the preferred topics of the features differ significantly. As noted earlier, there tends to be quite a range of domains covered in *NW*. While concentrating on male/female similarities and differences, the magazine often addresses these themes through features dealing with workplace issues and socio-political issues (*Flirting at work: risky business*). In *SHE*, the unavoidable theme is 'sex gone wrong', occasionally relieved by a feature about cultures or societies gone wrong. Preferred locations differ markedly: most *NW* features deal with everyday, familiar, urban Australian environments, whereas *SHE* prefers features set in exotic and unfamiliar places (the Middle East is a favourite choice). If familiar environments are chosen, they are usually seedy and rundown (such as Sydney's King's Cross area).

Visual analysis shows that the images accompanying *SHE* features tend to be either photos of women on their own, or ones which emphasize the difference or incompatibility between female and male roles, desires, and concerns. A feature of a woman who became a prostitute shows only her (or, more probably, a model's) legs on a bed; a feature on *Prisoners of love* shows two women visually framed ('imprisoned') by the wealth given to them by their Arab boyfriends. A feature on alcoholic women shows a model (presumably) on her own at a café table with an empty glass in front of her. A feature on power couples, *When sparks fly*, shows photos of famous couples, but the accompanying captions spell out why the couples broke up. So, generally, *SHE* does not favour representing successful relationships.

The visuals accompanying *NW* features, on the other hand, suggest relative success: a woman making herself up at work and a man comes walking in (*Chemistry between colleagues can be one of the most erotic things going*). *NW* may also present the negative side of relationships, such as a woman behind bars (*My life in a harem*) or women on the phone (*Friends and breakups*). Generally, however, the negativity is dynamic, not static: the woman behind bars is looking out; the women on the phone are in some form of contact, they are talking. The visuals always offer some form of 'way out (to another or others)'. Where the visuals accompanying features in *SHE* tend to present a static, resigned and negative view on social relations, their *NW* counterparts are frequently positive, sometimes negative, but generally dynamic in their presentation.

Discussion: the significance of difference

Our analysis has suggested that despite the magazines' similarities, they display clearly differentiable and coherent editorial styles. In this section we explore the significance of these styles, drawing on the socio-semantic theory of Basil Bernstein.

Editorial style and socio-semantic coding orientation

In mapping out the different styles, we were struck by the parallels with Bernstein's (1971; 1975; 1990) socio-semantic coding orientations, the restricted and the elaborated.

It is the strength and types of boundaries enacted in the socio-semiotic environment ('boundarization') that provides the basis of Bernstein's code theory. Bernstein (1971; 1994a) argues that different coding orientations predispose users to classify and frame experience differently. Essentially, the concept of code refers to the degree of socio-semiotic *possibility* available to a speaker.

Elaborated code both enables and allows verbal elaboration of ideational and interpersonal relations and encourages a focus on ideational and personal difference, and permits a degree of social reflexivity:

> Where codes are elaborated the socialised has more access to the grounds of his [sic] own socialisation and so can enter into a reflexive relationship to the social order he [sic] has taken over. (1971, cited in 1994a: 175)

In contrast, restricted code involves the relative absence of such a verbal negotiation of ideational-personal relations, and foregrounds non-negotiated (and non-negotiable) social positions, or 'status arrangements' (1990: 96ff).

Critics of Bernstein's work have generally interpreted his theory as operating with a deficit model (for example, Rosen, 1972; Labov, 1972; Wardhaugh, 1986; Edwards, 1987; Huspek, 1994; 1995). Bernstein has repeatedly pointed out, however, that his code theory does not make any psycho-cognitive claims. On the contrary, its claims are purely socio-semiotic:[11] the kinds of meanings people make and the way they make them tend to be conditioned by their social background (Bernstein, 1971; 1975; 1990; 1994a; 1994b; 1996; also Hudson, 1980; Hasan, 1989; 1992; Halliday, 1995).

It is Bernstein's attention to differences in degrees of boundarization which provides the point of contact with the study presented here. It seemed to us that the clusters of meanings made in the magazines indicate that while *NW* is a text which presumes access to or identification with elaborated code, *SHE* relies on restricted code. A striking dimension of this is that the negativity and firm boundaries in *SHE* seem to be related to what Bernstein (1990: 96) called a 'positional' orientation or a relatively non-negotiable social positioning, while *NW*'s positive, optimistic and more transgressive outlook parallels what Bernstein labelled the 'personal' orientation, that is a positioning that allows for a broader set of social relation types.

The different coding orientations displayed by the magazines instantiate not merely different interests, but divergent views of acceptable and accepted female behaviour and notions of femininity. *SHE* presents a static world in which women as a generic class are warned of the negative consequences of stepping outside feminine sex roles. Its voyeuristic preoccupation with the negative consequences of transgression defines all that which deviates from the norm as other, and thus as 'newsworthy'. Its concern with topics like *Female transvestites who drive women wild, My brother is my lover,* and *Fathers who steal their own children* is fuelled not by a desire to understand or identify with the subjects involved, however (all stories are in 'distant' third person), but by a macabre fascination with that which is or should be 'not-us' (compare the eighteenth and nineteenth century 'crime pamphlets' which were 'both a frank commercial speculation and a form of social control': Chibnall, 1980: 185).

NW, on the other hand, presents a more complex case. While this magazine would seem to embrace feminist calls for women's empowerment through individual change, it nevertheless subtly neutralizes the possibility of real emancipation.

First, *NW*'s 'dynamism' identified above is always framed within the same expensive multi-modal technology which defines most women's magazines: a glossy and visually enhanced presentation containing perhaps three or four feature articles, each one or two pages long, with the rest made up of fashion photos of posing women, ads for status sensitive health care products and other consumer items emphasizing wealth. Like its competitors, it suggests an absence of care, critical focus and political engagement. Thus, the action or dynamism which *NW* encourages is premised on both social indifference and egocentric preoccupation.

Second, brief comparison of *NW* with pre-1960 magazine examples suggests that the influence of feminism is confined to two main areas:

1 The recognition that women (must) work for money outside the home. However, the workplace is turned into another domain for patriarchal femininity to flourish, for example one article about setting up your business office dealt mainly with what kind of desk to choose, deciding on the colour of furnishings; articles about being a successful businesswoman focus on the choice of clothes and

hairstyle, and features on workplace issues sexualize work relations (*How to flirt at work*).

2   The representation of women who are more sexually assertive than was possible in pre-second-wave times. However, sexually assertive women are women who can get and satisfy a man more actively without challenging his position or the dominance of heterosexual monogamy (*How to sustain the passion, How to flirt at work*).

Even articles which appear to represent women behaving non-traditionally (such as refusing to have sex or children) continue to mark that behaviour as marginal (*Learn to say NO (and feel great about it*) or *The 'no kids' option: what you must know*). This pattern of the appropriation or 'recuperation' of feminist ideas is noted by Macdonald as:

> a manoeuvre [which] pretends to respond to the competing ideology but ignores its ideological challenge . . . The compromise is to adopt the surface terminology, without taking on board the ideology that underpins it. (1995: 91)

This is brought out both linguistically and visually. An article on learning to surf, *Not drowning but waving* (*NW*, November 1994), has the subtitle *A babes' guide to surfie culture*, positioning the learning women as 'babes' and surfing as the exclusive domain of male 'surfies' (a term now eschewed by surfers for its sexist and red-neck associations). The article includes a half-page 'surfie dictionary', comprising slang items 'required' to break into 'surfie culture'. The title is double-edged: on the one hand, implying that women who surf may get into trouble, but on the other hand, appealing to the well-read middle class reader who may recognize the play on Stevie Smith's famous poem.

The surfing article in question manages to subvert its 'activity' focus visually as well. It presents a large action shot of a woman surfer whose body and board replicate vectors along the horizontal and vertical axes, that is 'the paths of greatest stability' (Arnheim, 1982: 107), thereby infusing stasis even into an action shot of a woman. The article includes shots of successful woman surfers, but only at the end of the article in very small photos at the bottom of the page, with two out of three *carrying* their boards. The third page has a large photo of Pixie (a fat woman comedian) dressed up as a surfer and carrying a board. Thus, even articles which might harbour the promise of portraying active women successfully breaking into domains traditionally controlled by men ultimately marginalize, even ridicule, the notion of a learning, enterprising and active woman.

Compared with *SHE, New Woman* could be seen to present a dynamic world in which women are offered positive enticements to take on male gender (do what the boys do) and to be self-empowered (learn new things). It appears however, on closer inspection, that its tendency towards transgression and development is held in check by the ways in which these enticements are framed. There is a mismatch, a contradiction, between *NW*'s emphasis on change and transgression, and the disempowering nature of the devices it uses to realize these concerns, as discussed below.

Elaborated coding orientation and contradiction

We have suggested above that, on the one hand, *NW* seeks to liberate women, while on the other hand it reinforces their subordinate position within patriarchal consumer society. Its emphasis on change and engagement is at the same time neutralized by its embeddedness within the already familiar capitalist-patriarchal institution of magazine publishing. Having noted this tension, the parallel between *NW*'s meaning style and Bernstein's elaborated coding orientation can now be taken one step further. Bernstein notes that

> The new middle class . . . are caught in a contradiction: for their theories are at variance with their objective class position. A deep rooted ambivalence is the ambience of this group. On the one hand, they stand for variety against inflexibility, expression against repression, the inter-personal against the inter-positional; on the other hand there is the grim obduracy of the division of labour and the narrow pathways to its positions of power and prestige. (1975: 126, cited in 1996: 186)

In general, and as pointed out above, *NW* presumes access to certain levels of education because of its specialized lexis, its use of macro-genres (cf. Martin, 1994), and its demanding patterns of internal reference and coherence. In addition to that, *NW* requires that the reader be able to deal with the contradictions between the overt message (*change, empower yourself!*) and the covert message (*but don't really threaten the status quo*). This involves a continuous double reading, which as Bernstein notes is inherent in an elaborated coding orientation. More specifically, *NW*'s meanings are infused with ambivalence: the possibility of freedom is always kept in check by boundaries not realized simply and congruently as in *SHE*, but in more complex and covert ways.

As shown above, *SHE* sets up redundancies between its meanings ('don't', 'bad'), its structures (linguistic and visual distance achieved through objectifying devices, boundaries), and its overall organization and sequencing ('us' as given; 'other' as new). By contrast, *NW* plays its linguistic semantics of freedom off against other devices, such as aspects of its visual representation and structural organization.

The *NW* article discussed above, *Not drowning but waving*, was shown to be a clear example of this. Its verbal exhortation is that women should go out there and do something, which initially appears to be matched in its visual representation of surfing women. And yet this message is undermined by depicting the women as static, incapable

(Pixie), and through its emphasis on men as naturally controlling the domains of action under focus (as 'surfies' or 'bosses' whose knowledge and behaviour are taken as benchmarks).

While the positive and transgressive meanings are realized explicitly, that is linguistically, the negative and static are realized implicitly, that is visually. As Kress and van Leeuwen (1990: 2) point out, visual representation in our culture tends to be seen as 'natural', and therefore as less deserving of or necessitating critical interpretation, with visual grammar thus more unconscious for most people.

In addition to the contradictory meanings being made linguistically and visually, a further contradiction is achieved covertly through structural organization. While *NW* claims to be about *new* women, in fact its point of departure is invariably women who can't do the things they need to do – that is the unknowing, the incapable. There are few articles dealing with women who have successfully transgressed gender boundaries and challenged the status quo. The incapable, inexperienced woman constitutes the theme/given in linguistic structures (occupying first position in the clause) and is represented on the left of images (the position of given).

This structural strategy also functions to restrict the new woman's scope of change and transgression by defining what is worthy of her attention, or 'news' ('where she might go'). Thus, for *NW* learning and change concern a specified and limited degree of practical change, excluding radical transgressions of patriarchal definitions of womanhood.

Conclusion: difference, reading habits and consumer choice

We have suggested so far that the two magazines exploit visual and linguistic patterns consistent with particular coding orientations, and we have considered some of the contradictions this involves for the elaborated coding text, *New Woman*.

However, in Bernstein's account, the two codes have always been associated with different socio-economic classes, with middle class speakers having access to both elaborated and restricted coding orientations, while working class speakers are limited to the restricted coding orientation. Despite the fact that the magazines we analysed were remarkably consistent in terms of each coding orientation, the demographic data researched by magazine publishers did not suggest clear class differences between buyers of these magazines.

It thus seems that although the variation is patterned in a culturally relevant way, it does not seem to differentiate readers. The study does not support the view that choice of a magazine is simplistically associated with coding orientation. Rather, it suggests that reader choice may be 'heteroglossic' (Bakhtin, 1981: 273), that is that readers can choose to access a variety of meaning styles. Thus, readers' choice does not represent a monologic identification with the coding orientation of a text.

The lack of apparent correlation between reader background and particular magazines leads us finally to reflect on the meaning of variation in popular texts. Recognizing the 'instability of gender/media consumption' (Ang and Hermes, 1991: 323), we accept the position that the reading practices generally associated with these popular cultural products are themselves integral to the meaning of a text. Different types of popular text appear to get read/used in different ways, as Hermes found in her study of readers of women's magazines: 'The most important difference between women's magazines and other popular genres . . . seems to be that women's magazines are read with far less concentration and much more detachment than other popular genres' (1995: 14). Hermes's interviewees led her to conclude that: 'women's magazines are valued most of all because they are easy to put down' (1995: 67). Women's double, perhaps triple, responsibilities at home, at work and for children often leave little time and space for extended engagement with books, magazines, or other media. Their busy and fragmented lives enable at most a casual consumption of precisely those products whose meanings do not further problematize or complicate the nature of their social relations. It is the format of women's magazines which most suit the kind and degree of attention afforded in these conditions.

However, in a consumer culture the reader expects variety, and it may well be that coding orientations provide ready-made frameworks for consumer choice while reinforcing patriarchal definitions of femininity. The casual reading habits associated with these products make it possible for readers not to claim any strong identification with the magazines' meanings, and to avoid dealing with the texts' contradictions.

We can now return to the questions with which we began this chapter. The fascination (if the relevant reading practices warrant the use of that term) which these magazines exert over their audiences is an outcome, we suggest, of two factors. Firstly, the magazines instantiate consistent and distinguishable coding orientations, which realize social difference and give the buyer a sense of control over her consumption. Secondly, the format of the magazines is appropriate to the lifestyles of their women readers. None of the texts in this genre demand sustained attention.

Difference, therefore, is neither unproblematically related to the readers' social backgrounds, nor meaningless variation. Instead, differences in coding orientation may now have become tools of marketers for generating consumer choice. Thus, difference becomes a resource used to gloss over the basis of women's relation to the status quo. What women's magazines offer, ultimately, is difference without diversity.

Notes

1. For further background to the semiotic theory relevant here see Lemke (1984; 1995) and Thibault (1991; 1997). For further examples of applications of the model see Iedema (1997) and Eggins and Slade (1997).

2. See Halliday (1978), Martin (1992), Eggins (1994), Thibault (1997) for more detailed explanations of this stratal view of semiosis.

3. 'Redundant' is here used in Bateson's (1973) and Lemke's (1984) sense: a meaning realized in one semiotic modality (such as image) is reflected in some way in another semiotic modality (such as language).

4. 'In reality, every time it is confronted with objective conditions identical with or similar to those of which it is the product, habitus is perfectly "adapted" to the field without any conscious search for purposive adaptation, and one could say that the effect of habitus is then redundant with the effect of field' (Bourdieu and Wacquant, 1992: 129).

5. The two magazines differ slightly in size: *New Woman* is 27 cm × 20.5 cm, while *SHE* is 29.5 cm × 22.5 cm.

6. Note that although we consider decisions about advertising to be an important part of a magazine's 'style', we did not specifically look at advertising in this study, as that was not part of our brief.

7. Kress and van Leeuwen (1990; see also 1996).

8. For reasons of space we cannot here present results for the fiction or editorial statement sections, which were the briefest sections. However, patterns displayed there were consistent with those identified in other sections.

9. Boundaries are a sign of order. Their absence will create a degree of disorder. The tension between order and disorder however is a potential: 'Granted that disorder spoils pattern; it also provides the materials of pattern. Order implies restriction; from all possible materials, a limited selection has been made and from all possible relations a limited set has been used. So disorder by implication is unlimited, no pattern has been realised in it, but its potential for patterning is indefinite' (Mary Douglas, 1966: 94). Douglas concludes: disorder 'symbolises both danger and power' (1966: 94).

10. 'Through the ages and in most cultures, the central position is used to give visual expression to the divine of some exalted power' (Arnheim, 1982: 72). The parallels between magazine covers and medieval (pre-perspectival) forms of representation are striking (Iedema, 1994).

11. With reference to empirical research results, Bernstein remarks: 'The difference between [subject] is not a difference in cognitive facility-power but a difference in recognition and realisation rules used by [subjects] to read the context, select their interactional practice and create their texts' (1987: 568).

References

Ang, Ien and Hermes, Joke (1991) 'Gender and/in media consumption', in James Curran and Michael Gurevitch (eds), *Mass Media and Society*. London: Edward Arnold. pp. 307–27.

Arnheim, Rudolf (1982) *The Power of the Center: a Study of Composition in the Visual Arts*. Berkeley, CA: University of California Press.

Bakhtin, Mikhail (1981) *The Dialogic Imagination*. Austin, TX: Texas University Press.

Bateson, G. (1973) *Steps Towards an Ecology of Mind*. New York: Granada.

Bernstein, Basil (1971) *Class, Codes and Control. Vol. I: Theoretical Studies towards a Sociology of Language*. London: Routledge & Kegan Paul.

Bernstein, Basil (1975) *Class, Codes and Control. Vol. III: Theoretical Studies towards a Sociology of Language*. London: Routledge & Kegan Paul.

Bernstein, Basil (1987) 'Social class, codes and communication', in U. Ammon, N. Dittmar and K.J. Mattheier (eds), *Sociolinguistics: an International Handbook of the Science of Society*, Vol. I. Berlin: de Gruyter. pp. 563–79.

Bernstein, Basil (1990) *The Structure of Pedagogic Discourse: Class, Codes and Control*, vol. VI. London: Routledge.

Bernstein, Basil (1994a) 'A rejoinder to Michael Huspek', *British Journal of Sociology*, 45(1): 103–9.

Bernstein, Basil (1994b) 'Edwards and his language codes: response to A.D. Edwards' "Language codes and classroom practice"', *Oxford Review of Education*, 20(2): 173–82.

Bernstein, Basil (1996) *Pedagogy, Symbolic Control and Identity: Theory, Research, Critique*. London: Taylor & Francis.

Bourdieu, Pierre and Wacquant, Loic (1992) *An Invitation to Reflexive Sociology*. Cambridge: Polity.

Chibnall, Steve (1980) 'Chronicles of the gallows: the social history of crime reporting', in H. Christian (ed.), *The Sociology of Journalism and the Press*. Sociological Review Monograph 29. pp. 179–217.

Douglas, Mary (1966) *Purity and Danger: an Analysis of Concepts of Pollution and Taboo*. London: Routledge & Kegan Paul.

Edwards, A.D. (1987) 'Language codes and classroom practice', *Oxford Review of Education*, 13(3): 237–47.

Eggins, Suzanne (1994) *An Introduction to Systemic Functional Linguistics*. London: Pinter.

Eggins, Suzanne and Slade, Diana (1997) *Analysing Casual Conversation*. London: Cassell.

Erbring, Lutz and Shabedoth, Eva (1993) 'Measuring editorial style in women's magazines'. Paper presented to the ESOMAR Seminar on Competition in Publishing: The Necessity for Research, London.

Frieden, Betty (1963) *The Feminine Mystique*. Harmondsworth: Penguin, 1965.

Gilbert, Pam and Taylor, Sandra (1991) *Fashioning the Feminine: Girls, Popular Culture and Schooling*. Sydney: Allen & Unwin.

Halliday, Michael A.K. (1978) *Language as Social Semiotic*. London: Edward Arnold.

Halliday, Michael A.K. (1994) *An Introduction to Functional Grammar*, 2nd edn. London: Edward Arnold.

Halliday, Michael A.K. (1995) 'Language and the theory of codes', in A. Sadovnik (ed.), *Knowledge and Pedagogy: the Sociology of Basil Bernstein*. Norwood, NJ: Ablex. pp. 127–43.

Halliday, Michael A.K. and Hasan, Ruqaiya (1985) *Language, Context and Text: Aspects of Language is a Social Semiotic Perspective*. Geelong: Deakin University Press.

Hasan, Ruqaiya (1989) 'Semantic variation and sociolinguistics', *Australian Journal of Linguistics*, 9: 221–75.

Hasan, Ruqaiya (1992) 'Meaning in sociolinguistic theory', in K. Bolton and

H. Kwok (eds), *Sociolinguistics Today: International Perspectives*. London: Routledge. pp. 80–119.

Hermes, Joke (1995) *Reading Women's Magazines*. Cambridge: Polity.

Hudson, R.A. (1980) *Sociolinguistics*. Cambridge: Cambridge University Press.

Huspek, Michael (1994) 'Oppositional codes and social class relations', *British Journal of Sociology*, 45(1): 79–102.

Huspek, Michael (1995) 'Oppositional versus reproductive codes: a response to Basil Bernstein's "Rejoinder to Michael Huspek"', *British Journal of Sociology*, 46(1): 127–32.

Iedema, Rick (1994) 'Textual meaning in visual representation'. Mimeo, Linguistics Department, University of Sydney.

Iedema, Rick (1997) 'Interactional dynamics and social change: planning as morphogenesis'. PhD thesis, Department of Linguistics, University of Sydney.

Kress, Gunter and van Leeuwen, Theo (1990) *Reading Images*. Geelong: Deakin University Press.

Kress, Gunter and van Leeuwen, Theo (1996) *Reading Images: the Grammar of Visual Design*, 2nd edn. London: Routledge.

Labov, William (1972) 'The logic of non-standard English', in Pier Paolo Giglioli (ed.), *Language and Social Context*. Harmondsworth: Penguin. pp. 179–215. Reprinted from *Georgetown Monographs on Language and Linguistics*, 1969, 22: 1–31.

Lemke, Jay (1984) *Semiotics and Education*. Monographs, working papers and publications, no. 2. Toronto: Toronto Semiotics Circle.

Lemke, Jay (1995) *Textual Politics: Discourse and Social Dynamics*. London: Taylor & Francis.

McCracken, Ellen (1993) *Decoding Women's Magazines*. New York: St Martin's Press.

Macdonald, M. (1995) *Representing Women: Myths of Femininity in the Popular Media*. London: Edward Arnold.

Martin, James R. (1985) *Factual Writing: Exploring and Challenging Social Reality*. Geelong: Deakin University Press. Republished Oxford: Oxford University Press, 1989.

Martin, James R. (1992) *English Text: System and Structure*. Amsterdam: Benjamins.

Martin, James R. (1994) 'Macro-genres: the ecology of the page', *Network*, 21: 29–52.

Plum, Gunter (1988) 'Textual and contextual conditioning in spoken English: a genre-based approach'. PhD thesis, Department of Linguistics, University of Sydney.

Rosen, Harold (1972) *Language and Class: a Critical Look at the Theories of Basil Bernstein*. Bristol: Falling Wall Press.

Sacks, Harvey (1972) 'On the analyzability of stories by children', in J. Gumperz and D. Hymes (eds), *Directions in Sociolinguistics: the Ethnography of Communication*. New York: Holt, Rinehart & Winston. pp. 325–45.

Thibault, Paul (1991) *Social Semiotics as Praxis: Text, Social Meaning Making and Nabakov's 'Ada'*. Minneapolis: University of Minnesota Press.

Thibault, Paul (1997) *Re-reading Saussure: the Dynamics of Signs in Social Life*. London: Routledge.

Wardhaugh, Ronald (1986) *Introduction to Sociolinguistics*. Oxford: Basil Blackwell.

8

'IT'S A GAME!': THE CONSTRUCTION OF GENDERED SUBJECTIVITY

Alyson Simpson

This chapter explores issues of power and subjectivity through data collected of a family interacting while playing a game. I will use linguistic analysis, read through a feminist poststructuralist framework, to tell a story about how discourses impact on each other. My aim is to highlight the negotiations for positions of power which exist within this family. The family in the study is my family and I am the mother of that family. Therefore, it could be suggested that I write with what feminists Thorne and Yalom refer to as 'the actual voice of mothers' (1982: 12). However, I acknowledge that there can be no one voice which could speak for all mothers, and that I speak here as a specific mother who is also a researcher. The combination of mother with researcher has proved to be a productive approach to this project.

Cixous said on the subject of mothers writing about the experience of being part of a family:

> Maybe mothers should write the truth about being mothered – that is, make open, show the family scene the family drama. I don't think it's ever been unveiled, we haven't got enough genius to be able to cope with a scene which is extremely contradictory, where everybody actually suffers. (1990: 24)

The chapter looks at a 'family drama' through excerpts of a text recorded when the family were playing a board game called *Babar Ups 'n' Downs*. (The game is a reworking of the traditional snakes and ladders, using elephant's trunks for ladders and crocodiles in place of snakes.) There are four people in the family: a mother named Alyson (A), a father, Guy (G), their six-year-old daughter, Heather (H), and four-year-old son, Toby (T). Whilst the family were playing the game the daughter was upset when she was chastised for trying to 'cheat'. Her desire to win the game was so strong that she was distressed and cried out, *I wanted to win!* The discourse of games was then constructed overtly by her parents as 'playing according to the rules'. However, this discourse was subverted at the end of the game when the father asked his daughter whether he won, when in fact he came last.

This text can be read as an example of strategic negotiation, what Foucault described as 'a series of localized strategies' (1988: xv). He maintained that it is most important to investigate how particular kinds of subjects are produced as effects of discursive and power relations. It is my intent that this chapter should construct multiple readings from data with which to tell stories about the negotiation of power relations within this family. However, as the institutional sites of the family and games are tightly embedded, it is necessary to tease out the theoretical implications of this conflation before attempting a close analysis of the text. Therefore, the chapter begins with an elaborated account of the theoretical framework chosen to support the detailed linguistic analysis of a text which records such conflicting interests as those signalled in the following lines when Heather attempts to rethrow her turn:

450   H: I want another go!
458   A: You threw five Heather that was the luck of the chance that you threw and that . . .
459   H: No!
460   A: . . . is how a game is played.
462   A: If you are going to be silly about it Heather you can leave the game.
463   T: She is being silly.
464   A: I know she is being silly Toby. You can't organize to win the game.
466   A: Heather it's a game! We've talked through this before.
468   H: It's not fair!
469   A: One, two, three, four, five, six. That's what a game is Heather. It's luck, it's chance, it's playing. You're supposed to be having fun. It's nothing to do with who wins. Four.

Theories of discourse

The term 'discourse' has two common usages. In linguistics, 'discourse' is traditionally understood to mean language as 'text'. This text may be a stretch of either spoken or written language. Emphasis is placed on the part language plays in the construction of meaningful communication created between writer/reader and speaker/addressee. Discourse analysis refers to textual analysis which is concerned with examining patterns and structures of language in use (Pennycook, 1994: 117).

The other use of 'discourse' originates within European philosophy. Foucault (1972; 1977; 1979), the French philosopher, describes discourse as ways of structuring knowledge and social practice manifested in particular ways of using language and other symbolic forms in specific institutional settings. His use of discourse

allows us to understand how meaning is produced not at the will of a unitary humanist subject, not as a quality of a linguistic system, and not as determined by socio-economic relations, but rather through a range of power/knowledge systems that organize texts, create the conditions of possibility for different language acts, and are embedded in social institutions. (Pennycook, 1994: 128)

The second meaning, that of discursive practice as constitutive of knowledge, is the one I adopt in my research where a discursive system constructs what counts in social and language practices as 'ways of being'. This proposal has been taken up by feminist scholars interested in theories of language and subjectivity such as Valerie Walkerdine and Linda Brodkey. Weedon (1987) calls discourses the conventions which to a significant extent govern what can be said, by what kind of speakers, and for what types of imagined audiences. And Brodkey suggests it is more useful to think of discourses as 'conceptual' rather than 'real objects', as 'world views or ideologies' (1992: 301). My research then is located within the poststructural project which aims to 'demystify the power of discourse in order to better understand the discursive practices that construct our sense of self, other and reality' (1992: 310).

Discourses operate as 'practices that systematically form the objects of which they speak' (Foucault, 1972: 49). In other words, they 'do not just reflect or represent social entities and relations, they construct them or "constitute" them' (Fairclough, 1992: 3–4). Here is the link between power/knowledge and discourse where our sense of self, other and reality can be seen as constructs which in some respect 'fit' the ways of seeing that have been accepted as suitable for the members of a particular institution. That is, discourses are shaped by the power relations in social institutions and in society as a whole such that 'power–knowledge relations are integral to the production and repro-duction of discourses' (Urwin, 1984: 284). If discourses are shaped by power relations then poststructuralist theories suggest that individuals are shaped (positioned) by their access to discourses and the subject positions made available to them in those discourses. The possibility of multiple positionings, otherwise known as 'ways of being', is relevant to a research project interested in children because, as Davies describes it, 'Any one child has access to a variety of ways of being dependent on who s/he is with, the particular context s/he is in and the discourse within which s/he is situated' (1982: 112).

The family as an institution

One of the most significant sites of the construction of subjectivity for the child is the family, as the modern Western childhood is a 'familialized and scholarized one' (Alanen, 1988: 54). A sociological view of the family suggests that in the early bourgeois family authority was invested as an internal control mechanism through the father figure whose power served to shape 'individuals to conform with the demands of the social system' (McNay, 1992: 100). This one-way view of authority structures in the family which proposed a transfer of the effects of power from the family to the social has been disputed by Foucault who suggests that, whilst the family exists as a self-regulated social structure, it has also been 'invested and annexed' by 'global mechanisms of domination' (1980: 99). It is viable then to propose another view, a contrasting view positioned within a poststructuralist framework which suggests that the family is an ideological and cultural construct, a political institution held together through power relations (Ochs and Taylor, 1992; Foucault, 1978).

In poststructuralist theory, social conditions are seen as constructions (Alanen, 1988: 61). Seen in this way, a family is a cultural construct bound by social apparatus which attempts to regiment the domestic life of ordinary people (Foucault, 1978) by making available a limited number of subject positions. These subject positions must be understood as 'historically produced and regulated' (Walkerdine, 1987: 10). As a site of production, the family constructs the subject positions of parent/child, sibling/sibling, partner/partner in relationships of power based on authority and age. These relationships are further complicated by social relations of gender, for example, mother/father and brother/sister. It is noted that within this historically and socially specific family a particular 'type' of discourse operates which supports a rationalist view of middle class values. In this respect, the discourse of rationality serves as one of many 'regimes of truth', sets of understandings which legitimate particular social attitudes and practices such as good behaviour, pride in achievement, respect for others through 'fair play', all of which are types of the moral/ethical judgements which justify restrictions of the player's actions and construct what it is to be a member of this family. The operation of this discourse can usually be seen in interactions concerning matters directly unrelated to the game, for example: comments related to behaviour, such as *That's quite enough shouting*; stories of achievement, such as *Toby counted up to ten in Greek*; and claims of *That's not fair!*

However, institutions do not operate in isolation and the family has embedded within it the social relations of games. That is, the negotiation of the subject positions within the game is partly dependent on the imposition of authority which enforces and is enforced by the structure of the family. In this sense, 'the authoritative word is . . . so to speak, the word of the fathers [and mothers]' (Bakhtin, 1994: 78). For it is within the context of the family that the game's interaction takes place and the relationship of support which exists between the two sites is important to the unproblematic progress of the game. These two institutions, that of the game and that of the family, operate together quite successfully to maintain stable relationships of power because they are premised on similar assumptions, for example, an acceptance of hierarchical authority structures.

The power of the instantiated authority can be observed when the players attempt to resist the structure of games. The institutionalization of both games and family can be employed to discipline them, as they are forms of authorized knowledge within the context of the family which are operationalized as a system of belief of how things ought to be constrained by adult sanctions (Urwin, 1984: 282). In this way the structures of family and games can be used as a means of social control which regulates the players', most often the children's, behaviour. As the breaking of rules signals, among other things, a challenge to authority, Gilbert's question 'who is authorised to break rules and who isn't' is relevant to a general discussion of the construction of subjectivity Gilbert 1993 and most relevant to the text below. What is important to note is that the discourses create the subject positions of 'fair player' and 'cheat', 'obedient' and 'naughty' daughter which operate as objective 'truths' despite being based on unproblematic assumptions of middle class rationality.

The conflation of the sites of family and games needs to be complicated further by social relations of gender. This move introduces relations which cut across age boundaries to work against assumptions of power based on seniority. In the next section gender is presented as a problematic concept which can be understood from two opposing views of socialization theory and feminist poststructuralism. Socialization theory presents gender as an inherent dualism. In contrast, feminists working with poststructuralism tend to view the socialization theory of gender as 'imposed effect' and propose instead a view of gender as a 'dynamic process' (McNay, 1992: 12). The significant effect which socialization theory has had on conceptions of gender in promoting difference as a central premise will be discussed and rejected from within feminist poststructuralist theories of multiplicity.

Gender and power

The role of language in the construction of gender difference has been a productive site for investigation, with a variety of viewpoints emerging from the research. One is the 'common-sense' view of child rearing which represents 'specific values and interests' (Weedon, 1987: 76). The prevalent notion concerning children and gender is that they are socialized into gender roles which place them into a polarized structure of difference and opposition, that is masculine versus feminine as exclusive categories. This theory depends on the acceptance of biological categories, boys and girls, as the basis for social activity. The problem identified by feminists with this approach is not that the biological is acknowledged, rather that it is privileged as the reasoning behind what then becomes an exercise in the normalization of human behaviour through gender differentiation. Gender differentiation is the construction of masculine and feminine in social life such that it results in limitations of social relations. Definitions of male/female behaviour can be seen in polarized comparisons which are used to differentiate between the sexes. These definitions are constructed in language and other semiotic systems from the moment the child is born.

This 'different culture' view is premised on the concept that boys and girls, who take on the unitary identities men and women, are socialized to use language differently. The approach suggests that there are cultural differences in girls' and boys' groups which give rise to different linguistic styles of interacting and creating meaning. From this perspective, girls are usually disadvantaged by these linguistic styles as the systems of communication within which they learn to operate pressure them to conform quietly, 'be nice' and choose the 'prestige of goodness' over the 'prestige of power' (Kohlberg in Maccoby, 1966: 105–6). Linguistic research carried out within this framework examines patterns of communication (and miscommunication) and finds gendered stereotypes as the norm (Tannen, 1990; Maltz and Borker, 1982).

Another view of the linguistic construction of gender, which proposes multiple femininities/masculinities, disagrees strongly with the promotion of difference as sufficient explanation for such complex issues as positions of power which may be contradictory and are continually negotiated (Walkerdine, 1986; 1990; Connell, 1987; Poynton, 1993). These researchers maintain that a theory of difference presupposing 'static and exaggerated dualisms' can lead to nothing but a 'conceptual dead end' (Thorne, 1993: 91). The political effect of accepting difference as the basis of gender relations is to maintain the imbalance of power as the status quo where the masculine is privileged within a patriarchal hierarchy.

In contrast to a theory of difference, a feminist poststructuralist perspective provides a theory of gender which proposes that gendered subjectivity is constructed through the individual's experience of a variety of subject positions which are created in discourse and constructed in language. This view 'explores the specific ways in which the gendered subject and his or her representations of reality are constructed within a social field' (Kinder, 1991: 10). The linguistic research supported by this framework examines patterns of communication as evidence of subject positioning in a number of social relations, not just gender. The position taken is that 'words are bi-polar, the people are not' (Davies, 1989: 9).

If we reject socialization as a theory which works to establish gender as a social division through which stereotypes are created as end products, then gender can be seen as something we 'do' which creates 'differences between girls and boys and women and men, differences that are not natural, essential or biological' (West and Zimmerman, 1987: 137). The concept of doing gender is supported by poststructuralists as the recognition of the construction of subjectivity as a process where an individual is positioned and repositioned through a variety of discursive practices (Thorne, 1993; Connell, 1987). The poststructuralist thesis that femininity and masculinity are constantly in process and subjectivity, which most discourses seek to fix, is constantly shifting. Support for this thesis will be provided by looking at two children as examples of 'actual boys and girls created at the intersection of multiple positionings and ascribed masculine/feminine' (Walkerdine, 1990: 75).

Methodology

The research has been designed as an ethnographic case study of one family. As mother/researcher, I am part of that family. I can speak from an 'insider's' perspective, as an embodiment of the participant observer of ethnographic research. A feminist ethnographic view of this kind of research is 'of great potential significance for rethinking ethnographic writing. It debates the historical, political constructions of identities and self/other relations, and it probes the gendered positions that make all accounts of, or by, other people inescapably partial' (Clifford and Marcus, 1986: 19). I have chosen my family as a research site in order to examine how the discursive structure of the social institution which is our family operates to construct positions of gendered subjectivity for my children. Rather than accepting the family as a given, I note Wodak and Schulz's warning that: 'the family cannot be considered as an autonomous social sub-system, nor can the division and definition of roles within the family be regarded as independent of social conditions' (1986: 12).

I locate my study within a feminist poststructuralist framework because of my concern with the political significance of personal lived experience. Kinder's description of poststructural feminism as 'exploring the specific ways in which the gendered subject and his or her representations of reality are constructed within a social field' (1991: 10) aptly describes part of the methodology I have chosen for my project. I combine feminist poststructuralist readings, however, with a form of detailed linguistic analysis. In their critique of the structuralist tradition of linguistics, Lee and Poynton (1995) advocate an approach to discourse analysis which enables the exploration of the linguistic construction of subjectivity through what they call 'feminist post-linguistics'. This approach seeks to 'produce readings of texts which indicate the ways individuals are positioned and take up positions within discourses' by combining both poststructural and linguistic analysis. Particularly useful work using linguistically based textual analysis read within a poststructuralist framework is being written by Australian feminists such as Threadgold (1986; 1988), Poynton (1985; 1993) and Lee (1996). Their work has established the viability of this kind of approach. My study serves as an example of the benefits of such research which addresses social and political issues, and is grounded in the everyday.

Two methods have been chosen to examine the discursive practices of the family, some fragments of which have been video recorded and then rewritten as texts. The first method is a type of close linguistic analysis which focuses on the language in the texts to find what Hodge and Kress refer to as 'enigmatic traces of process frozen in text, fossils of power preserved in linguistic amber' (1993: 159). This view of discourse analysis takes the linguistic definition of stretches of text to be discourse and sets out patterns of lexico-grammatical and semantic features as evidence of the negotiation of power in the dynamic interaction of game playing. Yet, as linguistic analysis does not attempt to interrogate the Foucauldian implications of discourse analysis which takes the poststructuralist definition of discourse as involving the construction of conflicting subject positions, it cannot supply the necessary detail to inform a critical reading of the data. Therefore, the model of critical discourse analysis chosen for this project is a response to Poynton's critique of linguistics and poststructuralist theory which states:

> . . . no linguistics which does not and cannot agree with central issues of feminist and poststructuralist theory concerning questions of subject production through discursive positioning can be taken seriously as a theory of language. [Nevertheless] there is a need for the recuperation within poststructuralist theory of certain kinds of linguistic knowledge, considered as technologies for understanding how the representations constituting discourses are actually constructed and the linguistic norms by which subjects come to be constituted in terms of specific power/knowledge relations. (1993: 2)

Taking this into consideration, the resulting analysis examines how the social is constituted in language to ask the question: how does language construct the conflicting subject positions which become labelled as gender differences? The proposal is made that the subject positions which speakers take up, as attempts to control others through power/ knowledge oppositions, are constructed in linguistic forms/textual strategies as a 'set of syntactic choices' (Kress and Threadgold, 1988: 239). It is the premise of this study that language as a semiotic system constructs ways of being which may be in conflict. This position has been developed out of Halliday's (1975) proposal that language is a meaning making potential with social implications. I have made use of Halliday's work on systemic functional linguistics as a framework which enables the identification of particular systems of choice in linguistic forms. The critical linguistic features chosen for analysis in this chapter from within that model of language are mood and speech function choice as these can be related to the negotiation of power relations.

It is mainly through an investigation of the use of rules in games texts that the negotiation of power relations is focused. The common grammatical category of mood associated with rules is the imperative. The linguistic 'rule' that matches a semantic coding with its congruent grammatical form suggests that most games rules would be recognizable as commands. Using speech function analysis, which categorizes the speech functions of command, statement and question as congruent or incongruent forms, it is possible therefore to examine the construction of positions of power in the discourse of games as made through strategic linguistic choices. For example, statements can be used to take up a position of knowledge within a discourse, for example, as expert or rule knower (Kress, 1985: 25). This is not to suggest that rules are the only means by which power relations may be constructed. Rather, they are the most obvious signal that power is being negotiated in the games interactions.

The games texts are not coherent within a unified text structure, but instead contain traces of a number of discourses. Each of these discourses is 'mixed into' the supra-discourse of games and may be identified by the particular lexical and syntactic choices speakers make. By examining the texts for the multiple discursive practices embedded within them, it is suggested that the structural patterns of text may be seen as what Kress and Threadgold describe as:

> a number of patterned processes by which systems of ideas and beliefs (ideologies/the world of common-sense reality) are constructed, transmitted and maintained. These processes involve institutions, power relations, questions of access and thus questions of the construction of social agents and subjects. They are not autonomous, or objective scientific categories for the analysis of texts: they provide no answers by themselves. (1988: 227)

The implication of the discussion above is that it is only through a combination of close linguistic analysis and poststructuralist reading that the identification of transitory subject positionings constructed in language in the playing of games is made possible. In this way the systemic functional approach to language adopted for the analysis will serve as a technology, a way of seeing how discourses work by looking at the language which constructs them. Recognizing the result as a form of analysis which works towards combining what have been described as 'incommensurable discourses' (Pennycook, 1994), it is acknowledged that there will be theoretical disjunctures. However, what is achieved is a critical perspective on the 'political quietism' of linguistic analysis which renders the familiar as unfamiliar, to examine how discourses construct our lives (1994: 133). As the purpose of the study is to investigate the construction of gendered subjectivity, the analysis of the data will illustrate how the children in the study are confronted by multiple positionings in conflicting discourses where gender is one of a number of social relations which impact on their everyday interactions.

Accepting these concerns, this study follows an ongoing set of positionings and repositionings between a girl and a boy, and the family of which they are a part. Recordings of the two children playing a variety of games with their parents were collected for one year. The utilization of mechanical means of recording enables the researcher to capture naturalistic speech to be used as a data base (Ochs, 1979: 43). Transcribing this text 'slows down' a conversation, making it possible to notice special aspects (Davies, 1982: 23). My decision to use video recordings of games as my sample of the total family talk available results in what Ochs (1979: 43) calls a selective observation of the data. I acknowledge that, by predefining my area of interest, I have limited the collection of data by my theoretical position to, as Bateson (1987) comments, 'determine what data we will see and what data will be *noise*' (Bateson's emphasis).

The games collected were then classified according to a schema which was sensitive to the existence of regulation. The proposed classification of games ranges from rule bound through format bound to open ended. There are three major games types in the classification:

1 Games with formalized rules, such as board games, are strongly routinized; in Kress's terms, they are 'closed' (1985: 26). There is a set pattern of action, imposed through external authority, which is accepted as 'playing the game properly' such that actions judged to be inappropriate are taken as resistance of the rules.
2 Format bound games, such as jigsaw puzzles, are governed by covert rules which are implied in the physical material themselves. Again these games are rated in Kress's terms as 'closed' because of the existence of imposed boundaries.
3 Open ended games, such as playing school, are governed by 'rules' of a different sort to the first category. These rules are most often openly negotiated and motivated by an order of discourse which has been taken up as suitable for the game. There is a marked slippage between discourses in this type of game, where the discourse of games becomes a metadiscourse, a means of organizing action, which enables the 'play' within other discourses. The categorization 'open ended' recognizes the multiple possibilities which exist within the frame of this game type. It is the most 'open' of Kress's types as power relations between players are negotiated.

The game I have chosen for analysis in this chapter is a rule bound board game, *Babar Ups 'n' Downs*. The capacity for negotiation of rules within the game type, if used as a measure of imposed authority, is directly relevant to the linguistic construction of the game and the negotiation of power relations. Board games such as *Babar Ups 'n' Downs* are the most easily recognized form of rule bound games. By definition the games are in the format of a board around which players move their pieces/counters/characters according to a prearranged pattern defined in the rules provided. One of the most obvious indicators of board games as rule bound games is the existence of formalized rules either on an instruction/rules sheet or printed on the game box. Board games can be sold in a boxed form with the pieces and moves preplanned so that players can learn them. The games are always played the same way – there is no creativity involved – and the rules are usually consulted in order to set the game up for the first time and referred to from then on as the external source of authority to which all participants must defer.

The importance of games

Recognition of the cultural potential of games is important. In both everyday life and scholarly discourse, games are rarely viewed as a form of interaction which has social implications. Reflecting the authoritative positions which adults take up to construct relations with children, this is partly due to the common-sense assumption that, as children play games, games can't be very important. A different view is proposed in this study which recognizes that games are examples of the kind of institutionalized structures in children's lives which Urwin problematizes as:

> events bounded by adult sanctions or constraints, or systems of belief about how things ought to be. Moreover, these systems of belief are not fixed, static or orchestrated from above. They are productive, and as such bear a particular relation to truth. It is at this juncture that a relation between regularized action and discourses regulating that action is produced. (1984: 282)

The relation which Urwin proposes between regularized action and regulative discourses is most applicable to the site of games as the regulatory nature of their structure is made obvious in rules.

The importance of rules to games cannot be denied. What my work seeks to establish is a link between the power/knowledge relationship, as elaborated by Foucault (1980), and the linguistic construction of that relationship in games. Following Foucault's theory, it is suggested that, as the instantiation of a body of knowledge which constructs power relationships, rules constitute games. Therefore, children cannot play games with others until they can both apply and be bound by rules. The proposal is made then that it is in learning the language of rules that social game play is made possible. In this way, rules can be viewed as one of the major linguistic practices which constitute games. In other words, rules make it possible to enact a particular set of linguistic and physical routines as a game. Therefore, through an examination of these routines in the form of a collection of texts which record children playing games, games will be discussed as the site of an investigation into the means by which language constitutes subject positions.

Within this discussion, rules are the most obvious control mechanism of games, but not the only one. It is also necessary to consider the constraints of the subject positions which are made available to children as players within the playing of the game. Again, it is through language that the existence and taking up of specific subject positions is made visible. Grounded in textual examples, the research carries out a close examination of how language constitutes alternative 'personas' for players to take up (for example, from the *Babar* game, the characters Babar, Celeste, Pompadour and Zephyr), and also the classificatory system of the progression of 'proper' game playing, for example: winner, loser, player, cheat. It is clear that the variety of possible subject positions in any game will present continual opportunities for changing relationships of power. It must also be remembered that, at the same time that each player is positioned within the games, there are other sites within which they are always already positioned, for example, within the site of family as sibling. Layered over these sites are other socially defined relationships such as gender and age. Because of the ongoing negotiation of subjectivity, a simultaneous investment in any number of the subject positions constructed in these sites and social relations will bring about a potential conflict of interests. It is the resolution of these conflicts and the resulting effects on the children's emerging subjectivity that is of interest to the larger study.

The bodies of knowledge on which the institution of games is built now need to be made explicit. The three terms 'play', 'games' and 'rules' will be discussed in this section to examine how their application is made specific to the discourse of games. The terms 'play' and 'games' are discussed as framing concepts which uphold socialization theory as ways of thinking about and being a child. These terms are rejected as insufficient to a poststructuralist theorization of games. 'Rules' are discussed as operating within functional social frameworks and then critiqued as an extension of the rationalist approach to child rearing practices.

The terms 'play' and 'games' form a semantic pair, the division of which for the purpose of discussion is not easily made as the relationship of meaning between the two terms is not clear. Before discussing the terms individually, then, it is necessary to tease out a potential distinction. In general terms, play is often viewed as more spontaneous, less bound than games. A useful distinction between games and play is made by Cheska who sees games as 'playfulness tamed' (1981: 24). That is, in games the spontaneous invention associated with play is bound by some sort of structure which limits what may or may not happen. This understanding is worded by Bateson as: 'the difference between a game and just playing is that a game has rules' (1987: 17). The relationship between the terms 'play' and 'games' is tightly interwoven and not easy to separate. It is possible to think of play as a process and games as a product. This distinction serves to justify the discussion of definitions based on a division of play read as 'content' (a problematic term implying unitary perspectives which will be addressed below) and games as 'form'. It is this contentious but common division which will be used to separate the discussion of play from games.

Play and games

One of the most accepted definitions of play is taken from socialization theory. This perspective is discussed below and critiqued as being an insufficient model for the study. The socialization approach to play suggests that play serves social purposes, whether it is skills based, is intended to expend physical energy, or is its own justification (Vygotsky, 1978; Cass, 1971). This approach to play suggests that play develops out of cooperative interaction which reflects social knowledge (Garvey, 1977; Willes, 1983). The evidence of this knowledge is found in linguistic routines where children share a common conception or 'script' for their play, for example, making telephone calls, organizing dinner (Garvey, 1977). It is the social view of play which Garvey adopts when she defines play as:

1 pleasurable for participants
2 engaged in by participation because of the intrinsic satisfaction generated, not for an extrinsic goal
3 engaged in spontaneously and voluntarily by participants
4 involving the active engagement of participants
5 systematically related to non-play activities.

Generally speaking, there are two major problems with a social view of play. The first is that the role of language in the construction of play is insufficiently attended to. Although Garvey refers to 'linguistic routines' and 'social knowledge', she does not see the relationship between the two as constitutive. A theoretical position which suggests that play 'reflects' social knowledge does not acknowledge play as discursive practice. The second problem with the social view of play, the denial of the political importance of play, is a result of the first. This perspective lacks awareness of discursive positioning as the ongoing negotiation of power/knowledge relationships. So that, although Willes speaks of the benefits of play as providing children with opportunities 'to explore their environment and their developing power to control it' (1983: 73, my emphasis), her conclusion presumes the existence of a unitary subject which might *explore* and *control* this 'thing' called power.

The term 'cooperative play' used above shows the influence of psychology on play theory. One of the most powerful psychological theories used as explanation of children's changing play behaviour has been Piaget's (1951) stages of cognitive development. This approach draws a developmental link between the age of the child and the type of play which is most common. The examples of individual play found amongst very young children are labelled 'parallel' because of the tendency for these children to play next to but not 'with' other children. According to Piaget (1951: 108), at this stage children are concerned with mastery of self, of things and of impersonation. In contrast, examples of social play found in older children are labelled 'coopera-tive' because the children play together. In Piaget's words, the child's early stages of play are purely for 'functional pleasure' (1951: 89) and only later, at around two to seven years, do they develop at the level of verbal and intuitive thought.

The inherent problem with this view of play is that it ignores the relevance of the linguistic development of the child in the constitution of social relations. In doing so, Piagetian based play theory posits the existence of something other than language, some mental capacity which mediates between social experience and the child, such that it is not until the correct stage is reached that the child can successfully take into account the views of others. The splitting of language from social relations is taken to be highly problematic in feminist poststructuralist research which supports the view that language is constitutive. The contrasting poststructuralist view of the role of language suggests that it is not possible for children to play socially until they have learnt the language of cooperative play. The concept of sharing, for example, belongs to a discourse of fairness which is constructed and can only be explained in linguistic terms. It is not a pre-existing mental capacity within a child which needs to be triggered by emotion, deprivation or growing older.

In a different way, Freud's work on the resolution of unacceptable desires has influenced the socialization theory of play. From Freud's concern with the mastery of disturbing events has developed a com-monly held view that play is a process of buffered learning (Millar, 1974: 29). Developed from this perspective, socialization theory sees children's play as being a direct reflection of adult culture (Good-enough, 1983: 156). From this theoretical perspective play serves the social purpose of enculturating children. According to this theory, children use role play to accustom themselves to the structures of the adult world. That is, the theory suggests that there may be a 'transfer' process at work in play where principles or concepts learnt during play in a 'real world context' will be assimilated. The problem with this view is the distinction drawn between 'reality' and play which seeks to naturalize a non-existent 'truth', that reality somehow exists 'outside' play. The implication of socialization theory is that the pre-socialized child operates in a different, even 'make-believe', social context which is somehow separate from the 'real' world in which adults operate. This view is supported by psychological theorists such as Vygotsky (1978) who suggests that play has no consequences for the 'real' world.

Whilst rejecting the view which postulates the possibility of 'reality' as a framing concept, it is possible to accept a view which separates one form of discourse practice from another. This view is found in Bateson's work on frames where he suggests that metacommunicative signals can construct boundaries to carry messages such as *this is play* (1987: 179). His work was taken up by Goodenough who describes play as 'a frame where children create their own rules' (1983: ix). That is, play can only occur if the participants agree to set their activity within a certain time and space as 'other than' that which is not play. For this to be achieved there needs to be what Cheska calls 'an awareness of alternatives: of two sets of goals and rules, one operating here and now, one that applies outside the given activity' (1981: 19). The play frame then 'brackets an encounter, setting it apart from ongoing, more "serious" life' (Thorne, 1993: 79). So, for example, it is understood that, when a group of people sit at a table moving small coloured pieces of cardboard over a larger piece of coloured cardboard, the activity is given the social meaning of playing a game. (Given a different cultural/historical perspective it could have equally been called 'war', 'trade' or 'economics'!) However, in this particular context the participants have agreed to play a game together. That is, they have set aside other activities and taken up the subject positions suitable to support the game scenario chosen.

In contrast to the view of play as 'make-believe' with a social purpose is a view of games as a social process. Sutton-Smith acknowledges the importance of looking closely at children's games as models of power, saying:

> Games serve to prepare children for expected life experiences. They are models of ways of succeeding over others, by magical power (as in games of chance), by force (as in physical skill games), or by cleverness (as in games of strategy). We have speculated that in games children learn all those necessary arts of trickery, deception, harassment, divination and foul play that their teachers won't teach them but are most important in successful human relationships in marriage, business and war. (1973: 356–7)

His definition fits within a socialization framework where games are seen to have the purpose of enculturating players into normalized social structures. It is clear within this perspective that there is a link between definitions of games and concerns with structure. This is found in Sluckin's (1991) definition of games as a method of socialization into structures of power. He labels games as:

> a distillation of human relationships particularly those to do with power. As models of power, games serve to prepare children for expected life experiences . . . for example, voluntary co-operation, regulated competition, contracts, a judicial system. These values are enshrined in rules systems. (1991: 163)

Like Sutton-Smith, Sluckin admits that power is part of the game playing context. What they both do not discuss is the potential of games as sites for the negotiation of power relations which have little to do with the actual game. Rather, they are only concerned with the possibility of players learning the already accepted, hierarchical models of power as established in society and interpreted through rules. This view of rules sees them as an unquestioned necessity.

It is noticeable that in definitions of games the link between rules and power is not often made visible. For example, as part of his definition of games, Denzin (1977) highlights the imposition of rules; however, he does not extend his discussion to include a consideration of the participation in games as having a political dimension with significance beyond the immediate boundaries of the game.

> A game shall be defined as an interactional activity of a competitive or cooperative nature involving one or more players who play by a set of rules that define the content of the game. Skill and chance are the essential elements that are played over. Played for the amusement of the players and perhaps also a set of spectators, games are focused around the rules that determine the role that skill and chance will have. The objects of action are predetermined (checkers, kites, chess players, dice). Furthermore, the elements of pretence are known beforehand and are specified by the rules of conduct deemed appropriate to the game at hand. These rules specify the number of players, tell the players how to play, and determine how they will relate to one another as game players. (1977: 20)

It is assumed then that the culturally learned view of games which depends on socialization theory sees games as socially purposeful but 'innocent' activity. This is a position questioned by poststructuralist theory which posits 'the end of innocence' (Flax, 1992). 'Innocence' is a problematic concept because of its assumption of the possibility of any action existing outside social relationships. Within this section it is sufficient to say that games are widely considered to be as unproblematic and innocent as reading is (Gilbert, 1987: 3) and therefore in need of theoretical disruption.

Playing by the rules

An alternative view of games to those expressed above is constructed within a poststructuralist framework which rejects the common-sense view of playing games as an innocent activity. From this perspective, games may be seen as systems of power/knowledge within which children take up subject positions. In contrast with the unpoliticized view of games, this suggests there is a multiplicity of subject positions available in the social activity of games played by children which are developed through specific discursive practices. The importance of rules to this problematized view of games is that they are forms of regulation which, while operating most obviously as overt forms of social control, may become internalized as a kind of disciplinary 'gaze' which is focused on the rational conduct of self (Foucault, 1977; Walkerdine, 1987).

Within the site of games, rules are a form of discursive practice which works against multiplicity as they are employed to establish a unitary power base in games by limiting the availability of subject positions within certain boundaries. It is this restriction of access through manipulative discursive practice to which Walkerdine refers when she proposes that 'examining the regulation of the specific practice allows us to examine how the subject is *inserted* as a participant in that practice' (1988: 115, my emphasis). One implication of the term 'inserted' in this statement is that the player could be seen to be controlled as a passive participant within games. To recognize the importance of rules in creating the subject positions within the site of games in which players are 'inserted', then, is to recognize the political strength of rules. A problematization of the acceptance of rules as non-political structures will aid in the investigation of games as a site of struggle, where relations of power are negotiated.

Rules have a central role to play in the construction of games as they define what is read as possible or sanctioned behaviour which facilitates the control and regulation of children (Wright, 1993: 28). That is, in games, rules govern the behaviour of the players and become the internalized authority to which all participants are expected to defer. Most definitions of rules suggest that they are 'imperative and absolute, beyond discussion' (Denzin, 1977: 21). Children are used to learning rules as directives concerning what is allowed within the social institution of the family. They are often told what to do yet, in their everyday experiences, these rules tend to be more negotiable, more 'messy', and hence more likely to have multiple interpretations. In contrast, rules in games serve the same function of telling children what to do, yet there is less room for negotiation. The contrast of the imperative of games structure as compared with rules for everyday life is recognized by Caillois, who observes: 'the confused and intricate rules of ordinary life are replaced in this fixed space and for this given time by precise, arbitrary, unexceptionable rules that must be accepted as such and that govern the correct playing of the game' (1961: 7). The acceptance of rules has constituted games as a form of ritual whose political structure is beyond question.

It is the explicit purpose of this study to question what has been ritualized for it is considered that, as rules serve as a form of power/ knowledge in games, they should be investigated. The danger of ignoring the force potential of rules is raised by Flax, who warns:

We cannot understand knowledge without tracing the effects of the power relations which simultaneously enable and limit the possibilities of discourse. Even consensus is not completely innocent, since traces of force may be found in the history of any set of rules that attain and maintain binding effects. (1992: 453)

It should be noted that games rules also apply to adults. Within the power relationships which the institution of games constructs at the beginning of a game, all participants may be positioned as apparent equals. The distinction of the set of subject positions made available in games from those in other sites is recognized by Denzin, who comments: 'location in these roles is determined by the game, not by relationships that exist between the players when they are not gaming' (1977: 20). That is, the imposition of a different social structure creates the possibility of new power relationships as, unlike the family, with its inbuilt age, generational and gender distinctions, the construction of the power relations in the games hierarchy depends on the progression of the game, not its initial organization. Within this view, the idealization of rules suggests that they maintain a prescribed order of behaviour which favours no single player. The view that rules serve to establish a kind of 'level playing field' and do not assign an order of power is supported by Suits, who states:

> rules are accepted for the sake of the activity they make possible. In games I obey the rules just because such obedience is a necessary condition for my engaging in the activity such obedience makes possible. The fact that the rules are already in existence for the game means that there is no need for negotiation and conflict resolution is made possible because of their acceptance. (1967: 154)

The assumptions which inform this statement are based on a non-critical awareness of rules which accredits them the value of creating a unifying structure within the site of games. However, rules are also associated with morality. A comparison of the application of rules in these two sites is given by Suits as: 'in morals conformity to rules makes the action right, but in games it makes the action' (1967: 154). A Foucauldian reading of this statement spells out the difference between morals and games as the difference between one as legitimated social attitude and the other as legitimated social practice.

A politicized awareness of the use of rules reads them as one of the means used to manage conflict through 'practices which depend on rendering invisible the power relation' (Walkerdine, 1988: 210). In contrast, in the non-politicized everyday living of this family, rules are treated as an unproblematic method of rational conflict control. It should be noted that the institution of the family is mapped onto the structure of games through a routinized acceptance of the discourse of rationality. When the family play a game, they all behave as if they have implicitly agreed to be bound by the rules listed as a kind of shared social norm. There is no discussion of the learning of the rules, merely explanation which serves as a form of enculturation of the children into rule bound behaviour within the limited number of subject positions which are made available. What counts as a satisfactory ending or an acceptable beginning, or a logical sequencing order of moves, is inevitably linked to dominant cultural knowledge. That is, in order for a game to proceed, participants need to agree with the rationalist discourse which allows there to be one and only one winner and only one way of winning the game.

A normative game text should proceed in ordered fashion. For most of the time, the text below follows that pattern exactly. However, what makes the text analysed so interesting is that, eventually, three of the players deliberately try to disrupt what, until the father's last move, had been treated as a tightly rule bound game. The contrast between Heather's attempted resistance to the rules and her subsequent accept-ance and then subversion of her father's subversive play shows up the shifts in the negotiation for power and the construction of subjectivity which is in process in the game. For when Heather attempts to resist her positioning in the game as loser, the subject positions of both games and family are employed to discipline her: she is no longer 'obedient daughter' or 'fair player'. Yet, when her father resists his positioning in the game, he attempts to make use of the subject positions of family to support his disruption. Heather is caught between being 'good' (obeying the rules) and being 'bad' (agreeing to let her dad break the rules), between winning and losing. Her creative resolution is to do both!

To investigate the conflict that Heather experiences I have adopted Lyotard's (1984: 10) extended metaphor around conversation as game playing. He comments: 'What is needed if we are to understand social relations . . . is not only a theory of communication, but a theory of games which accepts agonistics [jousting] as a founding principle' (1984: 16). Using Lyotard's trope of the 'taking of tricks', I have examined the moves as each speaker/player attempts to trump their communicational adversary within the conversation around the game. This is clearly evidenced in the many moves that each player makes to control the others through various discursive practices in the game and in the conversation.

Analysis

As an indication of the use of controlling moves, let us consider the introduction of text topics which have nothing to do with the game. Attempts to control topic function to position the speaker as one who knows and the listener as one who should be silent and attend (not necessarily as one who doesn't know). Early on in this episode, A begins to broaden the scope of the conversation by introducing ideas about the value of patience and the possibility of chance. G also comments on T's speculation about his moves. Whilst these comments do nothing to advance the game, they are still closely tied to the topic. It is later, when A relates a story to G, that a shift in discourse is found and a text within the text occurs at lines 276–302.

276	H:	One, two, three, four, five, six.
277	T:	One, two, three, four, five, six.
278	A:	Move your finger.
279	H:	Ow! That's what I do sometimes.
280	A:	Toby can count to six. He can count to ten. In fact he can count to ten in Greek.
281	H:	Hmm.
282	A:	We were in a maths shop yesterday looking at all these numbers and symbols and so on. Toby says 'that's ena' and I'm, 'sorry, pardon, what?' 'That's ena, that's three' or one or whatever it was. I can't remember myself.
283	H:	One, oh down the elephant.
284	T:	No!
285	A:	One, two, three.
286	H:	Hmm.
287	G:	[counts to himself]
288	A:	Do you remember what eight is in Greek, Toby?
289	T:	Yes.
290	A:	What is it?
291	T:	Otto!
292	A:	Otto, that's an easy one to remember.
293	H:	Otto is. Count up to otto, eight in Greek, Toby.
294	T:	Three.
295	A:	Wait a minute he's busy doing this.
296	T:	One, two, three.
297	A:	Heather, your turn.
298	H:	Count up to otto in Greek.
299	T:	No, no, no, no.
300	H:	But daddy would like to hear.
301	A:	He didn't hear when you turned out the light last night. You counted all the way up to eight.
302	T:	No, he was at work.

When H insists on showing T how to count to six, A reminds her that T can count to ten in Greek. A then begins to tell G about being in a shop with T and how he began counting in Greek and asks T to say the word for eight. T obeys but continues playing the game. H then commands T to count up to eight and he ignores her. A instructs H to leave T alone and reminds her to play the game. Again H orders T to count but he refuses. A reminds him that G did not hear and T agrees that he was at work. G does not speak at all.

Another way to indicate the dynamics of negotiation for control is to analyse the relational values of grammatical features. I have used a fairly simple analysis as a first run through the data to establish who orders, who questions and who answers or informs (Table 8.1). These grammatical forms may be viewed as constructing the power relationships between the participants.

In this moment, the institution of the family is foregrounded and the negotiation of family power relationships is highlighted. A patriarchal hierarchy is constructed through A's deference to G when she tells the

Table 8.1 *Speech function analysis of lines 276–302*

Name	Command	Question	Statement
A	2	2	11
G	0	0	0
H	2	0	3
T	0	0	1

funny story. In this excerpt H attempts to construct a hierarchical sibling relationship with T. This can be read in her use of commands and the way she both teases and patronizes him through her comments. A also attempts to control T, but in a less direct manner, by using questions which allow him to take up a position of power through knowledge. T refuses to be positioned by H but accepts his mother's authority to ask him questions. An analysis of the number of statements made by the participants shows that A makes the most comments overall in the collected data. This is also the case in this small excerpt. A uses commands to position H as one who requires direct control. The fact that G does not enter the conversation but only smiles and ruffles T's hair positions him as one from whom the others seek approval.

The next extract illustrates a more heated version of this negotiation process (lines 440–69).

440 H: I mean . . .
     [She throws the dice and when she sees it is not the number she wants she picks it up to throw again.]
441 A: Heather! You can't throw again.
442 H: Oh, but I wanted to win!
443 G: Five, one, two, three, four, five.
444 A: I'm sure you did but you can't . . .
445 H: No!
446 A: You can't make yourself win Heather.
447 H: I want to!
     [She cries.]
448 A: You can leave the game right now if you're going to be silly.
449 T: Daddy, that's not your one.
450 H: I want another go!
451 G: No!
452 T: That's your one.
453 A: You're not allowed to have another go.
454 H: That's not fair!
     [She cries.]
455 G: Well, leave the game then.
456 A: Off you go then. You're not playing any more. Give us the dice.
457 H: No!
458 A: You threw five Heather. That was the luck of the chance that you threw and that . . .
459 H: No!

Table 8.2 *Speech function analysis of lines 440–69*

Name	Command	Question	Statement
A	8	0	17
G	1	1	0
H	0	0	6
T	2	0	3

460 A: . . . is how a game is played.

461 G: Are you going to have five?

462 A: If you're going to be silly about it Heather you can leave the game.
   [Heather moves five in a sulky fashion.]

463 T: She is being silly.

464 A: I know she is being silly Toby. You can't organize to win the game.

465 T: So leave the game!

466 A: Heather it's a game! We've talked through this before.

467 T: Leave the game!

468 H: It's not fair!
   [She cries.]

469 A: One, two, three, four, five, six. That's what a game is Heather. It's luck, it's chance, it's playing. You're supposed to be having fun. It's nothing to do with who wins. Four.

By looking closely again at the words that are spoken in this short extract, we can examine who has what investments in the issue of control. H has tried to change her throw and is ordered by A and G to play according to the rules. T adds his opinion and tells A to follow through her threat to make H leave because she is being silly. It is clear that A is most concerned with controlling what is happening, as she uses the highest number of commands, many more than the number that G scores (Table 8.2). However, she also makes a large number of statements which operate in the discourse of games and attempts to position H as the obedient player. At this late stage terms such as *luck, chance, playing, win, game, fun* are used to establish a definition of the meaning of game. H capitulates sadly after protesting her feelings.

Daddy's girl: the construction of gendered subjectivity

This information only takes me so far into the purpose of this chapter. My main concern is to address a methodological issue. It is possible to see that I can achieve a certain 'result' from looking closely at my data. There are certain statements I can make about power and control. What concerns me more is what I do not say or see, by limiting the way I 'read' my data to a linguistic approach. I have always been aware that there was a question remaining after the counting stopped. To tell the story of this episode without looking further than how many times the parents correct the children or how the older female sibling speaks to the younger male sibling is to leave out the question of what this means to the relationships being constructed between the speakers. Such issues can best be addressed through a framework which raises issues such as subjectivity. From examining the data I suggest that the participants negotiate their way through varying relations of power. The positions involved are constructed by both institutions operating in the *Babar* text: that of family and that of games.

In the next two samples of text H wins the game 'fairly' and A comments on her previous behaviour as being inappropriate.

513	A:	One, two, three! There you go.
		[Heather throws the dice and throws the winning three that she needs.]
541	G:	Oh! Heather's won.
515	H:	I won.
516	G:	Heather won.
517	A:	There.
518	H:	Mmm.
519	A:	I don't know you deserved to after that display.

Then at last everyone finishes. Note what happens in the final moments at lines 644. G asks H if he won because he came last and H agrees.

639	A:	Everybody finished.
640	H:	Take off your thing.
641	G:	Yey!
642	A:	Hooray!
643	T:	Hah hah. Ooop!
644	G:	So did I win because I came in last?
645	H:	Yes.
		[Heather looks at Guy doubtfully.]
646	G,A:	Hah hah.

With all the anguish that H has been through concerning who will win, why does she agree to negate the right that she has to declare herself the winner? There is something more than an exchange of words happening here. H's desire to occupy the position of winner is in direct conflict with her desire to fulfil the position of obedient daughter. For H, her positioning within the game conflicts with her position within the family. She does not have the power to challenge the rules successfully so she chooses to abide by their restrictions. She could resist the gendered construction of her as 'good girl' but she chooses not to. Her change of heart about the value of winning the game reflects her acquiescence to her positioning within a particular set of family relations. Note that she had a very puzzled expression on her face when her father asks if he has won. By saying this, he has changed the discursive boundaries that they have been operating within. I suggest that she reacts to this move by repositioning herself, not as 'winner' in the discourse of the game, but firmly in the position of 'obedient daughter'. She gives into the emotional pull of letting the daddy she loves so much win even though she knows the 'rules' say he hasn't.

My reading of the text above is that, in more ways than one, her father is 'playing a game' with her. He is deliberately and mischievously breaking the rules. When the whole episode has been so tightly bound with concerns of playing fairly, this comment right at the end of the game seems way out of bounds. Is he trying to show her that the value of the win is not so great after all? Is he subverting the idea of who the winner is by suggesting it is an arbitrary decision? Is it a power game to make her prove her loyalty? Is it him being just as silly as Toby was when he talked earlier in the game about going down elephants and up crocodiles, and turning things back to front? I don't know the answer for sure. But it bothers me that she agrees to let him win, positioning herself so readily as 'daddy's girl'.

Such a positioning is not unique to H, however. Urwin explores this issue more generally in relation to:

> the child's developing gender identity in [the] different positions she takes up in language in relation to her mother and father. In the one case she assumes or fights for control over her mother; in the other case, her desire to please her father, to cater for his wants, perhaps, seems to undercut her demanding for herself. Is it not also possible then that in learning to manage interpersonal situations in accordance with what is allowed or expected, the production of language may itself enter into the production of culturally prescribed and proscribed aspects of masculinity and femininity? (1984: 274)

This statement explicitly describes the contradiction which exists for H between her desire to win and her reading of what her father has asked her. She is 'multiply constituted' within the sites of games and family, and visibly confused, she struggles with the solutions that her subjective position makes possible. It is clear evidence of the fact that, as Walkerdine suggests, 'children are multiply constituted subjects for whom the interplay of signs produces conscious and unconscious struggle' (1986: 58). H's resolution to the problem of how to please her father and still retain the upper hand is interesting, as it shows that she can subvert the rules for her own purposes. First, she arranges all the pieces, naming them all as winning (see line 647). However, at the last moment (on A's prompting) she quotes a humorous rhyme about finishing order she knows from school which recategorizes the winners. This rhyme enables her to reposition her father as someone with what to her is a funny characteristic: a hairy chest. She is making fun of him via an example of what she has constructed to be a resistant discourse. That is, she has changed the interpretation of the original text to suit her purpose, which serves to rename herself a winner, 'second the best', and her father simultaneously as 'first the worst' and 'the one with the hairy chest' (line 651). Through A's help, she is reminded of the possibility of resistance to patriarchal discourse.

647   H: The first to win, the second to win.
            [She points at the characters lined up on the board.]
648   A: What's that funny rhyme that you say Heather? Is it first . . .
649   H: First the worst, second the best . . .
650   A: Third the one with the hairy chest. Hah hah. Guess what Toby. Hah hah hah.
651   H: First the worst, me and Toby second the best, and daddy's the one with the hairy chest.
652   A: Haha hah.
653   H: Because you have got a hairy chest.

Conclusion

Davies remarks that 'Human subjects are not fixed but constantly in process, being constituted and reconstituted through the discursive practices they have access to in their daily lives' (1993: 11). Such a perspective informs my exploration of the construction of subjectivity through a number of readings of a small sample of data. Through this process I have shown what happens to one girl in the negotiation for positions of power within a family when they are playing a game. The conclusion from this discussion is that there is linguistic evidence of the construction of subject positioning through discursive and power relations. However, while individuals can be forced to conform to specific forms of behaviour, there are still possibilities for resistance. Weedon says, 'even in these instances, there is room for resistance by subjects who refuse to identify with subject positions which they are offered' (1987: 100).

I will continue to address this issue through further investigations of my data, for it seems clear to me that, as Fairclough proposes,

> constituted social subjects are not merely passively positioned but are capable of acting as agents and amongst other things of negotiating their relationship with the multifarious types of discourse they are drawn into. (1992: 61)

My investigation of Heather's story shows how a child can be constructed to have little power and a female child even less. Our particular family upholds some basic ideological concerns about morality which direct the ways we behave. Yet, as a feminist, I am also aware of the need to challenge notions of dualistic gender stereotypes and encourage multiple subjectivity. When I deliberately reminded H of the rhyme she knew from school, I created a position of solidarity with H: it was no longer her against the rest of us, but the two of us working in tandem to remove from G the power he had assumed. H employed the same tactics that G did, using language to disrupt the dominant hierarchy and reposition herself as more powerful. Sure, it was 'only' a game, but there was more at stake than just finishing first.

References

Alanen, Leena (1988) 'Rethinking childhood', *Acta Sociologica*, 31(1): 53–67.

Bakhtin, Mikhail (1994) 'Rabelais and his world' (1965), in P. Morris (ed.), *The Bakhtin Reader: Selected Writings of Bakhtin, Medvedev and Voloshinov*. London: Edward Arnold. pp. 194–244.

Bateson, Gregory (1987) *Steps to an Ecology of Mind: Collected Essays in Anthropology, Psychiatry, Evolution and Epistemology*. New Jersey: Jason Aronson.

Brodkey, L. (1992) 'Articulating poststructural theory in research on literacy', in R. Beach, J. Green, M. Kamil and T. Shanahan (eds), *Multidisciplinary Perspectives on Literacy Research*. Urbana, IL: NCTE. pp. 293–318.

Caillois, Roger (1961) *Man, Play and Games*. New York: Free Press of Glencoe.

Cass, Joan (1971) *The Significance of Children's Play*. London: Batsford.

Cheska, Alyce (1981) *Play as Context: 1979 Proceedings of the Association for the Anthropological Study of Play*. New York: Leisure Press.

Cixous, H. (1990) 'Difficult joys', in Helen Wilcox, K. McWatters, A. Thompson and L.R. Williams (eds), *The Body and the Text*. New York: Harvester Wheatsheaf. pp. 5–29.

Clifford, James and Marcus, George (eds) (1986) *Writing Culture: the Poetics and Politics of Ethnography*. Berkeley, CA: University of California Press.

Connell, R.W. (1987) *Gender and Power: Society, the Person and Sexual Politics*. Sydney: Allen & Unwin.

Davies, Brenwyn (1982) *Life in the Classroom and Playground: the Accounts of Primary School Children*. Boston: Routledge & Kegan Paul.

Davies, Brenwyn (1989) 'The discursive production of the male/female dualism in school settings', *Oxford Review of Education*, 15(3): 229–41.

Davies, Brenwyn (1993) *Shards of Glass: Children Reading and Writing beyond Gendered Identities*. St Leonards: Allen & Unwin.

Denzin, Norman (1977) *Childhood Socialization: Studies in the Development of Language, Social Behaviour and Identity*. San Francisco: Jossey-Bass.

Fairclough, Norman (1992) *Discourse and Social Change*. Cambridge: Polity.

Flax, J. (1992) 'The end of innocence', in J. Butler and J. Scott (eds), *Feminists Theorize the Political*. New York: Routledge. pp. 445–60.

Foucault, Michel (1972) *The Archeology of Knowledge*, trans. A. Sheridan. London: Routledge.

Foucault, Michel (1977) *Discipline and Punish: the Birth of the Prison*, trans. A. Sheridan. Harmondsworth: Penguin.

Foucault, Michel (1978) *The History of Sexuality. Vol. 1: An Introduction*. Harmondsworth: Penguin.

Foucault, Michel (1979) 'On power', in M. Morris (ed.), *Power, Truth, Strategy*. Sydney: Feral. pp. 96–109.

Foucault, Michel (1980) *Power/Knowledge: Selected Interviews and Other Writings 1972–1977*, ed. C. Gordon. New York: Pantheon.

Foucault, Michel (1988) *Politics, Philosophy, Culture: Interviews and Other Writings 1977–1984*, ed. L.D. Kritzman. New York: Routledge.

Garvey, Catherine (1977) *Play*. Cambridge, MA: Harvard University Press.

Gilbert, P. (1987) 'Post reader-response: the deconstructive critique', in B. Corcoran and E. Evans (eds), *Readers, Texts and Teachers*. Montclair, NJ: Boynton Cook. pp. 234–50.

Gilbert, P. (1993) 'Working with genre: reading place, parameter and play', in B. Cope and M. Kalantzis (eds), *Genre Approaches to Literacy Theories and Practices*. Sydney: Common Ground. pp. 101–8.

Goodenough Pitcher, Evelyn (1983) *Boys and Girls at Play: the Development of Sex Roles*. Sussex: Harvester.

Halliday, Michael A.K. (1975) *Learning How to Mean: Explorations in the Development of Language*. London: Edward Arnold.

Hodge, R. and Kress, G. (1993) *Language as Ideology*, 2nd edn. London: Routledge.

Kinder, Marsha (1991) *Playing with Power in Movies, Television and Video Games from Muppet Babies to Teenage Mutant Ninja Turtles*. Berkeley, CA: University of California Press.

Kress, Gunther (1985) *Linguistic Processes in Sociocultural Practice*. Geelong: Deakin University Press.

Kress, Gunther and Threadgold, Terry (1988) 'Towards a social theory of genre', *Southern Review*, 21(3): 215–43.

Lee, A. (1996) *Gender, Literacy, Curriculum: Rewriting School Geography*. London: Taylor & Francis.

Lee, A. and Poynton, C. (1995) 'Poststructuralist theory and literacy teaching'. Paper presented at the 21st ARA Conference, Sydney.

Lyotard, J. (1984) *The Post-Modern Condition: a Report on Knowledge Theory and History of Literature*, vol. 10, trans. G. Bennington and B. Massumi. Minneapolis: University of Minnesota Press.

Maccoby, Eleanor (1966) *The Development of Sex Differences*. Stanford: Stanford University Press.

McNay, Louis (1992) *Foucault and Feminism: Power, Gender and the Self*. Cambridge: Polity.

Maltz, D. and Borker, R. (1982) 'A cultural approach to male–female miscommunication', in J. Gumperz (ed.), *Language and Social Identity*. Cambridge: Cambridge University Press.

Millar, Susanna (1974) *The Psychology of Play*. Harmondsworth: Penguin.

Ochs, E. (1979) 'Transcription as theory', in E. Ochs and B. Schieffelin (eds), *Developmental Pragmatics*. London: Academic Press. pp. 43–72.

Ochs, Elinor and Taylor, Carolyn (1992) 'Family narrative as political activity', *Discourse and Society*, 3(3): 301–40.

Pennycook, Alistair (1994) 'Incommensurable discourses?', *Applied Linguistics*, 15(2): 115–38.

Piaget, Jean (1951) *Play, Dreams and Imitation in Childhood*, trans. C. Gattegno and F.M. Hodgson. London: Routledge & Kegan Paul.

Poynton, C. (1985) *Language and Gender: Making the Difference*. Deakin: Deakin University Press.

Poynton, C. (1993) 'Grammar, language and the social: poststructuralism and systemic-functional linguistics', *Social Semiotics*, 3(1): 1–21.

Sluckin, Andrew (1991) 'The culture of the primary school playground', in A. Pollard (ed.), *Children and Their Primary Schools: a New Perspective*. London: Falmer. pp. 150–64.

Suits, Bernard (1967) 'What is a game?', *Philosophy of Science*, 34: 148–56.

Sutton-Smith, Brian (1973) *Children Psychology*. New York: Appleton-Century-Crofts.

Tannen, Deborah (1990) *You Just Don't Understand: Women and Men in Conversation*. New York: William E. Morrow.

Thorne, Barrie (1993) *Gender Play: Girls and Boys in School*. Buckingham: Open University Press.

Thorne, Barrie and Yalom, Marilyn (1982) 'Rethinking the family: some feminist questions: introduction', in B. Thorne and M. Yalom (eds), *Rethinking the Family: Some Feminist Questions*. New York: Longman.

Threadgold, T. (1986) 'Semiotics-ideology-language', in T. Threadgold, E.A. Grosz, G. Kress and M.A.K. Halliday (eds), *Semiotics, Ideology, Language*. Sydney: Sydney Association for Studies in Society and Culture. pp. 15–60.

Threadgold, T. (1988) 'Language and gender', *Australian Feminist Studies*, 6: 41–70.

Urwin, Cathy (1984) 'Power relations and the emergence of language', in J. Henriques, W. Holloway, C. Urwin, C. Venn and V. Walkerdine (eds), *Changing the Subject: Psychology, Social Regulation and Subjectivity*. London: Methuen. pp. 264–322.

Vygotsky, L.S. (1978) *Mind in Society: the Development of Psychological Processes*, eds M. Cole, V. John-Steiner, S. Scribner and E. Souberman. Cambridge, MA: Harvard University Press.

Walkerdine, Valerie (1986) 'Post-structuralist theory in everyday social practices: the family and the school', in S. Wilkinson (ed.), *Feminist Social Psychology: Developmental Theory and Practice*. Milton Keynes: Open University Press. pp. 57–76.

Walkerdine, Valerie (1987) 'Surveillance, subjectivity and struggle: lessons from pedagogic and domestic practices'. CHS occasional papers no. 11. Minnesota: University of Minnesota Press.

Walkerdine, Valerie (1988) *The Mastery of Reason: Cognitive Development and the Production of Rationality*. London: Routledge.

Walkerdine, Valerie (1990) *Schoolgirl Fictions*. London: Verso.

Weedon, Chris (1987) *Feminist Practice and Poststructuralist Theory*. Oxford: Basil Blackwell.

West, C. and Zimmerman, D. (1987) 'Doing gender', *Gender and Society*, 1(2): 125–51.

Willes, Mary (1983) *Children into Pupils: a Study of Language in Early Schooling*. London: Routledge & Kegan Paul.

Wodak, Ruth and Schultz, Muriel (1986) *The Language of Love and Guilt: Mother–Daughter Relationships from a Cross-Cultural Perspective*. Amsterdam: Benjamins.

Wright, J. (1993) 'Regulation and resistance: the physical education lesson as speech genre', *Social Semiotics*, 3(1): 23–55.

9

TALKING POWER: GIRLS, GENDER ENCULTURATION AND DISCOURSE

Amy Sheldon

Children's worlds are arenas in which power, privilege and access are created, sought after, won and lost. Language is a major resource which allows children to make their way through the world. Language is also a powerful medium for teaching cultural novices, such as children, the community's tacit and dominant (that is, hegemonic) prescriptions for constructing gender (see Connell, 1987: 183ff for a discussion of gender hegemony). One of the major contributions of research on children's language is that it reveals how competent preschool children are with language, correctly encoding not only linguistic features, but also pragmatic and social features. Young children have a working knowledge of appropriateness, that is, of how talk should fit the context and addressee (Andersen, 1990; McTear, 1985). It should not be surprising, therefore, that young children's social uses of language would reflect tacit understanding of cultural prescriptions for the linguistic enactment of power and gender. I will discuss how gender can be 'done' in children's discourse, and will provide some examples. I will also discuss some of the challenges for future research on gender and discourse.

Theorizing gender differences

When we seek to understand how gender is reflected in discourse, and how discourse serves to maintain – or resist – gender arrangements, we need a working understanding of what the concept 'gender' means, what the local gender norms are, what the nature of discourse is, and what the local discourse practices are. In just about all cultures, females and males are theorized as being different from each other. This simply reflects a culturally constructed definition of gender as *difference*, usually *dichotomous, polar* differences rather than categories which have some area of overlap. Thus, speakers of English don't ordinarily notice anything peculiar about expressions such as 'the opposite sex', or 'the same sex', since these reflect shared, cultural beliefs that gender is about difference, if not dichotomy.

In addition, gender polarities are value-laden. Most cultures are androcentric rather than egalitarian or gynocentric. This is reflected in language. For example, even in an expression like 'androgynous', which refers to a balancing or mix of masculine ('andro-') and feminine ('gyn-') characteristics, the component which refers to masculinity occupies initial position in the word. There is no word 'gynandrous' in English. As reflected in English, male symbolism, male speakers, and masculine ways of speaking are considered normative and natural. Women as speakers and women's ways of speaking are seen as not fitting the norm and are often disparaged. The relative absence of positive feminine symbolism in language ordinarily goes unnoticed. Coates (1993: 16), in her review of academic writing and folkloric beliefs about women's and men's ways of speaking in English over the last few hundred years, sums up this systematic linguistic privileging as *The Androcentric Rule* 'Men will be seen to behave linguistically in a way that fits the writer's view of what is desirable or admirable; women . . . will be blamed for any linguistic state or development which is regarded by the writer as negative or reprehensible.'

Whereas gender polarization and androcentrism reflect and perpetuate a culture's definition of gender as difference, we can ask how and when these principles are learned and how they shape human interaction. Language is a powerful medium for teaching and perpetuating culture. Cultural prescriptions about gender norms are reflected in the tacit linguistic and social practices of mundane, everyday conversations.

However, a culture's gender ideology often takes the form of sketchy, oversimplified stereotypes. Are these stereotypes or prescriptions actually reflected and perpetuated in the context-sensitive discourse behaviours of hundreds, thousands, or millions of complex and diverse real females and males? What is the relationship between a community's gender norms and the behaviour of complex human beings in complex social situations? What model of gender should guide our research?

Critical discussions of gender theory have pointed out the descriptive inadequacy of theorizing gender as a dichotomy and of assuming that the categories 'woman/girl' and 'man/boy' refer to either natural or homogeneous social categories (for example, Bem, 1993; Connell, 1987; Deaux and Kite, 1987; Hare-Mustin, 1988; Scheman, 1997). These critiques of gender theory provide a cautionary message for sociolinguistic research which seeks to interpret gender in discourse. A complex enough understanding of gender as well as of the social matrix of language use are necessary in order to avoid perpetuating gender stereotypes in research, as recent critiques from researchers in the field of language and gender have also maintained (for example, Bing and Bergvall, 1996; Eckert and McConnell-Ginet, 1992; 1995; Freed, 1995;

Goodwin, 1980; 1995; Sheldon, 1992a; 1996b; Sheldon and Johnson, 1994; Thorne, 1990; Wodak and Benke, 1997).

Gender and conflict

One of the arenas in which the difficulties involved in interpreting gender in discourse are apparent is the study of gender differences in children's conflict talk. Conflict is a contest of wills. Gender ideology in many cultures gives males the license to argue in direct, demanding, and confrontative ways, with unmitigated rivalry. Girls and women do so at the risk of being called 'bossy', 'confrontational', 'bitchy', 'difficult', 'big-headed', or worse for the same behaviours that boys and men can garner praise for being 'manly', 'strong', or 'assertive'.

The gender ideology in many North American communities requires girls and women to 'be nice', or risk censure from peers and adults. Sachs (1987) finds that preschool girls have already learned to say things with a smile, pursuing their agenda and interests within the constraint that they not cause too much stress or jeopardize interpersonal harmony in their intimate groups. Baran (1987) hypothesizes that the pressure experienced by working-class and immigrant girls in London to not be adversarial or outspoken steers many away from competitive school subjects, such as science, shutting down future career choices. The pressure on teenage girls in a Detroit high school to find social success by constructing a pleasing, non-offensive personality (Eckert and McConnell-Ginet, 1995: 491) is part of this same theme. In communities in which there is a prescription that girls 'be nice', and where friendship ties are a crucial source of girls' social status and inclusion, it is clear that girls must learn to skilfully negotiate 'niceness', or risk censure. Being 'nice', which for females often means not being adversarial, is a norm that women are expected to adhere to, even if they have achieved institutionally derived status (see Sheldon and Johnson, 1994: 40–1 for an example).

Discussions of gender differences in verbal conflict management

The cultural ideology that frames gender differences in terms of polarities, and which is governed by a principle of androcentrism, is reflected in some previous descriptions of gender differences in the verbal management of conflict. Male groups and male conversations have been described in terms of *competition* and *hierarchy* (for example, Goodwin, 1980; Goodwin and Goodwin, 1987; Maltz and Borker, 1982). Female groups and female conversations have been characterized in an 'opposite' manner as *cooperative* and *egalitarian* (Kalčik, 1975; Maltz and Borker, 1982). Although many aspects of children's conflicts have been studied (Shantz, 1987), descriptions that focus on the discourse event, that is, the verbal tactics children use to construct and negotiate their way through conflict, are relatively new.

Another complicating factor is that much research has a male-centred bias. Boys' social behaviour has been well studied, with the result that, as Maccoby points out, 'we have a clearer picture of what girls' groups do *not* do than what they *do* do' (1986: 271). Androcentrism can also be seen in our cultural assumption that the norm for conflict involves aggressive, escalated or disruptive behaviours. Predictably, when measured against that norm, girls have been interpreted as *less forceful* (Miller et al., 1986: 543), or *less assertive* (Sachs, 1987: 185–8), or *unable to tolerate or resolve conflict on the playground* (Lever, 1976). An implication is that girls are not as effective or competent as boys at managing conflict. This is further reinforced by characterizing girls' same-sex interaction as emphasizing an ethic of *harmony* and *collaboration* (Miller et al., 1986: 547; Leaper, 1991: 796). Thinking dualistically about gender easily leads to mutually exclusive attributions of this sort.

Consistent with the view of how children's conflicts are gendered, some women in male-dominated business settings have described themselves as 'terrible at dealing with conflict', 'hating conflict', 'wanting people to get along', and 'behind the scenes peacemakers' (Kolb, 1992). Along the same lines, women colleagues in male-dominated academia have described themselves as 'not allowing our disagreements to reach the point of confrontation' and 'expert at developing strategies to avoid competition' (Keller and Moglen, 1987: 22). It has even been suggested that competition is a feminist taboo (Longino and Miner, 1987).

Add to this the observation by linguists (for example, Coates, 1993; Lakoff, 1992; 1995; Mendoza-Denton, 1995) and creative writers in male-centred cultures (for example, Rich, 1979; Russ, 1983; Olsen, 1978) that prescriptions of silence have historically restricted women and girls from expressing their authentic voice in speaking or writing. The expectation is that women and girls should keep quiet, should not be listened to, or, in comparison with men, should speak 'nicely', not disruptively.

Competition, conflict, and the exercise of power are complex social behaviours and psychocultural issues that are not necessarily well understood or described. Furthermore, if women's and girls' conflict episodes are described with reference points for conflict set at hegemonic, masculine conflict behaviours, feminine conflict will be less noticeable and less dramatic. Since conflict is defined through a masculine lens as escalated confrontation, even brute force, girls' conflict runs the risk of being interpreted as something else than conflict, or something 'less'. In an androcentric framework, it might be hard to imagine that girls could engage in oppositional and competitive behaviours, that they might have fights, arguments, and disputes. If we keep these androcentric and gender polarizing lenses on, we might conclude that girls were maladaptive in a world in which conflict is all around us and is unavoidable. But what if, instead of using prescriptions for hegemonic masculine conflict to define what we are looking for, we approached feminine conflict with the hypothesis that it will be *adaptive* to an androcentric gender order in which engaging in obvious conflict is a liability for girls and women? The outlines of a story of girls' effectiveness at managing conflict under such conditions might begin to take shape.

Ethnographies of speaking are important tools to get at the everyday practices of speech communities. Discourse studies have a great deal to contribute to our understanding of how gender is actually 'done' in the world. Recent studies of the discourse of girls and boys in the early, middle and teenage years leave no doubt about the importance of competition and the existence of oppositional talk in girls' social interaction. These studies underscore the importance of explaining the relationship between gender and context. Interactions are governed by the conversational norms and practices of the local community. Goodwin's studies of the playground games of girls from the Central American community in Los Angeles (1995), and of street games of African-American girls in urban Philadelphia (1980), contradict the notion (see Lever, 1976) that girls' gaming behaviour and their concomitant talk is in any way sugar-coated or deficient when compared with boys'. In these activities in these speech communities, girls' arguments are 'richly textured'. They are as direct and unmitigated as boys' arguments, and their competitiveness can be as fierce.

To illustrate how cultural and situational differences can shape different contexts for talk, note that Goodwin's findings contrast with those of Hughes (1988), who found middle-class, white girls' playground conflict talk to be highly mitigated. In a study of talk in school, Camras (1984: 263) notes that between preschool and second grade, socially dominant middle-class girls learn to 'mask their exercise of power during conflicts with polite language'.

As researchers broaden the contexts in which conflict talk is studied, we find more variation. In a study of siblings in unstructured play at home (DeHart, 1996) a great deal of similarity between girls' and boys' discourse and conflict talk was found. Girls used a higher rate of unmitigated imperatives, prohibitions and directives than have been found in girls' peer play (Sachs, 1987). Both girls and boys used a lower rate of mitigated forms, such as joint directives, pretend directives and permission questions, than had been found in studies of peer play. Killen and Naigles (1995) find that girls and boys also use more similar speech patterns to negotiate conflict when they play in mixed-sex groups, while a comparison of speech patterns in same-sex groups show greater divergence and contrast between girls and boys.

The conclusion we might draw from this research is that if we looked at talk in enough different contexts within a culture and across cultures,

we could show that girls and boys have the same discourse com-
petencies, although they may draw on them differently, as their culture
allows, depending on the context for talk and the sex of their co-
participants. In some cultures, street play and playground games might
allow girls to engage in tougher talk than they could do in classrooms or
more formal settings. Sibling imaginative play at home in a white
Midwestern American community seems to be a context in which girls
can use less mitigated talk than they might attempt if they were playing
with friends. We need more of these cross-context and cross-cultural
comparisons.

Another way that recent work has challenged prior thinking about
gender and discourse are studies which have demonstrated that girls
often use a complex style of dispute talk, so that they can display
themselves as nice *and* be powerful at the same time. This seems to be
an accommodation to a gender system which values feminine silence
and propriety (in comparison with what is allowed males). Research is
finding that girls' competitive and oppositional behaviours often *co-
occur* with cooperation and mitigation (Eckert, 1990; Goodwin, 1980;
Hughes, 1988; Modan, 1994; Sheldon, 1992a; 1996a; Sheldon and
Johnson, 1994). In addition, studies of the discourse of Jewish women
(Modan, 1994; Schiffrin, 1992), Greek women (Kakavá, 1994), Samoan
women (Ochs, 1987), Tzeltal-speaking Tenehapan women (Brown,
1993), and others, show that women's freedom to be oppositional in
discourse (compared with men), and the contexts for it, varies from
culture to culture. Gendered speech is culturally relative to, and
historically situated in, a community's cultural practices. Looking at
speech communities across cultures and languages (or dialects), therefore, is an essential step to seeing the range of adaptations in female and
male discourse behaviours.

Restoring a more complex perspective: double-voice discourse

My own programme of research with a community of Midwestern
American preschoolers (Sheldon, 1990; 1992a; 1996a; Sheldon and
Johnson, 1994) questions the view that females are not effective at
managing conflict, or that they lack a competitive dynamic, when
compared with males. I come to this work not only as a linguist but as
the mother of daughters, having spent countless hours watching girls
interacting as siblings, in friendship groupings at home, on the
playground, and watching girls and boys inside a child care centre
and in school classrooms. In the remaining part of this chapter I turn to
an illustration of this complex conflict talk style, which I call *'double-
voice discourse'* (Sheldon, 1992a: 99). I argue that the claim that girls are
not as effective as boys in pursuing their agendas when faced with

opposition is false. Quite the contrary, girls in this community were extremely skilful in managing dissent. They got their agendas met without running amok of feminine cultural prescriptions to 'be nice' and to 'get along'.

It is my hypothesis that double-voice discourse is characteristic of *solidarity-based* groups – *male or female* – which are relationship-based, and in which harmony and collaboration are especially valued. Since 'being nice' is a gender prescription for girls in the Midwestern culture (as well as other cultures), my hypothesis is that this talk style is used more frequently by girls. However, boys do use it too when they have *the same social goals*. Double-voice discourse is a form of problem solving through dialogue in which the speaker demonstrates an orientation to the addressee's interests and goals. It is a conflict style in which the 'voice' of mitigation and social sensitivity is bound up with the 'voice' of self-interest and egocentricity. Direct confrontation is regulated so as not to get out of hand. Getting along relatively harmoniously and collaborating are highly valued norms in girls' groups. Unmitigated confrontation is, therefore, socially risky female behaviour because it flouts norms for feminine behaviour. By using double-voice discourse, girls can skilfully navigate between Scylla and Charybdis in dangerous social waters, adhering to gender prescriptions yet acting powerfully at the same time. Double-voice discourse is an important discourse practice that shapes and regulates girls' power struggles.

In groups and contexts, such as boys' indoor play groups, or girls' and boys' street play, where interaction might not be closely regulated by the goal of maintaining solidarity but where individual performance and achievement are legitimated and foregrounded, direct and aggravated forms of conflict talk, and the direct expression of confrontation and competition, may be socially acceptable. I call this latter talk style '*single-voice discourse*'. Interactants have the single orientation of pursuing their own self-interest without orienting to the perspective of the partner or tempering their self-interest with mitigation. The following are illustrations of these two styles. Double-voice discourse is a more elaborate and linguistically more complex style than single-voice discourse. This is not surprising, given the more complex agenda and the deep intersubjective waters which are being navigated.

The theory of double-voice discourse reorients the debate about gender differences in talk from one described simplistically in terms of gendered polarities to one that reframes the issues and behaviours in a more complex way. Double-voice discourse reflects the active engagement of the speaker, usually female, but not necessarily so, in verbal power plays and competition for access and privilege. It embodies conflict mediation skills in which the speaker confronts without appearing confrontational, clarifies issues without backing down, and uses linguistic mitigators to soften the blow, while pursuing her (or his) own wishes and making their agenda matter. In double-voice discourse, the speaker is responsive to the companion's point of view even while pursuing her own agenda. Self-assertion is mitigated and contextualized, but nevertheless effective.

The research

The conversations to be discussed here come from 36 middle-class, predominantly white, three-, four- and five-year-old preschool children in the Minneapolis–St Paul area of Minnesota. They were grouped into all-girl or all-boy triads and videotaped during unsupervised play at their day care centre for more than thirteen hours (Sheldon, 1990 and 1992a, contain discussions of the procedures used). The examples of conflict discussed here both involve one child's attempts to enter the play of another child. The conflicts include disagreements about sharing playthings. Entry into play with another child is often a difficult achievement even for socially competent children, and it is a process which often gives rise to conflict (Corsaro, 1981; Garvey, 1984).

Aggravated conflict talk among preschool boys

By way of contrast, consider an example of a dispute from a boys' triad that fits a familiar, hegemonic masculine cultural model of conflict, in which insistence and brute force can be acceptable strategies for trying to get what one wants. Examples of men in such conflict are not infrequent on television and in the movies. Linguistically aggravated and physically aggressive conflict exchanges of the sort in Example 1 have been found more often in boys' interaction than in girls' in this and other communities (see Goodwin, 1980; Leaper, 1991; Miller et al., 1986; Sheldon, 1990; 1992a). This conflict talk style uses direct, unmitigated, confrontational speech acts (also found for girls by Goodwin, 1980; Goodwin and Goodwin, 1987; 1995; DeHart, 1996; Killen and Naigles, 1995).

Examples 1: Boys' single-voice discourse. 'That's my phone'
Charlie (4.0) and Tony (4.1) are together. Tony is sitting on a small foam chair/couch and is pushing the buttons on a touch tone phone base that is on his lap. Charlie is nearby. (Emphasized words are capitalized.)

1 Tony: I pushed two squares [*giggles*], two squares like this. [*pushes phone buttons*]
2 Charlie: [*comes closer, puts his fist up to his ear and talks into an imaginary phone*] Hello!
3 Tony: [*puts his fist up to his ear and talks back*] Hello.
4 Charlie: [*picks up the receiver that is on Tony's chair*] No, that's my phone!

5 Tony: [*grabs the telephone cord and tries to pull the receiver away from Charlie*] No, Tha- ah, it's on MY couch. It's on MY couch, Charlie. It's on MY couch. It's on MY couch.

6 Charlie: [*ignoring Tony, holding onto the receiver, and talking into the telephone now*] Hi. [*walks behind Tony's chair, the telephone base is still on Tony's lap*]

7 Tony: [*gets off the couch, sets the phone base on the floor*] I'll rock the couch like this. [*he turns the foam chair over on top of the telephone base and leans on it as Charlie tries to reach for it under the chair*] Don't! That's my phone!

8 Charlie: [*pushes the chair off the telephone and moves it closer to himself, away from Tony*] I needa use it.

9 Tony: [*kneeling, sits back on his heels and watches Charlie playing with the phone*]

In this conflict each child tries to physically overpower the other in order to use the telephone. Neither child negotiates or tries to verbally persuade the other for a turn. No one voluntarily reconciles their wishes with the other child's. Insistence escalates rather than ends the opposition and leads to aggressive responses and a forceful resolution. Only a limited range of problem solving strategies are tried here. This pattern of conflict management among boys is discussed further by Coie (1987) and D. Shantz (1986).

Double-voice discourse in girls' conflict talk

The girls in the larger sample in this study also engaged in directly insistent confrontations, but in the more than six hours of social play that was recorded with the girls, no oppositional exchanges were found in their groups that even compared with Example 1, whereas similar instances of highly aggravated talk, insistence, or physical force occurred in other boys' examples. (For a further discussion of gender differences see Sheldon and Johnson, 1994.) Girls' solidarity-based conflict often involved a great deal of verbal mediation and negotiation, demonstrated a variety of verbal problem solving strategies, and showed an awareness of the other person's needs while trying to achieve one's own ends. As a result, some of the girls' exchanges became very long and verbally complex.

The following episode demonstrates the elaborate linguistic and interactional skills that four-year-old girls can use and the difficult and artful work they do in mediating opposition. It also shows the workings of a peer culture which contradicts cultural stereotypes that portray girls as passive, yielding, weak, or conflict-avoidant. Instead, we see a culture in which girls do resist and oppose one another in order to further their own wishes. This is one of several long episodes co-constructed by girls' groups in this study.

Example 2: Girls' double-voice discourse. A negotiational tour de force: 'Nurses getta do shots'

This conflict takes place between Arlene (4.9) and Elaine (4.6); Erica (4.2) is present briefly. They have been pretending that some dolls are sick children and they are nurses who are caring for them. A conflict develops over who will use some medical implements that are in the room. Elaine, who started enacting the role of nurse earlier than Arlene did, wants to keep control of the equipment. But Arlene wants to use something too. (Various techniques of double voicing are underlined and loud speech is indicated by capital letters. In addition, there are various techniques of unmitigated self-assertion.)

1   Arlene: Can I have that- that thing? [*referring to the blood pressure gauge in Elaine's lap*] I'm going to take my baby's temperature.
2   Elaine: [*looking up from talking on the telephone*] You can use it- you can use my temperature. Just make sure you can't use anything else unless you can ask. [*turns back to talking on the telephone*]

In 1, Arlene asks permission to use the blood pressure gauge. She gives a reason for her request. In 2, Elaine gives qualified agreement. She lets Arlene use the thermometer with restrictions, telling her to ask before she uses anything else. Although the girls are competing for goods here, there is an attempt to allow for a fair distribution. Elaine shows some flexibility by offering a concession, establishing 'a middle ground which moves toward the other position but still opposes it' (Vuchinich, 1990: 126). However, a mutual opposition subsequently unfolds.

3   Arlene: [*picks up thermometer from a nearby table and takes her baby's temperature*] Eighty-three! She isn't sick. Yahoo! May I? [*she asks Elaine, who is still on the telephone, if she can use the needle-less hypodermic syringe*]
4   Elaine: No, I'm gonna need to use the shot in a couple of minutes.
5   Arlene: But I- I need this though. [*asks in a beseeching tone, picks up the hypodermic syringe*]
6   Elaine: [*firmly*] Okay, just use it once.

In 3, Arlene makes a polite request to use Elaine's syringe, 'May I?', but in 4, Elaine denies the request with a flat 'no' followed by a qualification of her refusal; she explains that she will need to use the shot soon. In 5, Arlene returns with an opposing move, adopting Elaine's reason, insisting that she also 'needs' it, softening her demand with 'though' while she picks up the contested syringe. In 6, Elaine reluctantly agrees to let her use it, again offering a concession that establishes a middle ground, but she firmly constrains the use to 'just' one time.

7 Erica: [*whispers*] Arlene, let's play doctor.
8 Arlene: [*to Erica*] No, I'm gonna give her a shot on the-
9 Elaine: Hey, I'm the nurse. I'm the nurse. [*she puts down the phone and comes over to Arlene and the crib in which her doll is lying*] Arlene, remember, I'm the nurse, and the nurses getta do shots, remember?
10 Arlene: But I get to do some.
11 Elaine: Just a couple, okay?

In 8, Arlene starts giving her baby a shot, but in 9 Elaine wants to be in control of the syringe. First she responds directly. She addresses Arlene by name and requests that Arlene 'remember' Elaine's role. 'I'm the nurse,' Elaine asserts. She has adopted Arlene's pretend play frame of reference. Having a common frame of reference is a useful strategy for gaining entry to Arlene's play because it increases mutual involvement. This also provides a rationale for Elaine's access to the syringe: nurses have a certain role to play, namely, they 'getta do shots'. She follows this justification with a tag question 'remember?' which is intended to elicit agreement. It does elicit Arlene's token agreement and a request for another concession in 10 when Arlene says 'But I get to do some.' This is a mitigating response, here called a *yes-but strategy*, in which agreement prefaces disagreement (discussed further in Sheldon, 1992a; 1996a; Pomerantz, 1984). It is a partial agreement and partial disagreement, in which Arlene backs off a bit, acknowledges that Elaine will use the syringe, yet still pursues her own agenda and states her intention to use it too. The yes-but strategy allows for an appearance of agreement, while the partners continue to negotiate their action plans. In 11, Elaine again offers a concession, telling Arlene that she can do 'just a couple'. She follows this directive with a tag question that solicits agreement, 'okay?', although Arlene offers none.

All of Elaine's concessions with constraints allow her to hold onto her own agenda while accommodating her partner's agenda also. This is a form of double-voice discourse. However, although Elaine is accommodating Arlene's wishes, competition between the girls is actually escalating and intensifying because Arlene is pressing to keep control of the syringe for her own use and to administer to the doll in other nurse-like ways. The opposition over who has exclusive rights to administer to the doll grows. Whereas in 3 Arlene started out by asking permission to use the needle ('May I?'), she has now moved to directly asserting what she'll do, as in 12.

12 Arlene: I get to do some more things too. Now don't forget- now don't touch the baby until I get back, because it IS MY BABY! [*said to both of the other girls*] I'll check her ears, okay? [*puts down the syringe and picks up the ear scope*]
13 Elaine: Now I'll- and I'll give her- I'll have to give her [*the same doll*] a shot. [*picks up the syringe that Arlene has put down*]

14   Arlene: There can only be ONE thing that you- that- NO, she- she
               only needs one SHOT.
15   Elaine: Well, let's pretend it's another day that we have to look in
               her ears together.

At this point Elaine wants to give the doll a shot but in 12 Arlene has
ordered her not to touch 'her' baby. She announces she is not
constrained in what she can do with the baby and that she will check
the baby's ears. As Elaine has done previously, Arlene adds a tag
question, 'okay?', a marker that solicits agreement. Although Elaine
does not directly respond to the tag question, she continues to act as a
participant. In 13, she renounces her plans to give a shot, 'Now I'll- and
I'll give her- I'll have to give her a shot.' In two indirect statements in
14, in which no agent is mentioned, and the responsibility for deciding
who gives a shot is vaguely expressed, Arlene tries to cut Elaine out of
the action by stating that 'There can only be ONE thing' and the baby
'only needs one SHOT'. Both girls are equally determined to have their
own way. In 15, Elaine tries to get Arlene to consider an alternative
in which they can both participate. She reframes the situation and
responds in multiply mitigated ways. She opens with a delay, 'Well'.
She uses a joint directive 'let's' and introduces a new pretend scenario:
she displaces the time to 'another day' and the medical problem to her
'ears', in an effort to induce cooperation on a combined agenda, that is,
that 'we' will work 'together'.

In 16, the conflict continues to heat up. In answer to Elaine's suggestion that they look in the doll's ears together, Arlene replies with a
token agreement, 'yeah but', and nevertheless continues to demand to
examine the ears herself, directly ordering Elaine not to 'shot her'.

16   Arlene: No, no, yeah but I do the ear looking. Now don't SHOT-
               [lowering her voice but still insisting] DON'T SHOT HER! I'm
               the one who does all the shots, 'cause this is my baby!
17   Elaine: [whispers] Well- I'm the nurse and nurses get to do the
               shots.
18   Arlene: [spoken very intensely] An' me'- And men- well, then men
               get to do the shots too even 'cause men can be nurses.
               [taunting, slightly sing-song] But you can't shot her.

In 17 Elaine continues to mitigate by delaying, 'Well', and countering
with a reason for why she should give a shot, 'nurses get to do the
shots.' In 18, Arlene counters with a competing justification, that is
intended to take some of the force out of Elaine's claim: 'well, then men
get to do the shots too even 'cause men can be nurses'. Arlene indirectly
questions whether Elaine, as a female, has an exclusive right to give
shots. Arlene again orders her somewhat indirectly not to give a shot,
'But you can't shot her.'

19 Elaine: I'll have to shot her <u>after- after- after you listen- after you look in the ears</u>.
20 Erica: She [*Arlene*] already shot her even.
21 Elaine: We have- <u>she didn't do a shot on her finger</u>.
22 Arlene: But she did- she did- I DID TOO! Now don't shot her at all!
23 Elaine: We hafta do it- <u>Well</u>, I'm going to keep do it after she- this baby.
24 Arlene: [*intense but <u>lowered voice</u>*] Now DON'T YOU DARE!

In 19, Elaine insists 'I'll have to shot her', and also continues to offer a concession, that she will give the shot 'after you look in the ears'. When Erica says that Arlene 'already shot her', Elaine assertively persists within the pretend frame, inventively countering (by noting a shortcoming in Arlene's procedure) in 21 that 'she didn't do a shot on her finger', that is, that Arlene missed a spot and it needs to be done by Elaine. Thus, Elaine resists Arlene's attempts to exclude her, and instead creatively offers alternatives in which she can share in the action too.

Although both girls are developing a complex negotiation in double-voice discourse, Arlene, however, is gaining more in this struggle than Elaine is. In line 24, Arlene persists: she intensely, directly and threateningly orders Elaine to stop, 'Now DON'T YOU DARE!' Arlene doesn't shout, but instead mutes her voice by lowering it. As the confrontation reaches its peak of insistence, the girls' voices get lower and lower, not louder and louder with anger. In 25, Elaine directly orders Arlene, in an even lower voice:

25 Elaine: [*voice lowered more than Arlene's but equally intense*] Stop saying that! [*pause*] <u>Well, then</u> you can't come to my birthday!
26 Arlene: [*voice still lowered*] I don't want to come to your birthday.

Finally, Elaine leaves Arlene at the crib and goes back to the table.

As Elaine and Arlene escalate their dispute with words, instead of raising their voices in shouts or screams, which happens in the boys' example, their speaking voices paradoxically become more and more muted. There is a lack of consonance between the girls' angry words and their quieter and quieter tone. It is a dramatic example of the mitigation of the voice of self in their double-voice discourse. It seems that the muting of their speaking voices allows them to escalate the directness of their words and the confrontational nature of their demands and assertions. Notice also in 25 that the kind of threat that Elaine uses is one of social ostracism, 'you can't come to my birthday!', not one of physical attack which we saw in Example 1, 'I'll rock the couch like this.'

Gender differences in use of double-voice discourse

I have described a vivid example of double-voice discourse to give the reader a sense of the linguistic and interactional phenomena that may be involved. One can ask how characteristic double-voice discourse is for the preschool girls in this study compared with the boys. Two coders compared transcripts of half the girls in this study (nine) to those of half the boys in the study (nine). The girls were eight months younger, on average, than the boys. Although the boys had more mutual conflicts (56%) than the girls (44%), more of the girls' conflicts were sites for double-voice discourse (60%) than the boys' were (45%) (see Sheldon, 1992a for further details.) In addition, in more than thirteen hours of conversational interaction, no boys' conflict has been found which comes close to matching the girls' for elaborateness or length of double-voice discourse. On the other hand, there are a number of similar complex examples of girls' conflicts, both long and short, which contain elaborate examples of double-voice discourse.

Double-voice discourse as a powerful persuasion mode

The negotiation of the conflict between Elaine and Arlene is an example of the linguistic and pragmatic complexity that is often involved in double-voice discourse. The girls use multiple argument strategies which involve a variety of linguistic devices that can be used to soften conflict in order to be effective. In this example, Arlene was successful in getting what she wanted in part because Elaine was willing to negotiate numerous concessions. For the most part, the girls resist without being confrontational, justify themselves rather than give in, and use linguistic mitigators while trying to get what they want. Although both girls use double-voice discourse, the differences in how much they use and when they use it reflect differences in their ongoing successes in getting their way during the negotiation.

Double-voice discourse enabled the girls to have an extensive interaction even though they disagreed. It extended their involvement with one another as they negotiated access to the syringe, and particularly as Elaine tried to balance her own interests with Arlene's interests. It allowed play to go on without disruption.

Conclusion

The analysis of the conflict episode between Arlene and Elaine raises a number of issues for the study of gender and discourse. First, it demonstrates the communicative competence, attainable in early childhood, which these girls display in attempts to get their agendas met when they are faced with opposition (that is, 'managing conflict'). Instead of finding girls avoiding conflict or incompetent at resolving it, we find preschool girls who go to great lengths to develop complex ways to negotiate their dissent, maintaining involvement and avoiding social breakdown. They are skilfully using a variety of language resources to mediate and overcome opposition. The exchange between Arlene and Elaine demonstrates the challenge of self-assertion: staking out one's point of view or goal, motivating it with justifications in an attempt to persuade or deflect the person who is opposing the speaker, communicating in clear verbal terms, all the while maintaining a modicum of 'niceness'. This work requires a great degree of attentiveness to discourse processes in order to properly frame responses, and to maintain thematic cohesion and relevance. Responses are produced to a partner's prior move and are framed to accommodate or distance the partner's next move.

The length of the girls' negotiations reflects Elaine's persistence in creating conditions which will overcome Arlene's resistance and convince Arlene to accept her. It also shows an awareness of her partner's needs, and the utility of framing her needs in terms of her partner's and providing justifications (see Kyratzis, 1994 for a discussion of gender differences in preschoolers' use of justifications). The length of the negotiation is also an index of the importance to Elaine of joining in play with Arlene as well as the complexity of the social task they are trying to accomplish. The girls demonstrate a variety of problem solving strategies. This example is one of a number of long conflict episodes found in this study, primarily in girls' discourse. Such episodes are extremely complex for analysts to work with. But if we want to understand discourse practices in girls' groups then we have to pay attention to these longer and more elaborate oral texts.

Second, whereas these girls' conflict talk is not directly confrontational in the ways that boys' conflict can be, any claim that girls or women operate within an ethic of unalloyed 'harmony', 'cooperation', or 'collaboration' (Kolb, 1992; Leaper, 1991; Miller et al., 1986) must be rethought in the light of such examples of elaborate verbal work. There are dialectical forces operating in conflicts. Example 2 shows that the achievement of equilibrium and the construction of reciprocality is a delicate and fluid process that proceeds *simultaneously* in the dual directions of self-assertion *and* mitigation.

Third, the close analysis of conflict reveals complexities of human interaction that should make us cautious in undertaking evaluations or making generalizations about females and males which are drawn from studies using measures of central tendencies based on aggregated data and which do not describe actual interactions in any detail. Long and complex interactions, which are rarely studied in developmental conflict research, not only give us important insights into social processes, but also raise questions about individual variation, which as yet have not been well addressed in the gender and discourse literature. Analysis of such interactions demonstrates the wisdom of resisting simple labels for gendered behaviour. Our understanding of gender can be well served by explicit and extensive analysis of examples. This chapter provides the kind of situation-specific sequential analysis that is called for (for example, in Putallaz and Sheppard, 1992) in order to better understand children's social competence.

Fourth, Arlene and Elaine are not equally successful in getting their agendas met. One reason why this example is so interesting is because of what it shows us about girls' resistance to opposition. Whereas Elaine's accommodation in the face of opposition may be familiar to those of us in this culture (or similar ones), and whereas her accommodation certainly fits cultural stereotypes of female behaviour, the tenacity and resistance that are shown here in different ways by *each* girl as she pursues what she wants is a subject that is hardly discussed in the literature on the discourse of girls and women (exceptions have been noted in the work of Goodwin, for example 1980). In our collective cultural imagination, as well as in the conflict literature, we have a clearer sense of females as accommodating and flexible than we have of females as resisting and defending self-interest, particularly someone like Arlene.

When gender is defined as a polarity, such a framework doesn't theorize competition and control in female interaction, or harmony and cooperation in male interaction. Hence, we do not *expect* to find non-theorized behaviours for either category, such as resistance and competition among girls. This discussion shows that on both empirical and theoretical grounds a dualistic framework for theorizing gender is inadequate. We need to reframe our thinking about girls and women so that we can begin to see the constructive and powerful ways that they put opposition and resistance to work in their discourse and social interactions. We also need to see beyond the hegemonic stereotypes for boys and men.

I have demonstrated that close analysis of discourse can form a partnership with the construction of feminist theory and a more sophisticated theory of gender. Discourse analysis is a powerful tool that can reveal the complexity of everyday practices that are involved in 'doing gender', and can call into question generalizations about gender differences (about boys as well as girls) that simplify rather than reveal the intricacies of human behaviour.

Discourse is a complex human activity. Close analysis of the negotiation for access and control in the discourse of girls' social interaction can help us to reconsider claims about girls' management of dissent and expressions of power. It also brings the study of child language squarely into the middle of feminist theory-making.

This chapter has illustrated the sort of investigation that is necessary to counteract stereotypical and androcentric views of gender (both folkloric as well as academic) which privilege male talk and discount or overlook female talk. A culture prescribes norms of gender appropriateness.

However, we do not have enough empirical work to understand how, why, and when speakers accommodate to or resist these norms in social interaction. Some of the greatest challenges to future research on discourse and gender will be these: (1) developing a richer concept of gender that is consistent with the complexity and diversity of female and male behaviours in the world; (2) incorporating work on the discourse of gender resisters and reformulators, or those whose talk appears to not fit gender norms; (3) increasing our data base by studying more speech communities, and more varied ones, so that we can observe cross-community similarities and differences in discourse norms and practices; (4) studying the discourse of individuals who have experienced gender desocialization or resocialization, such as individuals in transgender communities but also individuals whose attitudes towards gender change in the course of a lifetime and who take up different alignments to gender stereotypes, norms, and practices; and (5) demonstrating the role that context plays in gendering discourse, for example, comparing the behaviour of individuals across contexts in which their speech might vary. There is much exciting work to be done.

Notes

Parts of this paper are from Sheldon (1992b).

References

Anderson, Elaine (1990) *Speaking with Style: the Sociolinguistic Skills of Children*. London: Routledge.

Baran, G. (1987) 'Teaching girls science', in M. McNeil (ed.), *Gender and Expertise*. London: Free Association Books.

Bem, Sandra (1993) *The Lenses of Gender*. New Haven: Yale University Press.

Bing, Janet and Bergvall, Victoria (1996) 'The question of questions: beyond binary thinking', in Victoria Bergvall, Janet Bing and Alice Freed (eds), *Language and Gender Research: Theory and Method*. London: Longman. pp. 1–30.

Brown, Penelope (1993) 'Gender, politeness and confrontation in Tenehapa', in Deborah Tannen (ed.), *Gender and Conversational Interaction*. Oxford: Oxford University Press. pp. 144–62.

Camras, Linda (1984) 'Children's verbal and nonverbal communication in a conflict situation', *Ethnology and Sociobiology*, 5: 257–68.

Coates, Jennifer (1993) *Women, Men and Language*, 2nd edn. London: Longman.

Coie, John D. (1987) 'An analysis of aggressive episodes: age and peer status differences'. Paper presented at the Biennial Meeting of the Society for Research in Child Development, Baltimore, MD.

Connell, Robert (1987) *Gender and Power*. Stanford: Stanford University Press.

Corsaro, William (1981) 'Friendship in the nursery school: social organization in a peer environment', in Stephen R. Asher and John M. Gottman (eds), *The*

Development of Children's Friendships. New York: Cambridge University Press. pp. 207–41.

Deaux, B. and Kite, M.E. (1987) 'Thinking about gender', in Brenda Hess and Mary M. Ferree (eds), *Analyzing Gender: a Handbook of Social Science Research.* Newbury Park, CA: Sage.

DeHart, G. (1996) 'Gender and mitigation in 4-year-old's pretend play-talk with siblings', *Research on Language in Social Interactions,* 29(1): 81–96.

Eckert, Penny (1990) 'Cooperative competition in adolescent "girl talk"', *Discourse Processes,* 13(1): 91–122.

Eckert, Penny and McConnell-Ginet, Sally (1992) 'Think practically and look locally: language and gender as community-based practice', *Annual Review of Anthropology,* 21: 461–90.

Eckert, Penny and McConnell-Ginet, Sally (1995) 'Constructing meaning, constructing selves', in Kira Hall and Mary Bucholtz (eds), *Gender Articulated: Language and the Socially Constructed Self.* New York: Routledge. pp. 469–507.

Freed, Alice (1995) 'Language and gender', *Annual Review of Applied Linguistics,* 15: 3–22.

Garvey, Catherine (1984) *Children's Talk.* Cambridge: Harvard University Press.

Garvey, Catherine and Eisenberg, Ann (1981) 'Children's use of verbal strategies in resolving conflicts', *Discourse Processes,* 4: 149–70.

Goodwin, Marjorie H. (1980) 'Directive–response speech sequences in girls' and boys' task activities', in Sally McConnell-Ginet, Ruth Borker and Nelly Furman (eds), *Women and Language in Literature and Society.* New York: Praeger. pp. 157–73.

Goodwin, Marjorie H. (1995) 'Co-construction in girls' hopscotch', *Research on Language and Social Interaction,* 28: 261–81.

Goodwin, Marjorie H. and Goodwin, Charles (1987) 'Children's arguing', in Susan U. Philips, Susan Steele and Christine Tanz (eds), *Language, Gender and Sex in Comparative Perspective.* New York: Cambridge University Press. pp. 200–48.

Hare-Mustin, Rachel (1988) 'The meaning of difference: gender theory, postmodernism, and psychology', *American Psychologist,* 43(6): 455–64.

Hughes, Linda (1988) 'But that's not *really* mean: competing in a cooperative mode', *Sex Roles,* 669–87.

Kakavá, Christina (1994) '"Do you want to get engaged baby?": the cultural construction of gender in Greek conversation', in Mary Bucholtz, Anita C. Liang, Laurel Sutton and Caitlin Hines (eds), *Cultural Performances: Proceedings of the Third Berkeley Women and Language Conference.* Berkeley, CA: Linguistics Department, University of California–Berkeley. pp. 344–54.

Kalčik, Susan (1975) '". . . like Ann's gynecologist or the time I was almost raped": personal narratives in women's rap groups', *Journal of American Folklore,* 88: 3–11.

Keller, Evelyn F. and Moglen, Helene (1987) 'Competition: a problem for academic women', in H.E. Longino and V. Miner (eds), *Competition: a Feminist Taboo?* New York: Feminist Press. pp. 21–37.

Killen, Melanie and Naigles, Letitia (1995) 'Preschool children pay attention to their addressees: effects of gender composition on peer disputes', *Discourse Processes,* 19: 329–46.

Kolb, Deborah (1992) 'Women's work: peacemaking behind the organizational scene', in Deborah Kolb and Jean M. Bartunek (eds), *Hidden Conflict in Organizations: Uncovering Behind-the-Scenes Disputes.* Newbury Park, CA: Sage.

Kyratzis, Amy (1994) 'Gender differences in the use of persuasive justification in children's pretend play', in Kira Hall, Mary Bucholtz and Birch Moonwomon (eds), *Locating Power: Proceedings of the Second Berkeley Women and Language Conference*. Berkeley, CA: Linguistics Department, University of California–Berkeley. pp. 326–37.

Lakoff, Robin (1992) 'The silencing of women', in Kira Hall, Mary Bucholtz and Birch Moonwomon (eds), *Locating Power: Proceedings of the Second Berkeley Women and Language Conference*. Berkeley, CA: Linguistics Department, University of California–Berkeley. pp. 344–55.

Lakoff, Robin (1995) 'Cries and whispers: the shattering of the silence', in Kira Hall and Mary Bucholtz (eds), *Gender Articulated: Language and the Socially Constructed Self*. New York: Routledge. pp. 25–50.

Leaper, Campbell (1991) 'Influence and involvement in children's discourse: age, gender and partner effects', *Child Development*, 62: 797–811.

Lever, Janet (1976) 'Sex differences in the games children play', *Social Problems*, 23: 478–87.

Longino, Helen and Miner, Valerie (1987) 'A feminist taboo?', in Valeria Miner and Helen E. Longino (eds), *Competition: a Feminist Taboo?* New York: Feminist Press. pp. 1–7.

Maccoby, Eleanor (1986) 'Social groupings in childhood: their relationship to prosocial and antisocial behavior in boys and girls', in Dan Olweus, Jeanne Block and Marion Radke-Yarrow (eds), *Development of Antisocial and Prosocial Behavior*. San Diego: Academic Press. pp. 263–84.

Maltz, Daniel and Borker, Ruth (1982) 'A cultural approach to male–female miscommunication', in John Gumperz (ed.), *Language and Social Identity*. Cambridge: Cambridge University Press. pp. 196–216.

McTear, Michael (1985) *Children's Conversation*. New York: Basil Blackwell.

Mendoza-Denton, Norma (1995) 'Pregnant pauses: silence and authority in the Anita Hill–Clarence Thomas Hearings', in Kira Hall and Mary Bucholtz (eds), *Gender Articulated: Language and the Socially Constructed Self*. New York: Routledge. pp. 50–66.

Miller, Patrice, Danaher, Dorothy and Forbes, David (1986) 'Sex-related strategies for coping with interpersonal conflict in children aged five and seven', *Developmental Psychology*, 22: 543–8.

Modan, Galey (1994) 'Pulling apart is coming together: the use and meaning of opposition in the discourse of Jewish American women', in Mary Bucholtz, Anita C. Liang, Laurel Sutton and Caitlin Hines (eds), *Cultural Performances: Proceedings of the Third Berkeley Women and Language Conference*. Berkeley, CA: Linguistics Department, University of California–Berkeley. pp. 501–8.

Ochs, Elinor (1987) 'The impact of stratification and socialization on men's and women's speech in Western Samoa', in Susan U. Philips, Susan Steele and Christine Tanz (eds), *Language, Gender, and Sex in Comparative Perspective*. New York: Cambridge University Press. pp. 50–70.

Olsen, Tillie (1978) *Silences*. New York: Dell.

Pomerantz, Anita (1984) 'Agreeing and disagreeing with assessments: some features of preferred/dispreferred turn shapes', in J. Maxwell Atkinson and John Heritage (eds), *Structures of Social Interaction: Studies in Conversation Analysis*. New York: Cambridge University Press. pp. 57–101.

Putallaz, Martha and Sheppard, Blair (1992) 'Conflict management and social competence', in Carolyn U. Shantz and Willard W. Hartup (eds), *Conflict in*

Child and Adolescent Development. New York: Cambridge University Press. pp. 330–55.

Rich, Adrienne (1979) *On Lies, Secrets, and Silence*. New York: W.W. Norton.

Russ, Joanna (1983) *How to Suppress Women's Writing*. London: Women's Press.

Sachs, Jaqueline (1987) 'Preschool boys' and girls' language use in pretend play', in Susan U. Philips, Susan Steele and Christine Tanz (eds), *Language, Gender and Sex in Comparative Perspective*. New York: Cambridge University Press. pp. 178–88.

Scheman, Naomi (1997) 'Queering the center and centering the queer: reflections on transsexuals and secular Jews', in Diana Tietjens Meyers (ed.), *Feminists Rethink the Self*. Boulder, CO: Westview Press. pp. 124–62.

Schiffrin, Deborah (1992) 'Taking the role of another', in Kira Hall, Mary Bucholtz and Birch Moonwomon (eds), *Locating Power: Proceedings of the Second Berkeley Women and Language Conference*. Berkeley, CA: Linguistics Department, University of California–Berkeley. pp. 515–27.

Shantz, Carolyn U. (1987) 'Conflicts between children', *Child Development*, 58: 283–305.

Shantz, David W. (1986) 'Conflict, aggression and peer status: an observational study', *Child Development*, 57: 1322–32.

Sheldon, Amy (1990) 'Pickle fights: gendered talk in preschool disputes', *Discourse Processes*, 13(1): 5–31. Reprinted in Deborah Tannen (ed.) (1993), *Gender and Conversational Interaction*. Oxford: Oxford University Press. pp. 83–109.

Sheldon, Amy (1992a) 'Conflict talk: sociolinguistic challenges to self-assertion and how young girls meet them', in *Talk in the Study of Socialization and Development*, special issue of *Merrill-Palmer Quarterly*, 38(1): 95–117.

Sheldon, Amy (1992b) 'Preschool girls' discourse competence: managing conflict', in Kira Hall, Mary Bucholtz and Birch Moonwomon (eds), *Locating Power: Proceedings of the Second Berkeley Women and Language Conference*. Berkeley, CA: Linguistics Department, University of California–Berkeley. pp. 528–39.

Sheldon, Amy (1996a) 'You can be the baby brother but you aren't born yet: preschool girls' negotiation for power and access in pretend play', *Research on Language in Social Interaction*, 29(1): 57–80.

Sheldon, Amy (1996b) 'Constituting gender through talk in childhood: conversations in parent–child, peer and sibling relationships', *Research on Language in Social Interaction*, 29(1): 1–5.

Sheldon, Amy and Johnson, Diana (1994) 'Preschool negotiators: gender differences in double-voice discourse as a conflict talk style in early childhood', in Blair Sheppard, Ron Lewicki and Robert Bies (eds), *Research on Negotiation in Organizations*, vol. 4. Greenwich, CT: JAI Press. pp. 37–67. Reprinted in Jenny Cheshire and Peter Trudgill (eds) (1997), *The Sociolinguistics Reader*, vol. 2. London: Edward Arnold.

Thorne, Barrie (1990) 'Children and gender: constructions of difference', in Deborah Rhode (ed.), *Theoretical Perspectives on Sexual Difference*. New Haven, CT: Yale University Press.

Vuchinich, Samuel (1990) 'The sequential organization of closing in verbal family conflict', in Allen Grimshaw (ed.), *Conflict Talk*. New York: Cambridge University Press. pp. 118–38.

Wodak, Ruth and Benke, G. (1997) 'Gender as a sociolinguistic variable: new perspectives on variation studies', in Florian Coulmas (ed.), *The Handbook of Sociolinguistics*. Cambridge, MA: Blackwell. pp. 127–50.

10

WOMEN'S FRIENDSHIPS, WOMEN'S TALK

Jennifer Coates

In this chapter I shall explore the links between gender, talk and friendship. Having friends is something most of us take for granted. This means that the things we do in order to make friends and to sustain friendship are so much part of our everyday social practice that they are pretty much invisible to us. But doing friendship is a significant accomplishment: some people find it difficult, or get it wrong; others never grasp what it means to be 'a friend'.

Friendship, according to recent research, involves some or all of the following components: taking part in shared activities; developing a sense of trust and mutual support; being able to relax and 'be yourself'; having your sense of who you are validated (see Faderman, 1985; Hey, 1996; Johnson and Aries, 1983a; Kennedy, 1986; O'Connor, 1992; Wulff, 1988). But friendship varies from group to group, and seems to be gendered. Contemporary accounts of male and female patterns of friendship (Johnson and Aries, 1983a; 1983b; Pleck, 1975; Miller, 1983; O'Connor, 1992; Seidler, 1989) suggest the following contrasts: women's friendships are characterized by intimacy, mutual self-disclosure and a focus on talk, while men's friendships are characterized by sociability, a lack of self-disclosure, and a focus on activity.

The distinction between intimacy and sociability comes from the work of Joseph Pleck, who argues that, in the case of the American male, friendships are sociable rather than intimate: 'Male sociability is closely connected with male sex-role training and performance and is not characteristically a medium for self-exploration, personal growth or the development of intimacy' (1975: 233). Stuart Miller says in the preface to his book on men's friendships: 'Most men . . . will admit they are disappointed in their friendships with other men . . . [these] are generally characterized by thinness, insincerity, and even chronic wariness' (1983: xi). The findings of these American researchers are echoed by Victor Seidler, a social theorist working in Britain. Seidler argues that 'masculinity is an essentially negative identity learnt through defining itself against emotionality and connectedness' (1989: 7), and goes on: 'We [that is, men] learn to identify our sense of self so strongly with our individual achievements and successes in the public world of work that we do not realise the damage this may do to our capacities for open and loving relationships with others' (1989: 18).

Fern Johnson and Elizabeth Aries carried out a study to investigate the meaning of friendship for American adults. They gave a questionnaire on same-sex friendship to 176 college students, as well as interviewing twenty women and twenty men in a New England city. Their findings support those of other researchers. About men, they say: 'To the degree that activity, behavioral exchange, and light conversation replace a deeper sharing between male friends, their abilities to articulate personal concerns and to engage close friends in the solving of personal problems are probably diminished' (Johnson and Aries, 1983b: 235). One of the most interesting findings of their study was that talk is 'the substance of women's friendship' (1983a: 354).

This chapter will draw on a corpus of spontaneous conversations between women friends, and on a series of ethnographic interviews with women.[1] I shall attempt to show that, for women, talking with friends is constitutive of friendship; it is through talking that we do 'being friends'.

Women's friendships

Throughout history and in vastly different cultures, friendship between women has been a significant part of our lives. This was largely ignored – or denied – until recently. With the upsurge of interest in women's lives, women's friendship has become a topic of interest to historians, literary critics, philosophers, theologians, sociologists, anthropologists and folklorists. Social historians, for example, have discovered the lost history of women's friendship and have demonstrated that, while it may take different forms in different periods of history, it is a permanent strand in the social tapestry (Faderman, 1985; Smith-Rosenberg, 1975). Feminist philosophers and theologians have discovered in female friendship a source of inspiration, a model for good human relationships (Hunt, 1991; Raymond, 1986). Sociologists have carried out research on, and have thus made visible, the friendship patterns of young women, older women, working class women, middle class women, heterosexual women and lesbian women (Gouldner and Strong, 1987; O'Connor, 1992; O'Neill, 1993; Rubin, 1985; Wulff, 1988). Anthropologists have explored the way friendship varies from culture to culture, but at the same time have demonstrated the key role female friendship plays in women's lives, whether on Crete, where the harshness of women's circumscribed lives is made bearable by friendship with other women, or in central Australia, where solidarity and mutual support are vital in the maintenance of aboriginal women's traditional practices (Bell, 1993; Hamilton, 1981; Kennedy, 1986). Folklorists have asserted the value of women's culture, the collaborative folklore enacted in the privacy of the home, among women friends (Jordan and Kalčik, 1985).

Friendship is unlike other close relationships we have in our lives: there are no formal contracts, no socially accepted rituals, no rites of passage associated with it. It is also unusual in that the relationship of friendship is based on equality. Even when there are differences of age of social class or ethnic background, friendship can only be sustained – will only deserve the name – if participants treat each other as equals, and adhere to an ethic of reciprocity. In other words, friendship is a symmetrical relationship. Most relationships in our lives are asymmetrical: parent–child, employer–employee, customer–shop assistant, etc. And it can be argued that, as long as societies construct women and men as unequal, then heterosexual partnerships are also asymmetrical.[2]

This means that friendships have a key role in our lives, providing us with an arena where we give and receive support and where we explore ideas about the world and our place in it. But it is all too easy to take friendship for granted. This point is forcefully made by Drusilla Modjeska in her book *Poppy*:

> Whatever has happened to me, or has not, with lovers and husbands . . . continuity and security have been built on the excellence of friendship; and when I look at [my mother]'s life I can see that this was so for her too. Yet these connections between women are taken for granted, a backdrop to the real business of life: husbands, children, jobs. It takes only the slightest change of focus to see that these neglected intimacies . . . can offer the terms on which we best learn to be ourselves. (1990: 309)

This claim – that it is friendship with other women which offers us 'the terms on which we best learn to be ourselves' – is a very strong one, but it is surely part of the feminist enterprise to attempt the 'change of focus' that Modjeska speaks of. So we need to ask how friendship is able to offer us the terms on which we can best learn to be ourselves. I would argue that it is language, the interactive talk that goes on between people, which plays a key role in our learning to be ourselves (see Gergen, 1987; Harré, 1987; Taylor, 1991). The self, it is argued, does not pre-exist conversation but arises dialogically within conversation. As Weedon (1987) puts it, language is 'the place where our sense of ourselves, our subjectivity, is constructed'.

The centrality of talk to women's friendships is a key finding of research in the area (Hey, 1996; Gouldner and Strong, 1987; Johnson and Aries, 1983a; McCabe, 1981; Rubin, 1985; Wulff, 1988). This finding was supported by the responses I got in interviews. When I asked women what they did with their women friends, they said 'Talk', or, more emphatically, 'We talk, primarily we talk, we never stop'. One young woman said: 'For me just what I remember about the relationship is . . . you know the amount of time we just spent sitting around and talking'.

Moreover these women are adamant that their conversations with each other are fundamental to their friendships, and that these conversations give them a very particular sort of pleasure. One of them said to me about evenings in mixed company: 'I mean, you know at the end of the evening you feel, yes, dissatisfied . . . whereas when I [spend an evening] with Anna and Liz I come home and I feel like we've talked about what we wanted to . . . it's undescribable'.[3] Another woman described conversation with women friends as 'absolutely fundamental . . . the blood of life'.

Women's talk

In this section I will summarize the linguistic strategies women use in talk with friends. These linguistic strategies are not arbitrary, but highly functional in terms of the goals of women's friendship. The primary goal of talk between women friends is the construction and maintenance of close and equal social relationships. This means that the linguistic strategies deployed by women friends are designed to construct and maintain connection and to minimize social distance. (The conventions for the transcriptions are given in the appendix to this chapter.)

Telling stories

Stories are an intrinsic part of the talk of women friends. Telling stories fulfils women friends' need to keep in touch with each other's lives; moreover, hearing about others' experience helps to place our own experience in an explanatory framework. The exchange of stories follows a pattern of mirroring, a significant strategy in women's friendly talk where speaker A's contribution is matched or mirrored by speaker B. In particular, the anecdotes which are told as part of reciprocal self-disclosure are a key way of 'doing' friendship. Stories also serve to introduce new topics or to develop topics. The following two stories, from a conversation between two friends, are part of the topic 'Illness'. They illustrate the way stories are balanced as women friends mirror each other's contributions. This topic was initiated by Karen with a story about her father and his recent attacks of abdominal pain. Despite the humour of parts of her story, it is apparent that she is worried about these attacks. Here's the second part of this story:

> Anyway Doris phoned me Friday
> and he's only had one attack in the last two weeks
> and she's- I said, 'He told me it was wind'.
> She said, 'Well I know you're going to think this is crazy
> but since he's had his new teeth he's only had one attack'.
> I said, 'Pardon?'

She said, 'Well if you think, if you've got teeth that don't fit properly you
   can't chew.
So you take your f- '
You know what it's like when you don't chew your food,
and since he's had these new teeth he's had the one attack.

Pat responds with a story which not only mirrors Karen's, but which is
designed to reassure her, that is, to confirm her hypothesis that her
father's problem is to do with his digestion rather than his heart. Here is
Pat's mirroring story:

You know Bob Parry who used to live next door to us at Norton Road, the
   butcher,
He had- oh years ago, he had two or was it three terrible attacks where he
   passed out.
And the first time it happened it was in the middle of the night.
He woke up in bed with this excruciating pain in his chest,
staggered out of bed and collapsed
and went unconscious on the floor,
and he and his wife obviously thought he's had a heart attack
[. . .]
and it- that was indigestion.

Pat's story mirrors Karen's: hers, like Karen's, involves an older male
protagonist, and he too has an acute attack involving pain in the chest/
abdomen. In Pat's story, the diagnosis is known: the pain was the result
of indigestion, and was not a heart attack. With their emphasis on
people and places, women's stories function to ground us in the everyday world and allow us to reflect on our everyday experiences. They
allow us to explore themes of connection, of the importance of acting in
conjunction with others and of the foolhardiness of acting alone.
Through story-telling we can draw on humour to talk about problematic
issues. Story-telling plays a very important part in our construction of
ourselves as women and as friends.

Hedging

Hedges (words and phrases such as *maybe, sort of, I mean*) have multiple
functions: they can express shades of doubt and confidence; they allow
us to be sensitive to others' feelings; they help us in the search for the
right words to express what we mean; they help us to avoid playing the
expert. The first of these functions – to express doubt and confidence –
is basic, but less significant in terms of women's friendships. The other
three functions all have an important role in the maintenance of
friendship.

If friendship is the arena in which we can most completely 'be ourselves', then obviously we need to be able to draw on resources to protect ourselves when we make ourselves vulnerable. But we also need to be sensitive to our friends' feelings. In the following example, Bea and her friends are discussing child sexual abuse, and are trying to work out why girl victims of abuse are often treated unsympathetically.

> Bea: what happens to women sexwise is their fault/ and I mean I think it's just that taken down- extending it to little girls/

Bea is aware that this is a sensitive topic, and the hedges she uses – *I mean, I think* and *just* – signal sensitivity to her addressees (who might find the position controversial) as well as sensitivity to her own need to protect her face. Because we often discuss sensitive topics with our closest friends, and because mutual self-disclosure is criterial for female friendship, then linguistic forms which allow us to pay attention to the face-needs of all participants are a vital part of our repertoire.

Being able to search for the right words to say what we mean is also important in establishing a close relationship. In the following example, Helen is talking about her younger daughter. She is trying to describe the bad situation that had existed at her daughter's primary school, and contrasts this with how well she's settled down at her new secondary school:

> Helen: she really loves it/ and she's somebody that was really being . sort of labelled as somebody that wasn't really- was anti-school almost at Riversdale Road [*primary school*]/

Helen searches for a word to describe what was happening to her daughter at Riversdale Road school, and settles on *labelled*. Notice that in this example, the pause precedes the hedge *sort of*, but Helen's struggle for words has already been signalled by the hedge *really*. As she continues to describe this situation she begins an utterance *somebody that wasn't really-*. Her search for words leads her to the term *anti-school*, which expresses what she is trying to say, but which means she has to rephrase her utterance, changing *wasn't* to *was*. The hedges here also arise from the sensitivity of the topic, and from Helen's need to protect her own face. It is characteristic of hedges that they perform several functions simultaneously: they are extremely versatile linguistic forms.

Women friends allow each other time to 'struggle with words', as one of the women put it in her interview: 'Talking with women I'm- I'm much happier about struggling around how to say things . . . and also women give you time to struggle with it'. Inasfar as talking with others gives us the opportunity to explore possible selves, different versions of 'I', then feeling accepted, feeling confident that we can say anything and not be judged, allows us space to grow. It also allows us space to rehearse existing knowledge and to explore new knowledges. These are important claims which I shall come back to later in the chapter.

Hedging also allows us to avoid expert status. In order to 'do' friendship, we want to avoid anything that will increase social distance between us and our friends. Talking about a subject where we have some expertise can potentially open up distance, but the evidence is that women friends use hedges judiciously to downplay their expert status. In the example below, the speaker (Meg) is a psychologist who is familiar with the process being described in the discussion of child abuse. Her use of *sort of* makes her appear less fluent, and thus avoids opening up distance between participants.

[discussion of child abuse]

Meg: they can <u>sort of</u> um test that out by . showing people <u>sort of</u> video tapes/

In terms of the goals of friendship, it is more important to preserve equality with friends than to gain status as individuals.

Hedges also play an important role in the maintenance of the collaborative floor (see below). They help to preserve openness and to avoid closure and conflict. In a collaborative floor, the group voice takes precedence, which means that speakers need to avail themselves of linguistic forms like hedges which enable them to say what they mean without blocking others from making their own personal statements.

Questions

Questions, like hedges, are multi-functional. Many of these functions construct and sustain friendship. For example, both questions and tag questions function to draw speakers into conversation and to keep conversations going. They help us to check that we are still 'in tune' with each other, and allow us to ask for help when we're stuck for a word. Questions are also used to invite friends to tell stories. Moreover, they are a useful resource for speakers who are trying to protect their own face and that of their addressees: asking a question is much less threatening than making an assertion. We also use questions in the discussion of controversial topics to introduce a different point of view without overtly disagreeing with another speaker. In this way we maintain the collaborative floor (see below).

Rhetorical questions are used frequently in the talk of women friends. They are a way of expressing general truths, which assert the groups' world view and check that consensus still exists. In a discussion of a headteacher accused of abusing children in his care, Sue asks: *but how could the staff not know?* She doesn't expect an answer, but uses the question as a way of expressing the moral indignation of the group. Tag questions are also used to check the taken-for-grantedness of what is being said. Liz, for example, says *it's strange isn't it? the life some people lead*. Again, she doesn't expect an answer, but uses the tag as a way of confirming the shared world of the group of friends.

In terms of avoiding playing the expert, questions are a valuable resource, emphasizing the shared quest for answers rather than individual knowledge. Fundamentally, questions are a way of expressing solidarity and connection. They are used with great skill by women who exploit them at the interactional rather than the informational level, as part of 'doing' friendship.

Repetition

Repetition is a regular feature of the talk of women friends. It is a powerful way of affirming the group voice, since it means that two or more speakers say the same thing in some form or another. Repetition can take place at the level of words or phrases or clauses; it can involve grammar and meaning as well as vocabulary. In the following example, Bea's utterance repeats what Mary says lexically, syntactically and semantically, with just a minor change of wording in the verb (underlines indicate repetition):

```
[topic: child abuse]
- - - - - - - - - - - - - - - - - - - - - - - - - - - - - - - - - -
Bea:    I mean in order to accept that idea you're
- - - - - - - - - - - - - - - - - - - - - - - - - - - - - - - - - -
Bea:    having to .                        ⌈ completely
Mary:           mhm . completely review your ⌊ view of your
- - - - - - - - - - - - - - - - - - - - - - - - - - - - - - - - - -
Bea:    change your view of your husband/
Mary:   husband/
- - - - - - - - - - - - - - - - - - - - - - - - - - - - - - - - - -
```

Repetition functions primarily to signal solidarity between women friends. Because women treat talk with friends as a kind of jam session, repetition – that is, saying the same things as each other and using the same linguistic patterns as each other – becomes a powerful symbol of the connection we feel with each other.

The collaborative floor

When speakers choose to establish a collaborative floor (Edelsky, 1993; Coates, 1997) rather than a one-at-a-time floor (Sacks et al., 1974), they are choosing to do friendship or intimacy. While the single floor prioritizes the individual speaker and the individual speaker's turn, the collaborative floor prioritizes the group and symbolizes connection between speakers.

The collaborative floor in the talk of women friends is characterized by two strategies in particular: the shared construction of utterances and overlapping talk. When friends share in the construction of utterances, they are demonstrating in a very concrete way that they can operate as if they were a single speaker: operating as a single speaker is a powerful way of doing friendship. Further, women friends use overlapping speech as a way of joining in together, of sharing the floor (not as a way of grabbing a turn). In the example above (where Bea and Mary talk about child abuse), the two friends share in the construction of an utterance: Bea begins with *I mean in order to accept that idea you're having to* and Mary continues *completely review your view of your husband*. They also overlap, as Bea says *change your view of your husband*, while Mary is still talking. As this example illustrates, when two or more friends speak at the same time, on the same theme, the resulting polyphony is iconic of connection. Women friends also use minimal responses and laughter to assert their presence in the shared conversational space, and to maintain connections between each other.

The work required to establish and maintain a collaborative floor is work that is constitutive of friendship. Every linguistic strategy typical of the collaborative floor serves this purpose: this includes the strategies mentioned already (jointly constructed utterances and overlapping speech) as well as others such as shorter turns, repetition between speakers, and joking and teasing. The collaborative floor is qualitatively as well as quantitatively different from one-at-a-time turn-taking. Fundamentally this is because the collaborative floor is a shared space: what is said is construed as being the voice of the group rather than of the individual. This emphasis on the connection between speakers makes the collaborative floor a powerful way of doing friendship.

Communicative competence and friendship

This summary of linguistic strategies and their role in doing friendship is potentially misleading. I don't want to give the idea that to accomplish friendship through talk, women speakers just help themselves from a smorgasbord of linguistic features such as stories or hedges or questions. Knowing how to be a friend involves more than this. Knowing how to be a friend is a crucial part of our communicative competence. The phrase 'communicative competence' was coined by Dell Hymes (1971) to describe the repertoire of skills that each of us develops as we take our place in a particular speech community. Linguists often restrict their attention to linguistic competence, that is, a native speaker's knowledge of the grammatical structure of their language. But Hymes pointed out that even if you had perfect linguistic competence in a given language, but you didn't know when to join in talk, when to remain silent, when to tell a joke, when to laugh (all crucial aspects of communicative competence), then you would not be judged a competent member of that particular speech community.

The women whose conversations I have analysed demonstrate their communicative competence, both in the broad sense outlined in the previous paragraph, and in the more specialized sense of knowing how to be a friend. One strong piece of evidence for the idea of a specialized competence for 'doing friendship' through talk is that, as competent members of the speech community, we are immediately aware if someone gets it wrong.

One group of people who consistently 'get it wrong' is the group who suffer from autism. Psychologists working on autism argue that one reason no one understands this condition is that no one really understands the processes involved in becoming a healthy well-functioning human being. One of the most striking features of people suffering from autism is their inability to make friends, or even to understand what a friend is. Peter Hobson, a developmental psychologist working on autism, describes a twenty-year-old man he was involved in caring for at the Maudsley Hospital in London as follows:

> this individual had a number of preoccupations, but foremost amongst these was his inability to grasp what a 'friend' is. He would ask again and again: 'Are you a friend?', 'Is he a friend?', and so on. The ward staff made every effort to teach him the meaning of the word 'friend', they even found someone to act as a 'befriender' to accompany him on outings to the local shopping centre. All this was to no avail – he seemed unable to fathom what a 'friend' is. (1993: 5)

This experience and subsequent reflection on the nature of friendship and the nature of autism led Hobson to interrogate more closely the concept of 'friend'. How do we come to understand it? What is it that we 'do' in order to be 'friends' with someone? He makes the important point that you can't get to know what a friend is simply by observing. In order to know what it means to be a friend, you have to 'do' friendship, that is, be involved in interpersonal relationships of a particularly close and reciprocal kind. And this means talking. People suffering from autism have difficulty with interpersonal relations of all kinds, but, in Hobson's view, their inability to understand what a 'friend' is is fundamentally related to their 'deficient sense of self' (1993: 3).

These new insights into the nature of autism suggest that the talk we do with our friends is profoundly important. It seems that 'doing friendship' is vital to development and vital to our becoming well-functioning human beings. It is ironic that women's talk has over the centuries been viewed as trivial or self-indulgent. Women's subcultures revolve around talk: this should now be recognized, not as one of our weaknesses, but as one of our strengths.

Women's friendship, women's knowledge

Friendship is a powerful interpersonal relationship which provides us with a safe enough space to talk in ways we might not be able to elsewhere: I mean, to talk in ways that are exploratory and contingent. In our talk with our friends, we both confirm and resist our existing sense of our selves and our world, and also explore new ways of knowing or apprehending the world (see Weedon, 1987).

This makes the talk of women friends sound very serious: but exploratory talk is as likely to be playful as serious. The following example comes from a conversation involving three friends, Sue, Anna and Liz, and begins with Sue telling a story about a husband who was not allowed to play his guitar.

> I told you I went round to a friends who had ((a)) guitar.
> [. . .]
> The wife right- his wife would not let him have a guitar.
> She said no [A and L laugh]
> and he's so obedient.
> She's- she said, 'You're not having a guitar',
> so he didn't have one,
> he just didn't play it ever.
> and then for Christmas she allowed him to have a guitar
> as long as he didn't play it in front of her.

This story leads into discussion about marriage and ideas of obedience and rebellion. Although these are talked about in a very playful way, with lots of laughter, there is no doubt that important work is being done here by the three women friends. Discussion is sustained and well focused. The heart of this segment of conversation seems to be the friends' exploration of the meaning of 'obedience', both in terms of its appropriateness in a relationship between two adults and in terms of its congruence with (currently accepted forms of) masculinity. The couple Sue describes are a potent trigger for discussion because the expected pattern, the pattern normalized by dominant discourses, of a 'strong' husband and an 'obedient' wife is reversed here. It is the wife who makes decisions, who says how things are to be, and the husband who obeys. Initially Sue's description of the husband as obedient is challenged:

```
Sue:   but you've got to see it to
- - - - - - - - - - - - - - - - - - - - - - - - - - - - - - -
Sue:   believe it because he's just . obedient/ and she- ⌈and she
Liz:                                                      ⌊WHY did
- - - - - - - - - - - - - - - - - - - - - - - - - - - - - - -
Sue:   just-                                   ⌈what/ obedient?
Liz:   you use that word/ that's a dreadful    ⌊word/         obedient/
- - - - - - - - - - - - - - - - - - - - - - - - - - - - - - -
Sue:   yes ((xx))                          yes but he is/ that's what
Liz:   makes him sound like a pet rabbit/
- - - - - - - - - - - - - - - - - - - - - - - - - - - - - - -
```

```
Sue:    he's like/ he's obedient/ ⌈he just does as she says/
Anna:                            ⌊oh how aaww-ffuull/
Liz:
```

They deal with their horror (*oh how aaww-ffuull*) of this overturning of the 'natural' order by playing with the image of the husband as a pet rabbit, drawing on a theme from an earlier part of the conversation. This leads into a more general discussion of whether partners in a couple are ever equal, and whether living on your own is preferable to being part of a couple. Their talk becomes less playful; they reflect in a more sombre way on the difficulty of achieving equality in relationships and on the problems of 'coupledom', as Anna calls it.

This extended passage from the talk of these three friends demonstrates how friendship provides an arena where we can explore alternative ideas and forge new understandings of our social world. I want to look at an example from the talk of a different group of women friends. This example is more serious in tone throughout: there is none of the laughter or joking found in the talk about the obedient husband. Discussion of the topic 'child abuse' involves this group of friends in helping each other to work through distressing ideas and to think about the question of abuse in new ways. The collaborative floor plays an important role in providing these friends with a supportive space to take risks in their thinking and to push at the boundaries of existing knowledges.

Meg initiates this section of discussion with the statement *you remember that little boy that was um . in Brighton that was um . carried off and sexually abused*. This leads to a series of questions where the friends jointly take responsibility for answering Sally's question: *did they ever find the people that did that?*

```
Meg:    you remember that little boy that was um . in Brighton that

Meg:    was um . carried off=    =and sexually abused/    everyone was
Sally:                  yes/                      yes/
Mary:         mhm/          =yes=

Meg:    outraged about ⌈that=
Sally:                 ⌊did they ever find the people that did that?
Bea:            =mhm/

Meg:    yes they did didn't they?
Sally:                                        yeah/
Mary:                              did they?      yeah/ I remember/ yes/

Meg:                                                      yes/ they
Sally:                                                     really?
Bea:    did they find them?
Mary:                        they were in France weren't they?

Meg:    were part of a pornographic set-up/
```

Questions are used here to promote the group voice, and to avoid any one of the women being positioned as an expert. These questions also set up a frame where not knowing and wanting to know are salient. The discussion proceeds as follows:

```
- - - - - - - - - - - - - - - - - - - - - - - - - - - - -
Meg:                                              yeah/
Mary:  but I mean so much research is male-dominated/ I mean it just-

Meg:                    =mhm=      ((such see-through
Bea:                    =but also when you get down to
Mary:  it's staggering isn't it?=    = I mean ((xx))
- - - - - - - - - - - - - - - - - - - - - - - - - - - - -
Meg:   blinkered-))
Bea:   it/ . if you began to even have the faintest suspicion that
Mary:      that's right/
- - - - - - - - - - - - - - - - - - - - - - - - - - - -
Meg:             mhm/
Bea:   your husband . was interfering with . your- the two of
- - - - - - - - - - - - - - - - - - - - - - - - - - - -
Bea:   you's daughter/ . how quickly- . I mean in order to accept
- - - - - - - - - - - - - - - - - - - - - - - - - - - -
Bea:   that idea you're having to .
Mary:                    mhm/      completely review your
Jen:                    yes/
- - - - - - - - - - - - - - - - - - - - - - - - - - - -
Bea:   ⌈completely change   ⌉ your view of your husband=
Mary:  ⌊view of your husband⌋=                     =that's right=
Sally:                 =yes/
Meg:                    yeah/         mhm/
- - - - - - - - - - - - - - - - - - - - - - - - - - - -
Bea:   =and to have him become a person who can do . the undoable=
Meg:              mhm/
- - - - - - - - - - - - - - - - - - - - - - - - - - - -
Bea:              =and how easy is it to do that?=
Mary:  =that's right=                        =mhm/
- - - - - - - - - - - - - - - - - - - - - - - - - - - -
```

Bea and Mary are the main speakers in this extract: they articulate a series of linked ideas on the topic of child abuse. But the support of the other three women is important in sustaining them through this process, support provided in the form of frequent and well-placed minimal responses. (Through their minimal responses, these three speakers signal their continued presence in the collaborative floor, and thus take joint responsibility for what is said.) There are many linguistic features present which suggest that finding the right words isn't easy. For example, Bea initially says *your* to convey 'belonging to you and your husband', but amends this to *the two of you's daughter*, a nonce form which has the merit of making clear that she intends the possessive pronoun to be plural (*your* is ambiguous between singular and plural). She doesn't complete her rhetorical question *how quickly-*, as she struggles to express herself, and only later does she return to this structure, asking *how easy is it to do that?* (that is, how easy is it to realize that your husband is capable of doing the undoable?). As she struggles for words, Mary joins in the construction of the key utterance *you're having to completely change your view of your husband*.

Bea's words are punctuated by pauses, indicating the care she is taking in expressing herself. Examples, with pauses indicated by the symbol (.), are: *if you began to even have the faintest suspicion that your husband . was interfering with . your-;* and *and to have him become a person who can do . the undoable*. While 'interfering' is a euphemism, and shows there are areas of discussion which the friends find too painful to name directly, Bea's solution to naming what it is the husband does – 'the undoable' – is very powerful. She sets up a tension between the possible and the impossible. Her utterance is a semantic contradiction: your husband becomes a person *who can do* (who is capable of doing or who finds it possible to do) *the undoable* (that which it is not possible to do). This moves the talk into a new space: in talking about *the undoable* these women become able to say the unsayable. The women friends move on to a new understanding of why women don't recognize the signs that should tell them their daughter is being abused:

```
------------------------------------------------
Meg:  you don't- you don't assume it's possible/
Bea:                              and- and your husband has
------------------------------------------------
Meg:
Bea:   become a monster/
------------------------------------------------
```

At a superficial level, these two utterances are incoherent: Meg's refers to a world where your husband being an abuser is an impossibility, while Bea refers to a world where *your husband has become a monster*. How can these two utterances be joined by the coordinator *and?* Bea's utterance appeals to our common-sense knowledge that husbands and monsters are two non-overlapping categories – but what she is saying is that the one can become the other. In other words, at a profound level of understanding, these two utterances are totally coherent and express the group's new understanding of the schizophrenic position of the woman married to a child abuser.

Conclusion

When I asked the women I interviewed to describe what women's talk is like, Rachel characterized it in terms of 'warmth and nurturing and closeness', while Jo gave a list of adjectives: 'intimate, exploratory, provisional – I mean, open-ended'. These two responses focus on two sides of women's talk: its intimacy, the sense of connection between women that it engenders, and also its potential as a collaborative tool for exploring our world. The first of these is what we understand by saying that talking with our friends is constitutive of friendship, because talking with friends accomplishes intimacy and connection. But in an important sense, friendship is equally 'done' in talk which explores ourselves, the world and our place in the world: with our friends we are able to be reflexive in a way which is rarely possible in other, less safe, contexts. Out of these reflexive practices we are able to arrive at new understandings of ourselves and of the world we live in.

One of the great debates about women's friendships is whether they are a conservative or a liberating force. This simple binary distinction is too crude. Over the centuries, friendship with other women has offered women 'societies of consolation', to use Carolyn Heilburn's (1988: 10) phrase, meaning that women have always provided each other with a space where we can share our everyday experiences and problems as women living under patriarchy. The evidence of my research is that women do talk to each other about our lives and our problems. In part, this makes women's talk a conservative force because, through providing an emotional outlet, women's friendships help to support and sustain the heterosocial order (see Wilton, 1992). But there is a great deal of evidence in the conversations and interviews I've collected which suggests that friendship with other women offers us far more than simply 'consolation'. It also offers us the possibility of resistance and change.

Change cannot take place as long as an oppressed group accepts the status quo, that is, accepts the values of the oppressor. But women's friendships with each other provide us with a positive sense of who we are and enable us to develop solidarity. Solidarity with each other is a prerequisite for change.

And it is the talk that we do with our friends that makes resistance and change possible. Our jam sessions with women friends provide a context for risk-taking and experimentation. So in the playful conversational practices of women friends, we can try out different discourses, different positions in relation to the world. Subversive discourses can be nurtured and patriarchal discourses can be challenged. Through reflecting on our lives, we come to a greater understanding of ourselves. And through playing with the collaborative strategies which allow us to share the conversational floor, we can jointly move to a new awareness of how things might be, a new understanding of the patterns we observe. In the talk of women friends, new selves are forged and new knowledges are developed.

Appendix: transcription conventions

The transcription conventions used for the conversational data are as follows:

1 A slash (/) indicates the end of a tone group or chunk of talk, e.g.:
   she pushes him to the limit/

2   A question mark indicates the end of a chunk of talk which I am analysing as a question, e.g.:
    do you know anyone who's pregnant?

3   A hyphen indicates an incomplete word or utterance, e.g.:
    he's got this twi- he's got this nervous twitch/
    I was- I was- I was stopped by a train/

4   Pauses are indicated by a full stop (short pause, less than 0.5 seconds) or a dash (long pause), e.g.:
    he sort of . sat and read the newspaper/

5   A broken line marks the beginning of a stave and indicates that the words enclosed by the lines are to be read simultaneously (like a musical score), e.g.:

    -
    A: *the squidgy stuff that they put on pizzas/*
    B: *Mozarell* ⌈ *a/*
    C: ⌊ *Mozarella/*
    -

6   An extended square bracket indicates the start of overlap between utterances, e.g.:

    -
    A: *and they have newspapers and* ⌈ *stuff/*
    B: ⌊ *yes very good/*
    -

7   An equals sign at the end of one speaker's utterance and at the start of the next utterance indicates the absence of a discernible gap, e.g.:

    -
    A: *because they're supposed to be* =
    B: = *adults/*
    -

8   Double round parentheses indicate that there is doubt about the accuracy of the transcription:
    What's that ((mean))/ gayist/

9   Where material is impossible to make out, it is represented as ((xx)), e.g.:
    you're ((xx))- you're prejudiced/

10 Angled brackets give clarificatory information about underlined material, e.g.:
    why doesn't that creep – start to go wild/ <LAUGHING>
    I can't help it <WHINEY VOICE>

11 Capital letters are used for words/syllables uttered with emphasis:
    It's in MExico/

12 The symbol % encloses words or phrases that are spoken very quietly, e.g.:
    %bloody hell%

13 The symbol .hh indicates that the speaker takes a sharp intake of breath:
    .hh I wish I'd got a camera/ <LAUGHING>

14 The symbol [. . .] indicates that material has been omitted, e.g.:
    Tom [. . .] says there's a German word to describe that/

Notes

1. My corpus consists of twenty recordings of naturally occurring conversation between women friends, recorded by them in their own homes, collected by me between 1983 and 1992. This was supplemented by a series of ethnographic interviews with girls and women (many of whom had taken part in the conversations I'd collected) in which I asked them about the nature of friendship and its role in their lives (for full details of the methodology, see Coates, 1996, Chapters 1 and 2). I'd like to place on record my gratitude to all those who participated in this research.

2. The evidence of *The Hite Report* (Hite, 1989) is that in the USA 87% of married women and 95% of single women claimed that their deepest emotional relationship was with another woman.

3. The names of all participants and of people mentioned in the conversations and interviews have been changed.

References

Bell, Diane (1993) *Daughters of the Dreaming*, 2nd edn. St Leonards, NSW: Allen & Unwin.

Coates, Jennifer (1996) *Women Talk: Conversation between Women Friends*. Oxford: Blackwell.

Coates, Jennifer (1997) 'The construction of a collaborative floor in women's friendly talk', in T. Givon (ed.), *Conversation: Cognitive, Communicative and Social Perspectives*. Amsterdam: John Benjamins. pp. 55–89.

Edelsky, Carole (1993) 'Who's got the floor?', in Deborah Tannen (ed.), *Gender and Conversational Interaction*. Oxford: Oxford University Press. pp. 189–227.

Faderman, Lillian (1985) *Surpassing the Love of Men*. London: Women's Press.

Gergen, Kenneth (1987) 'Toward self as relationship', in Krysia Yardle and Terry Honess (eds), *Self and Identity: Psychosocial Processes*. New York: Wiley. pp. 53–63.

Gouldner, Helen and Strong, Mary Symons (1987) *Speaking of Friendship*. New York: Greenwood.

Hamilton, Annette (1981) 'A complex strategical situation: gender and power in Aboriginal Australia', in Norma Grieve and Patricia Grimshaw (eds), *Australian Women: Feminist Perspectives*. Melbourne: Oxford University Press. pp. 69–85.

Harré, Rom (1987) 'The social construction of selves', in Krysia Yardle and Terry Honess (eds), *Self and Identity: Psychosocial Processes*. New York: Wiley. pp. 41–52.

Heilbrun, Carolyn G. (1988) *Writing a Woman's Life*. New York: Ballantine.

Hey, Valerie (1996) *The Company She Keeps: an Ethnography of Girls' Friendship*. Buckingham: Open University Press.

Hite, Shere (1989) *The Hite Report: Women in Love*. Harmondsworth: Penguin.

Hobson, R. Peter (1993) *Autism and the Development of Mind*. Hove: Lawrence Erlbaum.

Hunt, Mary, E. (1991) *Fierce Tenderness: a Feminist Theology of Friendship*. New York: Crossroad.

Hymes, Dell (1971) 'On communicative competence', in J.B. Pride and Janet Holmes (eds), *Sociolinguistics*. Harmondsworth: Penguin.

Johnson, Fern and Aries, Elizabeth (1983a) 'The talk of women friends', *Women's Studies International Forum*, 6(4): 353–61.

Johnson, Fern and Aries, Elizabeth (1983b) 'Conversational patterns among same-sex pairs of late-adolescent close friends', *Journal of Genetic Psychology*, 142: 225–38.

Jordan, Rosan and Kalčik, Susan (eds) (1985) *Women's Folklore, Women's Culture*. Philadelphia: University of Pennsylvania Press.

Kennedy, Robinette (1986) 'Women's friendships on Crete: a psychological perspective', in Jill Dubisch (ed.), *Gender and Power in Rural Greece*. Princeton: Princeton University Press. pp. 121–38.

McCabe, T. (1981) 'Girls and leisure', in A. Tomlinson (ed.), *Leisure and Social Control*. Brighton Polytechnic: Chelsea School of Human Movement.

Miller, Stuart (1983) *Men and Friendship*. San Leandro, CA: Gateway.

Modjeska, Drusilla (1990) *Poppy*. Ringwood, Vic.: McPhee Gribble.

O'Connor, Pat (1992) *Friendships between Women: a Critical Review*. London: Harvester Wheatsheaf.

O'Neill, Gilda (1993) *A Night Out with the Girls*. London: Women's Press.

Pleck, Joseph (1975) 'Man to man: is brotherhood possible?', in N. Glazer-Malbin (ed.), *Old Family, New Family*. New York: Van Nostrand.

Raymond, Janice (1986) *A Passion for Friends*. London: Women's Press.

Rubin, Lilian (1985) *Just Friends: the Role of Friendship in Our Lives*. New York: Harper Row.

Sacks, Harvey, Schegloff, Emanuel A. and Jefferson, Gail (1974) 'A simplest systematics for the organisation of turn-taking in conversation', *Language*, 50: 696–735.

Seidler, Victor (1989) *Rediscovering Masculinity*. London: Routledge.

Smith-Rosenberg, Carroll (1975) 'The female world of love and ritual: relations between women in nineteenth-century America', *Signs: Journal of Women in Culture and Society*, 1(1): 1–29.

Taylor, Charles (1991) 'The dialogical self', in David Hiley et al. (eds), *The Interpretive Turn: Philosophy, Science, Culture*. Ithaca, NY: Cornell University Press. pp. 304–14.

Weedon, Chris (1987) *Feminist Practice and Poststructuralist Theory*. Oxford: Blackwell.

Wilton, Tamsin (1992) 'Sisterhood in the service of patriarchy: heterosexual women's friendships and male power', *Feminism & Psychology*, 2(3): 506–9.

Wulff, Helena (1988) *Twenty Girls Growing Up: Ethnicity and Excitement in a South London Microculture*. Stockholm Studies in Social Anthropology 21.

11

STORY-TELLING IN NEW ZEALAND WOMEN'S AND MEN'S TALK

Janet Holmes

Everyone loves a story and perhaps for this reason people use stories for many purposes: to instruct, to entertain, to illustrate arguments and to establish social connections. Stories can be used in all kinds of social contexts from the most formal presentation to the most casual conversation, and they can generally be relied on to (re)capture the audience's attention. There are many different kinds of stories from artistically crafted cultural myths to conversational accounts of mundane everyday experiences. This chapter focuses on the latter end of this continuum, on naturally occurring stories in the relaxed conversations of New Zealanders. In particular, the analysis explores the ways in which New Zealand women and men use stories in their daily interactions.

It has been suggested that New Zealand is a particularly gendered culture, 'a culture in which the structures of masculinity and femininity are central to the formation of society as a whole' (James and Saville-Smith, 1989: 6). Gender has been identified by feminist sociologists as the major preoccupation of New Zealand culture. Because of the pervasive influence of symbols of the pioneer origins of New Zealand Pakeha[1] society such as 'man alone' and 'dependent women', it is suggested that women and men are more effectively trapped in gender roles still in New Zealand than in European societies such as Britain. Gender is a salient dimension in New Zealand Maori culture, too. Metge describes male and female roles as functionally complementary, and, though she argues that female influence is pervasive and highly valued, it is clear that women's role is appropriately in the background in many social contexts (1995: 91–8).[2] Indeed, Fitzgerald (1993) emphasizes the extent of male dominance and points to the exclusion of women from many traditional Maori religious and political activities. Hence a feminist poststructuralist analysis would identify female–male relationships in New Zealand as still very traditional, with males dominating most overtly authoritative and statusful positions and formal speech events, while females generally take a less prominent role. Traditional gender roles are emphasized and reinforced, and most areas of public discourse represent women in what Weedon describes as their 'primary role – that of wife and mother' (1987: 3), suggesting that New Zealand society may be a particularly productive source of insight into expressions of femininity and masculinity.

Stories provide one way in which women and men construct their gender identity. Within a social constructionist framework, language is viewed as 'a set of strategies for negotiating the social landscape' (Crawford, 1995: 17). Language is the site of the cultural production of gender identity: subjectivity is discursively constituted (see also Weedon, 1987; Butler, 1990). In other words, each person's subjectivity is constructed and gendered within the social, economic and political discourse to which they are exposed (Weedon, 1987: 21). Using this approach people operate within subject positions, positions created and sustained by the use of language (Fairclough, 1989; 1995); speakers are regarded as constantly 'doing gender', and the different ways in which women and men behave are accounted for by the gendered social contexts in which they operate. This approach examines 'what speakers "mean" in their situated utterances' (Eckert and McConnell-Ginet, 1992: 474) and 'how gender is constructed in social practice' (1992: 472). In their stories, New Zealand women and men actively construct their gender identities, reproducing and reinforcing societal gender divisions, and sometimes challenging and changing traditional patterns. In the stories analysed in this chapter, I will show that New Zealand women and men tend to construct relatively conservative gender identities for themselves within the social contexts they select for their narrative settings, though there are also indications that feminist ideology has had some influence on women's perceptions of appropriate gender identities.

What counts as a story?

Many analyses of narrative in the sociolinguistic literature use elicited stories as data. These are stories produced in response to a question or request for an account of some experience: for example, the famous 'danger of death' question which has been used with varying degrees of success in so many social dialect surveys. The structure of such elicited narratives is fundamentally influenced by their function as 'answers' to a question in an interview context (see, for example, Wolfson, 1976; Schiffrin, 1994). The stories analysed in this chapter were not elicited in this way; they occurred spontaneously in conversations.

The use of spontaneously occurring, rather than elicited, stories raises the issue of what counts as a story. There is a very extensive literature analysing narratives and I do not intend to review it here. Like most previous researchers, I began from Labov's classic definition, since, as Linde notes, it was developed to account for oral narratives of personal experience, and has proved the most useful for studying 'naturally occurring oral data' (1993: 67–8). Thus a narrative of personal experience is

> one method of recapitulating past experience by matching a verbal sequence of clauses to the sequence of events which (it is inferred) actually occurred. (Labov and Waletzky, 1967: 20; Labov, 1972: 359–60)

In other words, a narrative uses a sequence of temporally ordered clauses to recapitulate past experience. Minimally, the structure of a story involves two narrative clauses which provide the story with a beginning, a middle, and an end. Here is an example with three clauses.

Example 1

I went down the shops yesterday
but I forgot my purse
so I ended up back home without achieving anything

A 'more developed', 'fully-formed' narrative would include all of the six components identified by Labov (1972) and used extensively in narrative analysis over the last 25 years (abstract, orientation, complicating action, evaluation, resolution, coda).

While this definition has been widely adopted (for example, Polanyi, 1985; Bell, 1991; Johnstone, 1993; Linde, 1993; Rymes, 1995; Coates, 1996), it is clear that the issue of what counts as a story differs between different social and cultural groups. Goodwin (1991), for example, notes that the 'instigating' stories told by working class young black girls do not fit Labov's definition. She describes them as emerging from the social action in which talk is naturally embedded, and comments that stories might better be described as 'cultural objects designed to operate in ongoing social projects' (1991: 275–6). In fact, most people's conception of what counts as a story in white Western culture differs from Labov's definition, as he acknowledges with the distinction between evaluated and unevaluated stories. The lay-person's definition of a story is generally much closer to Labov's evaluated stories which 'make a point'.

> Pointless stories are met (in English) with the withering rejoinder, 'So what?' Every good narrator is continually warding off this question. (1972: 366)

In Example 1, the evaluation is contained in the third clause. The question of what counts as a story is greatly complicated by the issue of whether or not the evaluative component is optional or not. Since, as Labov points out, the evaluation may be embedded rather than explicit, identifying it may not be straightforward. Moreover, in my observation, the evaluation may be conveyed entirely prosodically, or paralinguistically, or non-verbally. Recognizing this, it seems likely that unevaluated stories are extremely rare. The issue of embedded evaluations is discussed and exemplified further below.

Brief description of the data

The stories analysed in this chapter occurred spontaneously in the course of excerpts from a sample of 30 conversations between friends which were collected for the one million word Wellington Corpus of Spoken New Zealand English (WCSNZE).[3] Each conversation was a relaxed chat between two friends of the same age, gender, social class and ethnicity: that is, there were 60 contributors in all. Two ethnic groups were involved: 24 of the conversationalists were Maori and 36 were Pakeha. Half of the conversationalists were women and half men. This conversational data base yielded 96 narratives. In this chapter, I focus on similarities and differences in the stories produced by the women compared with the men.

There was no great disparity in the number of stories which occurred in the female versus the male conversations. While the women produced more stories than the men, the difference was not great: the women produced 55 stories compared with 41 from the men. And, given the problems of deciding where to draw boundaries between stories, the greatly differing lengths of stories, and the fact that the excerpts in the WCSNZE were generally taken from longer conversations, no particular weight should be put on this difference.

Not all conversations are equally conducive to story-telling. Conversational topics and 'moods' differ greatly, though in fact all but two of the recorded conversations (one male and one female dyad) included at least one story. In both these storyless interactions the conversations developed into task-oriented discussions of the merits and demerits of a proposed course of action – one concerning plans to buy a piece of land, the other about plans to build a ramp. The remaining conversations include a range from one story to nine. The men's stories tend to be shorter, the women's longer, but there is a large area of overlap: both women and men produced very short and very long stories. Indeed, in relation to story length, age was a more relevant factor than gender: older contributors tended to produce longer stories than younger ones.

The analysis which follows examines just two gender-differentiated features of these stories: the interactive structure of the stories, and the kind of gender identity constructed by narrators.

Constructing a story

Spontaneous conversational stories can often be analysed as joint productions or interactive achievements, involving both the narrator and the addressee to varying extents. There is a good deal of research illustrating the ways in which the audience contributes to the creation of a story. Wolfson (1976), Bell (1988) and Riessman (1993: 41) discuss the ways in which the structure of a narrative is influenced by the form of the interviewer's questions. Focusing on spontaneous narrative, Corston comments that it is 'interactive in nature, rather than mono-logic' (1993: 70). And Duranti provides extensive evidence of 'the symphonic quality of verbal performance' (1986: 245), with Goodwin demonstrating that the meaning of a story

> emerges not from the actions of the speaker alone, but rather as the product of a collaborative process of interaction in which the audience plays a very active role. (1986: 283)[4]

Coates (1996), however, makes the point that within the women's conversations she analysed, the structure of stories is unusual. Stories are much more of a solo performance than other parts of the conversations where a genuinely collaborative floor develops, which she describes as 'polyphonic talk' analogous to a musical 'jam session' (1996: 117, 133). She points out that, in terms of their structure, stories

> differ significantly from the surrounding conversation in which they are embedded. When someone starts to tell a story, we listen to them in a way that is quite different from normal. (1996: 95)

Labov too notes the power of the story to compel attention:

> [Narratives] will command the total attention of an audience in a remarkable way, creating a deep and attentive silence that is never found in academic or political discussion. (1972: 396)

Commenting on Labov's quotation, Coates (1996: 95) points out that *audience* is a key word:

> In friendly conversation, the idea of participants functioning as an audience while someone speaks is nonsensical for most of the time . . . Story-telling is the exception. When someone starts to tell a story, the other conversational participants withdraw temporarily from active participation and give the story-teller privileged access to the floor. (1996: 95)

While this accurately describes many of the conversational stories in the New Zealand data, where the co-conversationalist's role was largely restricted to indications of interest and attention, there are also some stories to which both conversationalists contribute. These could be better described as collaborative, interactive or 'dialogic' in structure (Cheepen, 1988).[5] Hence, in analysing this aspect of the New Zealand data, it was useful to consider two distinct continua, the first relating to the role of narrator, the second to the role of addressee or listener. The continuum for the *narrator role* may be represented as follows:

Solo construction ——————— Joint construction

At one extreme a narration may be completely solo, quintessential 'one-at-a-time' talk (Coates, 1989), as when a story is read aloud. At the other, a story may be co-constructed from contributions by two or more subjects. In theory, the way in which these contributions are integrated is another area of potential variation: they could, for example, be sequential, as in games where each contributor must pick up the story from where the previous person stops, or, at the other extreme, contributions may be simultaneous, with co-construction an ongoing dynamic process (for example, Sheldon, 1996).

Turning to the role of the listener(s) or audience, one continuum on which this role can be evaluated is the degree of support that the addressee gives to the narrator in telling the story. This continuum for the *listener role* may be represented as follows:

Supportive ——————— Unsupportive

The two continua are obviously closely related in that one extreme type of supportive behaviour might be to share the narrator's role. But, while this may accurately describe verbal interaction in some social and cultural contexts, it is not always the case, and at the conceptual level it is useful to distinguish the two roles. There are certainly some social contexts where the most supportive audience behaviour involves allowing the narrator uncontested access to the floor, and there are also contexts where a completely silent response can be totally supportive, indicating appreciation, respect or understanding.[6]

The narrator's role

The New Zealand corpus illustrated a range of points on both the narrator and the listener continua. Each of the conversations involved only two contributors, and the most common pattern was for stories to clearly 'belong to' one or other speaker. On the other hand, there were examples of jointly constructed stories. These were typically reminiscences of shared experiences or relivings of past shared adventures. Earlier research suggests that a collaborative approach to a story might be considered more typical of women's talk, a specifically female way of interacting. Coates comments, for instance:

> women friends prefer a way of talking which emphasizes the collaborative and which is antipathetic to monologue. So although storytellers are granted a more privileged floor, this often lasts only for a brief period at the beginning of a story. (1996: 111)

But a collaborative approach was not confined to women in this New Zealand sample. Where they occurred, jointly constructed stories tended to reflect the length and closeness of a friendship, rather than the gender of the contributors. Typically, shared stories consisted of collaboratively constructed reminiscences. The following example with its two compressed mini-stories is part of a long sequence in which two young men are reliving past shared escapades (transcription conventions are given in Appendix 1).[7]

Example 2

B: and we tried to take spoons remember /[laughs]\
A: /[laughs]\
B: trying to wire up the game /eh [laughs]\
A: /[laughs] yeah with a spoon\ it's just you actually think about it eh
A: /[laughs]\
B: /[laughs]\
A: we're the spoons trying to fucking we were the spoons [laughs] all right oh what eggs man
B: I- I felt like crying one time when we lost you know we [laughs] died fuck we got to walk all the fucking way home [laughs]
A: [laughs] yeah I'll say we had to walk all the way home
B: fucking hell we only got down with eighty cents and that was about bloody four or five games worth

The joint construction of stories is one way of expressing friendship and rapport. This function is emphasized in Example 2 by the shared overlapping laughter throughout, as well as by the use of other-oriented pragmatic particles such as *you know* which appeal to shared experience (Holmes, 1986), and by various repeated lexical units, including the echo by A (*we had to walk all the way home*) of B's description of what happened (*we got to walk all the fucking way home*). In this corpus, however, such examples were not common. There were relatively few instances where the stories were jointly owned in the sense that both subjects had been involved in the relevant experience, and thus there was the possibility of a joint reconstruction.

The addressee's response

Much more common was a pattern where the narrator told her or his story and the addressee took the listener role, reflecting the fact that the narrator was describing an experience which the other person had not shared. It was in this area that gender differences were most apparent. Women and men differed not only in the amount of verbal feedback, but also in the kind of feedback they provided.

There is considerable evidence that in conversational contexts women tend to provide a greater number of minimal responses (*yeah, mm*) than men (for example, Strodtbeck and Mann, 1956; Zimmerman and West,

1975; Fishman, 1983; Leet-Pellegrini, 1980). More recently, analysts
have begun to examine the function of verbal feedback, including a
larger and more open-ended set of short utterances, often together with
vocalizations such as laughter (for example, Stenstrom, 1994; Reid,
1995), and distinguishing supportive positive feedback from neutral or
non-committal responses (for example, Pilkington, 1994). Analysing the
conversations in this New Zealand sample, Maria Stubbe (forthcoming)
distinguished supportive from neutral minimal responses, as well as
more extended overtly supportive feedback, such as cooperative overlaps, from neutral verbal feedback. Stubbe summarizes the results of
this analysis as follows:

> there is a clear tendency for the men to respond more neutrally and minimally,
> while the women's feedback includes a greater proportion of responses which
> are both overtly supportive and more extended and contrapuntal in nature.

Doing gender for a woman clearly involved providing ongoing explicit
verbal support for a co-conversationalist.

More detailed qualitative analysis suggests that feedback is sensitive
to a range of further factors such as the nature of the relationship
between the conversationalists, and the type of talk in which they are
engaged. It appears, for example, that as the topic of the narrative
becomes more personal, the feedback becomes more explicitly supportive. In other words, personal topics elicit more supportive and
reassuring responses (Stubbe, forthcoming). One factor accounting for
the greater incidence of feedback in the women's interactions, then, is
the fact that the women's stories tend to focus on more personal topics,
or be treated from a more personal perspective than the men's (see
below).

Gender differences were also apparent in the more extended
responses provided to story-tellers in this sample – the questions and
comments offered by listeners. Some questions and comments were
clearly experienced by the narrator as helpful and structurally cohesive:
they assisted the story's development. Others were distracting or
disruptive, or, in some cases, challenging. In the following example,
where Mona is recounting the story of her hair colouring experience,
Carol's feedback and her questions are facilitative and encouraging.

Example 3

    M: and I haven't heard /from him\ today
    C: /tut oh\
    M: so I'm going to phone the salon tomorrow and speak to the owner if
       she's there
    C: yeah
    M: and um just ask her to do something about it
    C: gosh that's pretty poor isn't it
    M: well I don't have his home phone number or I'd phone him at home

C: yeah [tut] oh so they're trying to avoid you
M: I don't know I mean it might just be that that it hasn't been convenient to phone me but he hasn't phoned work or there would have been a message left for me
C: yeah yeah

In Example 4, an excerpt from a story about a friend's marriage, Meg's comments and questions are clearly experienced by Vera as supportive and constructive.

Example 4

V: did I tell you Jude's got married
B: JUDE
V: yeah
M: when did that happen?
V: last week she- she met a guy at church camp which was um two months ago they got engaged the week before last and they got married last week
M: OH MY GOODNESS what's he like
V: oh I've only met him once I don't know him
M: mm
V: at all but-
M: THAT'S AMAZING 'cause last time she was up here wa- she wasn't going out with anybody was she when I spoke to her
V: no and like it's sort of- it's really sad because I think she's made a really big mistake um because th- like they don't know each other they've only- they only met two months ago they don't know each other AT ALL hardly
M: far out

Similarly, in the story told by Helen to Joan which is analysed in some detail in the next section, and which is provided in full in Appendix 2, Joan's contributions are uniformly supportive and encouraging. In addition to much well-placed and appreciative laughter, and minimal feedback (*mm, yeah, oh, right*), she makes comments such as the following: *oh good on you, I know, goodness me, that's terrific, good on her, that's so good*. These are carefully placed to be non-disruptive of Helen's story. One more elaborated comment (*she's very good with adults isn't she*) is clearly welcomed by Helen, as indicated by the fact that she expands on it.

The men's questions, by contrast, sometimes appeared to distract the narrator from his story, and could be regarded as unhelpful.[8] In Example 5, Joe is telling a story about how his soccer team got beaten recently. Michael's comments are uttered in a jeering tone and – since he guesses inaccurately – they are unhelpful in terms of the development of the story.

Example 5

> J: we got DONE [laughs]
> M: oh no oh no
> J: we played- [laughs] played the top team
> M: /who- who are they?\
> J: /it was a good\ game
> M: Petone no doubt yay
> J: nope
> M: oh serious
> J: no Seatoun (we played right up) at Seatoun right on the waterfront

Similarly in the next example, which is taken from an excerpt which is provided in full in Appendix 3, Gary asks questions, intent on getting accurate information rather than responding to the point of Tom's story.

Example 6

> T: and I picked up the video thingy you know the
> G: is this the G code?
> T: the remote one no no
> G: no
> T: no no just the just an ordinary remote

And, at a later point, Gary attempts to guess what has gone wrong before Tom tells him.

Example 7

> T: and do you know what went wrong 'cause it you know that some-
>   thing went /wrong otherwise\
> G: /[laughs]\
> T: I wouldn't be telling you this story (quite-)
> G: /you got\ the wrong channel
> T: /quite pointless if nothing\ no no no everything was perfect

This could be regarded as unsupportive behaviour since Gary's guess, if correct, would have undermined Tom's denouement, and prevented him from presenting the point of his story in the climactic fashion he clearly planned. So while supportive questions and comments which appeared to facilitate the narrator's story were used by both women and men, challenging, undermining and disruptive questions and comments occurred exclusively in the men's stories in this sample.

Finally, and briefly, in considering the addressee's responses, perhaps the most extensive positive response to a friend's story is to 'mirror' it, that is to tell a similar story, reflecting parallel concerns and indicating understanding of the narrator's point. Mirroring at all levels of discourse is extensively discussed by Coates (1996). It is a way of expressing connection and empathy, and where appropriate may serve to reassure the original story-teller about some of the concerns expressed in their story. Coates notes many instances of this phenomenon in her women's group data, and there were a few examples of mirroring stories from both women and men in the New Zealand sample. Once again, this kind of supportive response to another's story was found more frequently in the female than the male conversations.

Constructing gender identity

Stories serve many concurrent functions in conversation. They may be intended to entertain, amuse or amaze those listening; they may be used to socialize others, to instruct, to indicate appropriate ways of behaving, or alternatively to contest societal norms; they may function interpersonally to praise others, to establish or consolidate connections and links, or perhaps to flatter, to build up the narrator's ego or that of the addressees (for example, Heath, 1982; Labov, 1972; Riessman, 1993; Schiffrin, 1994). Stories may also be used to draw distinctions and emphasize the boundaries between groups such as women and men.

In this section, focusing on two specific examples, I look in more detail at the ways in which women and men use narratives to construct gendered identities. Generally, the most relevant subject will be the narrator, but story-tellers may also construct gendered identities for others in their stories, as I will illustrate. Telling a story is one means of presenting oneself and others as appropriately feminine or masculine in terms of current societal ideology, or alternatively, a story may be used to subvert or contest the dominant ideology.

The women in the New Zealand sample tell stories about the small events which characterize their daily activities, and which often reflect their relationships with others. The main characters are themselves, their family members and their friends. The stories relate minor mishaps and small successes; they document embarrassing experiences rather than major disasters. The events recounted are mundane every-day occurrences. The topics include children's illnesses, giving blood, a good experience at the dentist, a bad experience at the hairdressers, failing a driving test, buying gifts for friends and family.

In this sample, talking to a friend in a relaxed social setting, men also tell stories about everyday events, but their stories tend to focus on work and leisure activities. They describe successes and achievements, sporting prowess, and the resolution of problems, often due to their own ingenuity, skill or competence. The topics include sitting exams, taking sick leave, playing soccer, sky diving, hiking, painting the bathroom, and playing video games. While particular items could potentially have appeared in the list of topics associated with the other gender, the cumulative effect is telling, and the way a topic is treated differs between women and men. Through their choice of story topics, as well as their different treatment of these topics, New Zealand women and men construct themselves as differently gendered.[9]

Female identity

Coates (1996; see also Chapter 10 in this volume) points to the importance of narrative in women's lives as a way of keeping in touch with friends. For women, updating friends on the ongoing story of one's life is an important component in 'doing friendship'. The narratives in the New Zealand corpus illustrate this very well. Without exception, at least one, and typically most, of the women's stories in each of the recorded conversations functioned to update the other person on recent events in the narrator's life (cf. Linde, 1993). But, of course, when we update someone on our life story we are inevitably selective. We can choose to focus on successes and events that have gone smoothly, for example, or we can focus on disasters and worries. Similarly, we can present ourselves as 'in charge', controlling events, or as the hapless victim of circumstances or luck. The aspect of this selection process that I want to highlight in this section is the ways in which women and men use stories to 'do gender'. In a variety of ways, the stories told by the New Zealand women functioned to construct or reinforce a particular kind of gendered identity for the narrator. This identity was typically a rather conservative one, even when the protagonist was a professional woman working full-time. As Weedon points out:

> As children we learn what girls and boys should be and, later, women and men. These subject positions – ways of being an individual – and the values inherent in them may not all be compatible and we will learn that we can choose between them. As women we have a range of possibilities. In theory almost every walk of life is open to us, but all the possibilities which we share with men involve accepting, negotiating or rejecting what is constantly being offered to us as our primary role – that of wife and mother. (1987: 3)

The first narrative portrays the narrator as not just accepting, but even embracing that primary role.

'We tried to go to the pool today'

This narrative occurs in a conversation between two close friends, Helen and Joan, both middle-aged Pakeha women pursuing professional careers. The first part of the conversation consists of Joan describing her newly established cottage garden. She then asks, 'but tell me about Jason I was thinking about him as I came up.' Jason is Helen's father who has been very ill. The story 'We tried to go to the pool today' is embedded within a long discussion of Jason's state of health, including a description of ways in which Helen is looking after him (with visits and meals), what his doctors have recommended, and so on. The conversation develops into a general discussion of the way doctors treat old people, and then moves to a discussion of Helen's mother's final illness. It provides an excellent example of the way women's conversations often move easily back and forward between descriptions of specific experiences and discussion of more general issues, and particularly of the way a specific story can lead into a more abstract discussion, as described by Coates (1996).

The story which is the focus of discussion is an account of Helen's attempt to take herself and her children to the swimming pool (see Appendix 2). The pool story is a classic narrative, recapitulating past experience using a sequence of temporally ordered clauses to do so (Labov, 1972: 359–60). Its structure is in some respects reminiscent of that of many fairy stories: the protagonist makes three attempts to achieve her goal and succeeds only on the third attempt. It can be summarized as follows:

1   I wanted to go to aqua-fitness at the Kilbirnie Pool – but didn't succeed.
2   I tried the Freyburg pool – but that wasn't satisfactory.
3   I decided to go to the Karori pool:
    (a) on the way we stopped in and saw Jason;
    (b) Andrea did seven lengths of the pool.
4   Resolution: it all ended up fine.
5   Coda: Jason's state of health.

The resolution completes both subsection 3 and subsection 3(a), each of which could be regarded as mini-stories, as well as rounding off the whole story. The coda relates the story back to the larger response to Joan's initial inquiry about Jason's health.

A superficial look at this story might leave one wondering what was its point. The most important 'point' is far from explicit: the evaluative component is deeply embedded in the context within which the story is told. At one level, its point is simply to bring Joan up to date on what Helen has been doing: it is a story about a visit to the swimming pool. At another level it is one component in a complex answer to Joan's inquiry about Jason's health. At yet another level (the level on which I am focusing), the story constructs Helen's identity as a 'good' daughter and a 'good' mother.[10] Both these identities are very important to her. Of three daughters, she is the only one who lives near her father; and she is a solo parent. Though in many respects her life does not conform to the norms of conservative New Zealand society, in these two areas she clearly strives to so conform. She takes her roles as 'daughter' and 'mother' very seriously, and likes others to recognize and appreciate the extent to which she meets society's prescriptions in these areas. This message is conveyed in the story 'We tried to go to the pool today', but it is not always conveyed explicitly. It is also worth noting that Joan is a much more conservative woman than Helen in a number of respects, and it is probably not accidental that she is the audience for this particular story. (As Linde, 1993: 72, points out, participants must agree on the evaluative component of a narrative.)

Helen first presents herself as a good mother, concerned for her children's comfort and well-being. This is most obvious in the following three utterances:

> so we gathered up Susie and everybody and their togs . . .
> it's lane swimming only which is no good for the little kids . . .
> and actually it was rather sort of muggy and hot to be driving round Wellington with a car full of children . . .

While the message is easily inferred from the latter two utterances, it is not quite so clear from the first. In fact, this utterance indicates Helen's willingness to take an extra child Susie on this outing, thus providing a playmate for her youngest child, Andrea, another indication of her thoughtful mothering.

Helen also constructs her identity as a good daughter. Here the most obviously relevant sections of the story are:

> so on the way to the Karori pool we stopped in and saw Jason . . .
> and I said why don't you stay with Jason and make him some lunch
> so we went in and visited him
> and I said Annie'll stay with you and make you some lunch
> and she gets on quite- and she chats away with Jason . . .
> so she stayed with him for an hour . . .
> so Annie stayed there and made Jason some lunch
> and then we went back afterwards . . .

These utterances represent Helen as looking after her father's needs: he is provided with the companionship of his granddaughter, with whom we are told he gets on well, and also with his lunch.

More subtly, Helen constructs her identity as good mother and daughter in the account she provides of the way she 'manages' Annie, and in the analysis she presents of Annie's relationship with Jason. Annie is a somewhat difficult teenager, as Joan knows, and as indicated earlier in this story by her reluctance to cooperate with Helen's attempts to rescue their outing:

> so then we get I don't want to go to – Annie didn't want to go to Freyburg
> . . .

and later

    and Annie was saying I don't want to go in will you drop me home

Helen presents herself skilfully persuading her daughter to look after her grandfather's needs, and, at the same time, she constructs a much more positive identity both for her difficult daughter and for her rather grouchy father:

    and she gets on quite- and she chats away with Jason
    and they have quite a nice . . .
    well she's good with him too
    I don't know they sort of get along nicely
    and um better than the other two do really you know
    she sort of somehow gets it right with him
    and he seems to make an effort too

Similarly, the picture Helen presents of her youngest daughter is extremely positive:

    Andrea did SEVEN lengths
    with a little breaks in between
    but she's never swum a length of that pool before
    and she just suddenly discovered she could swim a length [laughs]
    and got so keen she didn't want to stop
    she said I'll just do another one and then I'll do another one
    so that was quite sweet she looked like a [laughs]
    s- Liz was there with her friend John
    and he said she looked like a goldfish you [laughs] know
    s- (there's) a little head (rolling) in the water
    [laughs] and legs sort of sagging in the water o-
    and breaststroking away you know
    but she was obviously really sort of getting a kick out of the achievement

There is firstly an explicitly admiring account of Andrea's achievement, but, in addition, this section of the story achieves its effect through the use of diminutives and attenuators which construct Andrea's identity as a small, sweet, endearing little girl. The positive effect of the explicit phrase *quite sweet* is further supported and developed by attenuating words such as *just* and *little*, the pragmatic particles *sort of* and *you know*, the adverb particle *away* in the phrase *breaststroking away* and the repetition of phrases and syntactic patterns (*I'll just do another one and then I'll do another one*). These components all contribute to Helen's affectionate picture of her little girl swimming gamely away, as does the paralinguistic laughter, and the attribution to an observer of a comment (*there's a little head*) that emphasizes how sweet and amusing Andrea's behaviour is.[11]

In this story, we see some of the ways in which Helen presents herself to her friend in her role as a loving mother and daughter. But, there are hints of another discourse here, too. As David Lee points out:

> Texts are typically the site of contestation between conflicting perspectives, and linguistic processes constitute the mechanism for the resolution of these conflicts. (1992: 136)

The conflicting discourse is kept relatively suppressed, but it surfaces at various points. It is a discourse which on other occasions Helen may choose to voice more extensively and explicitly – the expression of Annie's lack of cooperation, the glancing reference to the fact that her other two children do not get on so well with Jason, the presentation of herself as authoritative and decisive, brooking no argument (*so I said 'we're going to Freyburg we've got this far'*), and the implied criticism of her father, the hint that he is not always cooperative *(he seems to make an effort too)*. From a poststructuralist perspective, there is some evidence here of the relative nature of the individual's identity, of reflexivity and slippage (Weedon, 1987: 106). Ultimately, however, this particular narrative resolves into Helen's construction of herself as a normatively good mother and daughter, and in addition, she constructs conservatively gendered identities for her two daughters.

Many of the New Zealand women's stories in the sample can be similarly interpreted as underlining and emphasizing the women's roles as 'good' mothers, daughters, wives and friends. One young woman, Alison, constructs herself as a caring and careful mother, describing how she kept her child at home when he had chicken-pox, and comparing herself favourably with another mother who sent her daughter to the child care centre when she was still infectious. Another older woman, Kay, tells the story of how her son Sam met his wife, Lynnette. The story is constructed as a romantic love story with Sam in his 'officer's uniform', wooing Lynnette with flowers and expensive restaurant meals. Kay describes Sam's success, the happy wedding and the subsequent birth of a baby. Lynnette, however, refuses to fit the conservative identity Kay thinks appropriate, and the story ends with a wry coda, *I can see though she needs to be using her brain you know and she's not gonna be just a mum at home*. In all these cases the stories construct conservative gender roles for the protagonists. Helen and Alison present themselves as good mothers; Kay presents Sam as an ardent lover and Lynnette as his maidenly conquest. And, interestingly, in all these stories, the seeds of an alternative conflicting discourse are apparent, though they are not allowed to flourish.

But of course, this is not the whole story either. In other contexts, Helen tells stories that emphasize different identities and roles. In her women's group she tells stories, for instance, about how people respond to her arrival at social events with her lesbian partner; with other friends she describes the day-to-day frustrations and successes of her high level management job. As they construct their gender identity in ongoing interaction, people may reinforce norms at one point, but challenge and contest them at others. In the pool story, on this particular occasion, talking in her kitchen with a relatively conservative friend, Helen constructs a predominantly conservative gender identity. In other contexts with different participants, the gender identity she constructs is much more radical.

There is also evidence of the seeds of change and the impact of new gender ideologies in the stories of some of the younger women.[12] One area where this is evident is in stories which celebrate women's power, where women are presented as influential protagonists, or where women construct a positive powerful identity for themselves as they tell their stories. One example describes a confrontation with a woman who had physically abused her children. The story focuses on the fact that although the abuser's behaviour was rejected, she was treated caringly and with respect. The narrator presents herself as compassionate, but firm and authoritative. Another story describes the role played by a young lawyer, Kathryn, in protecting her family's rights. The story constructs Kathryn's identity both as 'family' and as an intellectually sharp, helpful young lawyer. Other stories describe women's successes at work, including an effective campaign to create a smoke-free area, and a young woman's enjoyment in putting in his place an older man whom she constructs as bothersome and rather stupid.

Example 8

    A: old um John Smithson came up to me today and said oh do I pay my
        thirty dollars to you and I said [tut] well have you been receiving
        letters to say that you owe them thirty dollars and he goes oh yeah
        and I went well THAT'S who you pay it to
    B: [laughs] (smarmy)
    A: [laughs] that's eXACtly how I said it too I said it to him like that oh it
        was so funny

Just as the seeds of an alternative discourse were evident in the conservative stories, there are often elements of conservatism and conformist behaviours in these more radical stories. Example 9 provides an excerpt from a long story describing a confrontation between the narrator, Fran, in her role as teacher, and a belligerent pupil at a school camp. For most of the story the narrator presents herself as dealing in an authoritative way with an uncooperative and resentful young man.

Example 9

> F: they weren't pulling their weight and I no- I noticed it a bit later- a bit later on but I sort of said to them hey look come on everybody's got to do their bit and you're not
> K: yeah
> F: and he was going oh what and I was going no there's no need for that kind of lip
> K: mm [laughs]
> F: now come on snap out of it Joe and he was going MAN [imitates Joe complaining] and I says I'm not saying this just for the hell of it
> K: yeah
> F: I don't see that you're doing any work   everybody else is and you're leaving three people to do the work that six people should be doing
> K: yeah
> F: now just get over there

Up to this point, the story constructs Fran as competent and decisive, exercising her authority fairly but firmly. As she moves towards the story's climax, however, she begins to question her method of dealing with the problem.

Example 10

> F: I was starting to get really pissed off with him and I said get over there   I mean there was w- one thing in particular that I think did-didn't deal with very well in that I started to raise my voice in front of the other kids (so you)
> K: [laughs] yeah
> F: don't do that in front of senior kids in front of secondary s- school kids
> K: oh yeah
> F: and I know you don't but he wasn't listening he was pissing me off and as far as I was concerned you know pulling him aside 'cause he was just going leave me alone and just get over there and it'll be the end of it
> K: mm
> F: all he had to do was wash the bloody pots

The story moves to a conclusion in which we are told that Joe did not hold a grudge and he pulled his weight for the rest of the trip. Once again the narrator is presented as in control and the pupils are constructed as appropriately respectful and mindful of her authority. In the final section, however, the same ambivalence surfaces once again.

Example 11

> F: man he was in there so I made a point of going - I don't know whether this is talking down to him but I made a point of praising him 'cause I don't think sometimes secondary school kids get enough praise you know

I am not suggesting that it is inappropriate for Fran to reflect on her behaviour and consider whether it was effective and reasonable. What is interesting is that this reflection is built into her story so that the gender identity she constructs is complex; it includes evidence of her acting in powerful traditionally 'masculine' ways, as well as evidence of a more 'feminine' reflective and somewhat less decisive identity.[13]

These excerpts illustrate the contested ongoing nature of identity construction: elements of traditional, unconfident, self-questioning femininity can be found alongside the construction of a more assertive, powerful identity. As Cameron says

> one is never finished becoming a woman, or a man. Each individual subject must constantly negotiate the norms, behaviours, discourses, that define masculinity and femininity for a particular community at a particular point in history. (1995: 43)

Male identity

The men too used stories to construct a gendered identity for themselves and others. But they tended to do so in rather different ways than the women, and in a different overall context. Men's stories were generally not ways of bringing their addressees up to date on the story of their lives as the women's usually were. There were certainly stories which recounted recent events in the men's lives, but these were decidedly a minority. Often the men would use stories to illustrate more general points, or as ancillary devices in the discussion of an issue such as 'urban transport' or 'homosexuality', or a particular topic such as 'painting the house' or 'developing a good football team'.

On the other hand, like the women's stories, the men's stories constructed a clearly gendered identity for those featuring in their stories. The two young men quoted in Example 2, reflecting on their earlier escapades, present a picture of themselves on one level as 'dumb', which they clearly find amusing. In the process they indicate their current level of sophistication while also conveying a sense of their earlier behaviour as appropriately wild and 'crazy' for young city boys. Other men's stories underline their control of a situation, their competence, their awareness of what they portray as female 'wiles', their resistance to what is presented as unreasonable authoritarianism, their status as 'good keen Kiwi blokes',[14] and so on. The stories often reflect a concern with status, and with giving an impression of worldly wisdom. In men's stories, 'doing gender' involves presenting themselves as in control, knowledgeable, competent or, if things go wrong, as self-aware, sophisticated, and reflective.

'I drove our video last night'

These points are illustrated in a male narrative from a conversation between two friends and colleagues, Tom and Gary, both middle-aged

Pakeha men who work in salaried professional jobs. This is one of the relatively few male conversations which focus on recent activities. In the first part of the conversation they talk about what they have been doing earlier in the day. It is probably not irrelevant that this conversation takes place over a coffee at work, rather than in one of their homes. The identities constructed in the stories told in this conversation are no doubt influenced by the social context. Tom introduces the first topic by volunteering to explain 'Why I haven't been in my office all day'. He then gives an account of meeting a visitor at the airport, chairing a meeting, and solving problems for clients. By contrast Gary frames his day as 'much more prosaic', but goes on to provide a similarly detailed account of his activities. The story 'I drove our video last night' follows a discussion of the tape recorder and similar technical apparatus.[15] Tom tells how he eventually overcame the problem of getting his video machine to record a film, and his story is followed by a discussion of the inadequacies of the television company in providing accurate programme information to viewers.

In this video story, Tom constructs himself as competent and intelligent by describing in detail his achievement in mastering the programming of the video (see Appendix 3). He describes each step in the process, giving the impression of an orderly, methodical approach to the challenge he faced.

> I looked at- looked up where the programme was on in the pap- you know in the paper
> I picked up the video thingy you know the the remote one . . .
> I pushed the appropriate buttons
> and it ALL worked

The use of the same syntactic pattern through several constructions reinforces Tom's presentation of his behaviour as orderly and systematic. Utterances like

> I had to set the time and the date from scratch . . .
> I set it up and it recorded at exactly the right time . . .
> everything was perfect . . .

underline the complexity of the task and the level of his achievement. As he presents it:

> th- the whole point about this is
> I solved the technology problem
> I had programmed the video

Tom is constructing his identity as a competent manager of technology. He also indicates, however, that external forces undermined his best efforts.

> and do you know what went wrong . . .
> the p- programme schedule was completely screwed up . . .

The interfering factors are constructed as beyond his control and the word *silly* recurs repeatedly in his account (*it was silly, the silly (remote), the silly rugby sevens*), expressing his attitude to the subverting factors.

One of the most interesting aspects of this story is the fact that, having clearly framed it as a triumph of his skill over modern technology, Tom then admits in the course of the account that things were not quite as much under his control as he had suggested – nor as he had intended to convey when he began the story. This subsequent undermining of the identity he has constructed is presented in a rather wry and somewhat self-conscious manner, and, interestingly, this too is not atypical of the men's stories. There was often an ironic comment or an indication that the constructed identity of an effective or powerful person, totally in control of events, did not represent the whole picture. The mocking attitude to their younger selves apparent in Example 2 is somewhat similar, though the narrators maintain distance by telling a story about an earlier time. In a number of cases, as in Tom's narrative, the story peters out towards the end with qualifications and caveats, as the narrator permits reality, or some degree of reflexivity, to intervene and prevent the story reaching a heroic climax.[16]

> no that's right I couldn't undo the programming
> 'cause having programmed the damn thing
> having got all that set up I couldn't then undo the programming
> I couldn't figure out how to do it
> I tried that I tried I I I
> in the end I decided I have to undo the whole lot start again
> but I couldn't change anything . . .
> no I solved part of the of 'cause I couldn't figure out to turn it off
> I couldn't undo the programming once it had started once it started . . .
> I thought it was just me
> maybe maybe it's the way the Japanese make videos

So, in the men's narratives too there is often an alternative discourse competing with the explicit message – a slightly ironic, self-mocking discourse. In Tom's story it is hinted at in the comic framing of his story with the introductory utterance (*I drove our video last night*), but it gradually becomes more evident and almost takes over at the end of the story, suggesting Tom is aware of an alternative view of his behaviour. It is further indicated by words such as *thingy* to refer to the digital scanner, as well as by the somewhat wry tone with which some utterances are imbued. Another male conversationalist, Ken, tells a story about recording a radio programme without a script. Ken's story appears to be making the point that because he was an experienced broadcaster he managed to achieve this goal, thus proving undeserved the scepticism expressed by the producer. But in fact, as the story progresses, Ken admits that things did not go as smoothly as he had intended, and some patching up of his presentation was necessary. Nevertheless, at the most obvious level, Tom's story is intended to demonstrate his competence, just as Ken's ends with a statement emphasizing that the results of the recording session were fine. Tom presents himself as an able person who has successfully mastered the workings of a complex piece of machinery. The reason all does not go well is due to forces beyond his control. This is as much a gendered identity as that reflected in Helen's story which presents her as a paradigmatically dutiful mother and daughter. Tom's story emphasizes a typical normative masculine identity in New Zealand culture – someone who can control modern technology.

It is possible, though not common, to find stories in which men present themselves in ways more usually framed as 'feminine'. One man recounts a story about the rejection of his work by an expert, clearly seeking his friend's sympathy; another's story describes a problem at work. But such stories are exceptional. It seems likely that stories constructing alternative, less stereotypically masculine identities occur in more intimate contexts. This is an obvious area for further research.

One final feature worth comment which is illustrated by these stories is the extent to which the evaluative component of the women's stories was more likely to be relatively implicit or embedded in the story structure, while the men were more likely to make the 'point' of the story explicit. Labov suggests that explicit or 'external evaluation' is a common trait of middle-class narrative (1972: 372). Middle-class narrators, he claims, frequently interrupt their narratives to underline the point of the story, ensuring that their audience is not missing it. By contrast, he illustrates how the young working-class black men he recorded tend to embed their evaluations within the narrative: they may quote themselves responding at the time to the events described, or, more subtly, they may attribute the evaluative component to a co-participant in the events. This kind of embedded evaluative component was common in the New Zealand women's stories: another participant is often quoted expressing astonishment at what the narrator has experienced, or admiration for what the narrator has achieved. In the pool story, this process is taken one step further. At one level, the pool narrative, like the video narrative, is a success story – Helen finally managed to get to the pool. But I have suggested that its main function is to construct Helen's identity as 'a good mother' and 'a good daughter'. In the pool story Helen constructs these identities without drawing explicit attention to the process, either through her own commentary or through the words of another. The point is conveyed very indirectly.

Tom, by contrast, makes the point of his story quite explicit. Despite all the odds, and the interference of external forces beyond his control, he succeeded in 'driving' his video machine. He draws explicit attention to this point at two different stages in his account. The first is when the interfering forces are introduced:

> and do you know what went wrong
> 'cause it you know that something went wrong
> otherwise I wouldn't be telling you this story
> (quite-) quite pointless if nothing

And the second is at the end of the story when he again underlines his point quite explicitly:

> but BUT th- the whole point about this is
> I solved the technology problem
> I had programmed the video

While there is clearly an element of subjectivity in identifying the main point of a story, especially when it is not made explicit, there is nonetheless evidence in the sample that men were generally more likely than women to assert the point of their stories explicitly. In a number of ways, then, these two stories serve to illustrate gender-differentiated patterns which are typical of a number of stories in the sample.

Conclusion

The stories told by women and men in the New Zealand sample used in this analysis indicate the range of ways in which conversationalists construct gendered identities in their everyday interactions with friends. Though the material consists of routine, mundane events in the lives of the protagonists, it is transformed in their narratives into the building blocks of stereotypical and, more rarely, radical female and male societal roles.

In talk between friends, stories express shared values and attitudes. Both women and men expect their friends to express empathy and understanding in their responses to such stories. In some cases, where experiences are shared, the story itself may be a joint construction. In others, the addressee provides varying degrees and types of support. Positive feedback and supportive questions and comments were used by both female and male addressees, but they were more frequent in the women's conversations, while men were more likely to make challenging comments and ask sceptical questions. And though both female and male listeners sometimes produced a sympathetic mirroring story, this pattern occurred more often in women's conversations.

The analysis has also demonstrated how stories may serve to construct and reinforce the dominant societal ideology concerning gender roles, reaffirming conservative normative social and cultural values. As Coates says:

> through our story-telling we create and re-create our identities and experiment with possible selves, in a context of mutuality and trust. Conversational narrative is our chief means of constructing the fictions that are our lives and of getting others to collude in them. (1996: 115)

The topics of women's and men's narratives assert the fundamental importance of everyday experience and activities. But they also reflect the different preoccupations of the daily lives of women and men. The women focus on relationships and people, affirm the importance of their family roles, family connections and friendships. The men focus on work and sport, events, activities and things, and affirm the importance of being in control, even when they don't achieve it. These different preoccupations contribute to and reinforce the gender identities women and men construct through their talk.

Stories also offer a site for contesting the dominant ideology, and there was some evidence in the analysed texts of alternative discourses, different voices expressing different constructions of the world and of gender roles. The way narrators position themselves in a story is often complex. There was evidence of subversive and, for feminists, more optimistic elements even in conservative texts, as well as some stories celebrating women's power and autonomy, providing indications of the gradual emergence of a more feminist ideology, and indicating the potential of discourse to contribute and reinforce such change. By a variety of discourse strategies, then, both women and men in these New Zealand stories affirmed their gender identities, but also indicated an awareness of their confines.

Appendix 1: Transcription conventions

All names are pseudonyms.

YES   capitals indicate emphatic stress

[laughs]	paralinguistic features in square brackets
+	pause of up to one second
. . ./ . . . . . . \. . . . . ./ . . . . . . \. . .	simultaneous speech
(hello)	transcriber's best guess at an unclear utterance
?	rising or question intonation
-	incomplete or cut-off utterance

Appendix 2: The pool story

H: and so today we wen- we tried to go to the pool today I tri- I wanted to go to aqua fitness at eleven

J: oh good on you

H: well I wanted to go to aqua fitness at eleven so we gathered up Susie and everybody and their togs and we tear over there just- get there about three minutes before the class is supposed to start and the pool is all closed for some other spe- you know they're not /no\

J: /oh a\

H: aqua- aqua fitness is cancelled some

J: /sport thing\

H: /sporting thing\

J: oh

H: and I th- so I thought oh god I thought you know after we'd s- go- spent half an hour getting there so then I said let's go to Freyburg so then we get I don't want to go to- Annie didn't want to go to Freyburg and the other two DID and you know w- so I said we're going to Freyburg we've got this far /so we\ get round to Freyburg it's lane

J: /right\

H: swimming only which is no good for the little kids [tut] so I thought + oh god this really isn't working out at all and actually it was rather sort of /muggy an hot to be driving round Wellington with a car full of children\

J: /[laughs] I mean (only car) I know\

H: so then /I said oh well\ we'll go and we'll

J: /you've got to (deal)\

H: go to um the Karori pool what the hell\ we'll go to the Karori pool

J: mm mm

H: and we'll just swim there wh- well we could have done that in the first place except that I couldn't have done my class and /the\ w- and it's

J: /no\

H: not quite as w- good as those bigger pools so on the way to the Karori pool we stopped in and saw Jason and i- and Annie was saying I don't want to go in will you drop me home and I said why don't you stay with Jason /and\ make

J: /mm\

H: him some lunch

J: mm

H: so we went in and visited him and I said Annie'll stay with you and make you some lunch and she gets on quite- and she chats away with Jason and they have quite a nice-

J: /she's very good with\ adults isn't she

H: /yes she is\ she's- well she's good with him too I don't know they sort of get along /nicely\ and um better

J: /mm\

H: than the other two do really /you know\

J: /mm\

H: She sort of somehow gets it right with him and he seems to make an effort too so she stayed with him for an hour we went- the other two and I went and swam at the pool Andrea did SEVEN lengths

J: goodness me

H: with a little breaks in between but she's never swum a length of that pool before /and she just suddenly discovered\

J: /(that's so good)\

H: she could swim a length [laughs] and got so keen she didn't want to stop she said I'll just do another one and then /I'll do another one so

J: /that's terrific\

H: that\was quite sweet she looked quite sweet like a [laughs] s- Liz was there with her friend John and he said /she\ looked like a goldfish you [laughs]

J: /mm\

H: /know s- (there's) a little head (   )\

J: /[laughs]\ (he'd find out when we-) yeah

H: a- a (rolling) in the water

J: /[laughs] oh\

H: [laughs] and legs sort of sagging in the water o- and breaststroking away

J: /good on her\

H: /you know\ but she obviously really sort of getting a kick out of the achievements

J: /that's so good\

H: so Annie stayed there and made Jason some lunch and then we went back afterwards so I mean he's sort of all right he's pottering around but he's- he's walking with a stick

Appendix 3: The video story

T: I I drove our video last night

G: [laughs]

T: I did I I looked at- looked up where the programme was on in the pap- you know in the paper

G: mm

T: [drawls] and I picked up the video thingy you know the

G: is this the g code?

T: /the remote one no no\

G: /no\

T: no no no just [drawls] the just an ordinary remote and I pushed the appropriate buttons and it ALL worked and I had to set the time and the date from scratch and I set it up and it recorded at exactly the right time and do you know what went wrong 'cause it you know that something went wrong /otherwise\ I wouldn't

G: /(   ) [laughs]\

T: be telling you this story/ (quite-)\

G: /you got\ the wrong channel

T: quite pointless if nothing no no no everything was perfect

G: oh

T: no it was silly um the silly (remote) er

G: the programme schedule was /(   )\

T: /yeah the p- programme schedule\ was completely screwed up /the\ the um it was it was Channel Two and I

G: /yeah\

T: was supposed to be recording [film title] The Lair of the White Worm [laughs] it's a Ken Russell

G: oh

T: Ken Russell horror story and it was supposed to start at five to twelve ++ and instead the silly rugby sevens went on you know the rugby league sevens

G: mm

T: went on until twelve thirty so I'd carefully set this thing up now if I'd left it it wouldn't have mattered too much catching half an hour of the silly rugby sevens but I /didn't\ know when they finished

G: /mm\ yeah

T: and it was a three hour tape and I didn't know how long [film title] The Lair of the White Worm went on for /because Ken\ Russell can

G: /[laughs]\

T: make some pretty long movies

G: /[laughs]\ yes [laughs]

T: and so [drawls] um I had to take (undo- it) no that's right I couldn't undo the programming 'cause having programmed the damn thing having got all that set up I couldn't then undo /the\ programming

G: /yeah\ that's right you've got to unless you just undo the whole lot and start again

T: I couldn't figure out how to do it I tried that I tried I I I in the end I decided I have to undo the whole lot start again but I couldn't change anything so as far as I know having set it up it still turned itself off at two o'clock and there's probably another half an hour of [film title] The Lair of the White Worm

G: /(yeah)\

T: /unrecorded\

G: a- and and the thrilling climax

T: yes

G: (oh)

T: but BUT th- the whole point about this is I solved the technology problem I had programmed the video no I solved part of the of 'cause I couldn't figure out to turn it off I couldn't undo the programming once it had started /once it\ started

G: /yeah\ no I've had that problem with our o- o- original simple one

T: I thought it was just me maybe /maybe\ it's

G: /yeah\

T: the way the Japanese make videos

Notes

I would like to express my appreciation to Maria Stubbe and Ruth Wodak who read drafts of the chapter and provided valuable comments which have greatly improved it. The research was made possible by a grant from the New Zealand Foundation for Research, Science and Technology.

1. The term 'Pakeha' is used in New Zealand to describe those of European

(mainly British) origin, who colonized New Zealand in the nineteenth century. Maori are the indigenous people of New Zealand.

2. Differences between Maori and Pakeha narratives will be the focus of subsequent analysis.

3. Half of the Corpus consists of excerpts from informal conversations between adult New Zealanders (see Holmes, 1995). In collecting these conversations we developed techniques aimed at ensuring that they were as unconstrained as possible, and the excerpts were selected from the most relaxed sections of the recordings (see Holmes, 1996).

4. See also Goodwin (1990), Dubois and Horvath (1992), Schiffrin (1994) and Rymes (1995).

5. 'This dialogic form of story telling means that the distinction between "storyteller" and "audience" becomes blurred, because what is happening in such a situation is that the speakers are collaborating in a story-telling' (Cheepen, 1988: 54).

6. In some Maori contexts, for instance, silence is interpreted positively, speakers are allowed to continue uninterrupted until they have finished, and there is no expectation of verbal feedback.

7. The texts of stories are slightly edited to make them easier to read. Transcription conventions are described in Appendix 1. Names are changed to protect people's identities.

8. Any interpretation will be subjective and this is a real problem in gender research (see Hay, 1996). However, there was often prosodic and paralinguistic evidence on the tapes to support my interpretations: for example, a disruptive question or critical comment would often be followed by a pause or a vocalization from the narrator which suggested a disrupted train of thought.

9. It has often been noted that the topics of women's and men's conversations tend to differ (Kalčik, 1975; Aries, 1976; Wodak, 1981; de Boer, 1987; Coates, 1989; Dorval, 1990; Sheldon, 1990; Tannen, 1990). Hence, it is not surprising that the topics of women's and men's spontaneous narratives reflect different interests and concerns.

10. This story is thus a clear, specific illustration of Linde's claim that narrative is 'an extremely powerful tool for creating, negotiating, and displaying the moral standing of the self . . . the most basic moral proposition, which is contained in some form by all first-person narratives, is "I am a good person"' (1993: 123).

11. Rymes (1995: 505ff) illustrates the use of hedges and mitigating devices for broadly parallel functions in a very different type of discourse in which high school drop-outs convey their sense of moral agency through their narratives.

12. This is especially true of the Maori women. The issue of cultural differences is too complex to explore in this chapter. See Holmes (forthcoming) for an analysis of cultural differences in narratives.

13. It is worth noting too that a more complex identity for Joe is constructed in the concluding section. His one-dimensional role as teenage rebel is developed into something less stereotypically masculine as he 'pulls his weight' and gets 'in there', behaving in a helpful and cooperative manner for the rest of the trip.

14. The 'good keen bloke' is a widespread stereotype of Kiwi (New Zealand) men which portrays the model New Zealand male as taciturn, unemotional, and very practical, and expert at home maintenance or do-it-yourself.

15. In general the men were much more conscious of the tape recorder than the women – a methodological problem discussed in some detail by Hay (1996).

16. The seeds of discontent or areas of potential challenge to the gender identity specified by the dominant culture are even more explicit in some stories, but the selected texts are more typical and representative of the majority of narratives in the sample.

References

Aries, Helen (1976) 'Interaction patterns and themes of male, female and mixed groups', *Small Group Behaviour*, 7(1): 7–18.

Bell, Allan (1991) *The Language of News Media*. Oxford: Blackwell.

Bell, Susan E. (1988) 'Becoming a political woman: the reconstruction and interpretation of experience through stories', in Alexandra D. Todd and Sue Fisher (eds), *Gender and Discourse: the Power of Talk*. Norwood, NJ: Ablex. pp. 97–123.

Butler, Judith (1990) *Gender Trouble*. New York: Routledge.

Cameron, Deborah (1995) 'Rethinking language and gender studies: some issues for the 1990s', in Sarah Mills (ed.), *Language and Gender: Interdisciplinary Perspectives*. London: Longman. pp. 31–44.

Cheepen, Christine (1988) The *Predictability of Informal Conversation*. London: Pinter.

Coates, Jennifer (1989) 'Gossip revisited: language in all-female groups', in Jennifer Coates and Deborah Cameron (eds), *Women in their Speech Communities*. London: Longman. pp. 94–121.

Coates, Jennifer (1996) *Women Talk*. Oxford: Blackwell.

Corston, Simon (1993) 'On the interactive nature of spontaneous narrative', *Te Reo*, 36: 69–97.

Crawford, Mary (1995) *Talking Difference: on Gender and Language*. London: Sage.

de Boer, Mieke (1987) 'Sex differences in language: observations of dyadic conversations between members of the same sex', in Dédé Brouwer and Dorian de Haan (eds), *Women's Language, Socialisation and Self-image*. Dordrecht: Foris. pp. 148–63.

Dorval, Bruce (1990) *Conversational Organisation and its Development*. Norwood, NJ: Ablex.

Dubois, Sylvie and Horvath, Barbara (1992) 'Interviewer's linguistic production and its effect on speaker's descriptive style', *Language Variation and Change*, 4: 125–35.

Duranti, Alessandro (1986) 'The audience as co-author', *Text*, 6(3): 239–47.

Eckert, Penelope and McConnell-Ginet, Sally (1992) 'Communities of practice: where language, gender and power all live', in Kira Hall, Mary Bucholtz and Birch Moonwomon (eds), *Locating Power: Proceedings of the Second Berkeley Women and Language Conference*, vol. 1. Berkeley, CA: Berkeley Women and Language Group, University of California–Berkeley. pp. 89–99.

Fairclough, Norman (1989) *Language and Power*. London: Longman.

Fairclough, Norman (1995) *Critical Discourse Analysis*. London: Longman.

Fishman, Pamela M. (1983) 'Interaction: the work women do', in Barrie Thorne, Cheris Kramarae and Nancy Henley (eds), *Language, Gender and Society*. Rowley, MA: Newbury House. pp. 89–101.

Fitzgerald,Thomas K. (1993) *Metaphors of Identity: a Culture–Communication Dialogue*. New York: State University of New York Press.

Goodwin, Charles (1986) 'Audience diversity, participation and interpretation', *Text*, 6(3): 283–316.

Goodwin, Marjorie Harness (1990) *He-Said-She-Said*. Bloomington, IN: Indiana University Press.

Goodwin, Marjorie Harness (1991) 'Retellings, pretellings and hypothetical stories', *Research on Language and Social Interaction*, 24: 263–76.

Hay, Jennifer (1996) 'Problems and paradoxes of language and gender research'. Paper presented at Fourth Berkeley Women and Language Conference, 19–21 April 1996, University of California–Berkeley.

Heath, Shirley B. (1982) 'What no bedtime story means', *Language in Society*, 11: 49–76.

Holmes, Janet (1986) 'Functions of *you know* in women and men's speech', *Language in Society*, 15(1): 1–21.

Holmes, Janet (1995) 'The Wellington Corpus of Spoken New Zealand English: a progress report', *New Zealand English Newsletter*, 9: 5–8.

Holmes, Janet (1996) 'The New Zealand spoken component of ICE: some methodological challenges', in Sidney Greenbaum (ed.), *Comparing English World-Wide: the International Corpus of English*. Oxford: Oxford University Press.

Holmes, Janet (forthcoming) 'Narrative structure: some contrasts between Maori and Pakeha story-telling', *Multilingua*, 17.

James, Bev and Saville-Smith, Kay (1989) *Gender, Culture and Power*. Auckland: Oxford University Press.

Johnstone, Barbara (1993) 'Community and contest: Midwestern men and women creating their worlds in conversational story-telling', in Deborah Tannen (ed.), *Gender and Conversational Interaction*. Oxford: Oxford University Press. pp. 62–80.

Kalčik, Susan (1975) '". . . like Ann's gynecologist or the time I was almost raped"', *Journal of American Folklore*, 88(1): 3–11.

Labov, William (1972) 'The transformation of experience in narrative syntax', *Language in the Inner City*. Philadelphia: University of Pennsylvania Press. pp. 354–96.

Labov, William and Waletzky, Joseph (1967) 'Narrative analysis: oral versions of personal experience', in June Helm (ed.), *Essays on the Verbal and Visual Arts*. Seattle: University of Washington Press. pp. 12–44.

Lee, David (1992) *Competing Discourses: Perspective and Ideology in Language*. London: Longman.

Leet-Pellegrini, H.M. (1980) 'Conversational dominance as a function of gender and expertise', in Howard Giles, Peter Robinson and Philip Smith (eds), *Language: Social Psychological Perspectives*. Pergamon Press: Oxford. pp. 97–104.

Linde, Charlotte (1993) *Life Stories: the Creation of Coherence*. Oxford: Oxford University Press.

Metge, Joan (1995) *New Growth from Old: the Whaanau in the Modern World*. Wellington: Victoria University Press.

Pilkington, Jane (1994) 'Women, men and gossip: what's the story?', MA thesis, Victoria University of Wellington.

Polanyi Livia (1985) *Telling the American Story: a Structural and Cultural Analysis of Conversational Storytelling*. Norwood, NJ: Ablex.

Reid, Julie (1992) 'Gender differences in minimal responses', *La Trobe Working Papers in Linguistics*, 5: 107–32.

Reid, Julie (1994) 'Women, men and gossip: what's the story?'. MA thesis, Wellington, Victoria University of Wellington.

Riessman, Catherine Kohler (1993) *Narrative Analysis*. London: Sage.

Rymes, Betsy (1995) 'The construction of moral agency in the narratives of high-school drop-outs', *Discourse and Society*, 6(3): 495–516.

Schiffrin, Deborah (1994) *Approaches to Discourse*. Oxford: Blackwell.

Sheldon, Amy (1990) 'Pickle fights: gendered talk in preschool disputes', *Discourse Processes*, 13: 5–31.

Sheldon, Amy (1996) 'Sharing the same world, telling different stories: gender differences in co-constructed narratives', in D. Slobin, J. Gerhardt, J. Guo and A. Kyratzis (eds), *Social Interaction, Social Context and Language: Festschrift Presented to Susan Ervin-Tripp*. Hillsdale, NJ: Lawrence Erlbaum. pp. 803–29.

Stenstrom, Anna-Brita (1994) *An Introduction to Spoken Interaction*. London: Longman.

Strodtbeck, Fred L. and Mann, Richard D. (1956) 'Sex role differentiation in jury deliberations', *Sociometry*, 19: 3–11.

Stubbe, Maria (forthcoming) 'Active listening in conversation: gender patterns in the use of verbal feedback',

Tannen, Deborah (1990) *You Just Don't Understand: Women and Men in Conversation*. New York: William Morrow.

Weedon, Chris (1987) *Feminist Practice and Poststructuralist Theory*. Oxford: Blackwell.

Wodak, Ruth (1981) 'Women relate, men report: sex differences in language behaviour in a therapeutic group', *Journal of Pragmatics*, 5: 261–85.

Wolfson, Nessa (1976) 'Speech events and natural speech: some implications for sociolinguistic methodology', *Language in Society*, 5: 189–209.

Zimmerman, Don H. and West, Candace (1975) 'Sex roles, interruptions and silences in conversation', in Barrie Thorne and Nancy Henley (eds), *Language and Sex: Difference and Dominance*. Rowley, MA: Newbury House. pp. 105–29.

INDEX